Homosexuality
and Family Relations

Homosexuality and Family Relations

Frederick W. Bozett
Marvin B. Sussman
Editors

Homosexuality and Family Relations, edited by Federick W. Bozett and Marvin B. Sussman, was simultaneously issued by The Haworth Press, Inc., under the same title, as a special issue of *Marriage & Family Review* Volume 14, Numbers 3/4 1989, Marvin B. Sussman, Journal Editor.

Harrington Park Press
New York • London

ISBN 0-918393-70-1

Published by

Harrington Park Press, Inc., 10 Alice Street, Binghamton, New York 13904-1580
EUROSPAN/Harrington, 3 Henrietta Street, London WC2E 8LU England

Harrington Park Press, Inc., is a subsidiary of The Haworth Press, Inc., 10 Alice Street, Binghamton, New York 13904-1580.

Homosexuality and Family Relations was originally published as *Marriage & Family Review*, Volume 14, Numbers 3/4 1989.

Cover design by Marshall Andrews.

Library of Congress Cataloging-in-Publication Data

Homosexuality and family relations / Frederick W. Bozett, Marvin B. Sussman, editors.
    p. cm.
    "Has also been published as Marriage and family review, volume 14, numbers 3/4, 1989."
    Includes bibliographical references.
    ISBN 0-918393-70-1
    1. Gays – Family relationships. I. Bozett, Frederick W., 1931 – II. Sussman, Marvin B.
HQ76.25.H6744   1990
306.87 – dc20   89-26775
                                                         CIP

CONTENTS

ABOUT THE EDITORS

Frederick W. Bozett, RN, DNS, is a professor in the graduate program, College of Nursing, University of Oklahoma. He is editor of *Gay and Lesbian Parents* (Praeger, 1987) and co-editor of *Dimensions of Fatherhood* (Sage, 1985). He has published extensively in the area of fatherhood and gay fathers. Dr. Bozett is currently undertaking a longitudinal study of custodial gay father families, as well as studies of gay father-child relationships and gay grandfathers.

Marvin B. Sussman, PhD, is Unidel Professor of Human Behavior Emeritus at the College of Human Resources, University of Delaware. A member of many professional organizations, he was awarded the 1980 Ernest W. Burgess Award of the National Council on Family Relations, as well as a life-long membership for services to the Groves Conference on Marriage and the Family in 1981. In 1983, he was elected to the prestigious academy of Groves for scholarly contributions to the field. Dr. Sussman has published widely on areas dealing with family, community, rehabilitation, organizations, sociology of medicine, and aging. Dr. Sussman is the editor of *Marriage & Family Review.*

Homosexuality and Family Relations: Views and Research Issues

Frederick W. Bozett
Marvin B. Sussman

A COMMENTARY

Homosexuality has been documented since recorded history, and has not always had negative connotations. For example, in ancient Greece homosexuality was acceptable for adolescent males until completion of their military training (Bullough, 1979). It is primarily in cultures where Judeo-Christian monotheism is prevalent that homosexuality is most negatively labeled. Moreover, homophobia, the irrational fear of homosexuals and homosexuality (Herek, 1984; Weinberg, 1972; Jeter, 1988) appears to be especially virulent in the United States (Altman, 1982).

One of the main functions of the family is for it to be a "haven in a heartless world" (Lasch, 1977). It is within the supportive milieux of the family where all members are to be loved and nurtured so that healthy growth and development occurs. Social interaction outside the family may require that feelings and beliefs be suppressed, but within the family one anticipates they can be true to one's self, and honest with one's family members.

Although this may be an ideal rarely fully achieved, it is realized even less so for the gay or lesbian family member. Because of societal hostility toward homosexuality, growing up gay is often exceptionally painful, and is riddled with multiple problems. There are several theories that help explain the reasons for this. *Social reaction theory* (Weinberg & Williams, 1974) posits that the more prejudicial a society is toward a given group, the more difficulty its members have in adjusting to family and societal norms. In addition, the research of Ross (1983) supports the proposition that it is

1

not *actual* societal reaction that is critical but rather one's *perception* of societal reaction. Moreover, Lindesmith, Strauss, and Denzin (1977) make the point that "selves exist only in a social environment (from) which they cannot be separated. . . . Therefore "self" implies "others" and cannot be separated from them " (p. 322). In addition, Goffman (1963) remarks about the informing nature of the "with" relationship; that to be with someone is frequently used as a source of information concerning one's own social identity. Thus, the gay or lesbian family member, existing within the social environment of the family, being "with" the family, stigmatizes the family if they disclose their homosexuality (come out) to them. Moreover, nondisclosure is commonplace because it is assumed that rejection is a real possibility since the family is a microcosm of society. Hence, hiding sexual orientation which is central to one's core identity, makes it especially difficult for the gay adolescent to achieve or maintain a healthy self-esteem.

In addition, the absence of societal affirmation for being gay reinforces the notion that gay and lesbian individuals are not full members of society with the rights and privileges accorded the majority. Even though, in isolated sectors of the United States there has been a lessening of pejorative attitudes toward gays and lesbians, the oppression of gays continues to be a nationwide problem. To illustrate, the United States Supreme Court recently upheld the constitutionality of a Georgia law maintaining that the right to privacy does not extend to homosexual activity. Police harassment of homosexuals in gay settings such as bars is commonplace. Homosexuals may not marry one another and because of this are denied social security and insurance benefits, inheritance rights, and major medical benefits for live-in lovers. Gays are barred from military service. Some states ban gay adoptions and in some home ownership by unrelated individuals is illegal. Gay men and lesbians are not protected under Title VII of the Civil Rights Act of 1964 because it does not include sexual orientation. Public condemnation is also not infrequent. For example, a 1985 candidate for mayor of Houston, Texas joked that one way to reduce the crisis of AIDS (acquired immune deficiency syndrome) would be to "shoot the queers" (Walter, 1985). In addition, disapproval of homosexuality by both Christian and non-Christian religions further alienates gays from mainstream society (Bozett, 1988). Regarding gay and lesbian parents, Hitchens (1979/1980) writes that:

> Regardless of whether a parent has ever been involved in a court challenge, the threat of losing the custody of one's children . . . is an everyday reality for homosexual fathers and mothers. Gay parents are aware that their sexual orientation can all too easily be used against them by ex-spouses, family, or state authorities. Decisions about how to live, with whom to live, how to raise children, whether to "come out," and whether to become involved in political activities, all have potentially severe legal consequences bearing on the right to remain a parent. (pp. 93-94)

Even though non-disclosure of one's homosexuality creates a psychological distance between the gay person and his significant others, disclosure is risky. Response of others cannot be predicted. Rejection by others with the loss of their love and friendship is always considered a possibility. It is thought that men and fathers have more difficulty accepting a family member's homosexuality — especially a son's — than do women/mothers, yet research in this area is scant. Discovery that a family member is gay may cause the family to define itself as defective. Initially parents commonly consider themselves the "cause" of a child's homosexuality, and wonder where they went wrong. It is analogous to having the fantasy of the ideal child only to discover upon birth its defects. The family, parents and siblings alike, may need to go through a process of redefinition in order to regain equilibrium and to reestablish its definition of itself as healthy. Also, it is often thought there is conflict between a family member's role and his or her homosexuality. After being told of the mother's lesbianism a child has been known to ask "If you are gay are you still my mother?" (Back, 1985). The family needs to learn that there is no relationship between enactment of family roles and sexual orientation. These and other issues such as family acceptance of the gay member's lover or friends, or of not having grandchildren by the gay member, commonly need to be dealt with, and are usually resolved over time so that the gay member is reintegrated into the family, albeit with the new (to the family) identity of homosexual. The extent of reintegration into the family may depend on such factors as ethnicity, individual family culture, and degree of religiosity. Moreover, since persons who exhibit authoritarian personalities conform rigidly to middle-class values, have little tolerance for ambiguity, and have punitive attitudes toward non-conforming sexual activity (Babad, Birnbaum, & Benne, 1983), it is likely they will have great difficulty accepting a family member as gay.

There is very little science regarding homosexuality and the family. Only scant research exists. Thus, it behooves existing departments of family science, and departments of psychology, sociology, family nursing and medicine, and other academic units of universities concerned with the family to increase substantially their study of families and homosexuality, and to study the gay/lesbian *family* in its multiple variations. There is a sufficient pool of subject families and researchers for the development of a sub-specialty of family scientists to devote their research efforts exclusively to the study of the gay/lesbian family and the effect of homosexuality on the family. Although some suggestions for additional research have in the past been made (Bozett, 1985, 1987), we offer these additional recommendations.

RESEARCH ISSUES

In western societies there are few rites of passage for individuals entering man or womanhood. Confirmation rites are found in various religious faiths to mark the beginnings of pubescence and approaching young adulthood but these are not universally practiced. The closest to a universal practice of passage, and this is largely limited to the non-poor social classes, is obtaining a driver's license, and if at all possible the use of wheels. Even this dramatic life course event is devoid of myth and symbology which characterizes rites of passage in non-western and preliterate societies.

There is agreement, however, that the period of adolescence is one of turbulence, uncertainty, and volatile expressions of behaviors and feelings in the quest for identity, self-acceptance, self-esteem, personhood, and independence of the family. The search for "who am I" and how do I fit into a world of high technology and robotism, and at times bent on self-destruction, is highly influenced by one's peers and media images. Being in sync with peer expectations and the proper image is requisite for survival.

One research issue is whether homosexual adolescents have problems which other adolescents do not experience. If peer acceptance is unattainable and rejection of the homosexual identity prevails, can and how do homosexual adolescents acquire self-acceptance and self-esteem? What are the manifestations of rejection by non-homosexual adolescents? Do homosexual youth have higher rates of suicide, runaway youth, and drug dependency compared to straight adolescents? What are the options for homosexual youths to survive and to experience some quality of life enroute to adulthood? What are the responses of homosexual and non-homosexual parents to this situation? Is one, and perhaps a primary option, the formation by homosexual youth of a close knit in-group in order to receive nurturance, support, affection, caring, love, and help; acts we would expect to find in families? Do such groups exist, what is their incidence, and do they function to protect the homosexual adolescent on her or his personal journey to adulthood and to counteract and neutralize the discriminating practices of the larger society. Systematic quantitative and qualitative studies are indicated in order to confirm or reject the notion of the extra burdens experienced by homosexual youth on the road to adulthood.

It is believed that there is an increase in the incidence of lesbians becoming parents by artificial insemination or natural conception, generally, with a gay man. The reasons for this observed desire for parenthood are unclear. One neglected area of study concerns legal issues. If a lesbian of a couple becomes a parent, does the other member become a parent as occurs in any heterosexual marriage, *if* a break-up occurs? One legal issue is regarding custody and parental rights. Research is required involving the collection and analysis of cases in various jurisdictions on how such issues are resolved. Are the courts treating such cases similar to those involving cohabitation where parental rights are conveyed to the separated partner, if it is in the "best interest of the child?"

Other researchable issues include the response of the gay network to the expectant lesbian mother. How will this network react and will relationships and emotional support continue unaffectedly? The consequences of the absence of a male role model for a child is an issue for the lesbian and single parent family. Does the putative father, or some other male member of the gay network, play this role? Another issue concerns the explanations provided a child for the absence of a father. These phenomena are so recent that a collection of experiences in handling these issues will provide a description of appropriate techniques and strategies to maximize child rearing outcomes.

Relationships of lesbian mothers and their children with various publics: family of orientation, other lesbians, mothers, grandparents, relatives and non-lesbian friends, is an uncharted research area. One major question is how these families are treated by functionaries of a society's organizations and institutions, especially those in the human service area.

Adoption is a complex process fraught with contradictions and variable roles according to particular state jurisdictions. The frustrations experienced by non-gay couples are believed to be even greater when involved in the adoption process. Courts are reported to give short shrift to efforts at adoption by gay men and lesbians, and social service agencies have not demonstrated extreme enthusiasm either. Studies are needed on court decisions during the past ten years to ascertain trends and rationales resonated in the courts which establish the common law in this matter. Investigations on the perceptions and attitudes of functionaries of adoption agencies toward homosexuals will establish the level of homophilia and needed programs to enable non-heterosexuals to have options equitous with heterosexuals in adoption practices.

Another line of inquiry is on new paradigms which will effect a transformation of dominant values, perceptions, and behaviors of straight persons regarding homosexuality and its legitimacy as a life style. A paradigmatic revolution is underway worldwide. Individuals in varied walks of life are asking such fundamental questions on the nature of the cosmos: the threat of nuclear holocaust, creation of a worldwide community, depletion of the ozone, despoiling the globe, destruction of the rain forest, pollution, and overpopulation. They are seeking new paradigms and endemic transformed behavior. Such shifts from old to new paradigms may include gender and sexual preference. Assessment of this shift in paradigms, its direction and content, is currently needed.

Lifespan studies of gay males and lesbians, some using longitudinal designs are indicated. There is little knowledge of the life course and presumed changes in behavior over time. For example, does acceptance of one's homosexuality and concomitant disclosure occur at one particular life stage compared to another, at a later over an earlier age? Are there differences in life styles over time between the disclosing and non-disclosing homosexual?

Quality research on the effects of AIDS upon families, kin and social networks is required if we are to understand the profound social and psychic consequences of this disease for those involved. Qualitative studies, primarily, can reveal the stories; the burdens, burn outs, spiritual transformations, caring practices, coping techniques and strategies of the ill and concerned others. New definitions of family need to be conceptualized in order to describe the functioning members, those persons who give endlessly, care, nurturance, and love.

Married gay men and lesbians and their relationship in two worlds is another research issue. Little is known regarding the incidence and prevalence of this phenomenon, and the consequences for the families involved.

Religious institutions profile a moral position and voice, and can influence millions to maintain or change paradigms which condition adherents to a posture regarding homosexuality. Detailed studies are needed on positions of religious faiths and denominations regarding the accommodation of homosexuality, resolving conflicts among homosexual and heterosexual parishioners, meeting the needs of homosexual family members, and tolerating and accommodating the homosexuality of church functionaries.

REFERENCES

Altman, D. (1982). *The homosexualization of America, the Americanization of the homosexual*. New York: St. Martin's.

Babad, E. Y., Birnbaum, M., & Benne, K. D. (1983). *The social self: Group influences on personal identity*. Beverly Hills, CA: Sage.

Back, G. G. (1985). *Are you still my mother: Are you still my family*. New York: Warner.

Bozett, F. W. (1987). *Gay and lesbian parents*. New York: Praeger.

Bozett, F. W. (1988). Gay fatherhood. In P. Bronstein, & C. P. Cowan (Eds.), *Fatherhood today: Men's changing role in the family*. New York: John Wiley & Sons.

Bozett, F. W. (1985). Gay men as fathers. In S. M. H. Hanson and F. W. Bozett (Eds.), *Dimensions of fatherhood*. Beverly Hills, CA: Sage.

Bullough, V. (1979). *Homosexuality: A history*. New York: New American Library.

Goffman, E. (1963). *Stigma*. Englewood Cliffs, NJ: Prentice-Hall.

Herek, G. M. (1984). Beyond "homophobia": A social psychological perspective on attitudes towards lesbian and gay men. *Journal of Homosexuality, 10,* 1-21.

Hitchens, D. (1979/1980). Social attitudes, legal standards, and personal trauma in child custody cases. *Journal of Homosexuality, 5,* 80-95.

Lasch, C. (1977). *Haven in a heartless world: The family besieged*. New York: Basic Books.

Lindesmith, A. R., Strauss, A. L., & Denzin, N. K. (1977). *Social psychology*. New York: Holt, Rienhart, & Winston.

Ross, M. W. (1983). *The married homosexual man*. London: Routledge & Kegan Paul.

Walter, D. (1985, December 10). Troubled times for Texas gays. *The Advocate*, p. 11.

Weinberg, G. (1972). *Society and the healthy homosexual*. New York: Doubleday.

Weinberg, M. S., & Williams, C. J. (1974). *Male homosexuals: Their problems and adaptations*. New York: Oxford University.

Hidden Branches and Growing Pains: Homosexuality and the Family Tree

Erik F. Strommen

SUMMARY. In reviewing the effects of having a gay or lesbian member in the family of origin, one is repeatedly drawn to the central role played by the social stigma surrounding homosexuality. The present paper suggests that social stereotypes and prejudices toward homosexuals create an image of homosexuality as incompatible with the family, and that the family's reactions to having a homosexual member depend upon their acceptance or rejection of these prejudices. When homosexual family members are discovered, heterosexual family members experience a conflict between their conceptions of homosexual persons and the familiar family role of the homosexual member. The origin and nature of this conflict, and differences among family members in their reactions are reviewed. Long-term resolution and possible models of positive and negative outcome are also described. It is suggested that the conflict experienced by family members is in many ways similar to the "coming out" process of homosexual identity acquisition, and that this similarity may reflect common mechanisms for coming to grips with a pejorative, negatively labeled social identity.

When reviewing the growing literature on the psychological development of homosexual individuals and their biological families, one is repeatedly led to ask why a homosexual identity should be so terribly troubling to both gay individuals and their relatives. Homosexual individuals experience a difficult, often painful identity de-

Erik F. Strommen, PhD, is Lecturer in the Department of Psychology, Rutgers University. Correspondence may be sent to the author, Department of Psychology, Tillett Hall, Rutgers University, New Brunswick, NJ 08903.

The author would like to thank Robin Gates for his comments on an earlier draft of this article.

velopment process in coming to acknowledge and accept their sexuality. Similarly, the families of origin of homosexuals, when they discover a relative is gay, experience this discovery as a negative, disruptive event which is often followed by long-term distress. While it has been the rule to consider homosexual identity development as distinct from family member reactions to having a homosexual relative, the elements of both processes are so strikingly similar that they suggest a common foundation. This foundation is societal stigma. Being homosexual, or having a homosexual family member, is disruptive only because society and its institutions view homosexuality in a powerful and pervasive negative light. The psychological adjustment of gay individuals and their families as it relates to this social stigma represents an understudied and poorly understood area of both social and counseling psychology. The existing literature, however, suggests a commonality of issues and themes in both individual homosexual identity development and family member adjustment to having a homosexual relative. This similarity of issues suggests that a profitable theoretical and practical synthesis of our understanding of personal family adjustment is possible. This synthesis is rooted in societal definitions of deviance, and their effects on personal and familial identity.

In the present paper, I will sketch out a framework for understanding the psychological adjustment of both homosexual family members and their relatives. This framework is developed on the basic assertion that the nature of family reaction, and its long-term effects, are both understandable and coherent when viewed as the product of having a major social deviance uncovered within the close environment of the family circle. The emphasis of this paper will be on family members, but the implications for the personal development of homosexuals themselves will be considered where appropriate. Under the present theory, the personal development of homosexual family members involves the rejection of societal values, and the creation of a self-identity that includes a positive affirmation of homosexuality as a component. For the family, the task is similar but more complex. Family members must both create a positive identity for the homosexual member AND create a place for this identity *within the family*. This process means reconciling two conflicting roles for the gay family member: The stigmatized social identity that comes with being homosexual and the familiar family role the gay member has held all along. To describe this process, I will first define the stigmatized image of homosexuals as a social identity or role, and how this stigma affects the personal development of a homosexual identity. Next, the invisible or unobtrusive nature of homosexuality within the family, and the effects on heterosexual family members of discovering a homosexual relative will be described. Finally, the long-term nature of the family's adjustment process and a portrait of the extremes of adjustment and their possible mechanisms will be presented.

SOCIAL STIGMA AND FAMILY VALUES

It is common knowledge that homosexuality is the subject of continuing and long-standing hostility on the part of the majority of Americans. Homosexuals are the focus of a complex set of social prejudices, prejudices which have increased in popularity since the advent of the AIDS epidemic (Bryant, 1982; Levitt & Klassen, 1979; Gallup Poll, 1987). A comprehensive treatment of these values, and their likely historical origins, is beyond the scope of this paper. (I recommend Boswell [1980] for a highly readable and informative treatment of this topic.) Knowledge of social prejudices is vital to an understanding of the family's perspective on homosexuality, however. Social prejudices provide a pre-existing model for the family to use in forming its attitudes toward homosexuals in general, and can govern their initial reactions toward homosexual family members in particular. Social stereotypes define what is "wrong" with homosexuals, and provide the family with expectations concerning their character and behavior (Gonsiorek, 1982). For present purposes, a consideration of four specific sources of anti-homosexual prejudice, which have direct implications for the family's misunderstanding of its homosexual member, is in order.

First, there is the popular social justification of prejudice against homosexuality on the basis that it is "unnatural" because it does not involve heterosexual reproduction (Boswell, 1980; Katz, 1983). This idea places homosexuals outside of marriage, dating, and other institutions for legitimizing intimacy. In families where these traditional rituals are given a high status, the need to adapt to a new, unfamiliar type of relationship, particularly a same-sex relationship, may be stressful and conflict-producing. More broadly, homosexuals are not generally thought of in terms of their having intimate relationships of any kind, familial or otherwise. Homosexuals are not thought of as brothers, daughters, mothers, etc. to other people; the public stereotype seems to be one of solitary, deviant individuals. Within the intimate confines of the family, then, homosexuality is seldom anticipated because societal prejudices lead family members to believe that those with whom they have close relationships cannot be gay.

The second social prejudice with relevance to the family is the widespread misconception that homosexuality constitutes a threat to children (Martin & Hetrick, 1988). This notion persists despite well-documented evidence that it is false (Burgess et al., 1978; De-Francis, 1966; Groth & Birnbaum, 1978; Kempe & Kempe, 1984). Fear for the safety of children, unfortunately, is a source of strong, irrational reaction on the part of the public. The notion that homosexuality is incompatible with children or child-rearing may contribute to the image of homosexuals as "family-less." Children are a major defining feature of the family (Skolnick, 1978). By characterizing children as endangered by homosexuals, homosexuals are dissociated from any loving, positive relationship with them.

The last two sources of prejudice against homosexuals are, unfortunately, the institutionalized value systems of religion and psychology. Outdated interpretation and inappropriate use of scripture to justify the persecution of homosexuals has a long tradition in Christian society (Boswell, 1980; McNeill, 1976; Martin, 1983). While a minority of Christian churches challenge anti-homosexual theology, the vast majority of Jewish and Christian faiths maintain a hostile attitude toward homosexuals in their flock (Hiltner, 1980). This doctrinal hostility means that families with strong religious convictions are likely to endorse this hostility within the family, even against one of their own. The significant hostility of established religions, supported by secular laws against homosexual behavior (themselves based on Christian traditions), also lends a powerful aura of veracity to the general idea that homosexuals are morally degenerate and a "threat to society."

On the secular side, religious bias is buttressed by that of science, especially clinical psychology and psychiatry. These professions continue to contribute an aura of "scientific" legitimacy to the view that homosexuals are both mentally and physically deviant (Bayer & Spitzer, 1982; DeCecco, 1987; Morin, 1977; Stoller et al., 1973). A recent survey of clinical psychologists in the United States found that more than one in five practicing therapists still treat homosexuality as a mental illness, despite the fact that it is no longer classified as such; in addition, fully 45% of those surveyed did not consider such behavior unethical (Pope, Tabachnick, & Keith-Spiegel, 1987). The religious and professional validation of anti-homosexual prejudice reinforces the general view of homosexuals as undesirable and deviant persons in general society, and by extension within the family as well. These twin sources of anti-gay condemnation mean that authorities to whom the family may turn for information about homosexuality are as likely as not to simply reinforce the family's misconceptions rather than encourage critical reflection on them.

Social stereotypes of homosexuals lie at the heart of why homosexuality is a psychological issue of such significance to both gay individuals and their families. Because the social stereotypes of homosexuality are so negative and so false, homosexuals must reject them in order to establish a self-affirmed, psychologically adaptive identity (Weinberg & Williams, 1974). Their families must experience a similar process. They must reject their own stereotypes and develop new values about homosexuality that do not stigmatize their homosexual relative. Before describing this process, however, the background against which it occurs must be explored in more detail.

HOMOSEXUALITY AS A PERSONAL ISSUE

In light of the strong, overt negative social prejudices against homosexuals, it is clear that homosexual family members must confront a variety of personal issues both in coming to terms with their sexual identity and with making their families aware of their feelings. There is no agreed upon model of "coming out," the process by which gay people come to define themselves and disclose their identities to others. There are many theories of this process, however (Cass, 1979, 1984; Coleman, 1982; DuBay, 1987; Martin, 1982; Minton & MacDonald, 1984; Sullivan, 1982; Troiden, 1979), which suggest several characteristic features of the attainment of a gay self-identity that have relevance for the family. The first of these is the emotional isolation engendered by the absence of other homosexuals in the immediate environment (Gagnon, 1977; Martin, 1982; Sullivan, 1984; Voeller, 1980). Because social values condemn homosexuality so severely, few positive role models are present in the public media for gay people to emulate. For the same reason, older, well-adjusted homosexuals in the community who may be more accessible are often concealing themselves as well. While this situation may be changing, it is still the case that there is a general lack of familiar, open gay people in the local community. This absence of role models can lead gay people struggling with their feelings to believe that they are alone in feeling as they do, and question whether they are deviant or mentally ill (Martin & Hetrick, 1988). The private guilt and fear of this situation can render them afraid to reach out to others in the family, for fear that others cannot understand and will simply verify what the homosexual person already dreads and fears: that he is abnormal and deserving of censure for feelings he cannot control or change. Thus, the homosexual member who is aware of his feelings often withdraws from the family for fear they will confirm society's attitudes.

An awareness of homosexual feelings and desires by no means implies that a homosexual identity has been achieved. There is significant evidence that a conscious homosexual identity is a psychologically late development, occurring anywhere from early pubescence to young adulthood, and sometimes much later (Bozett, 1982; Cass, 1979, 1984; Ponse, 1978; Ross, 1983). The late attainment of gay self-awareness of self-definition means that for a long period of time, typically *years*, homosexual family members are aware of their attraction to members of their own sex, but do not yet consider themselves to be "homosexual" or "gay" (Troiden, 1979; Cass, 1979). Part of the delay in acknowledging these labels may stem from an unwillingness to identify with the horrible image of homosexuality given by social stereotypes. To avoid identifying with this stereotype, homoerotic feelings are rationalized as transient or insignificant by homosexual family members, and their implications for personal identity are not contemplated. Active resistance and denial of one's homosexuality is also common. It is possible for a person to be actively engaging in homosexual encounters and yet repressing this side of themselves almost totally (Humphreys, 1970). This self-denial makes it possible for homosexual family members to dissociate their homosexuality from their family role, such that they can even practice concealment from the family without seeing it as duplicity (Humphreys, 1970; Ponse, 1978). Homosexual family members, then, struggle with their own desires and fantasies in a private conflict between their "good" family identities and the "bad" homosexual identity they are presented with by society. This conflict is resolved by "coming out" or rejecting social values, and accepting one's own homosexuality as a positive and desirable part of the self.

The attainment of a homosexual identity is an invisible event for others in the family. Only the homosexual member is aware that his or her identity has changed, and been redefined. Homosexual family members who have achieved a homosexual identity are thus confronted with two choices concerning the rest of the family: Revealing their new sexual identity (disclosure), or hiding the truth and perpetuating current family misconceptions (concealment). We do not have a clear idea why gay persons choose one option or the other. There is research evidence indicating that concealment is detrimental to psychological well-being, while openness is beneficial (cf. Chelune et al., 1979). To this end, homosexuals who choose to disclose often do so because they feel great personal anxiety over having to be covert, and feel guilt over deliberately misleading family members (Bozett, 1980, 1981, 1982; Coleman, 1982; Gagnon, 1977; Humphreys, 1970). Those who do disclose often say that they felt concealment placed a "distance" between themselves and their families, and left them unable to share personal feelings with family members (Bozett, 1980; Cramer & Roach, 1988; Hanscombe & Forster, 1982; Hoeffer, 1981; Maddox, 1982; Miller, 1979; Ross, 1983). There is also evidence, for both lesbians and gay men, that disclosure is positively correlated with mental health (Rand, Graham, & Rawlings, 1982; Schmitt & Kurdek, 1987; Weinberg & Williams, 1974).

If the decision to disclose is based on a desire to improve one's family relationships and mental well-being, the decision not to disclose appears to be based on more concrete and painful evaluations of oneself and one's family circumstances. The failure to reject societal values when one "comes out" can lead to adopting societal stereotypes as applicable to yourself. There is evidence that homosexual men who have internalized or adopted societal values feel shame and disgust over their desires, and conceal their "flaw" from their families for this reason (Bozett, 1980). More pragmatically, gay men and women who are well-adjusted often conceal their sexuality in order to avoid conflict or reprisal from alienated family members. Gay fathers and lesbian mothers, for example, often avoid disclosing to their ex-spouses because they fear custody battles, a fear amply justified by court statistics (Hanscombe & Forster, 1982; Hitchens, 1980; Hoeffer, 1981; Maddox, 1982; Pagelow, 1980; Whittlin, 1983). Recent evidence from a study of gay men has suggested that, at least for self-sufficient gay men, the decision is based not on fear of a negative reaction so much as a desire to avoid hurting or disappointing their parents (Cramer & Roach, 1988). For adolescents and young adults, however, whose financial and physical security often depends on parental goodwill alone, disclosure or discovery can mean loss of family support, loss of shelter and physical abuse (Bales, 1985; Hersch, 1988). In these situations, fear of the consequences of reaction make concealment a necessity; it maintains personal security and family stability by perpetuating the false image held by others in the family. Concealment always holds the risk of discovery, however, and discovery will initiate a family crisis just as surely as self-disclosure will.

HOMOSEXUALITY: THE INVISIBLE DIFFERENCE

In order to understand the advent of the family crisis over having a homosexual member, it is necessary to consider the striking nonphysical or psychological nature of homosexuality. Unlike gender, age, or race, which present outward physical indicators of social group membership, homosexuality is strictly a way of feeling and acting. Homosexuals are not distinguishable by any overt characteristics, and thus do not stand out as unique from other family members in any sense (Plummer, 1975; Warren, 1974; Weinberg & Williams, 1974). This physical invisibility is complemented by the fact that our society operates on a pervasive assumption of "straight until proven guilty," such that all persons are given the benefit of the doubt and presumed to be heterosexual. The homosexual family member thus is not only physically indistinguishable from others, but actively mis-identified by others in their daily interactions with him or her as well (Ponse, 1978, 1980). This indistinguishability and mis-classification means that to reveal their true identity, homosexual persons must act against current family roles and assumptions, and explicitly negate the assumed heterosexual identities with which they are endowed.

If we recall that a conscious awareness of one's "gayness," or "lesbianism" is a private, psychologically late development, then it is apparent that homosexual persons look and act no differently than other family members, but yet experience a growing psychological awareness that they "feel" different: They are attracted to persons of the same gender, while others around them are not. Taken together, the hidden or invisible nature of homosexuality and the late appearance of a self-conscious homosexual identity suggests that gay individuals "awaken" or develop their identities within a family setting in which other members of the family assume the homosexual member to be heterosexual, and only the homosexual member is aware of the fact that this assumption is incorrect. The disclosure of homosexuality by the family member, or the discovery of this homosexuality by others, is thus very likely to precipitate a crisis, since it means an unexpected challenge to the family's implicit understanding of the homosexual member.

THE REVELATION CRISIS

Thus far, I have tried to demonstrate how a false, stigmatized image of gay people, fashioned from social stereotypes, provides a model for understanding homosexuality that both the family and the gay individual must acknowledge. While family members may not actively accept this image, it is often the only one available to families who do not have any contact with openly gay people. Indeed, the invisible nature of homosexuality, which allows a personal gay identity to develop privately, may actually promote the maintenance of negative stereotypes by letting them go unchallenged within the family itself. The homosexual family member, eventually rejecting social values, either discloses to the family or is revealed accidentally. This unexpected revelation initiates two processes in heterosexual family members. First, heterosexual family members grope for a way to understand the homosexual member. The unfortunate result of this effort is that the homosexual member is often endowed with an identity *constructed from the family's own stereotypes of homosexuality*. Knowledge of family values may thus be of great assistance to the counselor or therapist involved with the family of a homosexual person, because the family's values form the hidden structure of the family's initial reactions, and govern the severity of their reactions as well: The more negative the family's values concerning homosexuality, the more severe the reaction. In extreme cases, family members are capable of irrational behavior such as physical abuse or throwing a previously intimate family member out on the street (Bales, 1985; Jones, 1978; Hersch, 1988; Martin & Hetrick, 1988).

Correlates of family member values which can help professionals predict the strength of family reactions have been identified. Collins and Zimmerman (1983) confirm that religious values play a large part in determining family member reactions: The more that family members rely on religious teachings as a source of moral strength and guidance, the more negative and severe the family's reaction to a homosexual member will be. There is also indirect evidence that family values regarding traditional gender roles interact with family values about homosexuality: Individuals possessing rigid, separate role definitions for the sexes are likely to react negatively to homosexuality in anyone, family member or otherwise (MacDonald, 1974; MacDonald & Games, 1974; Storms, 1978; Weinberger & Millham, 1979). How the family views itself in relation to society also plays a role in family member reaction. The family's view of itself in relation to the community is a major part of a family's "themes" or defining values and traditions. DeVine (1984) describes three family themes which have negative implications for family reactions: (a) "maintain respectability at all costs," which stresses conformity to societal norms; (b) "as a family we can solve our own problems," which implies resistance to outside information and assistance, and that the family need not change its values in any way; and (c) "be as our religion teaches us to be," which allows the family to draw on religious values to reject the homosexual member in good conscience.

Demographic variables such as age and gender can be useful as predictors of family member reaction as well. There is some evidence to suggest that younger children do not react to homosexuality with the same strong visceral negativism of adults (Moses & Hawkins, 1982). This may be due to their not having internalized societal prejudices, not having a clear understanding of sexuality and its relationship to social identity, or both. Whatever the mechanism, children show increasingly negative, adult-like reactions as they get older, with adolescents demonstrating attitudes quite similar to adults (Bozett, 1987; Schofield, 1967; Sorensen, 1973). (The children of gay parents show unique reactions, described below.) At the upper end of the age range, it is possible that older adults may react differently than younger or middle-aged adults. Life experiences are thought to give older adults extra insight or wisdom into personal relationships, social values, and decision making (Brent & Watson, 1980; Clayton, 1982). This extra insight and knowledge of social bonds and their vicissitudes may well moderate the reactions of older persons to homosexuality in the family.

There is abundant evidence that heterosexuals react more negatively to homosexuals of their own sex than those of the opposite sex (see the excellent review of this work by Herek [1984]). This fact means that one's same-sex family members are the ones likely to demonstrate the most difficult reactions. Men have a special problem in this regard: There is a notable tendency for men to react more harshly than women towards homosexual persons of both sexes, but especially towards gay men (Kite, 1984; Herek, 1988). Given this finding, it seems likely that male family members such as fathers, brothers, or sons can be expected to react more harshly than female members, no matter who is disclosing. Indirect evidence supporting this point is found in the fact that the husbands of married lesbians react more violently to disclosure, and maintain animosity towards their homosexual spouses longer than the wives of gay men (Hanscombe & Forster, 1982; Jones, 1978).

As the family struggles to find a way to integrate the homosexual member's new identity into the family system, the second component of family member reaction occurs. This is the negation of the homosexual family member's previous role as brother, wife, son, etc. by the new, homosexual identity the family is trying to define. This disruption in role definition is experienced by the rest of the family as a sudden alienation from the homosexual member, a feeling that the homosexual member's previous identity is lost, and that the "new" homosexual member is a stranger in their midst (Collins & Zimmerman, 1983; DeVine, 1984; Jones, 1978; Weinberg, 1972). This component of initial reaction is best understood with reference to the point of view of individual family members. Heterosexual family members each perceive the implications of homosexual identity differently, depending on the particular role relationship between themselves and the homosexual family member. Given the diverse variety of role relationships that comprise families it would certainly seem likely that individual family member reactions should be dictated by the particular relationship that the homosexual member has with that individual. Unfortunately, very few studies have concerned themselves with this issue, but the little information that is available is suggestive.

Beginning with the family of origin, parental experiences have been the most well-documented. Parents respond to their child's homosexuality and the alienation it brings with powerful feelings of guilt and failure. Parents apparently see themselves as somehow having contributed to their child's becoming homosexual, and from their perspective this makes them responsible for their child's deviance and abnormality (Fairchild & Hayward, 1979; Jones, 1978; Weinberg, 1972). Undoubtedly, the popularization of psychological theories that parental inadequacies "cause" homosexuality contributes to this feeling on the part of parents. (See Bieber [1962] for a classic example of this type of theory.) Fairchild and Hayward (1979) provide excellent firsthand accounts written by parents which eloquently capture the anguish parents feel, believing that they themselves have destroyed their children's lives and "made" them the abnormal, degenerate strangers of their own stereotypes.

Only a single author (Jones, 1978) has discussed sibling reactions in any detail. Jones reports that siblings, unlike their parents, often react with feelings of anger and confusion rather than guilt, and feel that the homosexual member is a stranger despite their shared childhoods. Considering the significant role that siblings play in each others' lives as sources of identity and intimacy (Schvaneveldt & Ihinger, 1979), it is likely that there are important effects on the siblings as a result of discovering that a fellow sibling is gay that have not yet been documented. DeVine (1984) and Jones (1978) have both suggested that family members are told incrementally, with the emotionally closest members (who are often siblings) being disclosed to first. The implications of this sequential disclosure have not been explored, but it seems likely that sibling reaction to the "advance notice" of homosexuality may play a role in overall family reaction, since the sibling disclosed to now has the option of telling the parents or modifying their reactions through his or her own reactions.

Members of the family of origin who have not been studied and whose reactions are of some interest are grandparents. Do homosexuals disclose to grandparents? Are grandparents told when the discovery of a homosexual family member is made? Are there homosexual grandparents who have told their children and grandchildren? It is known that grandparents exert significant influence over both their children and grandchildren, and that they function as important sources of influence within the family system (Matthews & Sprey, 1985; Troll, 1982). Grandparent reactions, as well as considerations of disclosure to grandparents by homosexual family members, is a topic that is in need of research.

When the homosexual family member is a spouse or parent, the effects of alienation on the family are more diverse. Because the foundations of marriage as an institution are heterosexual, it is to be expected that the partners of homosexuals in marriages should react strongly to the negation of the marital contract by the homosexuality of their spouse. A distinct literature has developed on gay men in marriages. The wives of gay men reportedly react in a manner similar to parents: They feel as if they have somehow caused their husband's homosexuality, and have failed in their duty and role as spouses (Gochros, 1985; Ross, 1983). The husbands of lesbians are more of a mystery. They avoid participating in research (Hanscombe & Forster, 1982), so we have only the reports of their lesbian ex-wives to go on, and they paint a disturbing portrait. In contrast to the wives of gay men, there is the possibility of actual physical abuse by the husbands, and long-term animosity is common (Hanscombe & Forster, 1982; Jones, 1978). Coleman (1985) has suggested that a wife's homosexuality is possibly viewed by her husband as a particularly onerous form of infidelity. Given the double-standard that a wife's indiscretions are more serious than a husband's, the reactions of husbands of lesbians may perhaps be profitably compared to the reaction of husbands discovering heterosexual infidelity on the part of their wives.

The children of gays and lesbians present a unique profile in the psychological literature. Much research has demonstrated no harmful effects on children of having or living with a homosexual parent (Golombok, Spencer, & Rutter, 1983; Green, 1978; Green, Mandel, Hotvedt, Gray, & Smith, 1986; Hall, 1978; Hoeffer, 1981; Hotvedt & Mandel, 1982; Kirkpatrick, Smith, & Roy, 1981). Little work has been done on these children's perceptions of homosexual identity or how they feel their parents' homosexuality affects them. Recent data, however, are intriguing. More than half of these children have an initially negative or uncertain reaction to parental disclosure (Harris & Turner, 1986). However, the majority of both gay mothers and fathers report that they are open with their children about their homosexuality, and that disclosure improved their emotional relationships with their children in the long term (Bozett, 1980; Hanscombe & Forster, 1982; Hoeffer, 1981; Miller, 1979). As noted above, age plays a role in children's reaction to their parents' homosexuality. Younger children, not having a clear idea of what homosexuality is, or its implications for personal identity, do not seem to experience the feeling of estrangement that older relatives do (Moses & Hawkins, 1982). However, recent research suggests that older children, especially adolescents, are at least aware of the stigma of homosexuality. A minority of these children fear "identity contamination," or being abused by others because their parent is homosexual. Some express resentment toward their parents for this social difficulty (Bozett, 1987), while others blame society (White, 1987). It is not surprising, given this problem, that homosexual parents practice and advise their children to practice discretion with peers (Golombok et al., 1983; Jones, 1978; Miller, 1979).

The revelation crisis is clearly the most severe and direct effect on the family of having a homosexual member. By drawing on social values to try and understand the homosexual member, the family experiences a conflict between the negative substance of social stereotypes and the homosexual member's previous identity. The severity of this conflict depends on many factors, but it is invariably perceived as disruptive and negative by the family. Once this initial crisis has passed, however, the permanence of the situation becomes apparent. The family must somehow come to grips with this change in its structure, and find a way to reclaim the homosexual member. This process is described in the next section.

THE LONG TERM

Several authors have noted that the effects of having a homosexual family member are not abrupt or transient, but extend beyond the initial discovery or disclosure as a significant issue (Collins & Zimmerman, 1983; DeVine, 1984; Fairchild & Hayward, 1979; Jones, 1978; Weinberg, 1972). DeVine (1984) has described this process as a progression through a series of stages. First, there is *subliminal awareness*, in which a family member's homosexuality is suspected because of specific behaviors, such as having many same-sex friends, not dating heterosexually, adopting particular fashions, etc., and changes in communication such as avoiding certain topics in family conversation. The second stage is *impact*, when the explicit, undeniable truth is made apparent; this is the phase of the revelation crisis described above. The third phase, *adjustment*, involves the family's initial attempts to adapt to the homosexual member. This usually takes the form of conservation of the family status quo in conformity with social values: The homosexual family member is actually pressured to change or at least hide his sexuality from others. The fourth phase, *resolution*, involves the family's discarding of their fantasized heterosexual identity for the homosexual family member. During this period, family members begin to examine their own values about homosexuality and possibly modify them in light of their new, intimate knowledge of homosexual persons. Finally, in *integration*, the family changes its values in order to accept the homosexual member's new identity within the family.

Additional evidence that the family's adjustment is a lengthy process comes from the fact that there are support groups for the relatives of homosexuals, founded and run by people who have been through the same experience. One such organization, P-FLAG (Parents and Friends of Lesbians and Gays) which was founded in 1973 in New York City, has over 150 chapters around the United States and abroad. By studying how families help other families to change and accept their homosexual members, it is possible to gain insight into the issues confronting the family and the mechanisms for their resolution. The New York chapter's charter challenges the families of gay and lesbian persons to examine their own and society's values about homosexuality, and to consider the effects of these negative values on their gay relative's self-esteem. P-FLAG's major focus is on dispelling myths about homosexuality, and helping family members to shed the deeply felt but inaccurate values concerning homosexuality that they are applying to their child, sibling, or spouse. The literature provided by the organization emphasizes taking the homosexual family member's perspective, considering what being a homosexual person is like in the United States, and how painful growing up can be under such circumstance. P-FLAG thus facilitates acceptance and family reintegration by addressing both of the issues noted in the family crisis; encouraging critical reflection on one's own prejudices addresses the stigmatizing of the homosexual member, and encouraging empathy addresses the alienation and estrangement of identity that accompanies the social stigma.

In preparation for this article, I telephoned the New York City chapter office as a family member would, in order to obtain more detailed information about the organization and its members. The person answering the phone, whom I will refer to as Mrs. B., identified herself as the mother of a gay man and an active member of P-FLAG for seven years. In the course of our conversation she offered her own observations to me as she would to any family member calling. Her remarks confirmed and extended current research. She told me that although there are individual differences, reactions are quite similar across families, indicating a common experience. To quote her excellent description of the revelation crisis, she said that family members often feel as if there has been a "death in the family" when a loved one is found to be homosexual. The family may react as if the member is lost to them, and they express angry, ambivalent feelings toward the "new" homosexual person who has taken his old place. Verifying the available evidence that families move through a complex series of phases of acceptance, Mrs. B. also stressed that there are "degrees of acceptance," and that family members make progress through these degrees slowly and haltingly, in their own time and their own way. She also echoed the literature on the often detrimental effects of religion, saying that it is often the most religious persons who have the worst time coping with a family member's homosexuality. To this end, P-FLAG recommends several books dealing with the question of having a homosexual family member from a religious perspective, and provides references to books dealing with religion and homosexuality in general. A key component of P-FLAG's doctrine is that homosexuality is not a choice or a sin, but rather an acknowledgment of one's own feelings. Mrs. B. stated that "having to come out and be who you are" means being true to yourself and honest with others, a comment echoing the literature which reports that homosexual persons feel they must disclose to their families in order to be open and honest about themselves.

Gay persons often attend P-FLAG meetings to gain information on how best to come out to their parents. Mrs. B. counsels that gay people must be happy and comfortable with themselves before revealing their sexual orientation to their families, otherwise they only make the family's confusion worse by communicating self-doubt and uncertainty in response to family member concerns and anxiety. She has also found that the quality of the relationships in the family, especially between parents and the homosexual member, plays a role in both disclosure and adjustment. Homosexual family members who do not disclose end up having a rather superficial relationship with others in the family, since they cannot share much of their emotional lives with them. Some gay people, Mrs. B. has found, are not close to their families and accept this type of distance without regret. More often, however, gay people desire to be truthful so they can have the honest and intimate relationship they are used to with their families. Mrs. B. also commented that gay persons whose parents are deceased have attended the meetings of P-FLAG and expressed regret that they had not told their parents while they were alive. She worried that there are many gay people, who have not disclosed, who will also regret having not told their parents after they have died.

MODELS OF ADJUSTMENT AND THEIR MECHANISMS

Having reviewed the psychological issues involved for both homosexual individuals and their families, it is clear that just as the acquisition of a homosexual identity is a lengthy process for the individual, the family's acquisition of a new identity for the homosexual member takes time as well. Two mechanisms of this process suggest themselves. First, family values toward homosexuality must be defined or redefined. The family has to either articulate an understanding of homosexuality that does not stigmatize the gay member, or change its negative values to the same end. Second, a new homosexual identity for the family member, one that includes the familiar features of the old family role, must be constructed. In this final section, I will synthesize the available evidence and attempt to create a portrait of the two extremes of adaptation: acceptance and support of the homosexual member on the positive end, and rejection and hostility on the negative. These models must be regarded as tentative, but hopefully they will provide working hypotheses of the causes and mechanisms of different long-term outcomes, and suggest possible routes of intervention for professionals treating such families in an official capacity.

Weinberg (1972) has suggested a broad interpretation of family issues in the adjustment to having a homosexual member that serves as a convenient basis for describing positive and negative family adjustment outcomes. Describing the adaptation process with reference to parents, Weinberg characterized it as a conflict between two "parenting themes": A love theme and a conventionality theme. The love theme compels parents to accept their children as they are, regardless of social values. Parent-child love and loyalty takes precedence over societal mores in the love theme. The conventionality theme, in contrast, compels parents to censure their children and line up in support of societal norms. This theme stresses parental adherence to community values: Parents should adopt a position against the homosexual member, in accord with social values and prejudices. Weinberg's analysis can be profitably extended to all members of the family, and used as a general characterization of the major issues in family adjustment. A broad interpretation of positive adaptation is that it relies on the ascendancy of the love theme over the conventionality theme. Specifically, these families create a new identity for the homosexual member, in defiance of social values, and modify their own attitudes toward homosexuality as well. Several authors have suggested that to establish the new family role for the homosexual member, the old role must not only be recognized as lost, but grieved over (DeVine, 1984; Collins & Zimmerman, 1983; Weinberg, 1972). This seems only natural. Family roles entail not only assumptions about current behavior but expectations for the future as well. For families, canceling a member's heterosexual identity often means additional revelations: no conventional marriage, no grandchildren (at least not conceived of in the traditional fashion), and the loss of a host of other milestones of family life as well. Recognizing their expectations and mourning for them apparently allows positively adjusted families to create a new role for the homosexual member, one that is an accurate and realistic characterization of the whole person. In accord with their refusal to reject the homosexual member, positively adjusted families work to modify their own values toward homosexuality. By rejecting the negative stereotypes of homosexuality, it becomes possible to integrate the gay member's homosexual identity and family role together. A key to this reconstruction of a family role may be the gaining of a perspective: Sexuality is only one part of an individual's total nature. De-emphasizing the small part of the homosexual member's identity that is different, and retraining the rest of the individual's already known and loved attributes, may represent a major feature of long-term positive outcome.

Attempting to create a picture of rejection is necessarily more risky than creating a portrait of acceptance. Those who reject their family members because of homosexuality also seem to avoid discussing it with researchers, leading to a dearth of information about these people and their feelings. Nonetheless, it is possible to create a picture of these people using Weinberg's competing themes as a general framework, filling in the details using the current model. In rejecting families, it appears that the conventionality theme dominates. The family appears to accept the negative social stereotypes of homosexuality, and uses these stereotypes to understand the gay family member. Rejecting families appear to resent the role negation caused by the family member's homosexuality, and blame the homosexual member for causing the disruption. The alienation and disruption of the revelation crisis give rise to bitter recriminations in these families. Both Collins and Zimmerman (1983) and DeVine (1984) have suggested that this negative outcome is due in part to the family's lack of effective mechanisms for managing crises. Scape-goating, avoidance, and other maladaptive strategies may contribute to failure to make progress in these families. Kramer (in press) has speculated that adult cognitive development may play a role in poor adaptation to changes in the family structure as well. Persons with static world views (often characteristic of young and middle age) may be less able to reorganize their values and attributions than other older, who have a more relativistic world view. Whatever the source of this inability to address conflict and change, rejecting families remain fixed at the initial conflict point, and the result is a failure to redefine the homosexual family member's role. These families reject their gay relatives, and maintain continuing anger, disappointment, and guilt over the "pervert" in the family. One of the mechanisms of acceptance, putting oneself in the place of the homosexual relative, or being able to identify with his or her feelings, seems closed to these families. The homosexual member's old family role is idealized and longed for, but not given up. Since the old role is not "laid to rest" and its invalid components discarded, the family is unable to gain a sense of perspective on their own expectations or the relative importance of sexuality compared to the rest of the individual as a whole person. Their image of the homosexual member thus remains negative and stereotypical, and they remain estranged from this image, without a new family role to replace the one canceled by it. Because they are unwilling or unable to reject the stereotype, and integrate a more positive understanding of homosexuality with a new family role for the homosexual member, no resolution is possible and a hostile, ambivalent situation becomes the normal state of affairs.

CONCLUSIONS

By using social values and their effects on family attitudes and identity as a unifying theme, it is possible to characterize the adjustment of both gay persons and their families with reference to the same basic processes. Whether the goal is the attainment of a personal homosexual identity or the creation of a family role for a homosexual individual, a positive outcome for both these tasks requires that (a) negative values toward homosexuality be rejected or modified, and (b) the gay person's new identity or role must contain a positive or at least neutral attitude toward homosexuality as part of its content. As has been shown, this process is hindered or facilitated by many variables which are as yet only partially understood. Closer study of these factors can only help us gain more insight into the nature of this learning process for the family, and improve our skills for intervention.

The immediate implications of this process for members of the helping professions are obvious. Family members undergoing this redefinition and development of new values and roles need factual, unbiased information about homosexuality to help them gain a balanced perspective on the trauma they are experiencing. Unconscious biases and unspoken expectations need to be made explicit and discussed. These families need to be assisted in discarding the old role for their homosexual members, and encouraged to develop a new understanding of these persons that does not stigmatize them for being what they cannot help being. By providing facilitating, nonpejorative assistance to the family we can lessen the confusion and uncertainty these families experience as they wrestle with the reconstruction of long-held but never-examined beliefs and assumptions, and help them to keep the intimate circle of the family intact and healthy.

REFERENCES

Bayer, R. & Spitzer, R. I. (1982). Edited correspondence on the status of homosexuality in DSM-III. *Journal of the History of the Behavioral Sciences, 18,* 32-52.

Bieber, I. (1962). *Homosexuality.* New York: Basic Books.

Boswell, J. (1980). *Christianity, social tolerance, and homosexuality.* Chicago: University of Chicago Press.

Bozett, F. W. (1980). Gay fathers: How and why they disclose their homosexuality to their children. *Family Relations, 29,* 173-179.

Bozett, F. W. (1981). Gay fathers: Evolution of the gay-father identity. *American Journal of Orthopsychiatry, 51,* 552-559.

Bozett, F. W. (1982). Heterogeneous couples in heterosexual marriages: Gay men and straight women. *Journal of Marital and Sexual Therapy, 8,* 81-89.

Bozett, F. W. (1987). Children of gay fathers. In F. W. Bozett (Ed.), *Gay and lesbian parents* (pp. 39-57). New York: Praeger.

Brent, S. B. & Watson, D. (1980, November). *Aging and wisdom: Individual and collective aspects.* Paper presented at the 33rd. Annual Meeting of the Gerontological Society, San Diego, California.

Brown, H. (1976). *Familiar faces hidden lives.* New York: Harvest/Harcourt Brace Jovanovich Co.

Bryant, C. (1982). *Sexual deviancy and social proscription.* New York: Human Sciences Press.

Burgess, A. W., Groth, A. N., Holmstrom, L. L., & Sgroi, S. M. (1978). *Sexual assault of children and adolescents.* Lexington, MA: D. C. Heath.

Cass, V. (1979). Homosexual identity formation: A theoretical model. *Journal of Homosexuality, 4,* 219-236.

Cass, V. (1984). Homosexual identity formation: Testing a theoretical model. *Journal of Sex Research, 20,* 143-167.

Chelune, G. J., Archer, R. C., Civikly, J. M., Derlega, V. J., Doster, J. A., Grzelak, J., Herron, J. R., Kleinke, C. L., Nesbitt, J. G., Rosenfeld, L. B., Taylor, D. A., & Waterman, J. (1979). *Self-disclosure: Origins, patterns, and implications of openness in interpersonal relationships.* San Francisco: Jossey-Bass.

Clayton, V. (1982). Wisdom and intelligence: The nature and function of knowledge in the later years. *International Journal of Aging and Human Development, 15,* 315-321.

Coleman, E. (1982). Developmental stages of the coming-out process. In W. Paul, J. D. Weinrich, J. C. Gonsiorek, & M. E. Hotvedt (Eds.), *Homosexuality: Social, psychological, and biological issues* (pp. 149-158). Beverly Hills, CA: Sage Publications.

Coleman, E. (1985). Integration of male bisexuality and marriage. *Journal of Homosexuality, 11*(1/2), 189-207.

Collins, L. & Zimmerman, N. (1983). Homosexual and bisexual issues. In J. C.

Hansen, J. D. Woody, & R. H. Woody (Eds.), *Sexual issues in family therapy* (pp. 82-100). Rockville, MD: Aspen Publications.

Cramer, D. W. & Roach, A. J. (1988). Coming out to mom and dad: A study of gay males and their relationships with their parents. *Journal of Homosexuality, 15*(3/4), 79-92.

DeCecco, J. P. (1987). Homosexuality's brief recovery: From sickness to health and back again. *Journal of Sex Research, 23,* 106-114.

DeFrancis, V. (1966). *Protecting the child victim of sex crimes committed by adults.* Denver: American Humane Association.

DeVine, J. L. (1984). A systemic inspection of affectional preference orientation and the family of origin. *Journal of Social Work and Human Sexuality, 2,* 9-17.

Fairchild, B. & Hayward, N. (1979). *Now that you know: What every parent should know about homosexuality.* New York: Harvester/Harcourt Brace Jovanovich Co.

Gagnon, J. H. (1977). *Human sexualities.* Glenview, IL: Scott, Foresman and Co.

Gallup Polling, Inc. (1987, March). Homosexuality. *The Gallup Report* (Report No. 258). Princeton, NJ: Author.

Gochros, J. S. (1985). Wives' reactions to learning that their husbands are bisexual. *Journal of Homosexuality, 11*(1/2), 101-113.

Golombok, S., Spencer, A., & Rutter, M. (1983). Children in lesbian and single-parent households: Psychosexual and psychiatric appraisal. *Journal of Child Psychology, Psychiatry, and Allied Disciplines, 24,* 551-572.

Gonsiorek, J. C. (1982). Social psychological concepts in the understanding of homosexuality. In W. Paul, J. D. Weinrich, J. C. Gonsiorek, & M. E. Hotvedt (Eds.), *Homosexuality: Social, psychological, and biological issues* (pp. 115-119).

Green, R. (1978). Sexual identity of 37 children raised by homosexual or transsexual parents. *American Journal of Psychiatry, 135,* 692-697.

Green, R., Mandel, J. B., Hotvedt, M. E., Gray, J., & Smith, L. (1986). Lesbian mothers and their children: A comparison with solo heterosexual mothers and their children. *Archives of Sexual Behavior, 15,* 167-184.

Groth, A. N. & Birnbaum, H. J. (1978). Adult sexual orientation and attraction to underage children. *Archives of Sexual Behavior, 7,* 175-181.

Hall, M. (1978). Lesbian families: Cultural and clinical issues. *Social Work, 23,* 380-385.

Hanscombe, G. & Forsters, J. (1982). *Rocking the cradle.* Boston: Alyson.

Harris, M. D. & Turner, P. H. (1986). Gay and lesbian parents. *Journal of Homosexuality, 12,* 101-113.

Herek, G. M. (1984). Beyond "homosexuality": A social psychological perspective on attitudes toward lesbians and gay men. *Journal of Homosexuality, 10*(1/2), 1-21.

Herek, G. M. (1988). Heterosexuals' attitudes toward lesbians and gay men: Correlates and gender differences. *Journal of Sex Research, 25,* 451-477.

Hersch, P. (1988, January). Coming of age on city streets. *Psychology Today*, pp. 28-32 + .

Hiltner, S. (1980). Homosexuality and the churches. In J. Marmor (Ed.), *Homosexual behavior* (pp. 219-231). New York: Basic Books.

Hitchens, D. (1980). Social attitudes, legal standards, and personal trauma in child custody cases. *Journal of Homosexuality, 5,* 89-95.

Hoeffer, B. (1981). Children's acquisition of sex-role behavior in lesbian mother families. *American Journal of Orthopsychiatry, 51,* 552-559.

Hotvedt, M. E. & Mandel, J. (1982). Children of lesbian mothers. In J. Weinrich, B. Paul, J. C. Gonsiorek, & M. E. Hotvedt (Eds.), *Homosexuality: Social, psychological, and biological issues* (pp. 275-285). Beverly Hills, CA: Sage Publications.

Humphreys, L. (1970). *Tearoom trade*. Chicago: Aldine.

Jones, C. (1978). *Understanding gay relatives and friends*. New York: Seabury Press.

Katz, J. N. (1983). *Gay/Lesbian almanac: A new documentary*. New York: Harper & Row.

Kempe, R. S. & Kempe, C. H. (1984). *The common secret: Sexual abuse of children and adolescents*. New York: W. H. Freeman and Co.

Kirkpatrick, M., Smith, K., & Roy, R. (1981). Lesbian mothers and their children. *American Journal of Orthopsychiatry, 51,* 545-551.

Kite, M. E. (1984). Sex differences in attitudes toward homosexuality: A meta-analytic review. *Journal of Homosexuality, 10*(1/2), 69-81.

Kramer, D. A. (in press). Change and stability in family interaction patterns: A developmental model. In D. A. Kramer & M. J. Bopp (Eds.), *Movement through form: Transformations in clinical and developmental psychology*. New York: Springer-Verlag.

Levitt, E. A. & Klassen, A. D., Jr. (1979). Public attitudes toward homosexuality. In M. P. Levine (Ed.), *Gay men* (pp. 19-35). New York: Harper & Row.

MacDonald, A. (1974). The importance of sex-role to gay liberation. *Homosexual Counseling Journal, 1,* 169-180.

MacDonald, A. & Games, R. (1974). Some characteristics of those who hold positive and negative attitudes toward homosexuals. *Journal of Homosexuality, 1,* 9-27.

Maddox, B. (1982, February). Homosexual parents. *Psychology Today*, pp. 62-69.

Martin, A. D. (1984). The perennial canaanites: The sin of homosexuality. *Et Cetera, 41,* 340-361.

Martin, A. D. & Hetrick, E. S. (1988). The stigmatization of the gay and lesbian adolescent. *Journal of Homosexuality, 15*(1/2), 163-183.

Matthews, S. H. & Sprey, J. (1985). Adolescents' relationships with grandparents: An empirical contribution to conceptual clarification. *Journal of Gerontology, 40,* 621-626.

McNeill, J. (1976). *The church and the homosexuality*. Kansas City, MO: Sheed, Andrews, & McMeel, Inc.

Miller, B. (1979). Gay fathers and their children. *The Family Coordinator, 28,* 544-552.

Minton, H. L. & MacDonald, G. J. (1984). Homosexual identity formation as a developmental process. *Journal of Homosexuality, 9,* 91-104.

Morin, S. F. (1977). Heterosexual bias in psychological research on lesbianism and male homosexuality. *American Psychologist, 32,* 629-637.

Moses, A. E. & Hawkins, R. O. (1982). *Counseling lesbian woman and gay men: A life-issues approach.* St. Louis, MO: C. V. Mosby Co.

Pagelow, M. (1980). Heterosexual and lesbian single mothers: A comparison of problems, coping, and solutions. *Journal of Homosexuality, 5,* 189-204.

Plummer, K. (1975). *Sexual stigma.* London: Routledge & Kegan Paul.

Ponse, B. (1978). *Identities in the lesbian world.* Westport, CT: Greenwood Press.

Pope, K. S., Tabachnick, B. G., & Keith-Spiegel, P. (1987). Ethics of practice: The beliefs and behaviors of psychologists as therapists. *American Psychologist, 42,* 993-1006.

Rand, C., Graham, D., & Rawlings, E. (1982). Psychological health and factors the court seeks to control in lesbian mother trials. *Journal of Homosexuality, 8*(1), 27-40.

Ross, M. (1983). *The married homosexual man.* Boston: Routledge & Kegan Paul.

Schvaneveldt, J. & Ihinger, M. (1979). Sibling relationships in the family. In W. Burr, R. Hill, F. Nye, & I. Reiss (Eds.), *Contemporary theories about the family. Volume I: Research-based theories* (pp. 453-467). New York: Free Press.

Schmitt, J. P. & Kurdek, L. A. (1987). Personality correlates of positive identity and relationship involvement in gay men. *Journal of Homosexuality, 13,* 101-109.

Schofield, M. (1967). *The sexual behavior of young people.* London: Longman, Green, and Co.

Skolnick, A. (1978). *The intimate environment: Exploring marriage and the family.* Boston: Little, Brown and Company.

Sorenson, R. (1973). *Adolescent sexuality in contemporary America.* New York: World Publishing Company.

Stoller, R. J., Marmor, J., Bieber, I., Gold, R., Socarides, C. W., Green, R., & Spitzer, R. L. (1973). A symposium: Should homosexuality be in the APA nomenclature? *American Journal of Psychiatry, 130,* 1207-1216.

Storms, M. (1978). Attitudes toward homosexuality and femininity in men. *Journal of Homosexuality, 3,* 257-266.

Troiden, R. R. (1979). Becoming homosexual: A model of gay identity. *Psychiatry, 42,* 362-373.

Voeller, B. (1980). Society and the gay movement. In J. Marmor (Ed.), *Homosexual behavior* (pp. 232-252). New York: Basic Books.

Warren, C. (1974). *Identity and community in the gay world.* New York: John C. Wiley & Sons.

Weinberg, G. (1972). *Society and the healthy homosexual*. New York: St. Martin's Press.

Weinberg, M. S. & Williams, C. J. (1974). *Male homosexuals: Their problems and adaptations*. New York: Oxford University Press.

Weinberger, L. & Millham, J. (1979). Attitudinal homophobia and support of traditional sex roles. *Journal of Homosexuality, 4,* 237-246.

White, K. (producer and director). (1987). *Not all parents are straight* [Film]. San Francisco, CA: Full Frame Productions.

Whittlin, W. (1983). Homosexuality and child custody: A psychiatric viewpoint. *Conciliations Courts Reviews, 21*(1), 77-79.

Married Homosexual Men:
Prevalence and Background

Michael W. Ross

One of the ways that a homosexual orientation may have on impact on family relationships is where a spouse is bisexual or homosexual. This paper investigates the situation where a married man has homosexual involvements while in a marriage, both in terms of the prevalence of such a situation and the dynamics associated with it. The literature on married homosexual men is also reviewed here.

The research literature on the married homosexual man falls into two categories: those studies which look at broader aspects of homosexuality, and incidentally provide information on the proportion of homosexuals who have married; and those which look at several cases in some depth. The former tend to be epidemiological, reporting useful statistics on prevalence and incidence, but not going any deeper into the phenomenon. The latter tend to be case-histories, usually of ten cases or less, which may not be particularly representative of married homosexual men and which tend to emphasize those who have problems. In general, the findings of those studies which look at prevalence are fairly similar across Western cultures, and their data can be assumed to be accurate, despite the fact that they are over-representative of the middle-class, educated individuals who are usually sampled through Gay organizations and public venues such as bars and social clubs.

Michael W. Ross, PhD, is Senior Research Fellow, The Sydney Hospital, Albion Street AIDS Centre, 150 Albion Street, Surry Hills, NSW 2010, Australia.

35

KINSEY INSTITUTE STUDIES
ON MARRIED HOMOSEXUAL MEN

The earliest formal research which casts any light on the issue of male homosexuality, and also on the prevalence of married homosexuals, was the famous Kinsey Report of the late 1940s (Kinsey, Pomeroy, & Martin, 1948). Kinsey et al.'s study is too well known to require any more than a brief description. The data, which included indepth interviews with over five thousand three hundred white American men, collected between 1938 and 1947 provided the evidence that homosexual behaviour was relatively common in the population, and it became clear that people were not "homosexual" or "heterosexual," but were placed on a continuum. This so-called Kinsey Scale is composed of seven positions, graded from 0-6. Individuals classified as 0 are described as heterosexual: they make no physical contacts which result in erotic arousal or orgasm with members of their own sex. Those rated 6 are the homosexual equivalent of 0, where the sexual preference is totally toward other men. While Kinsey et al. noted that some 37 percent of the male population (over one-third) had had at least one overt homosexual experience leading to orgasm between the ages of 15 and 56, when the married homosexual man is referred to, it is the individual who has a rating of 3 or higher who is the subject of this review. In addition, those referred to in subsequent research have also identified themselves as predominantly homosexual.

Kinsey et al.'s work, however, while including a breakdown of their data, do not label the individuals beyond their position on the Kinsey Scale. They also analyse their data in terms of the educational level of their subjects, which provides some interesting insights. Kinsey et al.'s data are of particular interest because unlike the data of other studies, which give us the proportions of homosexual men who have married, these data give us the proportion of married men who are homosexual, and also enables a check of one set of figures against the other.

For the age groups 20-24 to 45-49 of married men, an average of 1.7 percent of the primary school graduates, and 1.9 percent of the college graduates were at level 3 on the Kinsey Scale. In effect, given that this indicates that their homosexual experience was at least equal to their heterosexual experience and given that they were married, and had permanent access to heterosexual sex, their homosexual sexual experience must have been considerable. It is of interest that the highest figure (4.5 percent) is for the lower education group, and tends to decline after the age group 20-24; for the college-educated group, however, it tends to increase above the less educated group from the age group 25-29. What this suggests is that there are two different circumstances of married homosexual men, which to some degree depend on educational level, and therefore, the socioeconomic status of homosexual activity appears to peak in the late teens-early twenties, and decline following this period. This could well represent hustling or the opportunity for frequent and possibly relatively impersonal sex while the individual is young and attractive. On the other hand, the increase above the lower-educated by those who have a higher educational level, and thus higher socioeconomic status, from the 25-29 age group, suggests that homosexual activity is something which occurs much later, presumably as a function of an awareness of the individual; with the individual's homosexual sexual preference slowly developing. This conception of the two groups of married homosexual men fits in well with data of Humphreys (1970), reviewed below.

There is one subsequent study from the Kinsey Institute at Indiana University which has looked at epidemiological considerations in regard to married homosexuals. As a part of a larger study of male and female homosexualities, Bell and Weinberg (1978) obtained a sample of homosexual men both white and black, in San Francisco in the early 1970s. Sources of recruitment included public advertising, personal contacts, bars, public baths, homophile organizations and public places: in this way, interviews could finally be conducted with 3,854 homosexual men (3,538 white, 316 black). They noted that while marriage was not commonplace, nor was it unusual: however, they also noted that it was usually unhappy and short-lived and that almost all ended in separation or divorce. White homosexual men had a marriage rate of 20 percent, blacks 13 percent: average age at marriage was at 24. The fact that most marriages were short-lived and usually ended in separation or divorce is most probably a reflection of the nature of the sample, which was heavily weighted towards the more overt and better educated individual. The additional fact that the sample was predominantly from San Francisco, held by some to be the largest "Gay city" in the world, suggests a bias toward overt and better-adjusted homosexuals. It is perhaps significant that even in this sort of sample with this sort of environment, one-fifth had been married. This proportion is also roughly similar to that found by Saghir and Robins (1973) and Weinberg and Williams (1974).

Corroborating evidence comes from a study by Masters and Johnson (1979), who found that of their homosexual sample, 17 percent had been married previously: these marriages had lasted periods from one week to seventeen years! Of the bisexuals that Masters and Johnson studied, none had married. Further, nearly two-thirds of their homosexual men who had married (61 percent) had done so in an attempt to reverse their homosexual preference. This accords quite well with the reasons which Bell and Weinberg's sample report for marriage: attempting to hide one's sexual orientation, to test their heterosexual responsiveness, deny their homosexuality, accommodate to social pressures, disappointment with homosexual lovers (all negatively related to homosexuality). Other reasons given were more positive, including flight from an intolerable parental relationship, a desire for a stable and permanent relationship, affection for spouse, and a desire for children.

PREVALENCE OF MARRIAGE IN HOMOSEXUAL MEN IN OTHER COUNTRIES

It can thus be seen that in terms of the epidemiology of marriage in homosexuals, all the studies to date which have touched on the area produce substantially similar figures in different samples and in different Western societies. There is corroboration of the 1.7-1.9 percent which Kinsey et al., reported in 1948 from a Dutch study (Noordhoff, 1970), which indicated that 1.3 percent of married Dutch males were homosexual: this is all the more impressive given the differences in time and culture. Similarly, the figures of between 10 percent and 20 percent who had been married in the studies of homosexuals carried out in the United States, the Netherlands, Denmark, and West Germany are in substantial agreement. Again, some incidental corroboration of this is provided by Lautmann (1980-1), reporting on the persecution of homosexual males in concentration camps in Nazi Germany between 1933 and 1945. Lautmann notes in passing that of the data on some 700 homosexuals to which he had access, 16 percent had been married or widowed. The data available also suggest a strong social or societal component in the decision to marry. It is, therefore, necessary to follow through and to look in some detail at the marriage situation of married homosexuals and how this may be affected by the reasons for marriage, and the adjustments to marriage.

Only one study has been carried out to date to ascertain the distribution of homosexual and heterosexual behaviour in a random population. Ross (1988 a,b) carried out a doorstep interview with 2,601 randomly selected Australian adults over the age of 16 on attitudes towards AIDS, and an anonymous questionnaire was left with a prepaid return envelope which requested information on sexual behaviours in the past 12 months and over previously. Questions were included on homosexual and heterosexual contact, as well as marital status. Over 60 percent of questionnaires were returned, and there were few differences between returners and non-returners which might bias results.

Data suggested that Kinsey et al.'s (1948) figures (which were not based on random samples) were substantial overestimates of the amount of male homosexual behaviour in the community. However, it must be recalled that Kinsey et al. collected their data through the Second World War, when men were in large single-sex groups in the armed forces, and that the term "homosexual" was not widely recognized or applied to same-sex sexual contact at that date. It is, therefore, possible that sexual contact between men was more common since it did not carry a commonly recognized stigmatized label.

However, Ross (1988 a,b) did find that 11.2 percent of men had had sex with another male ever, with 6.1 percent having had sex with another male in the past 12 months. This did not differ significantly across states. Of those men who were currently married, 8.8 percent had ever had sex with a male, and 4.2 percent in the past year. Figures for single men were 16.1 percent (ever) and 9.8 percent (past year), and for previously married men 15.6 percent and 6.4 percent, respectively. These random data suggest that one in 24 currently married men was homosexually active in the past year, a figure which is higher than data extrapolated from non-random studies would suggest.

Analyzing these data further by breaking down data on men who were currently (or previously) married into those with homosexual experience and those without such experience, there were no differences in occupational status (as measured on Congalton's [1969] 7-point rating scale), or on age. Those married men with homosexual experience were, predictably, significantly more personally concerned about AIDS and more scared of the disease. They were more likely to know homosexual people, and less likely to think that sex should be limited to marriage. In terms of sexual behaviour, those with homosexual experience were also significantly less likely to have had sex with a woman in the past 12 months, and more likely to have ever used intravenous drugs. On the Kinsey Scale, predictably, they were more likely to consider themselves bisexual (although 63 percent now rated themselves as completely heterosexual; category 0). This last piece of data suggests that a substantial proportion of men who have had previous homosexual experience may now think of themselves currently as completely heterosexual, and that sexual behaviour is, as Kinsey et al. (1984) found, reasonably fluid across the lifespan.

STUDIES ON MARRIED HOMOSEXUAL MEN

There are, in addition, several theoretical issues which are helpful in examining the position of the married homosexual. Humphreys (1970) studied homosexual activities in public conveniences. While the main purpose of the study was to deal with stigmatized behaviour in terms of how it was organized and the rules for interaction within the public convenience, he also took the license plate numbers of the cars in which men came to the conveniences. From local records, he was able to obtain names and addresses, as well as marital and occupational status for the participants. Some fifty of the hundred license-plate numbers obtained led to indepth interviews with the men who had been observed having sex with other men in a public convenience, with the researcher posing as a market researcher in order to interview them in their homes.

Over half (54 percent) were married and living with their wives. There was no evidence that these marriages were any more unstable than other marriages, nor that the wives were aware of their husbands' secret sexual activity: in fact, he suggests that the public convenience was chosen for just this reason. In most cases, it was apparent that the respondent's desire for sex that was fast, impersonal, and did not lead to any identifying details being given was primarily to protect their families. However, when the interview schedules were analyzed, a pattern emerged which was referred to as "conjugal role separation," in which the predominant pattern of married life involved separate and different activities of husband and wife, but activities which fitted together to form a functioning unit. Thus, the marriage tended to be composed of separate but interlocking activities of husband and wife with a minimum of interaction. Some eleven (4 percent) of the homosexually active men's marriages were of this sort, compared with only three in the couples in a heterosexual control sample: it does suggest that this sort of compartmentalization may be one response to the situation of marriage in homosexual men.

The married men in Humphrey's sample could be divided into two groups in terms of their education and occupation: this division offers a classification which is remarkably similar to the education level classification of Kinsey et al. (1948). The first classification ("Trade," according to Humphreys), comprised 38 percent of the homosexually active group, and all were, or had been married. Most worked as truck drivers, machine operators, or clerical workers: one in six was black. There was an over-representation of Roman Catholics: in 63 percent of marriages, husband, wife or both were Catholic. Truck drivers were the biggest single occupational group in the "Trade" category: their median age was 38, with an average of 2.2 children. The group was called "Trade" because two-thirds took the active (insertor) role in fellatio in public conveniences, and because they would be classified in the homosexual subculture as such: men who do not consider themselves homosexual (or will not admit to it), as long as they do not take a passive role.

Humphreys considers that there is no indication that these men seek homosexual contact as such; rather, they want a form of orgasm-producing action less lonely than masturbation and less involving than a love relationship. On the other hand, one could argue that since one-third did perform fellatio in the receptive (insertee) role, and since the act of fellatio was performed almost invariably in silence and in the shortest time possible, it was so akin to masturbation that there must have been good reason to choose a male partner rather than to masturbate. Certainly in terms of sex of partner, these men who Humphreys calls "Trade" were homosexual. Length and degree of intimacy in any encounter are not what gives rise to the classification of homosexual or heterosexual: as Stern and Stern (1981) report similar heterosexual encounters on buses in Russia, it would seem unjustified not to classify them as heterosexual simply because they were anonymous and brief. The essence of the encounters described in the "Trade" group is perhaps denial of the homosexuality rather than anything else: denial by the participant as well as to his family, friends or even to other homosexuals.

The second classification group Humphreys describes are the ambisexuals. These married men had double the median income of the "Trade" group, 1.6 children on average, a median age of 43, and were usually Protestants. In terms of their observed role in fellatio, two-thirds were insertees, one-third insertors. Ambisexuals were much more likely to be middle class or upper-middle class, and to be more open about their homosexual preferences. He also noted that nearly two-thirds of the ambisexuals were college graduates, which tends to put them into the group described by Kinsey et al. (1948), which included those with tertiary education. However, in openness about their homosexual preference, they are open only to other homosexuals. In all the cases which are cited by Humphreys none of the spouses or heterosexual friends knew. Such ambisexuals are apparently not fleeing from unhappy homosexuals lives or sexless marriages, but usually express great devotion to their wives and families. The pattern for their sexual preferences was almost one of separation and compartmentalization: as Humphreys cites one of his ambisexual subjects, "You might think I live two lives, but if I do, I don't feel split in two by them." Such individuals recognized their homosexual activity as a part of their psychosexual orientation, and themselves as behaviourally bisexual. Contacts with other homosexuals (although not usually individuals from the more public homosexual subculture such as bars and clubs) were common, as is reading about homosexuality. These ambisexual individuals appear to cope because they do seem to have a significant degree of heterosexual responsiveness as well as homosexual preference, and thus the heterosexual marriage has rewarding aspects. The more the individual is homosexual in preference (that is, the closer he is to position 6 on the Kinsey scale), however, the more likely there will be pressure on the marriage and towards a homosexual emotional, as well as sexual relationship.

Perhaps the most startling aspect of Humphreys' study concerns what he calls the "breast plate of righteousness," or "refulgent respectability." By this, he refers to the cloud of propriety and respectability which surrounds the married homosexual. He suggests that the "covert deviant" develops a self-presentation that is overly respectable and orthodox: this includes often a highly conservative political and social stance. As with the actual marriage of homosexual man, this may also be seen in the light of overcompensation in one direction to hide the unconventional sexual orientation. The rationale is probably something similar to "if I express the view that civil rights for homosexuals are necessary, people may start to suspect I'm one." This, however, goes much further than issues with regard to sexuality: Humphreys found that on indices of liberalism relating to economic reform, the civil rights movement, the Vietnam war, and police practices, the married homosexuals, particularly the "Trade" group, were much more conservative than a matched control group. Even more surprising was the fact that those in the lower-middle class encouraged more vice-squad activity, and some could even be described as moral crusaders: several were also members of the right-wing John Birch Society.

These data underscore an important theoretical point with regard to married homosexual men. It became clear that overcompensation is occurring in an attempt to deny their homosexual orientation, to the extent that it could be described as reaction formation (a psychological defence mechanism in which the individual reacts to an event or state by moving to the extreme opposite state in terms of attitude and behaviour). That this occurs with sociopolitical attitudes in some married homosexuals does suggest another theoretical base for marriage. It could be postulated that those who are homosexual to some degree and who marry are not just reacting to their homosexuality by covering up with a "breast plate of righteousness," but that they were even prior to marriage conservative, and that their marriage was just one manifestation of this. The question is: Is this a function of marriage, or a reason for it?

ADJUSTMENT IN MARRIED HOMOSEXUAL MEN

In looking at data from studies which examine the married homosexual man with the context of the homosexual subculture, it is probable that only the more overt or well-adjusted married homosexuals have been sampled, and this bias must be taken into account when making conclusions. It is debatable whether any sample of homosexuals is representative, and any sample of convenience is likely to be even less so. Nevertheless, such selective research does produce a greater depth of information compared with the epidemiological survey.

The classic early study on the married homosexual man was that of Ross (1971). Ross studied the situations and modes of adjustment of eleven married homosexuals in Belgium. While noting that the married homosexual was an important but rather obscure social problem, and that no firm conclusions could be reached because of the small number and case-history method, Ross noted that subjects fell into two groups, those who discovered their homosexuality after marriage and subsequently redefined their status after a homosexual affair, and those who knew of their homosexuality prior to marriage, and who were possibly in a conscious flight from their homosexuality. Some of this latter group felt that orientation was situational and would disappear with marriage. In general, both groups had little sexual experience of any sort before marriage. The marriage had been a result of a number of factors, including advice from a doctor or priest, a rational choice because of the subject's family-centred values, social pressures from family and relatives, work and loneliness. Weinberg (1970) has noted that loneliness amongst homosexuals is most common in those under 25.

Several main sources of conflict within the marriage were also noted by Ross. Sexual problems tended to increase as the marriage continued: when the wives found out the husband was homosexual they felt defrauded and resentful, and any deep homosexual relationships on the part of the subjects were resented, while jealousy also occurred in some cases. However, the establishment of a homosexual liaison was often the greatest compensation for marital problems and sometimes, surprisingly, kept the marriage together. All his married subjects took part in the local "Gay life," but their spouses were suspicious and recriminating.

Four main modes of adjustment were noted among the subjects: first was separation, if there were no children of the marriage and no "satisfactions" of married life. Such satisfactions would include non-sexual and non-affective ones, such as a common home, division of labour, companionship and social respectability. Fear of a subject's inability to lead a separate and independent life, and an adjustment to the psychological peculiarities of the partner were also factors which led to separation. Second, there was the "platonic" marriage, which involved abandoning the sexual side of the marriage and concentrating on other marital satisfaction and outside interests, such as job, children, etc. Any sexual contacts occurred outside the marriage. Third, the "double-standard" marriage, which involved an outside homosexual liaison as well as marriage, occurred. This was probably the hoped-for ideal of the second type, "platonic" marriage. However, it was resented by the spouse, who felt a dual commitment was unable to be maintained. Fourth, the "innovative" marriage, characterised by frequent heterosexual relations as well as homosexual relations, all quite openly, was seen as a possible solution. In one case, a "menage a trois" occurred. In this type of marriage, true bisexuality rather than homosexuality could be said to be contributing factor to the adjustment.

The effectiveness of these adjustments, Ross felt, was variable. All adjustments occurred in the context of apparent near-complete acceptance of conventional norms by most of the subjects. Thus, they were rather poor solutions to conflict between heterosexuality and homosexuality. The "platonic" marriage engendered mutual dissatisfaction and a displacement from the marital tie. Biological and psychological frustration was the result, often overtly expressed and with mutual guilt. Devaluation of the spouse led to bitterness and aggression toward the husband. "Innovative" marriage appeared the most successful and free from interpersonal conflicts, but this depended on the versatility of the husband and the broadmindedness of the wife.

While the work of Ross contributes a great deal to the preliminary analysis of the situation of married homosexuals, it raises a number of points from which some testable hypotheses can be generated. Saghir and Robins (1973), in a comprehensive investigation of homosexuality, observed not only some aspects of the adaptations and factors affecting married homosexuals, but also those affecting homosexuals generally. While Saghir and Robins used a matched sample of 124 men (89 homosexuals and 35 heterosexuals), retrospective distortion occurred as a function of hindsight and rationalisation. This problem is a common one, and almost impossible to control for: Ross (1980) noted it could occur in three ways. First, faulty recall; second, intentional falsified reporting; and third, knowledge about the commonly held antecedents of a homosexual orientation. It is this last category which could conceivable bias recall, with individuals reporting common conceptions or misconceptions about married homosexuals.

However, results of Saghir and Robin's (1973) investigation showed some interesting facts. Fifty-nine percent of the homosexuals sampled showed, or had had, some romantic attachment of a heterosexual nature during their life. Forty-eight percent had had sexual relations with a woman. Data on stable heterosexual relationships also reflect these figures: 53 percent of the homosexuals had had one or more stable heterosexual relationships, either marital or non-marital, over a period of a year. On the basis of these data, it could be implied that a fair proportion of homosexuals could be in a situation in which marriage could occur. Of the total sample, 18 percent had been married. Broken down, these figures include: 12 percent married and divorce, 3 percent married and separated, 2 percent still married, 1 percent widowed. That nearly a fifth of this sample have been married suggests that the situation is not uncommon, even in such a relatively "overt" sample. Age at marriage was found to be under 25 (60 percent), 25-29 (13 percent) and over 30 (27 percent). That the majority marry under 25 could well be connected with the finding of Weinberg (1970) that most loneliness in homosexuals occurs in this period. It could be suggested that for those under 25, marriage is an attempt at heterosexual adjustment when loneliness or conflict about homosexuality is at its peak, or a result of family and social pressures.

Of those who married, and then separated or divorced, 70 percent had lived with their wives less than three years, 30 percent more than three years. Reasons for the break-up are very similar to those found by Ross (1971), most being because of emotional and sexual dissatisfaction. Nevertheless, while 76 percent of the homosexual sample described their wives as aggressive and unsympathetic, 75 percent of the heterosexual control sample describe their spouses as the same. Nevertheless, homosexual men who married often stated that the marriage was initiated by the wife.

Reasons for marriage were also similar to those found by Ross: 94 percent of the married sample gave the reason for marriage as social acceptance, family or girlfriend pressure, and domestic needs or a desire for children. Seventy-nine percent of the previously married homosexuals said they would not marry again, as did 71 percent of the unmarried homosexuals. Two of the total sample were still living with their wives. Both were leading successful homosexual and heterosexual lives without threat to the marriage and neither of the wives knew. In each case the subject preferred homosexual relations, although both types of relations were satisfying both emotionally and physically. Heterosexual relations were monogamous, homosexual relatively promiscuous. Only one subject was married to a lesbian, and the marriage broke up as a result of jealousy (on the part of the man).

Most of Saghir and Robin's subjects (62 percent) had desired a change in their orientation at some time in their life, and of these 67 percent desired it before the age of 25. And again, of these 62 percent, 45 percent (that is, 31 percent of the total sample) sought to de-emphasize their homosexuality by becoming involved heterosexually. These data amply demonstrate that a high proportion of homosexuals become heterosexually involved as an attempted compensation for their homosexuality. At the other end of the scale, some 28 percent of the subjects feared growing old and being lonely. It is possible that some later marriages may stem from this factor.

Confirmation of these findings is provided to a large extent by Weinberg and Williams (1974), who, using a large number (2,437) of homosexuals in the US, Denmark and the Netherlands, examined the adjustment and adaptation of these subjects in the light of societal reaction theory.

Societal reaction theory would expect married homosexuals to be less well adjusted than their unmarried peers, not only as a result of conflict between their orientation and existing situation, but also because of their different way of relating to the heterosexual world and a higher exposure to traditional values, which, in Western society, are anti-homosexual. Thus married homosexuals would be expected to be the most secretive of the sample, first to prevent the spouse's discovery and second because of their greater acceptance of current standards. Further, psychological problems of homosexuals tend to be greater without the support of others with the same status, and Weinberg and Williams (1974) have noted a bimodal distribution of relating to the homosexual subculture. That is, there are two groups in terms of relating to the "Gay scene": one bunched up at the top end of the scale who are strongly involved, and the other at the bottom end who have no, or almost no contact with the homosexual subculture.

Weinberg and Williams also note 17 percent of those sampled have been married, a proportion which agrees well with the findings of Saghir and Robins (1973). Of these, 49 percent of the wives knew their husbands were homosexual, 16 percent may have known, and 34 percent did not know. Such a high proportion of wives cognisant of their husbands' status is probably a reflection of the nature of the sample, which is biased toward those who are active in the gay subculture. Individuals in the subculture are more likely to be overt, and to have the necessary support to be able to "come out." Of those subjects married, the projected reactions of the spouse were 57 percent accepting to tolerant, 43 percent intolerant to rejecting. A tendency in the general sample with education controlled for, was for the younger homosexual man to be less well adjusted. Again this supports earlier findings.

A number of interesting findings which will be used to generate hypotheses with regard to married homosexuals, but which, in the work of Weinberg and Williams (1974) occur as factors in the adaptation of single homosexuals, will be discussed briefly here. They noted that the higher the level of adjustment, the lower the femininity of the subject, which confirms subjective findings of Hooker (1965) and others. A high commitment to homosexuality as a way of life was found to be correlated with higher psychological well-being and also with acceptance of homosexuality as normal. Infrequent (homosexual) sex, loneliness, and never having had an exclusive (homosexual) relationship correlated highly with a lack of psychological well-being. Worry about exposure of one's homosexuality and passing as a heterosexual, were compared, and it was noted that it was the worry about exposure rather than the passing as such which led to a higher proportion of psychological problems. It was consequently suggested that "compartmentalization" of interests and activities plays a large part in the adaptation of homosexual men to societal reactions. A further finding of interest was that those with low involvement in the homosexual subculture felt more threatened by the heterosexual world. It was suggested that greater involvement would mean more support and less threat. No great problems were noted for those who were bisexual (not married), however. Those subjects living at home did have a chronic fear of exposure.

Some specific factors were noted about those subjects who were, at the time of the study, living with their wives. These homosexual men were most likely to worry about exposure, be least known about by other homosexuals, highest in passing as a heterosexual, described themselves as bisexual, less likely to be involved with other homosexuals and less involved in the gay subculture, and had fewer close friends over two years. Weinberg and Williams (1974) suggest that married homosexual men obtain from their families and other heterosexuals the gratifications that other homosexuals with other living arrangements obtain from the homosexual world. In effect, the suggestion is that compartmentalization occurs in terms of sexual preference, and that gratification need not necessarily be associated with any particular source, male and female. While married homosexuals tend to show considerable amounts of guilt, shame and anxiety over their homosexuality, they appear to be within the normal range with regard to their other subscales measuring psychological adjustment. All these findings were controlled for level of social involvement. Weinberg and Williams (1974) found that, in general, their data were not as expected in terms of the societal reaction so much as to how the individual reacts to that societal reaction: in other words, the individual holds the clues to the situation.

Societal reaction theory holds that homosexuals in more anti-homosexual societies will have worse psychological adjustment, in particular be less self-accepting, have less self-esteem, and feel more badly about homosexuality, than those in more accepting societies. However, Weinberg and Williams (1974) found this was not the case in the three societies they looked at (the United States, Denmark and the Netherlands). Following this, Ross (1978) suggested that the critical variable was not the *actual* societal reaction, but the way the homosexuals *perceived* it. It subsequently turned out that perceived societal reaction did predict a significantly lowered state of psychological well-being, although actual societal reaction did not.

Degree of homosexuality is also an important variable which may have some bearing on marital adjustment. Imielinski (1969) studied the relationship between the degree of homosexuality in male homosexuals, and success of marriage. However, all of his twenty-eight subjects were clinical cases or prison-referred. Degree of homosexuality was measured on a modified Kinsey Scale, and it was found that only those subjects with position 1 and most with position 2 homosexuality had successful marriages: from position 3 on the success of marriage declined dramatically. Reasons for marriage in order of importance were (1) physician's advice; (2) desire for children; (3) emotional relationships with women; (4) need for somebody to keep house. No doubt this study reflects the greater condemnation of homosexuality in Eastern Europe (Warsaw) in 1969. Nevertheless, the point is made that the higher the degree of homosexuality, the less chance any marriage has of surviving.

Data similar to that found by Ross (1971) and Saghir and Robins (1973) is provided by the study of Dannecker and Reiche (1974) in the Federal Republic of (West) Germany. Dannecker and Reiche found that, of their sample of 789 homosexual males, 10 percent had been married or were still married (5 percent of each). It was suggested that the 1:1 relationship of existing to broken marriages showed that adaptation was not very successful, or that not many homosexual men had found what they were looking for in marriage. For some two-thirds, the spouse did not know of the husband's homosexuality at the time of marriage, and of these, half ever knew. Such an arrangement, and its correlated purpose of using marriage as a means of hiding homosexuality, caused marriage of homosexuals to be labelled a "collective neurosis" by the authors. Reasons for marriage were varied: the three most important were (1) to have a lifelong companion; (2) to have children; (3) to hide one's homosexuality. Fifty-six percent of married subjects ticked at least one statement which mentioned resistance to, or hiding of, homosexuality. Those who also said they married with the desire for "sexual intercourse with a woman" tended to rate their marriage as not very happy, perhaps indicating the sexual conflict met within the situation.

Subjects were further analyzed by degree of homosexual sexual activity. Those who had low homosexual activity also had low sexual activity with their wives, and those who showed a high degree of homosexual activity also had a high level of sex with their wives. An interesting corollary was that those subjects who regarded their marriage as happy had a higher degree of homosexual sex than those who regarded their marriage as not so happy. Married subjects did not differ appreciably from non-married homosexuals: age of coming out as homosexual was similar, all knew they were homosexuals before marriage, and no greater proportion wished to be "treated" nor disliked homosexual activities. Average age at time of marriage was 27. A certain degree of role-conflict was noted and discussed by Dannecker and Reiche (1974): homosexual men in society were, it was felt, socialized into the institution of monogamous marriage. The decision to marry would appear to be a "subconscious social process," forceful but beyond control, evidenced only as a "conformity" to the family life style. They claim that contradictions of heterosexual norm and homosexual abnormality exist in each homosexual who has married.

Bisexuality was not seen as a problem either in theory or practice by their respondents. Many subjects in Dannecker and Reiche's (1974) total sample (56 percent) had had sexual intercourse with women. This does not imply bisexuality, since many tried to overcompensate their homosexuality through excessive heterosexuality, or because of wavering between hetro- and homosexuality, in society in which heterosexuality is the favoured norm, to derive the "bisexuality" of a person from the amount of his homo- or heterosexual activity. Dannecker and Reiche (1979) suggest that all bisexuals are really predominantly homosexuals: some such people were referred to as "defence-bisexuals." However, while it is stressed by Dannecker and Reiche that married homosexuals were not a special group in many respects, they pointed out the importance of "illuminating and empirically working out the marriage motive." They did not believe that marriage was solely a defense mechanism against homosexuality, but more important objective or subjective reasons existed. Ross (1979) studied 42 married homosexual men, and found that the reasons for marriage included being "in love" (26.2 percent), thinking that homosexuality would go away if one married (16.7 percent), wife being pregnant (11.9 percent), pressure from girlfriend (11.9 percent), wanting children and family life (7.1 percent), it seeming the "natural thing" (7.1 percent), and everyone else getting married (4.8 percent). These data suggest that there are three main clusters of reason for marriage in homosexual men: heterosexual desires; trying to hide or remove one's homosexuality; and personal or societal pressure to marry. Ross (1983), in a detailed examination of married homosexual men, found that there were few differences between currently married and separated homosexual men, suggesting that the situation of marriage contributes little except for a slightly higher degree of depression. However, he also notes that those who remain married may be those who can better cope with the situation.

Ross (1983) also found that the homosexual "type" most likely to marry could be fairly clearly differentiated from those who do not. There are some differences in background, but the major factor differentiating the two samples was the measure of "expected societal reaction" and its associated scales measuring "anxiety regarding homosexuality" and "conception of homosexuality as normal." This hypothesis that homosexual men who marry will see social reaction against homosexuality as much stronger than those who do not marry was confirmed, although the mechanism underlying this finding was not readily apparent from the background data, even though some factors are suggestive of them. Nevertheless, it was clear that those homosexual men who marry are not only more open to social pressure but see social pressure as being more threatening towards their sexual orientation as well.

In terms of the professional approach to homosexual men who have married and who seek help, it is clear that the most effective approach will probably be to minimize the expectation of negative reaction of others and society in general to homosexuality and the guilt and anxiety about a homosexual orientation. A similar approach would probably be more effective in homosexuals who indicate that they intend to marry. Acceptance of a homosexual orientation within marriage, however, may ultimately lead to a breakdown of the marriage.

In the same study, Ross (1983) also investigated the influence of time of discovery of sexual orientation (before or after marriage). He found that those individuals who knew they were to some degree homosexual prior to marriage did tend to marry in order to de-emphasize their homosexuality. On the other hand, it also appeared that those whose homosexuality became obvious after their marriage may well have had some awareness of their sexual preference subconsciously, but that it was not thrust into importance until after marriage and recognized for what it was. The differences between these two groups would appear to be in terms of their thinking about their sexuality and the levels of that thinking before marriage, rather than in terms of the different effects discovery of sexual preference before or after marriage. In terms of these effects, the two groups were remarkably similar, and it can probably be concluded that discovering one's sexual direction after marriage does not lead to any great trauma compared with knowing something about one's sexual preference prior to marriage.

Comparing time of "coming out" to spouse, Ross also found that the differences between the three groups of individuals who had at some time been married and who had told their wives before marriage that they were homosexual, after marriage, or never told them, seemed to follow the same pattern. While those individuals who had never told their wives about their sexual preference were more anxious about their homosexuality being known about and expected a worse societal reaction to it, they did not suffer from what has been termed a "double life" at all. This led Ross to conclude that the difference found between the groups may be a function of the degree and particularly the time they "came out" as homosexual, and not of whether their spouse knows or when she was told. Thus the negative consequence of leading a supposedly conflicting existence were not at all obvious, and it can only be concluded that being married and having one's spouse unaware that her partner is homosexual does not lead to psychological problems.

There can be little doubt that, apart from individual differences in backgrounds and adaptation, the main factors implicated by Ross as important in the heterosexual marriages of predominantly homosexual men is their more anti-homosexual perception of the attitudes of their contemporaries and society, and thus the more negative consequences of living a homosexual lifestyle. In a study of married homosexual men in three societies (Australia, Sweden and Finland), Ross (1983) found that anti-homosexual social and societal environments lead to higher proportions of homosexual men marrying (and separating), as well as less openness about their sexual orientation to their spouses, but also that the variables of societal reaction, both actual and expected, were apparent as differentiators between groups and by implication as factors involved in the marriage of homosexual men. One factor which was particularly salient in the Scandinavian-Australian analysis was that of sex-role conservatism. While general conservatism was previously shown not be implicated (Ross 1978), sex-role conservatism is clearly an important predictor of marriage along with societal reaction. This is of particular interest since Ross, Rogers and McCulloch (1978) have indicated that they believe the two main factors which determine the role of homosexual projects in a society, or which a society projects on to the individual, are determined by the degree of anti-homosexual prejudice and the degree of sex-role conservatism in that society acting together. These findings would also suggest, then, that those two factors may be implicated in the role of homosexual male plays in more general terms, such as in marriage and remaining married as well.

An interesting finding by Bell and Weinberg (1978) was that those homosexuals who in later (homosexual) relationships were what they called close coupled and open coupled (that is, in monogamous and exogamous relationships, respectively) had married significantly younger than other groups. There is a hint in this that those who married younger may have done so because of their need or desire for a relationship and a need for affection and the stability of a partner. Bell and Weinberg (1968) also report that the homosexuals felt their marriage to be less happy than those of the heterosexual controls. This contrasts with the finding of Saghir and Robins (1973) that there was equal marriage dissatisfaction, and suggests that there may be some degree of rationalization in those who report an unhappy marriage. For example, they may justify their move to a solely homosexually sex object preference and separation from their wife by saying that "it wasn't really happy anyway." On the other hand, the heterosexual control group was more sexually active in both the first and last years of marriage, which does tend to suggest that heterosexual sex was less important for the married homosexuals, and for this reason, the marriages may well have been less happy. In addition, the Bell and Weinberg (1978) sample were predominantly positions 5 and 6 on the Kinsey Scale: one-third of the white and one-fifth of the black married homosexuals often fantasized that they were having sex with men while having sex with their wives; nearly half (40 percent) did so occasionally. More than a third had, in fact, told their wives of their sexual orientation prior to marriage (although not that they would do anything about it). Nearly half were married for about three years or longer, one quarter for only 1-2 years, one quarter for 11 years or longer. In over half the white (54 percent) and less than a quarter of the black (23 percent) married homosexuals, their homosexuality had something to do with the ending of the marriage. In particular, factors such as becoming involved with another male (48 percent), lack of interest in heterosexual sex (20 percent), the spouse finding out her husband was homosexual (18 percent), and being unable to sexually satisfy the spouse were mentioned. Half the white men had no children of the marriage, while half the black men had had one child. With regard to being aware of their homosexuality prior to marriage, only 15 percent of the white men and none of the black men had not been aware they were homosexual prior to marriage: this strongly suggests that social or societal factors may have played a major part in the decision to wed.

CONCLUSION

In summary, the data reviewed demonstrate that a significant proportion of married men (between 2 and 4 percent) may be homosexually active, and that between 10 and 20 percent of homosexual men will have been married at some time. However, there appear to be few obvious psychological costs associated with this, perhaps due to the defense of "compartmentalization." Much of the phenomenon of marriage is predominantly homosexual men appears to be due to social or societal pressures, and there would seem to be little difference between those who tell their spouses before or after marriage or never, or those who became aware of their sexual preference before or after marriage. It must be concluded that a significant source of homosexuality in the family may be the husband, and that this is likely to be due to pressures to marry.

REFERENCES

Bell, A.P. & Weinberg, M.S. (1978). *Homosexualities: A study of diversity among men and women*. Melbourne: Macmillan.

Congalton, A.A. (1969). *Status and prestige in Australia*. Melbourne: F.W. Cheshire.

Dannecker, M. & Reiche, R. (1974). *Der gewöhnliche homosexuelle: Eine soziologische untersuchung uber mannliche homosexuelle in der Bundesrepublik*. Frankfurt am Main: S. Fischer Verlag.

Hooker, E. (1965). An empirical study of some relations between sexual patterns and gender identity in male homosexuals. In Money, J. (ed.), *Sex research: New developments*. New York: Holt, Rinehart & Winston.

Humphreys, R.A.L. (1970). *Tearoom trade*. London: Duckworth.

Imieliński, K. (1969). Homosexuality in males with particular reference to marriage. *Psychotherapy and Psychosomatics*, *17*, 126-132.

Kinsey, A.C., Pomeroy, W.B., & Martin, C.E. (1948). *Sexual behavior in the human male*. Philadelphia: W.B. Saunders.

Lautman, R. (1980-1). The pink triangle: The persecution of homosexual males in concentration camps in Nazi Germany. *Journal of Homosexuality*, 6(1/2), 141-160.

Masters, W.H. & Johnson, V.E. (1979). *Homosexuality in perspective*. Boston: Little, Brown.

Noordhoff, J.E. (1970). (ed.) *Sex in Nederland*. Utrecht: Prisma-Boek.

Ross, H.L. (1971). Modes of adjustment of married homosexuals. *Social Problems, 18*, 385-393.

Ross, M.W. (1978). The relationship of perceived societal hostility, conformity and social adjustment in homosexual men. *Journal of Homosexuality, 4*, 157-168.

Ross, M.W. (1980). Retrospective distortion in homosexual research. *Archives of Sexual Behavior, 9*, 523-531.

Ross, M.W. (1983). *The married homosexual man: A psychological study*. London: Routledge & Kegan Paul.

Ross, M.W. (1988). Prevalence of risk factors for AIDS infection in the Australian population. *Medical Journal of Australia, 149*, 362-365.

Ross, M.W. (1988). Prevalence of classes of risk behaviors for HIV infection in a randomly selected population. *Journal of Sex Research, 25*, 441-450.

Ross, M.W., Rogers, L.J., & McCulloch, H. (1978). Stigma, sex and society: A new look at gender differentiation and sexual variation. *Journal of Homosexuality, 3*, 315-330.

Saghir, M.T. & Robins, E. (1983). *Male and female homosexuality: A comprehensive investigation*. Baltimore: Williams & Wilkins.

Stern, M. & Stern, A. (1981). *Sex in the Soviet Union*. London: W.H. Allen.

Weinberg, M.S. (1970). The male homosexual: Age related variations in social and psychological characteristics. *Social Problems, 17*, 527-537.

Weinberg, M.S. & Williams, C.J. (1974). *Male homosexuals: Their problems and adaptations*. New York: Oxford.

Guess Who's Coming to Dinner This Time? A Study of Gay Intimate Relationships and the Support for Those Relationships

Jan Meyer

SUMMARY. The need to "couple," to have that special person with whom we share not only sexual intimacy but a past, present, and future, is not limited to the "straight" world. Raised by heterosexual parents, gays (male homosexuals) desire that same type of intimacy. Given that intimate relationships provide a very necessary function for the larger community of heterosexuals, those relationships should provide the same function for gays. This paper examines the differences and similarities between long-term gay and heterosexual intimate relationships, and the support each of those types of relationships receives from the community in which they exist.

INTRODUCTION

"Everybody needs somebody sometime . . . " is more than an old popular song: it is a summary statement of the need we, as individuals, have to "couple," to have that special person with whom we share not only sexual intimacy but a past (no matter how lengthy), the present, and with whom we can look forward to the future.

That need is not limited to the "straight" world; raised by heterosexual parents, gays (male homosexuals) are conditioned by their culture and by their own basic human needs to desire, in fact seek

Jan Meyer, PhD, is Assistant Professor, College of St. Thomas, St. Paul, MN 55101, and President, Meyer Human Resources, 2203 Como, St. Paul, MN 55108.

out, that same type of intimacy. Given that intimate relationships provide a very necessary function for the larger community of heterosexuals, those relationships should provide the same function for gays. This paper examines the differences and similarities between gay and heterosexual intimate relationships, and the support each of those types of relationships receives from the community in which they exist.

Much of what has been written about homosexuality is not very positive:

> It is ironic that book after book has been researched and written examining why people are gay and whether lesbianism and male homosexuality are "morally acceptable," yet so little has been written to help lesbians and gay men lead happier and healthier lives. (Altman, 1971, p. 4)

Since Altman's statement, some authors have produced works which provide support for the individual gay (Walker, 1977; Silverstein & White, 1977; and others); however, few discuss the long-term male couple. Perhaps the best work on relationships of male couples is that completed by McWhirter and Mattison (1984); however, they only briefly address early formation of and community support for the relationship. This paper attempts to add to that body of literature which aids in understanding the success and failure of gay couples.

PROBLEM DEFINITION

Growing up, finding that certain someone, getting married, and living happily ever after is taken for granted as the ideal future for everyone in our culture. It is "normal and natural"; few question as they are growing up, or even after, that there are alternatives. It would be expected then, that like other common phenomena in any culture, there would be some underlying purpose (besides procreation: there need not be "permanent" relationships to procreate!) for the existence of this expectation, and that the support for continuation of such a phenomonem would be readily identifiable. In this problem definition section, the reasons and support for intimate relationships within the heterosexual community are identified as the starting point for comparison.

Reasons for Forming Intimate Relationships

Davis (1973) in his study of intimate relations reasons that the necessity for such relationships stems from the

> transformation of social life from that based on gemeinschaft (community) to that based on gesellschaft (society). It is this historical circumstance that accentuated the factors that, we shall see, pull the person apart, motivate him to search for intimates, and put problems in his path. (Davis, 1973, p. xx)

In other times, the community provided individuals with their identity and with their reality. With the breakdown of that community support, individuals became more uniquely individual and at the same time replaceable: he literally had no identity. This created psychological stress to the point that individuals "attempt to reconstruct around himself the community he feels he lacks – or at least a small-scale version of it, consisting of his personal relations" (Davis, 1973, p. xxii).

> The plausibility and stability of the world, as socially defined, is dependent upon the strength and the continuity of significant relationships in which conversation about this world can be continually carried on. . . . Marriage occupies a privileged status among the significant validating relationships for adults in our society. (Berger & Kellner, p. 221)

Though this one-on-one relationship is in itself precarious, the support of the community and the addition of children provide stability. Intimate relationships, most commonly known in our culture as marriage, therefore provide a more stable world for the individuals involved.

The Social and Legal Sanctions and Rituals and Symbols for Marriage

While "living together" has become more socially acceptable, any individual over the age of about 25 who is still unmarried, either never-married or divorced, recognizes firsthand the stigma still attached to the unmarried state in our culture. Ranging from discrimination in employment (illegal interview questions such as "when are you going to settle down and get married, have a family," etc.) to being shut out of the "couples" social life ("Well, yes, we did have a party but there were only couples there!"), these negative sanctions serve to reinforce the notion that paired (preferably married) is best.

Legal sanctions, both positive for and negative for not being married, also abound. Unmarried persons until recently suffered overt discrimination in attempts to own property and/or obtain credit ratings. Unmarrieds who attempt to own property together are still advised against same, for reasons varying from the "mess when one of the owners dies," to how to split up the property if the two separate for any other reason.

The obvious ritual for the establishment of a heterosexual intimate relationship is the time-honored courtship and marriage. Testimony to this is the number (and profit picture) of the "bridal houses" and the social pages of the Sunday newspapers. The engagement ring is followed in swift succession by other symbols of the process: showers, wedding invitations, the bachelor dinner, and the wedding, all of which are clear messages to the society that these two have publicly proclaimed their commitment, their intimate relationship. Everyone is happy and proffers their congratulations. These people are fulfilling the expectations of a culture for which they have received a lifetime of conditioning.

Family and Community Support for Intimate Relationships

One need not even search for examples of the obviously (though perhaps not realistically portrayed!) perfect couple and/or happy family: the media has until recently bombarded households with exclusively heterosexual and married intimate relationships, from

Ozzie and Harriet to their more contemporary counterparts. And, every mother's goal is to hear those wonderful words: "Mom, I'm getting married." (After all, the parents' [Mom's?] job is not done until the "child" is married.) More insidious is the negative sanction for not being half of a whole: getting the worst table in the dining room of the nice restaurants if eating alone, or discounts for married couples on travel arrangements, or "double occupany rates" as the only choice on tours as if no one would even consider travelling alone.

Length of Intimate Relationships

It is commonly expected in the heterosexual world that relationships are permanent; that is, they will last a lifetime. Though in practice this is no longer true, marriage is still the primary relationship and it is still entered into with the wish if not expectation that it will last forever.

Given the above needs from and expectations for intimate relationships among heterosexuals, what are the similarities and differences between those and gay intimate relationships: Do intimate relationships between male homosexuals differ? If so, how and why? What function does the gay intimate relationship serve? And, what support is there for such an intimate relationship?

METHODOLOGY

Data were gathered during interviews specifically scheduled for this research. For all of the interviews except one, notes were recorded as the interview progressed, and those notes were transcribed as soon as possible after the interview. For one, the interview was tape recorded for the first two hours (until the tape ran out); for the last hour, notes were recorded as in the previous interviews.

A total of twenty-four interviews were conducted, all subjects being acquired by referral (starting with two gay acquaintances, each interviewee was asked at the end of the interview whether he would refer the researcher to others; virtually all did, sometimes asking the potential interviewee to call the researcher, sometimes providing the name and contact to the researcher). Of the twenty-four, the age range was from 28 to 44. Educational level was almost uniform: all had a four-year baccalaureate degree and two had post-graduate professional degrees. Most had had a number of relation-ships: the minimum was four, the maximum of those interviewed was six (although they reported having had partners who had had up to twelve other intimate relationships). The length of these relation-ships varied from six weeks to seven years (again, subjects reported others in their acquaintances who had had much longer-term rela-tionships). All had had previous actual or attempted intimate het-erosexual relationships.

Interviews were held in various locations, both at the researcher's office and home, in a lounge, and in the interviewees' home; two were conducted via phone.

At the outset of each interview the researcher was candid about the purpose. This openness evidently aided in establishing rapport: there appeared to be no topics that were too "personal" for the sub-jects to discuss. The researcher remained constantly concerned about confidentiality. Not all of the subjects are "out of the closet," or at least not all of the way out. Care was taken not to violate their right to remain anonymous. There was one exception to the expectation that they would be anonymous: one couple, described in detail be-low, requested that their real names be used.

A possible problem in this research was the difference between the insider and the outsider, or the "insider/outsider myths." Styles (1979) suggested that "there are no privileged positions of knowl-edge when it comes to scrutinizing human life" (p. 147); therefore, the researcher must have the appropriate listening skills accompa-nied by a non-judgmental acceptance. A second problem identified by Styles was that of gaining acceptance: one doing research would "need informants who could give him detailed accounts of their . . . experiences as well as alternative interpretations of things he ob-served" (1979, p. 151). In this study, caution was taken to clarify definitions and behaviors with insiders.

Because of the small number of subjects in the group studied, no attempt is made to generalize these findings to any larger group.

ANALYSIS AND DISCUSSION OF THE DATA

Why Relationships Are Formed

> Having to live in the larger society . . . the adolescent soon feels the need for a "little world" of his own, having been socialized in such a way that only by having such a world to withdraw into can he successfully cope with the anonymous big world that confronts him as soon as he steps outside his parental home. (Berger & Kellner, 1975, p. 230)

Gays, having been reared in heterosexual households, are subjected to this same socialization process, and they, too, feel the need for a little world of their own. In this study, all reported expectations, or desires, of at least a semi-permanent relationship for specific reasons:

> *Researcher:* Why did you live together in the first place?

> *M:* It is something I always wanted. (He answered quickly with no hesitation. Then there was a short silence before he continued and his voice changed as he started talking about more practical reasons.) Living expenses. Companionship. There was love involved. I did love him. And a lot of caring. We just grew out of that.

Another was more direct:

> *C:* In the gay community there is a need to be with someone. So you just go for it. But it never materializes. The toothpaste cap gets left off and you realize you just can't live with this one. It seems gays are real quick to get into a monogamous situation without knowing the other person first.

Another related it to being married, saying most gays expect that (to move in together), to have someone there, not to have to go out hustling in the bars and "compete with all those other bitches."

The Cementing Bond in Relationships

"Heterosexual marriages are institutionalized by church and state. Heterosexual couples fit into society in numerous ways, both obvious and subtle, in which homosexual couples cannot partake" (Hoffman, 1968, p. 174-5). What, then, holds these relationships together? One interviewee reported the end of a relationship, saying there was no more sex so it was over:

> *Researcher:* What about companionship; isn't it still good without the romance?
>
> *T:* Well, I think it is different for lesbians; with males there is the constant search for the big O (orgasm), and when there isn't any, you have to look somewhere else.

This is consistent with reports in the literature: "Many men have both the ability, and often the preference, for engaging in anonymous or 'impersonal' sex. . . . Although women are socialized to believe that sex should occur within the context of love and commitment, men are seldom sensitized to such constraints" (Blumstein & Schwartz, 1976, p. 341).

Others reported similar experiences, saying that while they don't have "exclusive" relationships, they are "in love" with three — or two or four — different people but don't expect any exclusive rights over any of them. There appear to be some inconsistencies in these expectations, however, about what might hold a relationship together:

> *Researcher:* You said you wouldn't do it (have an intimate long-term relationship) again?
>
> *J:* Well, yes, I would. In due time. Certain things would have to be settled first. I'm not big on this idea of sleeping with everybody. You may start with magic but then you have to build on something more solid. For me the big issue is fidelity.

The common view of gays to have shorter-term intimate relationships has sometimes been attributed to the greater tendency of males in general to separate sex from affection, to estimate their personal worth on the basis of how often they "score," and to view fidelity as an undesirable restriction upon their freedom and independence. However, Bell and Weinberg (1978) suggest another reason:

> Society provides them (gays) with little or no opportunity to meet on anything more than a sexual basis. Driven underground, segregated in what have been termed "sexual marketplaces," threatened but perhaps also stimulated by the danger of their enterprise, homosexual men would be expected to have an enormous number of fleeting sexual encounters. (p. 101)

For all of these reasons, Hoffman (1968) has suggested that "The most serious problem for those who live in the gay world is the great difficulty they have in establishing stable paired relationships with each other" (p. 171). It has become a rather chicken-and-egg-like question: pairing is difficult due to the non-monogamous "nature" of males; they become more promiscuous because they have such great difficulty forming lasting relationships!

The Character of the Gay Intimate Relationship

Closely related to the cementing bond of the gay intimate relationship is the character of that relationship: there seemed to be a great deal of tension underlying most of these interactions.

Researcher: Do you plan for the future together now?

T: No, now we just take it as it comes. I'm saving my money so that I will have enough if I decide to go it alone again and leave him.

Another respondent said that the commonality between them "is sex, not feelings and concerns." Another put it in slightly different words:

Researcher: Do you think D's refusal to participate in this study is any reflection on your relationship?

T: Oh, yes, we don't talk together about anything so personal. I try to but he's comfortable with things the way they are so why should he?

The impermanence of the relationships seemed to be underlying much of the everyday behavior towards each other:

M: G kept it very tentative. At least once a week he would say, "Well, I may decide to end this." Maybe that was why we didn't buy things together. With him the whole thing was trauma.

And there was not much planning for the future:

T: I don't care what happens. He can just be an old man in his rocking chair.

"Every individual requires the ongoing validation of his world, including crucially the validation of his identity and place in this world, by those few who are his truly significant others" (Berger & Kellner, 1975, p. 220). One couple interviewed displayed that necessary validation:

Steve: Well, the primary relationship is that this is home.

Jason: This is ours together.

Steve: Yeah. I don't find a need to wander. (Jason nodded agreement.)

The back-and-forth, give-and-take just briefly demonstrated was characteristic of the entire interview with this couple. That give-and-take was reinforced by a great mutual sense of humor:

Jason: And . . . we're kind of an Oscar and Felix sort of thing. I'm a pig. (Much laughter.)

Steve: I believe everything has a place. (More laughter.)

For most of the relationships described then, they were characterized by tension and insecurity. One couple, however, did indeed fulfill the expectations that "home is our own special little world" which provides meaning for the participants.

Support from the Society, Friends, and Family

"Children, friends, relatives and casual acquaintances all have their part in reinforcing the tenuous structure of the new reality" created by intimate relationships (Berger & Kellner, 1975, p. 228). While this may be true for heterosexual couples, there appears to be little or no support from the society at large for gay intimate relationships. In response to a question about being out in public with his "significant other," one interviewee said "it just isn't done":

> *J:* Well, to begin with if by "in public" you mean on the street or in this bar, I couldn't take the chance that someone who knows someone from work, or whoever, might be over in that corner watching.

Most subjects responded that they have few friends:

> *J:* As I said, I pretty much keep friends separate from each other. I live in two different worlds.

and

> *Researcher:* When you decide to go into a relationship such as this one with D, do your friends change?
>
> *M:* We never had too many friends.

and

> *Researcher:* Is that lonely for you?
>
> *T:* Darn right. That's what it's all about. We (gays) are the most lonely people around. There's no one who really cares. Our few friends are really important.

Some reported support from their family:

> *Researcher:* What about your family?
>
> *R:* They are wonderful. They all know, of course. They said

after I had been in Europe for a long time that I didn't have to stay over there because of that (being gay). They are wonderful.

and

Researcher: Was your family very supportive of your relationship?

J: Very supportive. My grandparents were very fond of him, in fact, they were captivated by him. My parents, too. Though it is very interesting when they are talking with me after the fact. My father was very apprehensive: was it good for me?

Most reported little or no support from their families:

Researcher: Would you describe yourself as married?

M: Well, no, I don't feel that way. Because there is no blessing from my family. They don't approve. They want contact with me, but we have no discussion ever involving my personal life. Even at that I only see my folks about twice a year. And they only live 80 miles from here. I have no desire to ever set foot in my sister's home again. (He had reported being very close to his sister in the past.)

and:

Researcher: What about your family?

T: Well, they're another story. We're always fighting about something anyway. They pretend it (D and I) isn't so. But they still include him when social events come up. But we can't sleep in the same room when we stay at their house. And they're always trying to "line both of us up" with some daughters of their friends.

Because of the trauma associated in not getting support from their families, interviewees reacted in different ways:

J: I told my parents because I wanted to share with them. Now I would tell people NEVER to tell their parents. DO NOT. I suppose it depends on the family. If you have a working relationship or communication with them. No, I'd say keep the relationship you now have. They don't need to know. I remember all the agony I went through in telling them. . . .

The couple reported above with the give-and-take relationship spiced with humor reported an initial mixed reaction from the family but growing supportive climates:

Researcher: How about family? Do both of your families know?

Steve: Well, his is a little more receptive than mine is.

Jason: Well, mine is more open. . . . When I first told mine, well, have you ever heard the joke about what's different between being Black and being gay? When you're Black you don't have to tell your mother. Well, when I first told my mother she said, "Well, it's no news to me. You're the same person." When I told my sister and brothers, they were scared. But I told them that I didn't choose to be gay, but I do choose to be happy. But I made it very clear to them. I told them that if they couldn't accept me for the person I am and always will be, then that was too bad. . . . When my sister first met Steve, she loved him. She said, "You better hang onto him. You've really got yourself a catch!"

These support systems are vital to an individual's well-being: "One of the major factors contributing to the suicides of lesbians and gay men is our estrangement from the traditional support systems within our culture that people turn to in times of crisis (family, church and school)" (Rofes, 1983, p. 47). Rofes identifies many examples; interviewees in this study reported the same lack of support:

Researcher: Does your family ever see you together? Do they lend you moral support in tough times?

M: No, they have never seen us together. I get support only from my friends.

R: Do you get support from the gay community?

M: No, only from a few friends.

"All the world loves a lover" does not hold true for the gay lover, though

> after a time lovers have a real sociological need for that support that comes from being recognized as such. . . . We are all social animals, and highly dependent on the approval of others. Each time one's lover need be hidden, and jokes/excuses need be made about living with another man or woman, homosexuals feel the denial of what virtually all straights can take for granted—and thus usually miss the importance of. (Altman, 1971, p. 66)

Support from the Gay Community

> It was continually observed in the subject (gay) community that as soon as any two individuals entered into sexual or sociosexual relationship that was hoped to last for any period of time, these individuals rapidly withdrew from the activity of the community and decreased their participation in group affairs, regardless of how active or popular they had been before. (Sonenschein, 1972, p. 225-6)

This was also found to be true in the current study:

Jason: One of the biggest ways we protect our relationship is by staying away from the gay community.

Researcher: So you have little or no contact with the gay community?

Jason: Next to none.

Steve: It's really important that we don't go to the bars.

These sentiments were echoed by virtually all those interviewed in this study:

> *Researcher:* Why don't they (relationships) last long?
>
> *M:* The support group is not good. There is a lot of tearing apart in the gay community.
>
> *R:* What does that mean?
>
> *M:* Friends getting between two lovers.
>
> *R:* On purpose?
>
> *M:* They can't stand to have two people together.

and:

> *Researcher:* Oh, I thought that the community would be very supportive since you lack other kinds of support in the society?
>
> *T:* That's what I thought. When I first knew I was gay I thought, well at least I will have the gay community. But that doesn't happen.

and:

> *Researcher:* Were those friends you developed together supportive of your relationship?
>
> *J:* Most definitely. Most were straight couples. Well, maybe it was break-even between the number of gay friends and straight friends. The biggest issue in the gay community, anytime a single person is coming into a relationship a great deal of stress is involved.

And, probably the best summation was made by one of the interviewees:

> *N:* The gay community is a very unstable world. In the midst of all that instability, stability is a threat.

Perhaps this lack of support stems from a different cause: the literature abounds in arguments of whether or not there is such a thing as a gay community. Lee (1979) argues for the existence of a community by utilizing an ecological model, the energy source of which is sex. Hayes (1981) looks at the language of the gay community as proof that it is indeed a "culture." Glenn (1981) utilizes fantasy theme analysis as proof of the existence of a community. Whether or not it is a community, or culture, is outside the scope of this paper; however, appropriately, the question did arise:

> *Researcher:* What about support from the gay community?

> *R:* There is no gay community. A community is that which is held in common. We have nothing in common. Gay bars are controlled by the Mafia and organized crime. They are a commercial venture. Thirty-five percent of us are alcoholics. All drinks in gay bars are doubles. We get drunk faster. It's a glitzy glimmer world. *Gentleman's Quarterly* is our altar. Metropolitan Community Church is typical: there is no theology but people are there for the smells and bells. That's our tradition.

If there is no community, it cannot support its members in relationships.

Jason and Steve

One intimate relationship among the several examined during this study stands out as the "negative data" and thus deserves separate scrutiny. It was obvious to the researcher early that this was going to be different: the tone over the telephone was that of being welcomed to a "home," truly that sanctuary of special people who felt good about themselves and each other, and therefore could feel good about other people. In utilizing the framework already defined for looking at the "problem," it is useful to scrutinize the relationship of Jason and Steve separately but within that same framework.

These two suggested I use their real names: "I'll send my mother a copy." At another time during the interview, they related having been to visit Jason's sister:

> *Steve:* Her husband Al says "You two would be very good advertising for gays. The way you relate to each other."

Their reasons for forming a relationship appear to be the same as those of others, both heterosexual and gay, confirming the expectations of both Davis (1973) and Berger and Kellner (1975):

> *Jason:* I think a lot of people do that (jump into something) to have a first relationship. Kind of a love at first sight. That's the way mine was.
>
> *Researcher:* The first one after coming out?
>
> *Jason:* Yes. You have that need. People just need to have a mate.

While there is no legal sanction for their relationship, they function as a couple in all apparent aspects: they own things together, and talked about "our lease." They were in the process of buying a home together. Their relationship was formed in a different manner than any of the others included in this study: they met at work, and did not have a sexual relationship for several weeks after meeting. Steve was trying to "fix Jason up with a friend and nothing was working out. We became really good friends and started hanging around together. And that's how it started."

"Society has provided them (couples) with a taken-for-granted image of marriage and has socialized them into anticipation of stepping into the taken-for-granted roles of marriage" (Berger & Kellner, p. 224). While these taken-for-granted roles appear to be dysfunctional for both heterosexual and gay intimate relationships, Jason and Steve appear to have moved beyond role limitations:

> *Jason:* I started crocheting to keep me from smoking. (The researcher related the scene from *Torch Song Trilogy* in which Arnold had made an afghan and his mother made fun of it. Jason and Steve laughed.) I made one for my mother.
>
> *Steve:* I got a sewing machine and made a quilt for her.

While there was no ritual through which Jason and Steve must pass to become a couple such as the ceremonies that heterosexual couples experience, they and other gay couples reported symbols for their intimate relationships. Most wear each other's ring or an earring. Some reported wearing identical articles of clothing. Jason and Steve exchanged jewelry; they also wear each other's clothes. While it was reported as an item of convenience, it is quite likely at some point also symbolic.

Steve and Jason have developed a support network for their relationship. At work they are very open about their "significant other." They reported that their respective bosses made sure they had compatible schedules such as weekends off together. At social functions they are asked to bring the other. They have supportive joint and individual friends, most of whom are women, some are straight couples (though they reported that they usually become friends with the wife first—through their medical professional work—and then get to know the husband). They reported that the straight husbands are sometimes threatened:

Jason: Straight women seem to be much more accepting.

Steve: The straight men who have been our friends are very secure. And they know who they are. They're secure in their masculinity and don't find gays a threat. The real macho men see us as a threat.

And, for the most part, their families are supportive: Steve has never "come out" to his father, but "he knows. He's not dumb. He's pretending." But they reported that Steve's father loaned them the money for a car, even picked it out for them. They talked about visiting Jason's sister and husband, who made them feel very welcome ("How long can you stay?"). They play bingo with Jason's brothers and their "women." Relatives call them "the boys," as in "let's invite the boys to do this . . . " and it is felt to be an endearing term. And, family comes to visit, perhaps as Steve jokes, because they like his cooking.

As identified earlier, Jason and Steve "protect their relationship by staying away from the gay community." They confirmed the reports of others, that the fierce competition within the gay community would be destructive to their relationship.

While they both recognize the short-term nature of most gay relationships—they had both experienced that before—they clearly both hope to stay together a long time. When asked if they look to anyone else as role models, they clearly had someone in mind:

Jason: I would like our relationship to be like my aunt and uncle. They've been married almost 40 years and they're great together. . . . They've got ways to work things out.

They're proud of their communication style: they joked about "both coming from families of screamers," and they've both overcome and utilized that by being very direct and immediate about anything that might be bothering them; they both have an immediate say. They've found this alleviates pent-up problems which might surface later and tear the fabric of their relationship. And they've developed a sense of playfulness together, a step beyond simply a sense of humor; they related jokes they've made up, and laughed about Steve using a whole can of shaving cream playing in the bathtub.

How are Jason and Steve like or different from other intimate relationships? They appear to be the same in basic components to what Davis (1973) has described as intimate (Davis has been careful to identify that he did not use gender roles so that his model would indeed work for non-heterosexual pairs). They appear to be like any couple in which both partners like themselves and each other, and have worked out functional communication styles. They appear to be unlike most gay couples who have not identified support networks either in the family or in the community: support from people who share their value of a primary relationship based at least in part on fidelity. They perhaps are the individuals about whom Davis (1973) wrote:

> By being accepted in his personal relations as a unique totality, a person can overcome his isolation and merge with others into a larger unit, with all the increased relief, security and power that membership in such a supraindividual entity provides. In urbanized societies, then, personal relations permit a person to have his individuality and lose it, too. (Davis, 1973, p. xxii)

The Impact of AIDS on Intimate Gay Relationships

There is growing evidence that AIDS may be contributing to longer-term intimate gay relationships in at least two ways: first, the pressure for "safe sex" (including fewer anonymous partners) makes long-term relationships appear more attractive (Patton [1985], Blumenfeld & Raymond [1988], and Heeney [1988]). Second, "AIDS represents a unique assault on the newly emerging sexual identity and community in the U.S." (Patton, 1985, p. 120). When attacked, people respond, thus AIDS has served as a rallying point around which the gay community can unite. Examples of this abound: the "buddy system" (Cutler [1988]), functional wills and power of attorney or power of appointment documents in favor of lovers (Patton [1985]), and the NAMES quilt project (Jensen [1988]). Patton (1985) identifies an accompanying problem, however: " . . . the resulting changes in community are happening so rapidly. . . . changes on both the sexual and non-sexual levels of gay community must begin to integrate the growing standard of sensible sex as a method of maintaining the community" (p. 140). And Patton then adds her voice to the call for gay community support systems. As previously stated, the lack of support systems both within the gay community, from the family, and from society in general has been a major factor in the failure of intimate relationships.

CONCLUSIONS AND IMPLICATIONS

Several conclusions about this group might be drawn from the above study. First, there appears to be one primary difference between heterosexual and gay intimate couples: the support network available for both the individuals and for the relationships is missing for the gay couples. (McWhirter and Mattison [1984] indirectly confirm this: less than half of their couples "have talked with all or some family members about their homosexuality and their relationship. . . . The majority of our participants do not enjoy full family support or participation" [p. 238-9]). This single difference appears to lead to the other identifiable differences, such as the short length of the relationships and even possibly the apparently common factor of non-monogamy. As suggested above, McWhirter and Mattison (1984) confirm that lack of support, but do not suggest it as a deterrent to long-term relationships. They suggest, instead, that relationship survival and longevity is dependent upon compatibility, including complementarity (p. 289). However, virtually all of their recommendations are for various forms of support for gay couples, as are Patton's.

One important similarity between gay and heterosexual couples is that in both, successful relationships are characterized by open communication (the reverse is true for unsuccessful ones!), and supportive families, or substitute families.

There appears to be considerable tension within the individual between his conditioned need to be in an intimate relationship, and the pragmatic value or even possibility of imposing that heterosexual model on the gay community. Several gay writers have suggested that this is not practical; in fact, there may be evidence that the traditional model for couples has outlived its usefulness for even the heterosexual world. Many individuals are trying alternatives at least within some components of that model, such as role differentiation and authority structures. As stated, imposition of this model on gays, either voluntarily or subconsciously, may be a major factor in the almost permanent disorganization experienced by individual gays.

Individuals in this study appeared to be in two categories: first, some are comfortable with themselves and this seems to result in others being comfortable with them. This leads to a support network and also more possibly a relationship. The second category are those who are unhappy and uncomfortable with themselves, whether it be because they are gay or for some other reason (such as they don't like their physical appearance). They get no support, have a low trust of others, and see a rather bleak future. Quite obviously their relationships have no lasting duration. These differences might be identified also as categories of independence: the first is independent because they are so comfortable with the self that they have learned to be androgynous. The second is independent in a defensive manner: they don't trust anyone and will accept no restraints on their freedom. Again, a lasting relationship doesn't fit, or can't exist, within those constraints.

Since the size of the group studied is relatively small (24), it is not possible to generalize to the entire gay population or even to the educated gay population of the Twin Cities area (Minneapolis-St. Paul, Minnesota). However, there are important implications which might be drawn from this study. First, it is obvious that there is a need to develop support systems. Given the size of the gay population (the most conservative estimate is 10% and acknowledged to be much higher in the area of this study), there are a lot of people living very traumatic daily lives. This should be important information for those who set and implement social policy, and those who work with families. As Rofes (1983) suggests, this must be a conscious effort, since most homosexuals "find themselves estranged from their biological families and because none of us has been raised to see community building and relationship building as a valuable skill and activity . . . " (p. 122). As Schofield (1965) long ago suggested, "We should give up our attempts to eradicate the homosexual condition" (p. 213). Instead we should be looking for ways to make individuals, regardless of labels, better able to live their lives to their fullest potential. While AIDS may be the impetus for the emergence of some social support systems, more need to be consciously developed.

Another implication for this study is the need for a survey of the literature. Most publications from the '60s and early '70s focused on the sensational rather than on being helpful. Most focused on why people are gay, rather than with the impact on the individuals, families, and how to deal with it. Blumenfeld and Raymond (1988) provide a start on this survey, but end in 1978 by describing two books which "are both dismal pictures of gay social life" (p. 393). There is a need to identify the "gaps" in the gay literature: how did we get from the '70s to the late '80s, when most of the literature now appears to be written by gays? There appear to be definite trends; for those undertaking research in any of these related topics, and hoping to impact social change, this would be an important addition, particularly in view of the wealth of literature now being published about AIDS and its impact on gay life and community.

One interviewee said that in gay life "everyday there are people thrown away like toilet paper." That seemed so despairing that the researcher asked, "Then what is the redeeming grace?" He gave a quick reply: "Death. If you are isolated within and from the community and ostracized by the society, what else is there?" The researcher explained that what had been meant was what are the good things about gay life? His response: "There are lots of good things, like Arnold in bunny slippers (a scene from *Torch Song Trilogy*).

The real core in Arnold is seeking out the good things in life, with no dimensions or restrictions.'' So, it appears that success or failure, being happy or unhappy, will depend on the coping skills that the individuals, the families, and the community bring to or develop within the relationship. That's a very positive note for the future, because coping (communication) skills can be learned!

BIBLIOGRAPHY

Adair, N., & Adair, C. (1978). *Word is Out*. New York: Delacorte Press.

Altman, D. (1971). *Homosexual Oppression and Liberation*. New York: Avon Books.

Bell, A. P., & Weinberg, M. S. (1978). *Homosexualities: A Study of Diversity Among Men and Women*. New York: Simon and Schuster.

Berger, P., & Kellner, H. (1975). Marriage and the construction of reality. In Dennis Brisette, Ed., *Life as Theatre*. Chicago: Aldine Publishing Co. pp. 219-233.

Blumenfeld, W. J., & Raymond, D. (1988). *Looking at Gay and Lesbian Life*. New York: Philosophical Library, Inc.

Blumstein, P. W., & Schwartz, P. (1976). Bisexuality in men. *Urban Life*, 5(3). 339-358.

Bogdan, R., & Taylor, S. J. (1975). *Introduction to Qualitative Research Methods*. New York: John Wiley.

Chesebro, J. W. (Ed.) (1981). *Gayspeak: Gay Male and Lesbian Communication*. New York: The Pilgrim Press.

Cutler, M. (1988). Starting a buddy program. In Sasha Alyson, Ed., *You CAN Do Something About AIDS*. Boston: The Stop AIDS Project.

Davis, M. S. (1973). Intimate Relations. New York: The Free Press.

Emerson, R. M. (Ed.) (1983). *Contemporary Field Research*. Boston: Little Brown & Co.

Fisher, P. (1972). *The Gay Mystique: The Myth and Reality of Male Homosexuality*. New York: Stein & Day.

Heeney, T. (1988, November). *From abnormal identities to normal differences: AIDS and the ethics of community*. Paper presented at the meeting of the Speech Communication Association (SCA), New Orleans, LA.

Hoffman, M. (1968). *The Gay World: Male Homosexuality and the Social Creation of Evil*. New York: Basic Books, Inc.

Jensen, M. D. (1988, November). *Making contact: the NAMES project in comparison to the Vietnam memorial*. Paper presented at the meeting of the Speech Communication Association (SCA), New Orleans, LA.

Lee, J. A. (1979). The gay connection. *Urban Life*, 8(2), 175-198.

McWhirter, D. P., MD, & Mattison, Andrew M., PhD (1984). *The Male Couple: How Relationships Develop*. Englewood Cliffs, N.J.: Prentice-Hall, Inc.

Patton, C. (1985). *Sex and Germs: The Politics of Aids*. Boston: South End Press.

Rofes, E. E. (1983). *I Thought People Like That Killed Themselves: Lesbians, Gay Men and Suicide*. San Francisco: Grey Fox Press.

Schofield, M. (1965). *Sociological Aspects of Homosexuality*. London: Longmans, Green & Co., Ltd.

Silverstein, C., & White, E. (1977). *The Joy of Gay Sex*. New York: Simon & Schuster.

Sonenschein, D. (1972). The ethnography of male homosexual relationships. In Robert R. Bell and Michael Gordon, Eds., *Social Dimension of Human Sexuality*. Boston: Little, Brown & Co. pp. 215-227.

Styles, J. (1979). *Outsider/Insider: Researching Gay Baths. Urban Life, 8*(2). 135-152.

Walker, M. (1977). *Men Loving Men: A Gay Sex Guide & Consciousness Book*. San Francisco: Gay Sunshine Press, Inc.

White, E. (1983). *States of Desire: Travels in Gay America*. New York: E. P. Dutton, Inc.

Adoption and Foster Parenting for Lesbians and Gay Men: Creating New Traditions in Family

Wendell Ricketts
Roberta Achtenberg

INTRODUCTION

If we define the nuclear family as a working husband, house-keeping wife, and two children, and ask how many Americans actually still live in this type of family, the answer is astonishing: 7 percent of the total United States population. (Alvin Toffler, *The Third Wave*, 1980)

Recognizing human diversity is very different from making judgments about it [We need not] engage in the endless academic debate over the relative merits of different lifestyles, personalities, relationships, or types of family structures. Instead, [we can] focus on the importance of learning to live and work together constructively to solve problems. Pluralism has created

Wendell Ricketts is a writer living in San Francisco. Formerly the Manuscript Editor of the *Journal of Homosexuality*, he has previously published articles about foster care and adoption, homophobia, and lesbian and gay youth. Roberta Achtenberg has been the Directing Attorney of the National Center for Lesbian Rights since 1984. She has published and taught extensively in the areas of civil rights, reproductive issues, and lesbian and gay family law. Correspondence may be sent to the authors in care of the National Center for Lesbian Rights, 1370 Mission Street, San Francisco, CA 94103.

The authors would like to thank Donna Hitchens for her continuing support. In addition, we acknowledge the courage of Ann, Beverly, Chuck, Darby, Don, Linda, Meg, Michael, Nan, Rebecca, Ron, Steve, Tom, and the many others whose experience of lesbian and gay families has guided our work.

for us a strong society, and respect for human diversity is a prerequisite to tapping the full potential of our vast reservoir of human talent. (City of Los Angeles Task Force on Family Diversity, 1988)

Family experts have, for some time, been calling for flexibility in concepts of family—have been suggesting, that is, that legislators, courts, social service experts, and other policy-makers adopt definitions of family that simply reflect the ways in which people actually live. Given the mythical, emotional, and even patriotic symbolism with which "family" is imbued, however, it is not surprising that such a call has encountered hearty resistance.

The families created by lesbians and gay men are, of course, one of the "new" family's most controversial manifestations. Increasingly, lesbians and gay men are exploring an ingenious array of parenting options—including, to the extent they are permitted by law and policy, adoption and foster care.

For the most part, at least until recently, prospective lesbian and gay foster or adoptive parents have chosen to remain invisible. A few have actively misrepresented their sexual orientation, but most have simply made no mention of it. Caseworkers, courts, and administrative staff have either looked the other way or succumbed to their presumption of applicants' heterosexuality. The director of a foster home program in Washington, D.C., for example, commented:

> We've always had pairs of women providing foster care. In some instances, they have not been related. And of course, that always raises questions in some people's minds. But as far as we were concerned, they were two friends who lived together and wanted to do this together. I would assume that some of the people who apply to be foster parents might be gay. But if they are, we don't know about it.

It is essential to note, however, that the invisibility of lesbian and gay foster and adoptive parents—whether promoted by gay people themselves or by the "make no waves" ethic in many placement programs—can ultimately only contribute to stereotypes of homosexuals as child molesters, sex criminals, and emotional neurotics.

In virtually every case in which openly lesbian and gay parents confront the glare of media publicity or the scrutiny of judicial or administrative review, they must endure spoken and unspoken pre-judgments about their unfitness as parents—judgments that arise out of stereotypes to which invisibility and silence offer no chal-lenge. Given the deep entrenchment of homophobic prejudice, of course, there are compelling reasons for some prospective adoptive or foster parents to choose to remain silent about their sexual orien-tation. The result is an unfortunate Catch-22.

Gay and lesbian people who *can* be open about themselves, how-ever, deserve much credit for advances and victories in foster and adoptive parenting by lesbians and gay men. But none of them has had it easy. Fairly or not, lesbians and gay men often have the task of educating family court personnel, social workers, agency admin-istrators, and licensing programs, among others, that gay and les-bian people are as able to be fit, loving, and generous parents as anyone else. They must often be the "guinea pigs" for agencies trying to cope with the reality of new families. The goal of this article, then, is to provide as much encouragement and information as possible to gay men and lesbians in their efforts to become foster and adoptive parents.

Those who speak most eloquently of the joys and frustrations of negotiating "the system," of course, are those who have experi-enced it. We have quoted liberally herein from interviews with les-bian and gay adolescents in foster care, successful lesbian and gay adoptive parents, older heterosexual children in lesbian or gay step-parent families, and others. Their experiences are crucial in formu-lating the strategies that will benefit future lesbian and gay families.

THE RECENT HISTORY OF LESBIAN AND GAY FOSTER AND ADOPTIVE PARENTING

The few published reports on lesbian and gay foster and adoptive parenting have appeared largely in the gay press. Our research re-vealed a number of cases of interest.

1973: Chicago, IL The Director of the Department of Children and Family Services revealed that children with "homosexual ten-dencies" were being placed in homes with gay foster parents. Although *The Advocate* reported that this was the first time these placements had been made public, it acknowledged that "[g]ay organizations in several cities have quietly been arranging such placements [for some time] but have shunned publicity for fear an uproar would result which would wreck their work" ("Agency Reveals," 1973).

1974: Washington State The Department of Social and Health Services proposed new regulations that appeared to exclude gay men and lesbians from consideration as foster parents, although a number of gays were already acting as foster parents there ("New Rules," 1974). The section banning gay foster care was later stricken from the guidelines ("Ban on Gay," 1974).

1974: Oregon After a caseworker recommended to a circuit court judge that a 14-year-old "confirmed homosexual" be placed in a gay household, the Department of Human Resources prohibited the placement of any state-supervised children in gay foster homes ("Agency Backs Down," 1974).

1975: Vancouver, WA A judge ordered a 16-year-old gay youth to be removed from his four-month foster placement with a male couple, despite a lengthy hearing in which caseworkers, administrators, and expert witnesses all testified in favor of the placement (Shilts, 1975).

1976: California The Department of Social Services adopted a policy allowing gay people with "clean records" and without a "proclivity to sexually assault children" to be licensed as foster parents ("CA Gay Foster," 1976).

From 1974 through 1979, reports from New Jersey, Massachusetts, Minnesota, Pennsylvania, New York, and Washington, D.C. indicated that lesbians and gay men were being approved as foster parents for homosexual adolescents in those areas as well.

With regard to adoptions, however, the record is less clear. As early as 1976, the Los Angeles County Department of Adoptions put out an appeal to single men to apply to adopt its "bumper crop" of young boys over nine years of age. The Department stated, rather cryptically: "We seek the single adoptive parent who is comfortable in his sexual role and accepting of the opposite role" ("Los Angeles," 1976). It was not until March, 1979 that *The Advocate* reported what it believed to have been the first adoption by an openly gay couple in Los Angeles. In June of that same year, an openly gay man in Catskill, New York adopted the 13-year-old boy who had lived with him and his male lover for a year (Vecsey, 1979).

A GROWING TREND: OPPOSITION AND VICTORIES

What these accounts only hint at, but what has been true for many years, is that thousands of lesbians and gay men have, in fact, adopted children and been licensed as foster parents across the country. As noted previously, however, the issue of their sexual orientation has generally not been raised.

Family lawyers in such situations have consistently advised their clients not to volunteer information regarding their sexual orientation, but to tell the truth if asked directly. More recently, however, many lesbians and gay men have expressed a desire to present themselves in a clearer light, and choose to reveal their sexual orientation at the outset. In this way, they hope to avoid problems that can arise from withholding information that may be discovered later, and to protect themselves and any children who might be placed with them. Moreover, same-sex couples seeking to become foster or adoptive parents often do not want to pretend they are merely roommates, when in fact they are life-mates.

In addition to what might be considered the self-affirmative or even political goals of some prospective parents in making their homosexuality known to foster care or adoption workers, the recognition is also dawning that the phenomenon of secrecy, in and of itself, can be deleterious to children in a lesbian or gay home. Don Laterno, a Minnesota youth worker, for example, described several cases in which closeted homosexual foster parents refused to take gay or lesbian adolescents into their homes. Although the teenagers desperately needed to live where their homosexuality could be accepted, some gay and lesbian foster parents dismissed the possibility for fear their own homosexuality might be revealed. Laterno commented:

> When you're invested in protecting a secret, that secret some-
> times becomes a high priority in decisions you make regarding
> a child's welfare. If you're afraid that your social worker or
> the agency or whomever is going to find out about you, you're
> not in a good position to be an advocate for a child or to go to
> the wall, if need be.

Additional problems include the potential for disrupted placements when a parent's homosexuality is "exposed" and agencies
must respond to public outcry. The chances of an agency's defending a gay or lesbian placement are probably increased if the agency
has all the facts to begin with.

On the other hand, the issue of homosexuality and children is so
volatile, and homophobia in the child-welfare system so widespread, that no openly gay or lesbian parent can be assured of fair
treatment. Where previous successes are not in evidence or where
sympathetic social workers and administrators have not been identified, gay and lesbian would-be foster or adoptive parents enter each
situation blindly.

At the same time, those opposed to lesbian and gay foster or
adoptive placements commonly raise concern over the "trauma"
they believe will befall children raised in such homes. Massachusetts Representative Marie Parente put it quite succinctly when she
stated, in defending that state's anti-gay foster care policy,

> I'm not arguing homosexuality. I'm arguing children. I know
> homosexuals. They're very warm and caring and loving. But
> being a foster child of gay parents is just too much for a child
> to take. How could you people wish this on a child? Why
> would you let a little child go out on the playground and face
> this kind of ridicule? (Pincus, 1988)

Evaluating the potential impact on children of a prospective foster or adoptive household is, of course, the reason that home visits
and other investigations are conducted prior to a placement. Agencies *should* consider a parent's sexual and emotional adjustment,
along with all other factors, in determining the suitability of a particular home for a particular child. When *every* placement in *every*
lesbian or gay family is judged to be traumatizing for *every* child,

however, prejudice has eclipsed concern for children's best interests.

Parente's comments, moreover, which are echoed whenever the subject of homosexual foster or adoptive homes is raised, demonstrate ignorance of several key points. Because such arguments are so common, the following considerations are appropriate for discussion at every level of policy-making within the child-welfare system.

First, many children today already live in families in which at least one parent is homosexual, and their experiences are instructive. Such children may find that having a gay or lesbian parent is not the easiest part of growing up, but it is not necessarily the hardest. What is more, when parents are able to be open about being gay, the "terrible secret" of homosexuality is not one that children themselves must shoulder. (See, e.g., Gantz, 1983, and our interviews with "Dave" and "Alicia" below.)

Second, almost all children experience being different from others in one way or another. That sensation can be valuable or traumatizing or, occasionally, both. Many children today, for example, live in divorced, bi-racial, or single-parent families; alternately, their families may be culturally, ethnically, religiously, or physically different from those of classmates and neighbors. There can be no question that such children will be teased by playmates. Teasing is what children do. Does this mean that child-welfare policy must be set at a level no higher than the social interactions of children?

This is, of course, the logical extension of Parente's comments: the insistence that children be sheltered from every experience in which their difference might challenge prejudice, ignorance, or the status quo (or in which they would be "exposed" to the difference of others). Agencies conforming to such a standard must ask themselves whether it is their function to honor the system that generates stigma by upholding its constraints.

Clearly, assessing the impact on children of being raised by gay or lesbian foster or adoptive parents requires a complex and compassionate approach. Perhaps, however, there should be more to that approach than the suggestion that victims must change or that the oppressed must be denied opportunities. Perhaps, in fact, fostering respect for diversity can come to be seen as an important task for government, social welfare organizations, schools, churches, and, indeed, for society itself.

A heterosexual social worker, who has supported several lesbian and gay adoptions, had this comment:

> I came to this country as an immigrant from China, when I was a teenager. Because of being Asian and because I didn't speak English very well, I faced a lot of ridicule. So I am aware that this kind of thing happens, and that it doesn't necessarily defeat people. I raised my own children here, too, who were a minority in a Caucasian country, and they faced prejudice as I did. But there is no way you can protect your children from experiencing pain in their childhood.
>
> Of course, I think that gay people can definitely do things that make the situation more difficult — trying to raise children who are little gay rights advocates, for example, when they aren't gay themselves. But I think with empathy for what the child is going through, and knowledge that basically you're OK and that many children experience much worse things in their lives, then it can work out.

Case Studies

Alicia

Alicia has known since she was 7 that her mother was a lesbian. After her parents divorced, Alicia went to live with her mom and her mom's lover, Monica. Alicia is now attending her first year of college.

> Seventh grade was the first time I had problems with people knowing about my mom and Monica. I told one person and it got all over the school, and they teased me and said that I would be gay because of my mother. I learned my lesson in terms of knowing that you can't just tell anyone.
>
> After that, I only told one person up until my junior year. Then I told my best friend. She's someone I really wanted to tell, but her family is very, very Catholic, and I was afraid. I

knew she would understand, but what if she told her family and her family said, don't go out with Alicia anymore, don't go to their house?

The hardest part was basically always people's reaction — what they might think of the people who are special in my life. I think really highly of my mom, and for someone to criticize her or Monica — I've been afraid of that.

I think [lesbian and gay parents] have to be aware of their kids' need to have a "normal" house when their friends come over. For me, that was vital. To know that there are times when kids are going to want their parents not to act like they're lovers. When I was younger especially I was embarrassed by affection [between Monica and my mom]; I just didn't want to see it.

And they need to be really understanding about helping their kids figure out what they want to tell their friends. And they shouldn't be surprised if their kids just want to deny or ignore it. It's OK [for kids] to try and hide it for a while, until they feel comfortable.

I remember talking to my mom about feeling uncomfortable telling so-and-so, and having her say, "Well, just take your time. They don't have to know. Let them know when you want to tell them. There's no rush." It was important not to not have to open up to somebody right away. If my mom had pushed me to tell people, I think I would have had a much harder time.

If my mom hadn't been a lesbian, you could say that I'd have led a more normal life. You could say that if my parents hadn't gotten divorced, I'd have had a more normal life, but it would have been hell. I'm actually glad because I don't think I'm nearly as naive as I would have been. I think people who haven't had the same experiences are more judgmental and biased. I can get along with anybody, and I don't make judgments unless someone hurts me or does something I don't like. I get along with a lot more diverse crowd than most of my friends.

Basically, I have two of the greatest parents, and I find it hard when people judge them by what their sexual preference is. What I see from me and [other friends with gay parents] is that we're a lot more comfortable around adults, that we appear a lot more grown up in terms of responsibility and leadership. I'm much more supportive of women, too, and now that I can vote, I'm more aware of what I want to vote for. And it may very well have something to do with having grown up in this family.

Dave

After Dave's parents divorced, he and his sister went to live with his mom. Less than two years later, his mother's female partner, Susan, moved into the house. Now 18, Dave describes growing up with lesbian co-parents.

My mom first told me she was gay when she and my dad were getting a divorce, when I was in second grade. I didn't know what it meant — only that kids in school were always talking about fags and stuff. The hardest thing was trying to keep it a secret from other kids or trying to figure out who I could trust to tell.

Sometimes it was difficult, bringing new friends home, pointing out the rooms and stuff. Because they'd know that there was another person living there, but there was only one bedroom; so I wished I could make up a different room for Susan or something.

I guess it was more on my mind when I was younger that I might turn out to be gay, too. I never told anybody about my parents then, because I felt if they knew, they would stereotype me as being gay because of them. I think I used to make it more of a problem in my head than it ever actually was. Now I feel like if my friends can't deal with it, then that's their problem, because I'm not worried about my reputation anymore. But it was only recently that I came out and started telling friends about my mom and Susan. Most of them said, "Oh, that's cool," or "I figured that out a while ago."

I think what's important is if parents just explain [like my parents did] that they weren't trying to pressure me to be gay at all, that it was strictly my decision and they weren't even going to have anything to do with it. They always encouraged me to go out with girls and stuff. And my mom taught me how to be independent, which was really important to me. I don't know whether that has anything to do with having gay parents, but it's one thing parents should teach anyway.

I think parents should respect what their kids are going through, too. Because in a sense they do put their son or daughter in an awkward position. I mean, it's not like a life-or-death situation, but it does put pressure on a kid, and it's something that they obviously have to live with. And I'd tell them pretty early, so they know why their family's different.

If your parents get divorced, they'd still be dating new people anyway and maybe they'd get married again. So it's not that drastic a difference what sex their partner is. You're going through the same thing. I mean, you might not like who your parent dates or their new partner, whether they're gay or straight. Or you might have great families on both sides.

It seems to me that basically I have a family here, and it doesn't seem much different from any other person's family, except that some people don't accept it as a family. The only problem I ever had was just having to deal with other people dealing with my lifestyle.

FOSTER PARENTING AND GAY AND LESBIAN YOUTH

Finally, gay and lesbian adolescents are themselves among the most traumatized of all young people. What is more, they are a significant portion of the population requiring adoption and foster care. Although black children unquestionably suffer the effects of racism, for example, they grow up in families who understand what it is like to be black and to experience bigotry, who can provide the insulation of sympathetic support, and who can pass on a cultural heritage that provides some antidote to the enfeebling messages of racism.

Gay and lesbian children experience no such relief. They grow up harboring a shameful secret, even from the family members they love and depend upon most. When they reveal their homosexuality, they are quite frequently abused physically and emotionally and driven from their homes. When it comes to assessing trauma, the harm done to gay and lesbian adolescents in homophobic heterosexual homes is nearly incalculable.

Particularly with regard to foster care, then, a growing number of public and private agencies are beginning to view lesbian and gay homes as appropriate placements for homosexually-identified and other sexual minority youth. Welcome as such a trend may be, certain biases clearly lie beneath it. In most cases, agencies are reluctant to place "normal" adolescents with homosexuals — especially with those of the same sex as the child — for fear the lesbian or gay parent will "contaminate" the nascent sexuality of her or his charge (see Ricketts, 1986). Gay men and lesbians may be allowed to take in older adolescents, however, if caseworkers are convinced the youth are "confirmed" homosexuals.

In several cities, programs have sprung up whose specific purpose is to find placements for gay- and lesbian-identified youth who enter adoption or, more commonly, foster care programs. Frequently, such children have experienced a series of unsuccessful placements with families or in group homes in which their homosexual feelings and behavior were discouraged, ridiculed, ignored, or punished. They may enter the child-welfare system through the juvenile courts or through runaway and street-outreach programs. Indeed, youth workers in our informal survey estimated that from 30-70 percent of the juvenile prostitute, street, and runaway population are lesbian or gay adolescents. Others noted that the adolescent social service delivery system, particularly suicide-prevention work, is full of lesbian and gay youth. For these children, their experience on the street, their distrust of adults, and the trauma associated with multiple, unsuccessful placements frequently combine with sexual identity issues to make their needs complex and urgent.

Reluctance to recognize the unique problems of lesbian and gay youth has to do, in large part, with institutional homophobia. Steve Ashkinazy, a social worker at New York City's Hetrick-Martin Institute for the Protection of Lesbian and Gay Youth, comments on the Institute's training program for social service professionals in adolescent shelters and group homes:

We've had many situations where agency staff have blatantly told us that they were not interested in changing their attitudes. They didn't want us to tell them that homosexuality was OK, because they knew it was not. When you have staff who really believe it isn't OK to be gay, there's no real possibility that a gay person, especially an adolescent, could stay there without developing negative feelings about him- or herself. Some group homes are better than others, but there are no group homes in New York that are fully comfortable for a gay kid. In some, it would not be realistic to think a gay kid could survive there at all.

At the other extreme, Los Angeles' Triangle Project has been remarkably successful in recruiting and training gay and lesbian foster parents for children (both gay and straight) who need homes (see Ricketts, 1987). "Casey" and "Rhonda," for example (below), were both placed by Triangle. Efforts are underway in several other cities to establish similar programs.

Case Studies

Casey

Just after Casey turned 17, his mother ordered him out of their home in Texas. Less than a year later, Casey had entered a foster placement with a lesbian couple.

After my mom found out I was gay, we had lots of fights. She threw me out a bunch of times; I can't remember how many. During the last fight, the really big one, she took a shotgun and told me to leave.

At first I went to a group home, but after three days the caseworker said, "Casey, there's nothing we can do for you." And she dropped me off at the "Jesus House," which is where all the street people live downtown. So from there I walked back home to find all my things thrown out on the street. My mom had changed the locks and everything.

I had enough money to buy a bus ticket to California, so I took some clothes and stuff and boarded that night. I got to

California 3 days later. I had no money, I didn't know any-body. It was 7:00 on a Friday morning in downtown Los Angeles. I didn't know what else to do, so I went to Travelers' Aid and told them my story. They called my mother and she said, "He's there? Keep him, he's yours."

When I left, I was going to go to San Francisco and get into gay porn, be a hustler. And then on the way up here, I thought, I don't want that kind of lifestyle. That's not me. I just want to finish high school, go on and finish college, get into a career that I want. And I feel with help I'll be able to do it. I'll be the first one in my family to finish high school, and I'll be able to prove to my mom that being gay didn't stop me from graduating.

For me, being in a gay foster home is like being with my real mom and dad, but it's also like having a different set of parents who you can tell what you're really feeling, because you can never say what you're feeling in a regular home. When my mom found out I was in a gay [foster] home, she said, "Well, I guess you're not going to be straight. I guess you're going to be gay forever." I still think if she can accept me the way I am, I can accept her the way she is.

Rhonda

Rhonda is a 16-year-old black lesbian. When her grandmother died a few years ago, there was no one else to take Rhonda in and she moved into a youth shelter. Over the next 16 months, Rhonda says, she "went through every shelter and group home in Los Angeles." Several times, between placements, she wound up back on the street. At the time of this interview, Rhonda had been living with lesbian foster parents for about 7 months.

I've had counselors say, "What made you this way?" They assume it was my parents' fault and that it wasn't right and "you just haven't met the right guy" and all that. And I would say, "No, you just haven't been over to the gay side yet." And they would say, "You're very rebellious. You'll change." But they saw eventually that I didn't fall for that.

Some girls, they stop being gay and they're very unhappy, but not me.

Maybe a third of us that hung out on the street together were gay. A lot of them left home because their parents threw them out — "You're gay, that's a curse, get out." They treated it like a disease or something. And [the kids] came to California because there was a large population of gay people and they thought they could get help out here.

But a lot of gay kids would have problems because they wouldn't want to go into a straight [foster] home, so they didn't go anywhere. They'd say, either I get into a gay home or a shelter where I can be freely gay, or I'll stay out here.

But after several months of going from shelter to shelter, you want to say forget it, I'm not ever going to find a home, I'll make it on my own. I finally decided it was time for me to go into a straight group home, see how it was there and if I didn't get along, I'd just leave. And I did go and I saw what everybody was afraid of. It was very homophobic. They watched everything I did. They made me sign an agreement not to touch any other girl in the home. They totally blew the subject out of proportion.

I didn't even have to tell them I was gay, but I thought it was only fair. I thought, I must be truthful to myself, and say that I'm gay and that no one can change me. Because they were always saying shit like, "Oh, do you have a boyfriend?" and "Do you need birth control?" So I just said, "Look, let's just drop all this. I'm gay. I don't need that stuff."

When I moved in with Anna and Kris [her current foster parents], I didn't know at first if they were going to be friends to me or just foster parents. Because I've had foster parents where it's like, we'll give you a place to live and all, but if you have any problems, solve them on your own. But Anna and Kris, they're more friends. They treat me like I'm theirs, like they had me. Their parents call me their grandchild. It's wonderful living here. I kind of enjoy telling other people, "Well, I have two mothers." I would want them to adopt me if they could.

THE BOSTON FOSTER CARE CASE

One of the most dramatic examples of "official" response to gay and lesbian foster parents was the case of David Jean and Donald Babets, a Boston gay couple. In early 1984 the two men, who had lived together for more than ten years, applied to the Massachusetts Department of Social Services to be licensed as foster parents. In some ways, Babets and Jean were more stable, upstanding, and financially secure than many who applied for licensure in Massachusetts and across the country: Babets was a senior investigator for the Boston Fair Housing Commission and Jean was the business manager of a nursing home. Actively involved in community affairs and in local electoral politics, the men brought with them letters of recommendation from Mr. Babets' priest and Mr. Jean's minister.

Slightly more than a year later, after an evaluation period at least twice as long as that for most potential foster parents and a particularly extensive round of home visits and investigations, the DSS approved Babets' and Jean's application and granted them a license. Shortly thereafter, two young boys were placed in their home. The boys' mother had given written approval for the placement.

Less than two weeks after the children were placed with Babets and Jean, the Boston *Globe* broke the story on the front page of its "Metro" section (Cooper, 1985b). The *Globe* article created a flurry of activity within the DSS. On the morning of the day the story appeared, the Commissioner of Social Services assured Babets and Jean that the children would not be taken from their home (K. Cathcart, personal communication, July 7, 1986). But by the afternoon, as reporters and TV cameras descended on the scene, DSS officials abruptly removed the two boys.

Although the *Globe*'s original article did not identify Babets and Jean by name, there was no doubt that theirs was the home in question. Kenneth Cooper, the reporter who prepared the story, admitted that he had spoken to Babets before the piece ran. He recalled, "Babets suggested to me that if I did the story the kids could be taken out of the home. I wasn't persuaded of that. He was" (K. Cooper, personal communication, July 29, 1986). Cooper also informed Babets' and Jean's neighbors of the placement and solicited their reactions.

As the situation developed, the *Globe* remained a powerful influence. The editors' opinion of foster placements with lesbians and gay men was repeatedly expressed in a series of editorials. Said one, "The state's foster-care program . . . should never be used, knowingly or unknowingly, as the means by which homosexuals who do not have children of their own . . . are enabled to acquire the trappings of traditional families" ("A Model Foster-Care Policy," 1985).

Another, which marked the anniversary of the removal of the children from Babets' and Jean's home, opined, "As difficult as it might have been to envision then, the incident has produced major benefits for foster children" ("Foster-Care Lessons," 1986).

The "benefits" envisioned by the *Globe*'s editors included an emphasis on what it called "normal" families, in which the husband was employed and the wife stayed home to care for the children. Largely hypothetical, however, such families failed to provide relief for the more than 750 Massachusetts children then awaiting foster care in inappropriate or emergency settings. A December, 1985 report by the Commonwealth's Legislative Subcommittee on Foster Care noted that 50-58 percent of state and private placement agencies maintained significant waiting lists (Hildt, Kollios, Parente & Buell, 1985).

Like most states, it was true, Massachusetts made no mention of gay or lesbian applicants in its foster care policy. But Governor Dukakis and the DSS sheepishly accepted the *Globe*'s accusation — that the absence of a specific policy (particularly an exclusionary one) was evidence of negligence. Rather than affirm that Babets and Jean had more than adequately fulfilled all DSS protocols, the state set out to write a new and separate policy.

On May 24, 1985, the DSS announced its new preference system for evaluating prospective foster parents. Not surprisingly, gay men and lesbians were at the bottom of the list. Although homosexual foster parents were not technically excluded, Secretary of Human Services Phillip Johnston admitted, at the press conference announcing the new policy, that future placements with gay and lesbian foster parents were "highly unlikely" (Cooper, 1985a).

In January of 1986, Babets and Jean brought suit against Governor Dukakis and the DSS. They alleged that the intent of the priority system established by the new policy was to create an "arbitrary, invidiously discriminatory, and unreasonable classification of foster parents" based on sexual orientation. The litigation, now in its third year, is ongoing.[1]

Some Observations from the Boston Foster Care Case

Several aspects of the Boston experience are significant for lesbian and gay foster care applicants in other areas. These include:

1. Like Babets and Jean, many of the gay men and lesbians who successfully traverse the foster care system bring with them special skills, training, resources, and stability. Frequently, those who succeed in being licensed have, in addition to other abilities, a knowledge of how to work within bureaucracies that serves them well in social service delivery systems.

2. Perhaps the most important lesson of the Babets/Jean case is a demonstration of the way in which media attention thwarts the construction of rational child-welfare policies. When interviewed about his approach to the Babets and Jean story, the Boston *Globe*'s Cooper stated that "a reporter can get himself into an awful bind if he starts thinking, 'Well, if I write this, then that might happen.' [The possible impact of the story] didn't figure into our decision. I don't think it should" (K. Cooper, personal communication, July 29, 1986).

Shortly after the events in Boston, New Hampshire legislator Mildred Ingram proposed a ban on lesbian and gay adoption and foster care in that state. There, the *Manchester Union-Leader* newspaper took an aggressive role in supporting the bill and in whipping up fear and bigotry. Ultimately, its coverage made dialogue on the issue of homosexual foster parenting impossible.

Given these related experiences, the issue of media ethics necessarily arises. Obviously, it is not always clear when the press is merely "reporting" and when it is purposefully promoting a position that it advocates. "Objective reporting," however, does not exist – not even as an ideal. Where media coverage is inflammatory and inaccurate — e.g., the *Globe*'s editorializing, in the absence of any clinical evidence to support such a statement, that "married couple, wife stays at home" placements are better for children — that determination becomes somewhat simpler. In Massachusetts and New Hampshire, child-welfare experts were forced to abdicate their role while newspapers took over responsibility for shaping foster care policy. When media are, in effect, making decisions about the placement of children, they have blatantly transgressed their function.[2]

In ideal cases, of course, the thoughtful, affirmative strategies of groups working beforehand to construct policies that benefit lesbians and gay men are always preferable. Once a particular placement has become a media issue, however, agencies and politicians tend to respond in reactionary, defensive ways. Media attention in such circumstances may simply render after-the-fact salvage efforts impossible. More optimistically, groups such as the National Gay and Lesbian Task Force have developed considerable media expertise within recent years, and are an invaluable resource. In addition, foster care policy issues are being prospectively addressed by such groups as the National Child Welfare Resource Center for Management and Administration (Coleman, in press).

3. Equally frustrating, of course, is the recognition that even massive mobilizations in support of gay and lesbian rights issues are not always successful. In Massachusetts, for example, virtually every human service organization — including the National Association of Social Workers, the Human Services Coalition, the Society for the Prevention of Cruelty to Children, and the Massachusetts Psychiatric Society, to name a few — publicly opposed the new regulations. In New Hampshire, a similarly impressive roster of professional groups officially rallied against that state's anti-gay legislation. Sadly, information does not cure prejudice in every situation.

The mobilization of the lesbian/gay community, the formation of coalitions with supportive groups, and the dissemination of alternative information, however, are the only conceivable counters to media sensationalism and distortion. Obviously, such tactics may not have the opportunity of reaching as widely into the population as do the messages of the mainstream media. But the harnessing of the entire apparatus of the gay and lesbian community is both a means of protecting those who attempt to make advances and a way to ensure that the political clout and anger of the community are assessed.

Moreover, whether or not such efforts achieve a desired external result, they are always successful when they reinforce the dignity of gay and lesbian people themselves. Challenge, protest, and even civil disobedience are a dignified response to outrageous treatment. Where injustice prevails despite courageous efforts, lesbians and gay men can take heart from the community support that banishes isolation, alienation, and internalized oppression.

LEGAL BARRIERS TO LESBIAN/GAY ADOPTIVE AND FOSTER PARENTING

Only three states explicitly regulate the ability of homosexuals to become foster or adoptive parents. (South Dakota, in addition, requires foster parents to be married.) As discussed above, Massachusetts promulgated regulations in 1985 that effectively prohibited gays and lesbians from qualifying as foster parents. Those regulations have now been unofficially extended to adoptions. New Hampshire's ban on gay foster care and adoption became effective in 1987. Finally, the state of Florida has statutorily prohibited lesbians and gays from adopting since 1977. To date, no court challenges to the constitutionality of Florida's or New Hampshire's statutes have been initiated, although the justices of New Hampshire's supreme court offered their advisory opinion, in advance of the statute's enactment, that the New Hampshire law was soundly constitutional.

The "Sodomy Standard" and "Per Se" Rules

At this writing, 24 states and the District of Columbia continue to define sodomy as a crime. Although these laws are rarely enforced, their existence has had a significant negative impact upon judicial decision-making in the custody and visitation arena. There is, then, every reason to suspect a corollary effect with respect to adoption and foster parenting. In the case of the New Hampshire statute, for example, the legislature specifically formulated its intention to follow "public policy" as suggested by *Bowers v. Hardwick*, the now-infamous U.S. Supreme Court decision denying privacy rights to a gay man arrested for engaging in oral sex in his own bedroom in Georgia.

Another case-in-point arose in the Pima County, Arizona juvenile court in 1985.[3] In this instance, an openly bisexual applicant for pre-adoption certification was thoroughly investigated by the state DSS and was pronounced qualified. Upon discovering that the Department had recommended an admitted bisexual, a juvenile court judge took the unusual step of appointing independent counsel to represent both the court and the class of children that could potentially be adopted by the applicant. The judge's action was premised on the threat to children that he believed was posed by the applicant because of his sexual orientation. During the hearing, the judge asked the applicant whether he would molest a child placed in his custody or would attempt to "convert" a child to homosexuality. This line of inquiry was apparently prompted solely by the judge's antipathy toward homosexuals as a group, by his obvious dislike of the applicant, and by his total ignorance of issues of sexual orientation as they relate to one's qualifications to be a parent (or, in this case, an adoptive parent). The judge denied the application on the ground that "[p]etitioner is a bisexual individual who has had, and may in future have, sexual relationships with members of both sexes." In upholding the decision, the Arizona Appellate Court reasoned that while the applicant's bisexuality, standing alone, would be an insufficient basis on which to deny him certification, his homosexual conduct, proscribed by Arizona law, was. The court stated:

> It would be anomalous for the state on one hand to declare homosexual conduct unlawful and on the other hand [to] create a parent after that proscribed model, in effect approving that standard, inimical to the natural family, as head of a state-created family.

Statements like these, and those found in custody and visitation decisions in states where sodomy laws remain on the books, make approval of openly gay foster or adoptive parents less likely. The "sodomy standard" is not, of course, applied equally to heterosexual and homosexual "crimes against nature," since heterosexual applicants are not rejected because of their potential to commit the same illegal sexual acts.[4]

States in which the appellate courts have treated the homosexuality of a parent as a *per se* disqualification in custody or visitation cases should also be considered venues in which it is unlikely that openly lesbian or gay applicants will be treated favorably in their attempts to become foster or adoptive parents. In states where there are neither sodomy laws nor *per se* rules regarding homosexuality and child custody, lesbians and gay men have made the greatest progress in efforts to become foster and adoptive parents.

In California, for example, the sodomy law was repealed over a decade ago and appellate case law requires custody to be determined without undue emphasis being placed on the sexual orientation of the parent, unless a direct relationship can be shown to exist between the sexual orientation of the parent and active harm to the child.[5] The California DSS takes the position that it is required by California law to refrain from discriminating solely on the basis of a foster care or adoption applicant's homosexuality.[6]

Because the DSS is county-administered in California (as it is in 38 states), however, prospective adoptive or foster parents often find that this policy of nondiscrimination is enforced inconsistently. In the more conservative counties, for example, a tendency remains to restrict gays from becoming adoptive or foster parents. In counties where there are larger gay populations, and where social service agencies and courts are more familiar with gay people as parents, the resistance to lesbians and gay foster and adoptive parents is slowly breaking down.[7]

Nonetheless, even in San Francisco, where the oldest program exists for the licensing of gay and lesbian foster parents, and where single-parent adoptions by gays and lesbians are relatively common, homosexual applicants are scrutinized more carefully and are held to a higher standard than are their heterosexual counterparts.

Even more so than other single applicants, in addition, prospective homosexual foster or adoptive parents may find that only difficult-to-place children are made available to them, including older children or those who have been severely abused or neglected or who have serious emotional or physical disabilities. In a number of cities around the country, moreover, social service agencies are now encouraging the lesbian and gay community to adopt or to provide foster care for the growing numbers of babies and children with AIDS. This ironic and even slightly cynical turnabout comes after years of resistance, on the parts of some of the same agencies, to the idea of gay and lesbian adoptive or foster homes.

A SPECIAL WORD ABOUT ADOPTION

Rules regarding qualification for adoption vary considerably from state to state (see Achtenberg, 1985, Section 1.04[2]). Most states allow both agency and independent adoption. In the former, a private or public adoption agency evaluates the home and places the child with the prospective adoptive parent(s). The agency also makes a corresponding recommendation to the court, which has the ultimate discretion to grant or deny the adoption.

In an independent adoption the natural parent(s) choose for themselves the person(s) with whom they want the child placed. After the child is physically placed or, in the matter of an interstate adoption, after the placement has been chosen but before the child has been physically placed, a state or private agency investigates the prospective home and makes some form of recommendation to the court.

In either agency or independent adoption, however, a social worker's recommendation of a lesbian or gay placement is commonly reviewed at the highest levels of the evaluating agency. Those conducting the investigation often know little or nothing about homosexuality and about the impact of a parent's sexual orientation upon the psychological development of a child. Applicants may find it useful to offer to provide such information to the social worker and to her or his supervisor, particularly where lesbian and gay adoption is a new phenomenon. It is also during this period of evaluation that a prospective parent may need to retain a lawyer, if only to demonstrate that the applicant expects the same fair and impartial evaluation to which all applicants are entitled.

Generally speaking, independent adoption is preferable for lesbians and gay men who wish to adopt. First, the would-be parent avoids waiting in line at an agency that will invariably give prefer-ence to married couples. Second, once a child has been placed in an adoptive home by a natural parent, that living situation (and the bond that has developed between the child and the adoptive parents) is given weight in an ultimate determination by the court of the child's best interests.

Common practice, however, at least in the case of independent adoptions, has been to inform the birth parent(s) of the sexual orien-tation of the prospective parent(s). Generally, this is done pursuant to a regulation requiring "full disclosure" to the birth parent(s) before consent is given to the adoption. The disclosure "require-ment" can be abused, however, a fact of which lesbians and gay men desiring to adopt should be mindful.

Case Studies

Ken

Ken is a 32-year-old openly gay man who successfully adopted through his state's DSS. Along the way, however, Ken encountered considerable resistance from some personnel within the agency. He battled for more than a year before being allowed to adopt his son, Andrew.

> After my home study was done, it was just a matter of wait-ing for a call to say a child was available. Eventually it came, and my social worker, Mara, told me they had a 3-1/2-year-old boy. Of course I said, let's go.
>
> When Mara met with Andrew's welfare worker, though, his worker refused to read the home study. She said that because I was gay, it would be an inappropriate placement, that Andrew was especially vulnerable because of his background — I think she meant he might become gay, but she always just said "es-pecially vulnerable."
>
> So Mara went to one of their consulting psychologists, who read the home study, and he said, "There's no reason why this placement shouldn't occur." But Andrew's worker was still refusing to meet me. She was fighting tooth and nail. And it

turned into a big problem. Finally her supervisor told her, "You are to go and meet this man, and come back with a clinical reason why this placement should not take place—or else it will take place." It was ugly all the way through.

Well, she finally came to my house, and she was the coldest I have ever seen anyone be. During that meeting she said, "I'd like to know about your sexual history for the last 5 years." I was shocked, but I managed to say, "If you're interested in whether or not I'm HIV-antibody positive, I'm not. I've been tested and I'm not. But I'm not going to talk to you about my sex life." It wasn't pleasant. By the end of this meeting, she was saying all right, fine. But then she kept on fighting it.

Anyway, despite everything, the placement was finally made. The interesting thing was, although Andrew's worker did a terrible job all along, the last time she was here she couldn't say enough about how wonderful Andrew looked, and how great he was doing. So she did a turn around. It was kind of gratifying, but it didn't really make up for what she had done.

People try to make it seem much more bizarre and stressful [to have a gay parent] than it is. When it has to be a big secret, then it is an incredible burden on a child. But there isn't any secret here. In Andrew's day care program of 30 kids, he's one of four or five with gay or lesbian parents. Children who come from nuclear families are definitely the minority. A third or more are of mixed race, and at least half come from only-mother homes.

I also grew up in a single-parent household, so it seems real normal to me. But one thing I hear a lot is, "How can you raise a child without a mother? He's going to be disadvantaged because everybody else has a mother."

Well, of course, the truth is, almost nobody in this culture has a father. Even the ones who come from nuclear families, they have this guy who shows up in the evenings or on week-ends and maybe yells a little while watching football. So the tradeoff is that you get a full-time father, but you don't have a mother.

At one point somebody remarked that it was too bad I was raising Andrew without a mother, and my response was, "Oh, no. He has a mother. Would you like to hear about him? Would you like to hear what he's done?"

PROGRESS IN LESBIAN/GAY CO-ADOPTIONS

Where openly homosexual men and women succeed in adopting, however, they are forced to do so as single individuals—even if they live with family partners and even if their partners co-parent with them on an equal basis. It has always been assumed that no agency would recommend and that no judge would grant a joint adoption by an unmarried couple.

In 1986, however, in two Northern California counties, lesbian couples jointly adopted, each with a positive recommendation by the DSS.[8] California's adoption statute does not explicitly prohibit such a result, and the California courts have a long history of interpreting the adoption statute liberally in order to further the best interests of the child being adopted.

The DSS subsequently had second thoughts about these adoptions, however, and promulgated a policy to prevent both joint and second-parent adoptions by unmarried couples. The policy states, in part: "The best interests of [adoptive children] are served by placement in homes where the couple demonstrates a deep commitment to permanency. Couples who have formalized their relationship through a legal marriage reflect this desired commitment."

Although the policy applies both to homosexual and to unmarried heterosexual couples, it obviously has a vastly disproportionate impact on homosexual couples. Lesbian and gay family partners are prohibited by law from marrying. Thus, they do not have the option of demonstrating the desired "deep commitment to permanency" via "legal marriage" in the manner the state would prefer. Moreover, denial of an adoption petition does nothing to enhance the ability of lesbian or gay couples to engage in legal marriage and, in fact, it robs a child of the opportunity to have two legal parents.

In developing its new policy, however, the DSS was cautious not to appear to take a position against gay and lesbian co-adoptions *per se*, a posture that would have contravened California's Constitution and the holdings of its courts. Rather, the DSS attempted to focus narrowly on the issue of marital status. The new policy, of course, only emerged when a lesbian mother filed a second-parent petition to adopt her lover's child, a 4-year-old girl whom they had co-parented since her birth. Although the social worker who studied the home recommended the adoption, the application was stone-walled at higher levels of the Department. As one of the mothers in that case commented,

> We spent nearly a year collecting information [from the DSS]. All along, everyone kept insisting that [the denial of the petition] had nothing to do with the fact that we were lesbians, that it was strictly a marital status issue. Of course, we discovered that every document that came through the DSS — every internal memorandum discussing the policy — had "Lesbian Adoption" stamped all over it.

The new DSS policy appeared to come at least partly in response to concern that the approval of adoptions by homosexual couples might come under scrutiny by the media. At the time the policy emerged, in fact, the Department was weathering a particularly nasty spate of publicity.

In June of 1986, three months after the second-parent petition was filed in the above case, 14-month-old Nathan Moncrieff was beaten to death by foster parents in a neighboring county. It was quickly revealed that the foster parents, who had been in the process of adopting the infant, were not a married couple as the DSS had believed. Instead, both parties were men — one of them a transvestite posing as the other man's wife. The result was a full-scale investigation and widespread criticism of the DSS. As media and public attention bore down on the DSS, at least one of its reflexive gestures appeared to be the promulgation of the marital status policy.

Ironically, of course, such a policy would not have prevented the Moncrieff tragedy. Moncrieff's foster parents presented themselves as a married couple and were so approved. As one Bay Area adoption attorney noted:

The state never really looked at what went wrong with the Moncrieff placement, which was that [the DSS] failed to follow its own screening procedures. Apparently, they didn't even run a routine fingerprint check, which would have revealed the fact that the parents were both men and that one of them had a criminal record. Instead, they just looked at a label: "married couple." And [the two men] sailed through. By the time the issue had been kicked around the bureaucracy, however, the DSS had identified the problem as the fact that they couldn't be legally married.

More than anything, the state wanted to avoid the embarrassment of future media attention. By denying the petitions of all unmarried couples, then, the DSS gained the strategic advantage of forcing final determination of lesbian and gay joint or second-parent adoptions into the courts. If a media circus ever arose over a "bad" gay-couple adoption, the DSS could respectably maintain that their personnel had opposed it.

Since the advent of the new regulation, attorneys have successfully moved the court to order the DSS to study three prospective lesbian-couple homes and to present facts to support its denial of their adoption petitions. As of this writing, only one of these cases has progressed to trial, and the petition for a second-parent adoption was granted in that instance.

Case Studies

Beth and Liz

In 1983, Beth and Liz became one of the first same-sex couples in the country to succeed in a joint adoption. When they first applied to adopt their daughter, Laura, however, both women were blissfully unaware of the hurdles they would have to leap. As Beth noted, "When we originally thought about doing this, the idea of adopting a child as a couple seemed so sensible. We couldn't imagine it hadn't been done before!"

After several home studies, however, the court threw out all previous evaluations and ordered yet another. The new evaluator, Liz recalls, "asked us things like what would Laura be 'exposed' to in our household, whether she would have men in her life, what kind of touching she would see." At one hearing, Laura's county-appointed lawyer suggested that the four-year-old would do better in a "normal" family; later he asked whether two "strong women" would be able "to raise a little girl to be appropriately submissive."

At that point, Beth and Liz decided to retain an attorney to represent them during the rest of the process. "Our lawyer sent them a lot of information about gay and lesbian families and really demystified the whole thing," Liz remembers. "She got it away from people's worst fantasies and out of our bedroom, and refocused on Laura's best interests." Liz continues:

> We realized how critical it is for both parents to have full legal rights—the "right" to take Laura to the hospital or to enroll her in school. And it's good for Laura to have both of us recognized by other as her parents, because it affirms her perception of her family. It's hard for her, for example, when other kids don't believe that she really has two moms and was adopted. So we've tried to arrange the support of adults who can intervene when kids doubt her story. You know, they can just say things like, "No, she's telling you the truth."
>
> Throughout the legal process, Laura knew that she was being adopted, but she never went to court until the end. We always just told her that we were fighting for her. And we told her that they wanted us to make sure, because adoption was forever, so they kept calling us back and asking us if we'd changed our minds. We didn't want her to feel jeopardized. And we felt confident that we could win.
>
> On the day of the final adoption hearing, we did bring Laura with us. It was a very big day; so we all walked into the judge's chambers together. And the judge was really wonderful. It was as much a wedding ceremony as Beth and I will ever experience. He gave us a little lecture about loving one another and talked about the sacredness of the family, and about our responsibilities to each other and to our child. At the end, he invited Laura to come up and sign the adoption papers with us, but she said, "I don't know what it says!" And the judge told her, "It says that you're a family."

WHERE THERE IS ONLY ONE LEGAL PARENT

A final category of adoption involves cases in which a child's sole legal parent seeks to obtain recognition of the parental relationship that has arisen between the child and the child's non-legal (or non-biological) co-parent—usually, but not always, the legal parent's family partner. Particularly in situations in which children are born to lesbian couples via artificial insemination, and where the birth mother is the child's sole legal parent, the desire has arisen to validate in law the claims of both the child and the co-parent to an ongoing relationship with one another. What is crucial about second-parent adoption is that, like joint adoption, it provides a child with two parents recognized in law upon whom the child can depend for emotional, financial, and moral support. If anything happens to the birth or legal parent, nothing can interfere with the relationship between the child and the co-parent. Legally guaranteed and enforceable rights of the second parent add stability and permanence to a child's life and contribute to the child's healthy sense of self (see, e.g., Green, Mandel, Hotvedt, Gray & Smith, 1986; Patt, 1987-88).

Despite the obvious benefits to a child of second-parent adoption, these adoptions are not yet routinely available for securing the rights and obligations of a co-parent. Indeed, where such a formal or legal relationship does not exist, many lesbian and gay non-legal co-parents face the possible disruption of their relationships with the children they co-parent.

In a recent Nassau County, New York case, for example, a Surrogate's Court vacated a three-year-old adoption decree after it learned that the adoptive father had "concealed" from the court both his homosexuality and the fact that he shared a household with a male family partner of 13 years' standing who was also the child's co-parent (*Matter of Edward M. G.*, New York Law Journal, October 15, 1987). The issue came before the court when the relationship between the two men dissolved and the co-parent sought custody of their son.

On a more positive note, a California court recently considered the case of a four-year-old girl, Martha M., whose mother had committed suicide (*Guardianship of Martha M.*, 1988, 88 C.D.O.S. 6814). Although Martha's grandmother was appointed legal guardian, Kenneth T., a friend of the family, petitioned for visitation with Martha. Kenneth argued that he had contributed to Martha's support for more than three years, had developed a loving relationship with her, and considered himself her "psychological father." Martha's grandmother opposed the proceeding on the ground that Kenneth was a "stranger," but the court recognized the right of an interested but legally or biologically unrelated person to seek visitation with a minor child. Although decided in a heterosexual context, the case has important implications for gay men and lesbians who seek ongoing contact with children they have co-parented.

SOME AREAS OF CONCERN/SUGGESTIONS FOR FUTURE STUDY

1. There is a great need for human service workers to be educated about lesbian and gay families. Among social workers, psychologists, family court mediators, attorneys, judges, and others, for example, gay and lesbian parents continue to encounter such beliefs as these: same-sex couples assume exaggerated male and female roles; lesbians and especially gay men are sexually perverted and will engage in sexual activity in front of children; lesbian or gay parents or their friends or partners will molest children; the children of homosexual parents will be confused in their gender identity and will probably become homosexual themselves; and children will be harmed by witnessing affectionate behavior between two persons of the same sex.

The American Psychiatric Association, the American Psychological Association, and the National Association of Social Workers have all adopted official nondiscrimination statements (see, e.g., the American Psychiatric Association's foster parenting "Position Statement," 1986), but practice varies greatly. Lesbian/gay counsels within these professional assemblies must make a priority of educating their colleagues about issues relating to lesbian and gay parenting.

2. Because courts and agencies are, generally out of ignorance, concerned about the potential psychological harm to children who have lesbian or gay parents, there is a need for further research to show that such children are not adversely affected—particularly longitudinal studies and those that deal specifically with adoptive or

foster children. Although the extant literature is somewhat scattered, it is no longer scarce (see, e.g., Kirkpatrick & Hitchens, 1985; and Kleber, Howell & Tibbits-Kleber, 1986).

3. Agencies and groups that work with foster children must modernize their understanding of the children whom they serve. In several recent publications on homeless adolescents (National Network of Runaway and Youth Services, 1985), "multiple placement youth" (Pardeck, 1985), adolescents in unstable foster care (Taber & Proch, 1987), and disrupted older-child adoptions (Barth, Berry, Carson, Goodfield & Steinberg, 1986), the authors completely ignore the importance of sexual identity issues in understanding why some children experience ongoing problems in foster or adoptive placements, and are ultimately not helped by the system.

ADDITIONAL RESOURCES FOR LESBIAN AND GAY FOSTER AND ADOPTIVE PARENTS

The following organizations are able to provide information and advocacy to lesbians and gay men who hope to become foster (or, in some cases, adoptive) parents.

Gay & Lesbian Adolescent Social Services/The Triangle Project
8234 Santa Monica Boulevard, #214
West Hollywood, CA 90049 (213/656-5005)

Hetrick-Martin Institute/Harvey Milk High School
110 E. 23rd St., 10th Floor
New York, NY 10010 (212/473-1113)

National Center for Lesbian Rights
Adoption & Foster Parenting Project
1370 Mission Street, 4th Floor
San Francisco, CA 94103 (415/621-0674)

Lutheran Social Services
1201 Payne Avenue
St. Paul, MN 55101 (612/774-9507)

Sexual Minority Youth Assistance League (SMILE)
1638 "R" Street NW,
Washington, D.C. 20009 (202/232-7506)

The Shelter/Orion House
1020 Virginia Street
Seattle, WA 98101 (206/622-3187)

CONCLUSION

As we enter the 1990s, it has become fashionable to report that the American family is in revolution. The media, among others, remind us constantly of the "breakdown" of the nuclear family, but fail to describe the kinds of families that are evolving to take its place. At the heart of today's changing family, of course, is a simple observation: What was once considered "traditional" has become one of many variations on the modern theme of family diversity.

Yet despite these many changes, the family remains an institution cherished by all. Those men and women engaged in the formation of "alternative" families are not attempting to destroy the family. Indeed, they are some of its most ardent supporters. Despite the adversity they so often face, for example, lesbians and gay men continue to work toward progress in their efforts to become adoptive and foster parents.

These men and women may well hope that concepts of family will one day expand to include the relationships they create with their partners and with the children in their lives, but they do not depend upon such a sanction. In the end, they recognize, what truly informs the psychological health and even happiness of individuals lies not in how we define our families, but in how our families live.

NOTES

1. Additional information available from Gay & Lesbian Advocates and Defenders, P. O. Box 218, Boston, MA 02112, (617) 426-1350. For a more detailed examination of the case, see Ricketts and Achtenberg, 1987; and Uhl, 1986-87.

2. Media are powerful, but not always invincible. A coalition of groups was recently successful in persuading the *San Francisco Chronicle* to revise its policy regarding next-of-kin reporting in death notices of gay men and lesbians. After several meetings, the *Chronicle* agreed to stop excluding the names of surviving non-marital family partners from its obituaries.

3. In re *Pima County Juvenile Action*, 12 Family Law Reporter (BNA) 1557 (Arizona Court of Appeals, 1986).

4. The judge dissenting from the majority opinion in the Pima County case felt that the existence of the sodomy law put the state under no compulsion to deny adoption applications from homosexuals or bisexuals. He responded that, were such the case, every applicant's past, present, and future sexual conduct would have to be scrutinized by the court in order to ascertain the absence of other activity forbidden by Arizona law (e.g., adultery, cohabitation, and the *heterosexual* sex acts outlawed by the sodomy statute).

5. In *Nadler v. Superior Court*, 63 Cal.Rptr. 352 (1967), the Court of Appeal held that, in the case of a parent who is known to be homosexual, a custody decision cannot be made solely on the basis of that fact. The court must weigh all the evidence pertaining to the child's situation before making a custody determination.

6. In *Gay Law Students Assoc. v. Pacific Telephone and Telegraph Co.*, 24 Cal.3d 458, 136 Cal.Rptr. 14, 595 P.2d 592 (1979), the California Supreme Court held that arbitrary discrimination against an individual by a state or government entity due to homosexuality is impermissible and is a violation of the Equal Protection Clause of the California Constitution. Accordingly, the state DSS cannot discriminate against a homosexual petitioner for adoption by denying his or her petition solely on the basis of homosexuality without violating the constitution's Equal Protection Clause and the *Nadler* holding.

7. The National Center for Lesbian Rights has been contacted by people in San Francisco, Alameda, San Diego, Los Angeles, and Sacramento Counties who have succeeded in being licensed as foster parents or approved as adoptive parents. At the same time, complaints continue to emerge from Orange County, perhaps the most conservative California county, where agency personnel consistently discourage homosexual applicants by telling them that their applications for adoption or foster care licensure will stand no chance of being approved. The NCLR is contemplating a lawsuit in this regard. In the meantime, the NCLR is making efforts to require uniform enforcement of the adoption laws through its Adoption and Foster Parenting Project.

8. Additional information available from the National Center for Lesbian Rights. (See list of resources.) Other material available from the NCLR includes sample legal briefs, copies of published studies on the psychological health of children of lesbian and gay parents, and bibliographies.

REFERENCES

A model foster-care policy. (1985, May 28). *The Boston Globe*, p. 14.
Achtenberg, R. A. (Ed.) (1985). *Sexual orientation and the law*. New York: Clark-Boardman.
Agency backs down on foster children. (1974, July 17). *The Advocate*, p. 22.
Agency reveals kids placed with gay couples. (1973, August 15). *The Advocate*, p. 2.
Ban on gay foster care scratched from guide. (1974, July 17). *The Advocate*, p. 11.
Barth, R., Berry, M., Carson, M. L., Goodfield, R. & Feinberg, B. (1986).

Contributors to disruption and dissolution of older-child adoptions. *Child Welfare, 65*(4), 359-371.

CA gay foster homes approved. (1976, June 30). *The Advocate*, p. 11.

City of Los Angeles Task Force on Family Diversity. (1988). *Final Report: Strengthening Families – A Model for Community Action.* Los Angeles, CA: Author.

Coleman, L. (in press). Gays and lesbians as foster parents. (University of Southern Maine, Portland, ME 04103.)

Cooper, K. (1985, May 25). New policy on foster care: Parenting by gays all but ruled out. *The Boston Globe*, pp. 1, 24. (a)

Cooper, K. (1985, May 8). Some oppose foster placement with gay couple. *The Boston Globe*, pp. 21, 24. (b)

Families by adoption: A gay reality. (1974, August 28). *The Advocate*, p. 1.

Foster-Care lessons. (1986, May 11). *The Boston Globe.*

Gantz, J. (1983). *Whose child cries: Children of gay parents talk about their lives.* Rolling Hills Estates, CA: Jalmar Press.

Green, R., Mandel, J. B., Hotvedt, M. E., Gray, J. & Smith, L. (1986). Lesbian mothers and their children: A comparison with solo parent heterosexual mothers and their children. *Archives of Sexual Behavior, 15*(2), 167-184.

Hildt, B., Kollios, P., Parente, M. & Buell, C. (1985, December). *In the best interest of the children?* Boston, MA: Commonwealth of Massachusetts Joint Committee on Human Services and Elderly Affairs, Legislative Subcommittee on Foster Care.

Kirkpatrick, M. & Hitchens, D. J. (1985). Lesbian mothers/gay fathers. In P. Benedek & D. Shetky (Eds.), *Emerging issues in child psychiatry and the law* (pp. 108-119). New York: Brunner/Mazel.

Kleber, D., Howell, R. & Tibbits-Kleber, A. (1986). The impact of parental homosexuality in child custody cases: A review of the literature. *Bulletin of the American Academy of Psychiatry and Law, 14*(1), 81-87.

Los Angeles County Department of Adoptions. (1976, July 14). *The Advocate*, p. 10.

National Network of Runaway and Youth Services, Inc. (1985). *To whom do they belong? A profile of America's runaway and homeless youth and the programs that help them.* Washington, D.C.: Author.

New rules proposed: Seek to block gay foster homes. (1974, May 22). *The Advocate*, p. 8.

Pardeck, J. T. (1985). A profile of the child likely to experience unstable foster care. *Adolescence, 20*(79), 689-696.

Patt, E. (1987-88). Second parent adoption: When crossing the marital barrier is in a child's best interests. 3 *Berkeley Women's Law Journal*, pp. 96-133.

Pincus, E. (1988, July 31-August 6). Duke legislates foster care policy. *Gay Community News, 16*(4), p. 1.

Position statement on discrimination in selection of foster parents. (1986, November). *American Journal of Psychiatry, 143*(11), 1506.

Ricketts, W. (1986). Homosexuality in adolescence: The reification of sexual personalities. In P. Allen-Meares & D. Shore (Eds.), *Adolescent sexualities:*

Overviews and principles of intervention, special issue of *J. Social Work & Human Sexuality*, 5(1), pp. 35-49.

Ricketts, W. (1987, July 21). Triangle Project: Placing homeless gay youths with supportive gay parents. *The Advocate*, pp. 12-14.

Ricketts, W. & Achtenberg, R. (1987). The adoptive and foster gay and lesbian parent. In F. Bozett, (Ed.), *Gay and Lesbian Parents*. New York: Praeger Press, pp. 89-111.

Sencer, M. G. (1987) Adoption in the non-traditional family: A look at some alternatives. *Hofstra Law Review*, 16(1), 191-212.

Shilts, R. (1975, December 17). Foster homes for gay children: Justice or prejudice? *The Advocate*, p. 11.

Taber, M. & Proch, K. (1987). Placement stability for adolescents in foster care: Findings from a program experiment. *Child Welfare*, 66(5), 433-445.

Uhl, B. (1986-87). A new issue in foster parenting — gays. *Journal of Family Law*, 25(3), 577-597.

Vecsey, G. (1979, June 21). Approval given for homosexual to adopt a boy. *New York Times*.

The Married Lesbian

Eli Coleman

SUMMARY. The existing data on bisexual and lesbian women in heterosexual marriages is reviewed. The reasons for getting married in the first place, the quality of the marital relationships, the reactions of the husbands, and the relationships with children are described. Due to the inherent conflicts these women face in these situations, some useful therapeutic suggestions are offered.

One of the types of marital and family structures which is rarely described in the literature is the bisexual or lesbian woman in a heterosexual marriage. In sharp contrast, homosexual men who are married have been researched extensively (Gochros, 1978; Latham & White, 1978; Ross, 1971; Dank, 1973; Coleman, 1981/82; Ross, 1983; Matteson, 1985; Coleman, 1985; Wolf, 1985, 1986). In addition, a number of books have been written about the lives and relationships of homosexual men who are or have been married (Kohn & Matusow, 1980; Malone, 1980; Nahas & Turley, 1979). However, very little has been written about their female counterparts.

What is known comes from the large-scale studies of homosexuality which were conducted by Saghir and Robbins (1973); Bell and Weinberg (1978); and Masters and Johnson (1979). The other sources of information are based upon the various studies on lesbian motherhood (e.g., Green, 1978; Kirkpatrick, Roy & Smith, 1976;

Dr. Eli Coleman is Associate Professor at the Program in Human Sexuality, Department of Family Practice and Community Health, University of Minnesota Medical School. He is the author of *Psychotherapy for Homosexual Men and Women* and editor of the *Journal of Psychology & Human Sexuality*. Correspondence may be sent to the author at the Program in Human Sexuality, 2630 University Ave. S.E., Minneapolis, MN 55414.

Rand, Graham & Rawlings, 1982). Additional studies on bisexuality (e.g., Blumstein & Schwartz, 1976; Klein, 1978) provide additional information on lesbians, their sexual orientation, and their marriages. What is ironic about the lack of studies on this subject is that there is no indication that there are fewer homosexual women than men in marriage. In fact, some data suggest that the opposite might be true. Saghir and Robbins (1973) found that 25 percent of the women and 19 percent of the males had been previously married. Similar or higher percentages were found in the studies conducted by Bell and Weinberg (1978). A consistent pattern emerges in these large-scale studies: samples of homosexual women are equally or more likely to have been previously married than their male counterparts. So where are these women, and why are they not studied?

The answers to these questions may come from some of the data which has been collected. On the average, Bell and Weinberg (1978) found that males were married at the age of 24, compared to females who were married at the age of 21. This suggests that the females might have been less likely to be aware of their homosexuality prior to marriage. This is a result of simple age differentiation, as well as the fact that women become aware of their same-sex feelings later than do men (Coleman, 1981/82a). Bell and Weinberg (1978) suggest that women, because of sociocultural pressures and expectations, might experience a greater pressure to marry, and might not find sexual relations with men completely intolerable or impossible. Bell and Weinberg found that marriages in which the female was homosexual tended not to last as long as those of homosexual men. These authors concluded that females, more often than males, when they become aware of their homosexual feelings, develop an aversion to heterosexual relationships and quickly lose satisfaction with their marriage.

Since so little was known about these women, I initiated a research study (Coleman, 1985) by recruiting subjects through clinicians and personal contacts, attempting to identify bisexual and lesbian women who are or who had been married and to request their participation in this study. I prepared a questionnaire consisting of

26 items which the subjects could anonymously fill out and return to me by mail. Participation in this study was completely voluntary. It should be emphasized that the sample was based upon a selected clinic population where individuals with problems brought them to seek psychotherapy. Therefore, this represents a non-random sample.

Information was gathered about demographics, awareness of homosexual feelings and behaviors before and during the marriage, the husband's knowledge of the wife's homosexual feelings before and during the marriage, reasons for getting married, sexual difficulties or problems in marriage, attempts to eliminate homosexual feelings, attempts at counseling or therapy to deal with the conflicts resulting from their sexual orientation within their marriage; and Kinsey-type ratings of sexual orientation related to behavior, fantasy, emotional attachments before, during and after marriage (if applicable). One of the most significant results of the study was the finding that only four of the 45 participants were currently married. The most common response from the therapists who were involved in this study was, "I just don't know of anyone who is bisexual or lesbian and currently married. They don't seem to come to me while they are married." This may have been a factor in the sampling bias of this study, but it has been confirmed by a number of clinicians who continue to report that it is rare for bisexual or lesbian women who are married to identify themselves as such and to seek out therapy while they are married. To access this population, other types of studies using non-patient populations will be necessary.

While the same population in this study was predominantly previously married, the participants were able to give us some information, at least retrospectively, about their relationships before divorce.

REASONS FOR GETTING MARRIED

The great majority of bisexual or lesbian women reported that they got married because they were in love with their husbands and desired marriage. Respondents did not describe reasons such as coerced marriages or marriages of convenience. Marriage for most was a desired and deliberate decision. A pattern emerged from the respondents that their desire for marriage was no more influenced by cultural expectations than it is for heterosexual women.

Hypothetically, the bisexual or homosexual woman who adopts the male-defined adult identity might avoid the pressure to marry and give herself more time to become aware of her psychosexual identity development. However, in order to do this she must discount her socialized desire for relatedness and adopt a style of increasing individualization. This can result in the possible consequence of societal rejection and alienation (Browning, 1988).

Beyond the cultural identity expectations, many women are still involved in the developmental processes of parental separation. Because most family systems in American culture convey strong heterosexual messages, the emerging lesbian must face this conflict in living up to parental expectations. Again, once separation has taken place, the child is able to re-evaluate parental values and expectations and adopt those which hold relevance for her. This allows greater ability of the emerging lesbian to acknowledge her same-sex feelings and identity (Browning, 1988). It should be noted that the process of parental separation and questioning of parental values is not one that ends with chronological adolescence. Some children will be under greater influence for much longer periods of time. This can be one of the major struggles of identity development for anyone of any age. It is certainly an issue which many married lesbian women face in making the decision to leave or not to leave their marital relationship. Again, they are facing not only a conflict with cultural expectations, but familial ones as well. And they are having to face the conflict between the societally-determined female adult role and the definition of adult maturity—the latter based on relationship rather than an emphasis on sexual expression.

Essentially, many married lesbians avoid confrontation of societal and parental expectations and acquiesce to these expectations because of fear and disapproval or rejection. This results in the process of identity foreclosure (Marcia, 1980). Foreclosure prevents a congruence of one's feelings and behaviors with the essential process of identity formation.

QUALITY OF THE MARITAL RELATIONSHIP

As stated earlier, most of our information regarding women within marriage comes from the studies of lesbian mothers and lesbians who are no longer in their marriages. The information, therefore, is retrospective and admittedly flawed. However, from such studies we are able to put together a picture of marriage which is no more conflicted than is heterosexual marriage, and which endures the same length of time (Kirkpatrick, 1988). In one U.S. study, Kirkpatrick, Smith and Roy (1981) compared heterosexual women with children who had been divorced to homosexual women with children who had been divorced. These researchers found that the heterosexual women had endured stormier marriages but had been less likely to initiate divorce, while the lesbians regarded themselves as initiators of the divorce and blamed the failure of the marriage on the loss of intimacy rather than the abuse which occurred within the marriage. The heterosexual women were more bitter about the failure of the marriage and angry at men — relating it to their more highly reported incidences of abuse. Very few of the lesbian mothers in this study showed antipathy toward men. Lesbian mother studies such as Kirkpatrick et al. (1981) demonstrate that these women can live in satisfying lesbian relationships and are capable of living in satisfying heterosexual relationships for some time also. Kirkpatrick (1988) has also indicated that many lesbians who have been previously married often continue to have strong feelings of attachment for a former spouse and may be depressed or angry when the ex-husband remarries.

Reaction of the Husband

The information on the reaction of the husband is practically nonexistent. While we have some information regarding the reactions of women who learned that their husbands were bisexual (Gochros, 1985; Coleman, 1985; Wolf, 1985), I am not aware of any systematic study of the partner. In some ways this lack is similar to the paucity of knowledge about the male spouse of the female alcoholic, compared to that which we have for the female spouse of the male alcoholic. The problem seems to lie in some of the sex-role scripting of their roles, which have thusly been described in the alcoholism literature: the male spouse oftentimes has low tolerance for the "deviancy of his partner" and leaves; or because the "deviant" spouse feels that she has abandoned her prescribed role, she leaves herself in order to avoid further pain. On the other hand, the female spouse is likely to stay in the marriage with a "deviant" husband because that has been her socially prescribed role and one in which she can gain self-esteem and self-worth.

Therefore, the information which we have about the reaction of the husband is clinical and anecdotol. First of all, as indicated, the husband has a shorter length of time to deal with the wife's same-sex feelings, and there is a strong likelihood that he or she will terminate the relationship based on this factor alone (Coleman, 1985). In my clinical experience, the husband is totally shocked and in disbelief. Usually, he has not noticed any difficulty in sexual functioning, and therefore cannot understand this new revelation. Once the realization sinks in, however, he is likely to experience some feelings of shame. He is very likely to seek out the court and ask for help from anyone. He is likely to react to this by either passive acceptance or by anger and rage. Those who are passive tend to blame themselves for the change in their wife's sexual orientation. They struggle to please their wife in any way possible to avoid separation. The wife is the one who is most likely to terminate the relationship in these situations.

On the other hand, some men react to their shame with feelings of rage. If children are involved, the husband will, in some instances, threaten taking the children away from the mother and in some cases has been successful in gaining custody of the children. In these cases, the husband is likely to initiate the separation and divorce. Beyond this, the husband is unlikely to seek further counseling, whether it is taking a passive or an active stance. Again, this is in marked contrast to the female spouse of a bisexual or gay married man. Often she will continue to seek therapy to grieve the loss of her relationship, as well as to work on her self-worth and formation of her identity outside the relationship. More systematic study of the husbands of married lesbians is clearly needed.

Relationships with Children

It is important to note that no evidence supports the myth that lesbians reject feminine interests and activities (Kirkpatrick, 1988). It is true that entering the lesbian subculture, the tendency is to immerse herself in this subculture while withdrawing from her husband and family. In contrast to the majority of bisexual and gay married men who enter the subculture because of their sexual attractions, the bisexual or lesbian married woman usually is prompted by a relationship with another woman. In either case, this is a period of adolescence or exploration in a coming out process (Coleman, 1981/82a). It is very difficult for the husband and family to support the wife through this necessary phase. Often either the lack of support or the wife's guilt over her abandoned role terminates the relationship.

These women fear identification. Women living in metropolitan communities may feel less discrimination and loss of parental rights than those in smaller or more traditional communities. Women in metropolitan communities also have access to support groups and attorneys who have the experience to protect their parental rights. Knowing the cultural climate (and often changing climate) of one's community in regard to sexuality and lesbian parenthood may help the therapist empathize and support the family during such a time (Kirkpatrick, 1988). The studies of lesbian mothers have shown similar findings: these women have the same desire to bear and rear children as their heterosexual counterparts.

One question in the minds of many is whether a lesbian can be a good mother or not. Mucklow and Phelon (1979) indicated clearly a correlation between the child's self-concept and self-esteem and the mother's self-esteem, and did not find any correlation with the mother's sexual orientation. These researchers concluded that child-rearing style is clearly more a product of the mother's attitudes, values, and personality characteristics than of her sexual orientation. Hoeffer's (1981) study, which investigated parent-child relationships among lesbian mothers, eliminated another myth: that they might be less tolerant of cross-gender play and more supportive of girls developing male interests.

No study found lesbian mothers who hoped their children would be homosexual, but lesbian mothers were more inclined to not hold sexist views and ambitions for their children, and stated that they had no preference as to their children's eventual adult sexual orientation. Both groups of mothers were concerned about the children's development and turned equally often to professionals for help. (Kirkpatrick, 1988, p. 207)

The evidence has been clear in lesbian mother studies that there is no support for the notion that a lesbian mother's sexual orientation has any damaging consequences to the child's development (Golombok, Spence & Rutter, 1983; Kirkpatrick, Smith & Roy, 1981; Mandell & Hotvedt, 1980).

In my clinical experience, the factors of disturbed childhood development relate to the parents' personality characteristics, their manner of parenting, and the modeling of intimacy in the parental relationship. If there are negative effects on the children, these have more to do with the open displays of discord within the parental relationship, the neglect of the children's needs because of this conflict, and fears of the parental units separating. When talking to children of homosexual parents, one quickly realizes that the main trauma of growing up with a homosexual parent lies not with the parent's homosexuality but rather with the threat of dissolution of the marital relationship.

Disclosure to Children

It is rare that a bisexual or lesbian woman discloses to her children her sexual orientation while she is married. Our current research (albeit limited) indicates that the husband often does not even know. It is more likely that the bisexual or lesbian mother would disclose to her children her sexual orientation after leaving her marriage, but probably only when she is assured of protection of her parental rights. The issue of coming out to the children is probably more of an issue for bisexual or lesbian women who divorce and have children rather than for married bisexual or lesbian women.

Special Issues

A number of studies have indicated high incidence rates of alcoholism and other drug abuse among lesbian samples (Fifield, 1975; Lohrenz, Connelly, Coyne & Spare, 1978; Saghir & Robbins, 1973). We have no data which indicates the incidence rates of alcoholism or other drug addiction among bisexual or lesbian women who are married; however, we might suspect that this incidence rate is higher than in the general population. The reasons for this increased rate of alcoholism has been discussed elsewhere (Schaefer, Evans & Coleman, 1987). The marriage or family therapist must recognize that this might be an issue which needs to be addressed. Alcohol and other drug abuse could become a coping mechanism for the conflict between allegiance to the marriage and the merging interest in same-sex feelings and relationships. Drug abuse is also a natural part of adolescence, and if the woman is exploring her lesbian feelings, she may be doing this in bars or meeting places which promote the use of alcohol. The abuse of drugs can clearly interfere in the development of a positive and integrated identity (Coleman, 1981/82a); therefore, the professional should know as much as possible about alcoholism, its higher incidence among gay and lesbian populations, and its relationship to internalized homophobia (Kus, 1988).

IMPORTANT ELEMENTS OF THE THERAPEUTIC RELATIONSHIP

When a married lesbian presents herself in psychotherapy, she will often have difficulty entering into a therapeutic relationship because of the fear of facing herself, her own feelings, and, most importantly, the implications of these feelings. Oftentimes, women will present in psychotherapy at the point when they have resolved many of these issues and are looking for support as consolidation of these new awarenesses. They are also coming much closer to accepting the consequences for these awarenesses — essentially the understanding that their marriage might be over. Given cultural conditioning, the concerns are often for their partner and their children, and finally, for their economic security.

Internalized Homophobia

Regardless of where a client might be in developmental process, she is coping universally with the issue of internalized homophobia. Homophobia has been defined in different ways: as either analogous to other phobias or possessing negative attitudes toward homosexuality; usually there is a combination of both feelings, which need to be dealt with. Essentially, these women have internalized the negative attitudes and assumptions which society and their family culture have instilled. Internalized homophobia makes consideration of a lesbian identity extremely threatening to the individual's identity and self-esteem (Sophie, 1988).

The task of the psychotherapist then is to reduce the amount of internalized homophobia so that positive bisexual or lesbian identity can be considered. This positive identity is precluded as long as the internalized homophobia prevails. The goal in therapy is not to work on the achievement of a particular identity, but rather to address the issues of internalized homophobia. The therapist can help the individual understand where these belief systems were learned and can examine from her own experience as well the scientific information that allows for a challenging of the internalized assumptions.

Sophie (1988) has described a number of treatment methods which she has found helpful in working with the reduction of internalized homophobia in the emerging lesbian. She argues that the therapist is likely to be seen as the representative of society whose reactions may help the client dissipate the reactions of others in her life. The therapist is also seen as an authority figure and as a role model. All these aspects of the therapeutic relationship permit the therapist to convey an acceptance of homosexuality with the real homophobic environment in which we live. In attempting to reduce internalized homophobia, it is not helpful for the therapist to quickly dismiss the homophobic sentiment of society; it is more useful for the therapist to acknowledge and listen to the feelings which the client has and to acknowledge the negative societal attitudes which exist. In this way, the therapist acknowledges the feelings of fear and rejection while introducing the fact that we live in a pluralistic society and that different values regarding homosexuality do exist.

The client then is more able to decide to which value structure she wishes to adhere.

Disclosure of the Therapist's Sexual Orientation

In terms of the therapist's self-disclosure of his/her own sexual orientation, I have always taken the viewpoint that the client is looking for objectivity, and that the knowledge of the therapist's sexual orientation in early stages of therapy is an unnecessary burden for the client to struggle with. If clients know of the therapist's orientation, they will sometimes fear that the therapist will pressure them toward one direction or another. Awareness of this tendency is probably more important for an individual who is initially exploring her same-sex feelings than for one who has become more accepting of her own orientation, has already developed more of an internal frame of reference, and is less fearful of influence through acceptance or rejection of others regarding her orientation. Lesbians who are married and have accepted their identity will often seek out a lesbian-identified therapist to gain further support, or will choose a non-lesbian-identified therapist because they know that the therapist is a good therapist and will not threaten or question their identity.

A vexing question for the therapist is whether or not to respond to a direct request for information regarding the therapist's sexual orientation. A refusal to disclose may lead to distress, which could hamper the relationship; however, on the other hand, the client may not be ready to trust, given the outcome. Each situation must be handled individually, of course. I usually tend to recommend that the motivation for knowing this information be explored before the therapist makes his or her decision to respond. As Sophie (1988) recommends, if the client's motivation is based on homophobic and stereotypical assumptions or on distorted thought processes due to severe psychological disturbances, it is probably advisable to risk some distrust by refraining from responding to the client's direct questioning. Usually, in response to a direct question, I often recommend not responding directly and simply responding by saying,

My approach to therapy is not to reveal so much personal detail about my life. You are welcome to ask me questions about my professional credentials. While I understand your curiosity, I think it best to simply assure you that I work with a variety of clients with different sexual orientations, and I don't hold any moral judgement about whether an individual adopts a homosexual, bisexual or heterosexual identity. I am mostly concerned that people discover who they are and feel comfortable with themselves in their personal relationships.

This usually satisfies the client's curiosity but, more importantly, avoids the breach in trust and establishes appropriate professional boundaries of the therapeutic relationship. Therefore, this type of response in the initial stages of therapy serves several different purposes. It also serves as a model for the client that he or she can set boundaries for disclosure of her sexual orientation, when, and with whom. She is usually comfortable with this response.

Attitudes and Values of the Therapist

However, if the therapist does hold certain moral or value-laden views regarding homosexuality or homosexuality within a heterosexual marriage, it might be appropriate to acknowledge these biased values immediately and suggest alternative therapists from whom the client could choose.

This raises the subject of values and how these should be examined. The therapist first must examine his or her feelings about homosexuality, bisexuality and heterosexuality. Given our current socio-cultural climate, the therapist must acknowledge that several socially described forms of sexual expression exist and that there is no known scientific evidence which supports the view that any one of these identities is more or less pathological than the others.

Second, therapists must recognize that bisexuality is not simply some sort of "cop out" identity. While it is true that a bisexual identity for some people is a transition; for others it is a lifetime identity with which they can be comfortable. Further, a bisexual identity does not mean that the individual must engage in equal amounts of same-sex and opposite-sex activity throughout his or her lifetime. For most, it is a recognition of the capacity for relationships with either men and women and that their identity cannot be simply determined by their current partner choice (for a further discussion of the issue of bisexuality, see Klein, 1978; Klein & Wolf, 1985; Coleman, 1988).

The therapist must also realize that many people who have a predominate erotic orientation towards men or women do not necessarily use this as the sole basis for choosing a partner for relationship. There are clearly other more salient dimensions of partner choice than one's biological gender (Kaplan & Rogers, 1984; Ross, 1984). This may be more true for females than for males because of the sex role socialization process and the emphasis which is placed more on relational aspects of sexuality than on the visual and erotic. So the therapist must not immediately assume that because an individual's predominant erotic orientation is homosexual, he or she should adopt a homosexual identity, leave the marital relationship, and pursue a homosexual lifestyle.

Again, it is interesting to note in the studies of women who have been married and have developed a lesbian identity, that their decision to adopt a lesbian identity is usually based on the development of an emotional relationship rather than on the awareness of same-sex erotic feelings (Coleman, 1985). The therapist must recognize that individuals who could be classified as bisexual or lesbian by a number of different classification systems could lead satisfying marital relationships, as has been indicated in studies of gay and bisexual married men (Coleman, 1985; Wolf, 1987). In exploring the decision to remain in the marriage or to leave the marriage, the therapist serves the client best when he or she is not prejudiced in these general ways. The therapists' viewpoints regarding sexual orientation do affect their feelings in the therapeutic relationship. Therefore, if the therapist is a female who was married and decided to leave her marriage because of an emerging awareness of lesbian identity, she needs to be careful not to prejudge what is good for the client who is in the process of this struggle. Vice versa, if the therapist is predominantly heterosexual and has found that the societal advantages outweigh the exploration of same-sex feelings, this personal decision should not influence the objectivity of the therapeutic process.

Oftentimes clients urge the therapist to tell them what to do

("What is the best solution for me?"). The therapist needs to resist such questions and to take a more non-direct approach. Clients need to be the best expert about themselves, and the role of the therapist is to facilitate the emergence of the individual, as well as provide objective information about some of the advantages and disadvantages of the various options they are considering.

The Advantage of Group Therapy

I often find that this bind of the influence of the therapist over the client is diffused by treating these types of cases in a group therapy format. This format for bisexual and gay married men has been described elsewhere (Coleman, 1981/82b). In this approach, clients who are exploring decisions regarding their sexual identity and marital status are placed in a group to explore these issues. The heterogeneity of the group helps illustrate the variety of "solutions" different individuals have tried or are beginning to experiment with. This allows for the individual in the group to see the range of options and realize that there is no one "right way." The therapist role in this type of group is to consistently maintain the mixture of the group and the recognition of all valid options. The relevance of the therapist's own lifestyle, sexual orientation, and values is thus diffused. This type of group should be made more available to prevent the simple option of some type of conversion-type therapy or entering a "coming out group."

CONCLUSION

Bisexual and lesbian women get married because they love their husbands and desire marriage. However, there is evidence which suggests that societal and parental expectations influence their decisions on a subconscious level. Societal and parental expectations eventually come to play on a conscious level when same sex feelings are acknowledged in marriage and the conflict is recognized. Marriage results in an identity foreclosure and in congruence with one's feelings and behaviors. In spite of this, retrospective studies indicate that their marriages may be no more conflicted than heterosexual marriages. However, their struggles may be more difficult than gay or bisexual married men. Choices seem to be more limited. Greater stigma exists.

The research eliminated certain myths such as that lesbians reject feminine interests and activities. For example, there is no support for the notion that a lesbian rejects motherhood and, in fact, studies have demonstrated that one's sexual orientation has no bearing on her child's healthy development.

Certain problems exist and psychologists are in a good position to assist these women in resolving many of their struggles such as internalized homophobia and whether or not to remain in their marriages or pursue bisexual or lesbian lifestyles.

REFERENCES

Bell, A.P., & Weinberg, M.S. (1978). *Homosexualities: A study of diversity among men and women*. New York: Simon & Schuster.

Blumstein, P.W., & Schwartz, P. (1976). Bisexuality in women. *Archives of Sexual Behavior, 5*, 171-181.

Browning, C. (1988). Therapeutic issues and intervention strategies with young adult lesbian clients: A developmental approach. In E. Coleman (Ed.), *Psychotherapy with homosexual men and women: Integrated identity approaches for clinical practice* (pp. 45-52). New York: The Haworth Press.

Coleman, E. (1981/1982a). Developmental stages of the coming out process. *Journal of Homosexuality, 7* (2/3), 31-43.

Coleman, E. (1981/1982b). Bisexual and gay men in heterosexual marriage: Conflicts and resolutions in therapy. *Journal of Homosexuality, 7* (2/3), 93-103.

Coleman, E. (1985). Integration of male bisexuality and marriage. *Journal of Homosexuality, 11* (1/2), 189-208.

Coleman, E. (1988). Assessment of Sexual Orientation. In E. Coleman (Ed.), *Psychotherapy with homosexual men and women: Integrated approaches for clinical practice* (pp. 9-24). New York: The Haworth Press.

Dank, B.M. (1973). *The development of a homosexual identity: Antecedents and consequences*. Unpublished doctoral dissertation, University of Wisconsin. Madison, WI.

Fifield, L. (1975). *On my way to nowhere: Alienated, isolated, drunk*. Los Angeles: Gay Common Services Center.

Gochros, H. (1978). Counseling gay husbands. *Journal of Sex Education and Therapy, 4*, 6-10.

Gochros, J.S. (1985). Wives' reactions to learning that their husbands are bisexual. In F. Klein & T. J. Wolf (Eds.), *Bisexualities: Theory and research* (pp. 101-113). New York: The Haworth Press.

Golombok, S., Spence, A., & Rutter, M. (1983). Children in lesbian and single parent households: Psychosexual and psychiatric appraisal. *Journal Child Psychology and Psychiatry, 24*, 551-572.

Green, R. (1978). Sexual identity of 37 children raised by homosexual or transsexual parents. *American Journal of Psychiatry, 135*, 692-697.

Hoeffer, B. (1981). Children's acquisition of sex-role behavior in lesbian mother's families. *American Journal of Orthopsychiatry, 135*, 692-697.

Kaplan, G.T., & Rogers, L.J. (1984). Breaking out of the dominant paradigm: A new look at sexual attraction. *Journal of Homosexuality, 10*, 3/4, 71-75.

Kirkpatrick, M. (1988). Clinical implications of lesbian mother studies. In E. Coleman (Ed.), *Psychotherapy with homosexual men and women: Integrated identity approaches for clinical practice* (pp. 201-211). New York: The Haworth Press.

Kirkpatrick, M., Roy, R., & Smith, A. (1979, August). A new look at lesbian mothers. *Human behavior*, pp. 60-61.

Kirkpatrick, M., Smith, A., & Roy, R. (1981). Lesbian mothers and their children: A comparative study. *American Journal of Orthopsychiatry, 51*, 545-551.

Klein, F. (1978). *The Bisexual Option*. New York: Arbor House.

Klein, F., & Wolf, T. (1985). *Bisexualities: Theory and Research*. New York: The Haworth Press.

Kohn, B., & Matusow, A. (1980). *Barry and Alice*. Englewood Cliffs, NJ: Prentice-Hall.

Kus, R.J. (1988). Alcoholics Anonymous and gay American men. In E. Coleman (Ed.), *Psychotherapy with homosexual men and women: Integrated identity approaches for clinical practice* (pp. 253-276). New York: The Haworth Press.

Latham, J.D., & White, G.D. (1978). Coping with homosexual expression within heterosexual marriages: Five case studies. *Journal of Sex and Marital Therapy, 4*, 198-212.

Lohrenz, L., Connelly, J., Coyne, L., & Spare, K. (1978). Alcohol problems in several midwestern homosexual communities. *Journal of Studies on Alcohol, 39*, 1959-1963.

Malone, J. (1980). *Straight Women/Gay Men*. New York: Dial Press.

Mandel, J., & Hotvedt, M. (1980). Lesbians as parents. *Husarts and Praktijk, 4*, 31-34.

Marcia, J. (1980). Identity in adolescence. In J. Adelson (Ed.), *Handbook of adolescent psychology*. New York: John Wiley & Sons.

Masters, W.H., & Johnson, V.E. (1979). *Homosexuality in Perspective*. Boston: Little, Brown.

Matteson, D.R. (1985). Bisexual men in marriage: Is a positive homosexual identity and stable marriage possible? *Journal of Homosexuality, 11* (1/2), 149-171.

Mucklow, B., & Phelan, G. (1979). Lesbian and traditional mothers' responses to adult response to child behavior and self concept. *Psychological Reports, 44*, 880-882.

Nahas, R., & Turley, M. (1979). *The new couple: Women and gay men.* New York: Seaview Press.

Rand, C., Graham, D.L.R., & Rawlings, E. I. (1982). Psychological health and factors the court seeks to control in lesbian mother custody trials. *Journal of Homosexuality, 8* (1), 27-39.

Ross, H.L. (1971). Modes of adjustment and married homosexuals. *Social Problems, 18,* 385-393.

Ross, M.W. (1983). *The married homosexual man.* London: Routledge and Kegan Paul.

Ross, M.W. (1984). Beyond the biological model: New directions in bisexual and homosexual research. *Journal of Homosexuality, 10* (3/4), 63-70.

Saghir, M.T., & Robbins, E. (1973). *Male and female homosexuality: A comprehensive investigation.* Baltimore: Williams & Wilkins.

Schaefer, S., Evans, S., & Coleman, E. (1988). Sexual orientation concerns among chemically dependent individuals. In E. Coleman (Ed.), *Journal of Chemical Dependency Treatment* (pp. 121-140). New York: The Haworth Press.

Sophie, J. (1988). Internalized homophobia and lesbian identity. In E. Coleman (Ed.), *Psychotherapy with homosexual men and women: Integrated identity approaches for clinical practice* (pp. 53-65). New York: The Haworth Press.

Wolf, T.J. (1985). Marriages of bisexual men. *Journal of Homosexuality, 11* (1/2), 138-148.

Wolf, T.J. (1988). Group psychotherpay for bisexual men and their wives. In E. Coleman (Ed.), *Psychotherapy with homosexual men and women: Integrated identity approaches for clinical practice* (pp. 191-199). New York: The Haworth Press.

Lesbians and the Choice to Parent

Cheri A. Pies

Lesbians have been having and raising children for a long time (McCandish, 1987; Pies, 1985). Today, growing numbers of lesbians are having, adopting and raising children after "coming out" (Hitchens, 1986). Some are parenting with their primary partner, others alone, and still others with a male or female friend, or a family of friends (Pies, 1985). There are many types of lesbian family situations, each one distinctively different from the next (Pennington, 1987; Pies, 1987).

The subject of lesbians choosing to become parents frequently raises a number of compelling questions. For example, questions such as "Why do lesbians want to have children?" and "How will they do it?" are heard repeatedly. These are perhaps simple and straightforward questions to the curious observer. Placed in the context of childbearing and childrearing, however, such questions reflect what can be described as homophobic and antagonistic attitudes. Questions such as these are rarely, if ever, asked of a heterosexual woman and her partner choosing to become parents. Nevertheless, lesbians are expected to answer them, articulately and convincingly.

This article will address these questions, as well as a number of others, in an attempt to clarify the complex and challenging issues lesbians face as they grapple with the choice to parent. The quotations used in this article are from comments made by participants in workshops on lesbian parenting that the author has conducted since 1976.

The families that lesbians are building are often referred to as

Cheri A. Pies, MPH, MSW, is Health Education Specialist, Education Programs Associates, Campbell, CA 95008.

137

alternative or non-traditional families, but they are families none-theless. Despite the somewhat non-traditional nature of these families, lesbians approach the formation of their families in some fairly traditional ways. Lesbians have few role models for this task, thus there is a great need for sensitive support and informed guidance through the process.

A LOOK AT THE REASONS

Everyone always said I'd make a great mom. I love children. It doesn't make sense to give up my plan for having a child just because I am a lesbian.

I had a hard time as a child. My parents weren't around much. I want to do it differently and really love a child and give it a good home to grow up in.

We want to have a child together and share the ups and downs of being parents. We've been together over 4 years and feel we are ready to take on this experience.

Lesbians chose to parent for many of the same reasons as heterosexual women. They want children. They may have always wanted to be pregnant and bear a child. They may have had a memorable childhood they want to recreate for another young person. Or, perhaps they had a miserable and unhappy childhood and they want the opportunity to do it differently for another child. Some want to share the experience of parenting a child with their life partner, others hope that having a child will put a spark back into the relationship. Still others want to have a child for reasons that they are unable to explain; they simply know this is something they want to do.

The reasons for wanting children may be similar to those of their heterosexual peers, but that is where the similarity usually ends. Lesbians struggle with many of the same concerns as their heterosexual counterparts when it comes to choosing parenthood — time, work, emotional support from partner, responses of family and friends, raising a healthy child, etc. However, for lesbians, the issues are compounded by society's assumptions and biases about lesbians and especially lesbians choosing to parent.

All Things Considered, So to Speak

> We want our child to know the donor, but we want to do the parenting ourselves. Now we have to find a man who is willing to have that kind of arrangement.

> The people at my job know I am not married. What they don't know is that I am a lesbian. My lover wants to have a baby that we will parent together. How will I explain this new baby to my coworkers?

> I want to have a gay donor but I am worried about AIDS. This disease has changed the options available to those of us who want to use gay donors.

> My parents know I am a lesbian but they have made it very clear they do not approve. Now I want to have a baby and I don't even know how to talk to them about it.

For lesbians, the decision to become a parent requires a considerable amount of planning and coordination. A lesbian cannot simply say "I (or we) really want to have a baby, so I'm going to start trying to get pregnant (or adopt)." Instead, there are a series of complex questions and soul searching choices which must be reviewed and discussed. For lesbians, deciding to become a parent is a conscious choice; it rarely happens by accident. It is often a carefully orchestrated undertaking, with focussed attention to the personal, social, psychological, ethical and practical considerations.

The issues of concern vary for each lesbian or lesbian couple (Pies, 1987). Questions about donors, how to become pregnant, whether and when to tell families of origin, how to resolve legal issues if problems arise, are only a few that must be addressed and answered. Perhaps the most difficult however, are those which cause lesbians to question their right to have and raise children. These questions illustrate the internalized homophobia many lesbians live with every day of their lives.

Internalized homophobia is made up of the criticisms and doubts gay people have about themselves, their lifestyle and their peers. It is difficult to avoid internalized homohobia in a culture that assumes everyone is heterosexual and seeks to perpetuate negative attitudes and myths about gay men and lesbians. Perhaps the most obvious example of this is the repeated attempts by the media, clergy and others to categorize lesbians and gay men as only sexual beings.

Society has traditionally viewed lesbians in terms of their sexuality, rather than on the basis of their particular personal qualities, skills and capabilities. Judgments about their ability to be "good" parents have been obscured by deep-seated prejudice against and ignorance about homosexuality. It is as if sexuality is the yardstick by which one's skill as a potential parent is measured. As a result, there is a prevailing societal attitude that lesbians would not be "good" parents. Because of this lesbians often believe they must be more than simply "ordinary" mothers (Schulenberg, 1985).

Lesbians must be reminded repeatedly that they have a reproductive right to have children. And, at the same time, they must be reminded that they do not have to be "perfect" mothers.

It is not uncommon for lesbians considering parenthood to ask themselves many of the same probing and difficult questions that others ask. "Is it 'fair' to bring a child into the world and raise it in a lesbian family?" "Will the children of lesbians be discriminated against on the basis of the mother's sexual preference?" "Do children need male role models in the home on a daily basis in order to develop healthy identities?"

There are no right or wrong answers to these questions. Over the past 10 years a number of researchers have directed their studies to these areas of concern (Kirkpatrick, Smith & Roy 1981; Lewin & Lyons, 1982; Puryear, 1983; Steckel, 1987). As we learn more, it becomes apparent that children raised by lesbians have an equally good chance of developing into healthy, happy human beings as do children raised in heterosexual homes (Pennington, 1987).

Families of Origin

> When I mentioned I was planning on having a child my mother said, "Well, if we can put a man on the moon, I guess lesbians can have children." That was all she had to say.

No one in my family asked any questions. The truth is they didn't know what to ask. They never thought I would want to be a mother because I am a lesbian. In a way I think they hoped they wouldn't have to face this possibility.

I wanted my folks to understand that Sue and I were going to have a child, but Sue would be bearing the child. They didn't get it. They felt that if Sue had the baby, it was her baby, not *our* baby.

Parents and other family members have a wide range of reactions to the lesbian choosing to parent. For many family members, the decision is threatening and frightening. Perhaps they have just started getting used to the fact that their daughter (or sister or aunt) is a lesbian, and that may have taken time and effort. Now they are being asked to understand that she wants to become a parent. To family members, this may mean they will have to "come out" as the parent, brother or sister of a lesbian, thereby putting themselves in a situation with which they are not comfortable and ill-equipped to handle. For some, the decision may bring joyful and positive responses. Much depends upon the quality of the family relationships, religious values, moral rules, communication styles, and family traditions.

The lesbian who is planning to be a parent, must decide whether or not to discuss her sexual orientation with her family of origin. Some lesbians do not find it necessary or even relevant to talk with their families about their sexual orientation. Others choose to discuss it. It is not unusual for a lesbian to fear that her family will reject her totally if they learn she is a lesbian. Still others worry that their families will try to take their child away because of a daughter's lesbianism. Unfortunately, there is no way to predict how family members will act once they learn this information.

The lesbian planning to be the non-biological parent is faced with an even more complex task. She must convey to her family members that she will be the parent to a child that her partner is birthing. In addition, she may want to instill in her family a feeling of "relationship" to this child, so that the parents identify as grandparents, sisters as aunts, and brothers as uncles. This can be a frustrating task, especially if family members are uncomfortable with the idea of two women parenting a child together. Simply understanding and accepting the reality of a woman conceiving a child through artificial insemination could take time.

Needless to say, considerable strategizing is necessary to determine the most effective way of sharing this information with family members. Inevitably, it is a process. The lesbian choosing to parent has often spent a significant amount of time and energy making this decision. It is essential that she realize it may take her family equally as long to get used to the idea.

PLANS FOR PARENTING TOGETHER

I want a child and my lover does not. We have been together over 6 years and we are committed to this relationship. For me, this is a big problem.

I am not ready to have a child. I have many things I still want to do with my life, and having a child would be too disruptive. I know my partner wants to have a child, but she'll have to do it on her own. We can stay together, I just don't want to do this now.

The idea of having a child interests me, but who will people see as the "real parent." I mean, if my lover gives birth to this baby, how will the world see me?

We are going to adopt a child and raise it together. We come from very different family backgrounds. We each had very different experiences as children. I am genuinely worried about how we will work this part out.

We intend to have a legal agreement spelling out what will happen if we break up. We hope we never have to use it. But, we know it is a possibility. We have other lesbian friends whose relationships took a dive after they became parents. We want to protect our child and hope this will be the best way to do that.

Lesbian couples choosing to parent together may not always be in agreement about the process, timing, or choices. Do both want to have a child? Are both ready to parent a child together at this time? What if one urgently wants to parent and the other partner does not? Because becoming a parent doesn't just happen, lesbian couples rarely find themselves in a situation where they are already pregnant and have to decide how to proceed. The decisions about how to proceed take place early on.

Some lesbians believe the choice to parent must be shared equally by each partner. Many couples who have different levels of interest and readiness about parenting have developed creative solutions to this dilemma. One woman may choose to parent while the other is not a primary parent, but has some defined involvement in the childrearing. Some couples decide to begin parenting less than 50-50 with the understanding that they could shift the amount of participation as time goes on. In some situations, the lesbian couple has had to end their relationship because of this decision. In others, one partner has gone along with what the other partner wanted to do only to find that this did not work in the long run. And, in some situations, both women have wanted to bear the child and the couple has had to negotiate who will have the first child.

While some couples may have a difficult time because they are not in agreement about the decision to parent, others find their issues revolve more pointedly around the desire to gain societal and community recognition for the non-biological mother. Lesbian couples who have children through artificial insemination automatically have an asymetrical relationship with their child. That is, one woman is the birth mother and one is not. This often creates tensions within the relationship which are serious in and of themselves. However, the discussion here has more to do with how the outside world perceives the role of the non-biological mother and how that mother is treated by others.

We live in a culture that often identifies parents as those who have some biological connection to a child. To most, this means a man and a woman. When the parents are two women, most people have a very difficult time comprehending that the child then has two mothers. This is a serious dilemma. Society reinforces the role of the biological mother, while neglecting that of the non-biological mother. It is not uncommon for children to be asked to identify their "real" mother, thus suggesting that one is real and one is not. The non-biological mother then must find ways to insure that her role and position will be recognized and validated.

> My 6 year old daughter once said to me "You are not my *real* mother, Janis is because I was in her belly." I then asked her, "Does that mean you are not my *real* daughter?" The reply was a sharp "NO, I am your *real* daughter."

Because we are dealing with a culture-bound tradition — that a child only has one mother — it will take time and patience to educate family, friends, the community and the children about the validity of the role of the non-biological mother. Some lesbian couples have tried to address this dilemma by giving the child the last name of the non-biological parent. Others are pursuing a course which could enable the non-biological mother to legally adopt the child in a same-sex parent adoption.

Of even greater concern perhaps for the lesbian family, is the fact that the non-biological mother has no legally binding relationship with her child. Therefore, if something were to happen to the biological mother, it is altogether possible that the non-biological mother would not be recognized as the next-of-kin to care for the child. Biological grandparents have been known to file for custody of a child in the event of the death of their daughter, even when the non-biological parent is well and seeks to continue to raise the child alone. Such legal nightmares, as well as many others, make it essential for lesbians choosing to parent to have legal documentation of their parenting agreements (Hitchens, 1986).

The primary reason for legal agreements is based on the concept of promoting the "best interests of the child." If relationships change or end, one parent dies or becomes disabled, or if a donor seeks to change the relationship he has with the child, legal agreements spelling out intentions are of utmost importance. As one lesbian attorney aptly explained, "Judges understand contracts and legal agreement better than they understand artificial insemination" (Hitchens, 1985). Most lesbians find that drawing up legal documents and spelling out the exact nature of their agreements helps to clarify the parenting arrangement. Not all lesbians choose to have legal agreements with one another or with a donor. However, as questions concerning the use of reproductive technologies continue to be decided in the legal arena (Hornstein & Pies, 1988), it is imperative that lesbians carefully consider the risks of not having such agreements.

Contracts of this nature have yet to be tested in a court of law. Lesbians, their partners and donors who have had difficulties and differences have made efforts to resolve those differences outside of the courtroom. And, those cases which have been heard by a judge are often situations in which no contract was written. Whether such legal documents detailing a parenting agreement of this nature will be considered valid has yet to be determined.

Perhaps the most delicate and difficult legal situation arises when the lesbian couple decides to separate and the issue of child custody must be addressed. Certainly, if a contract has been written beforehand delineating the way in which such a situation would be handled, the individuals involved can follow the guidelines they established for themselves. However, what if one partner has had a change of heart? Are these contracts legally binding? What if the biological mother insists on sole custody of the child? How will the non-biological mother preserve her relationship with her child?

A few such cases have found their way into the court system, and by and large, they are being decided on a case by case basis. Regardless of how the adults perceive the situation, appropriate steps must be taken to promote and maintain the health and well-being of the child. The best interests of the child often dictate that adults make compromises with one another that they would not choose to make were there no children involved. Societal attitudes toward lesbians and gay men as parents and the widespread misunderstanding regarding the phenomenon of lesbian parenting on the part of key legal personnel, will certainly effect the course of any such litigation.

BECOMING A PARENT

I tried to get pregnant for about 11 months and finally stopped. I heard that I could adopt a child as a single mom, so I began the process of doing that.

Having an unknown donor was the only way I could see us having a child. We went to the Sperm Bank. Got the semen. After 3 tries, we got pregnant. I had our baby just over a year ago.

We had a known donor. In fact, he wanted to be involved in the parenting with us. We were thrilled. We tried to get pregnant, but it never happened. Turned out his sperm count was too low. We ended up with an unknown donor, but our first donor is actively participating anyway.

I want a gay donor, but I am worried about AIDS. We have talked to a number of our gay male friends, but a few are infected and others are not ready to take the HIV antibody test to find out. We understand, but it is very disappointing.

I am planning to get pregnant and I am going to have sexual intercourse with a man I know. We have talked about it. He is not interested in a relationship with me, nor I with him. The idea of artificial insemination doesn't feel right to me. My lover is willing to have this take place. I want to have a child and I want to do it *this* way.

We chose an unknown donor. Our daughter is now 6 years old. She often asks us about her "daddy." It is hard, we often wonder if we made the right decision. I think we did, but the questions will always remain.

Lesbians become parents in a number of ways. Some adopt or become foster parents. Others become pregnant through artificial insemination or sexual intercourse with a man. And others, as was discussed earlier, choose to be non-biological parents. Whatever the method, there are a number of practical, financial, emotional and ethical questions which must be answered.

For lesbians seeking to adopt children, they must decide which type of adoption agency to approach. There are a number of choices available today, however, not all welcome "single" parent adoptions. Then, there is the question of whether and how to "come out" to the adoption agency. Attorneys have frequently advised lesbians to answer all questions honestly. That is, if a question about the nature of one's intimate relationship is asked, it is best to tell the truth. Exactly how to talk about this to adoption personnel depends upon the agency, the area of the country, etc. Because many lesbians fear that this would decrease their chances of getting a child through adoption, sometimes only one partner in the couple applies to be an adoptive parent.

Some lesbians actively choose adoption instead of becoming pregnant. Sometimes neither woman wants to be pregnant. Perhaps one was adopted herself and wants to give a child a loving home. Others choose adoption because it insures a more equal relationship with the child. And, some lesbians choose adoption because they are unable to conceive a pregnancy but want to be parents.

Those choosing to become pregnant are faced with choices about whether to use artificial insemination or have sexual intercourse with a man, whether to have a known or an unknown donor, whether to have the donor involved in the parenting, whether to use fresh or frozen semen, and so on. And, since reproductive technologies have catapulted us into an age in which questions about biological parenthood are not as straightforward as they once were, lesbians choosing to conceive a child through alternative fertilization or artificial insemination face ethically challenging questions as they explore conception choices.

Do children have the right to know their biological father? Will a child be damaged psychologically if s/he is never able to know the biological father? How will parents explain who the "daddy" is? None of these is a simple question. And, once again there is no right or wrong answer, simply opinions and deep feelings on all sides of the issues.

There are specific and historical reasons why lesbians choose unknown donors. They want to be protected from legal battles and they fear losing their child to a man because they are lesbians. Many lesbians want to be identified as the primary parents and do not want to parent with a man they do not know. Others do not know a man they want to have as a donor or father and therefore choose to use an unknown donor. Although using an unknown donor has many benefits, it poses some risks as well.

What if the child begins to develop some unusual illnesses which are not in the biological mother's family? Or the child appears to be remarkably upset by not knowing who "daddy" is. Is it fair to bring children into the world when they will not be able to know their biological father? On what basis does one begin to address this question? Clearly, lesbians choosing to use unknown donors are making choices for their children. These are not easy choices and they are rarely made frivolously or without a great deal of forethought and discussion with others who have made and are making similar decisions.

Lesbians choosing unknown donors often utilize the services of a Sperm Bank or private clinician. In these settings, some basic information about the donor is available, his eye and hair color, his height, weight, some family history, special interests, hobbies, etc. Through some Sperm Banks, women can locate donors who agree to be known when the child turns 18. The donor is then "unknown" but with the possibility of being known to the child at a later date. This often provides women with just the balance they want in having an unknown, uninvolved donor who the child can have access to when they become an adult.

An unknown donor can also be located through friends. In this type of situation, the lesbian may not have full and complete medical information about the donor. And, although someone besides the woman receiving the semen may know who the donor is, there is no guarantee that she will be able to locate that man at a later date. For the woman who cannot afford the services of a Sperm Bank, medical doctor or nurse practitioner, however, this becomes the only option.

Within the past five years, the practice of using a known donor has increased. Some lesbians want their child to know the biological father. Some even want that person to have a role in the parenting relationship. Other lesbians have a male friend (gay or straight) with whom they want to parent. This may be a man one or both of the women knows well. Often, these individuals have discussed the pros and cons of this choice at great length, and have made a commitment to parent together. In some instances, lesbian couples decide to use semen from the brother of the woman who is not going to become pregnant. This is done so that the couple can create a situation in which both women have a direct blood relationship to the child.

Situations such as this, as well as many others, reinforce the necessity for writing a legal contract to clarify the roles and responsibilities of each individual involved. Legal documentation of agreements is especially important when the lesbian and her partner want a known donor and have specific ideas about the type of involvement they want this donor to have.

As the AIDS epidemic has become an everyday reality in all of our lives, the risk of HIV disease is another reality which lesbians who are choosing to become pregnant must address. Because there is a risk of transmission of the Human Immunodeficiency Virus through sexual contact (whether that be insemination or sexual intercourse) (Stewart et al., 1985; Eskenazi & Pies et al., 1989), lesbians choosing to become pregnant must take specific steps to verify that their donor is not infected (Women's AIDS Network, 1986). The AIDS epidemic has influenced choices regarding the use of gay men as donors. Prior to the epidemic, lesbians preferred to use gay men as donors (Pies, 1985). Today, because of the high infectivity rate in the gay men's community, lesbians are often forced to use an unknown donor or ask heterosexual men they know about their willingness to be a sperm donor. It is important to note, however, that not all gay men are infected with HIV. Nevertheless, this epidemic has had a profound effect on the course of the lesbian and gay parenting movement.

Practical Considerations — Work and Money

In addition to the wide range of logistical, social and ethical problems, a few practical concerns require attention. The lesbian choosing to become a parent must have a sense of how she will support herself and her child. And, even before that, if she plans to use the services of a Sperm Bank or private clinician, she must have resources to pay for the semen.

Taking time off work often requires an explanation for this request. If the explanation includes disclosure of pregnancy, and if the woman is "out" as a lesbian, co-workers may ask her how she became pregnant. Employers who were reasonably comfortable with an employee being a lesbian may not be as comfortable with her having a child. The lesbian parent-to-be could lose her job. For the woman who is not "out," she must decide how she will explain this pregnancy to an employer. And, what about the woman who will be the non-biological mother? If the woman has discussed her family situation at work, an explanation regarding a pregnancy may be less complicated. If she has not, she is often forced to hide the new child or find some way to explain the appearance of this child to co-workers. Lesbians must carefully review the risks they take in sharing information about their personal lives at work.

SUSTAINING AND MAINTAINING RELATIONSHIPS

Raising children puts a strain on intimate relationships for any number of reasons. Lesbians must deal with the usual stresses and strains of parenthood as well as the additional ones which arise because they are a lesbian family. Some lesbian relationships may not survive the first year of their child's life. With this as a risk, lesbians must take deliberate steps to plan for the survival of their intimate and emotional relationship in the face of what are often staggering odds.

> We never talked about what it would be like to have a child. We just knew we wanted to do it and do it together. I mean we talked about it, but we never discussed how it might throw our relationship off balance.

> My parents fought all the time when we were growing up. I didn't have any idea that would happen to us. But it did. We were totally unprepared for the way being parents brought up all those old issues from the past.

> What can I say? I loved our baby and didn't know how to love two people at the same time. I fell in love with the baby and my lover felt neglected, rejected and understandably abandoned. Sex was the last thing on my mind, I was too tired most of the time to even talk at night.

Lesbians choose to have children because they want to create families. Families need the continued participation of all members. They cannot survive unless there is open, frank and honest discussion beforehand about how couples will resolve conflicts, find time for intimacy, develop alternative ways for being intimate with one another that do not have to be sexual, and confirm the commitment that they have to one another.

Lesbians have found support for their relationships and their parenting choices through participation in considering parenthood groups (Pies, 1985), support groups for new parents, and individual and couple therapy (Hall, 1978). Groups provide lesbians with an opportunity to talk with each other about their decisions and the ways in which they have or plan to address specific situations. Talking with other parents, whether lesbian or heterosexual, is also helpful. Such dialogues offer participants an opportunity to explore the range of changes that can occur in a relationship after the arrival of a child. In addition, they provide couples and single parents with role models for problem-solving, coping, and surviving those early years.

Lesbians who choose individual or couple therapy often need validation of their choices and recognition of the multifaceted complexity of being a lesbian parent. Lesbians seek the guidance of therapists who are not homophobic and who may be parents themselves. Critical in the choice of a therapist is the skill of the practitioner to promote and encourage indepth exploration of the varied and complex issues.

IMPLICATIONS FOR COUNSELORS AND THERAPISTS

Above all, counselors and therapists choosing to work with lesbians considering or choosing parenthood must carefully explore their own feelings about such a choice. Identifying one's own homophobia regarding this issue is essential. Without an honest understanding of one's own attitudes and values about this choice, the course of the work may be negatively affected. In addition, therapists will want to explore their thoughts and feelings about parenting. Recognizing one's choices and reasons for those choices enables the practitioner to be more alert to possible counter-transference issues that often arise.

It is important to keep in mind that not all lesbians considering parenthood choose to become parents. After a careful review of the issues and possibilities, some find that they cannot resolve the internal conflicts. Others acknowledge that this does not seem to be the right choice for them in their life at this time. Some simply do not want to have children. Some lesbians find other ways to have children in their lives, realizing that they do not want the full-time responsibility of parenting. It is important for practitioners to be aware of the grieving process which such a decision can evoke. Directed discussion concerning this potential grief and loss will be useful in assisting the lesbian in accepting the choice she has made.

For lesbian couples who decide to become parents, it is not uncommon for deep-seated differences to affect the course of the parenting relationship. In the course of making their decision, inevitably some compromises have been made. Without a careful review and clarification of those compromises, problems may arise later. Counselors and therapists must assist couples in identifying those compromises as groundwork for preserving the parenting relationship in the future.

Practitioners can be pivotal in helping lesbians identify the parenting style of their families of origin. Discussions of the "ideal" or "dream" family prior to having a child can be vital to the health of the lesbian family-to-be.

Lesbians experience a great deal of pressure from their peers on both sides of the issue about becoming parents. How one's friends feel about the decision is critical. The lesbian community is heterogeneous, and each views lesbian parenting differently. Inevitably, friendship and support networks change when lesbians decide to become parents, thereby effecting the circle of people one has to rely on for emotional and social interaction.

Lesbians must be encouraged to explore the realities of being a single parent. All too often, lesbians planning to parent together imagine that they will ALWAYS have a partner. Each woman must be given ample opportunity to identify the pros and cons of single parenting, because one never knows when that may happen. And, for those lesbians choosing single parenting, deliberate identification of resources, plans for support and opportunities for respite deserve attention.

A thorough exploration of all the issues is essential. The issues of primary importance will be different for each person. Giving clients the opportunity to identify the issues and then exploring them in whatever order seems appropriate is perhaps the most straightforward way to address the decision-making process. The use of individual and couple exercises can also be helpful in assisting clients in sorting out their concerns, questions and fears. Above all, lesbians considering parenthood or choosing parenthood need a place to voice all the fears and pleasures of such a choice. The layers of complexity require this and such exploration and identification helps to insure healthy choices and conscious decisions.

CONCLUSION

As more and more lesbians choose to become parents, it is essential that therapists and counselors have a broad understanding of what is involved in this choice. The choices are not easy and there is no well-traveled road to follow. As has been illustrated throughout this article, the decisions lesbians are asked to make as they build families are challenging. And, although many lesbians have found support from their own community and those who have made these decisions before, there is still a great need for continued support of lesbians exploring the choice to parent.

There is no "typical" situation of a lesbian or lesbian couple choosing to be parents. There are as many different types of lesbian families as there are lesbians choosing parenthood. As more role models appear within this community, lesbians will have situations with which to compare and contrast their choices. Until that time, lesbians choosing to parent will continue to rely on the experiences of those others around them and the emotional support of sensitive and informed practitioners who can work with them as they explore the possibilities of being a parent.

BIBLIOGRAPHY

Eskenazi, B., Pies, C., Newsletter, A., Sheppard, C., & Pearson, K. (1989). HIV Serology in Lesbians Artificially Inseminated in *Journal of Acquired Immune Deficiency Syndrome*, pending in publication, May 1989.
Hall, M. (1978). Lesbian families: cultural and clinical issues. *Social Work*, 23, 380-385.
Hitchens, D. (1985). *Choosing Children: A Film About Lesbian Parents*. Klausner and Chasnoff, (Producers). Boston, MA.
Hitchens, D. et al. (1986). *Lesbian Mothers and Their Children: An Annotated*

Bibliography of Legal and Psychological Materials. San Francisco: Lesbian Rights Project.

Hornstein, F. & Pies, C. (1988). Baby M and the Gay Family in *Outlook: National Lesbian and Gay Quarterly* (1), 78-88

Kirkpatrick, M., Smith, K., & Roy, D. (1981). Lesbian Mothers and their children: A comparative survey. *The American Journal of Orthopsychiatry*, 51, 545-551.

Lewin, E. & Lyons, T. (1982). Everything in its place: The coexistence of lesbianism and motherhood. In W. Paul, J.C. Gonsioreck, & M. E. Hotvedt (Eds.) *Homosexuality: Social psychological, and biological issues*, 249-273. Beverly Hills CA: Sage.

McCandish, B. (1987). Against All Odds: Lesbian Mother Family Dynamics. In Bozett, F. (Ed.) *Gay and Lesbian Parents*, 23-38, New York: Praeger.

Pennington, S. (1987). Children of Lesbian Mothers. In Bozett, F. (Ed.) *Gay and Lesbian Parents*, 58-74. New York: Praeger.

Pies, C. (1985, revised 1988), *Considering Parenthood*. San Francisco: Spinsters/ Aunt Lute.

Pies, C. (1987). Considering Parenthood: Psychosocial Issues for Gay Men and Lesbians Choosing Alternative Fertilization. In Bozett, F. (Ed.) *Gay and Lesbian Parents*, 165-174. New York: Praeger.

Puryear, D. (1983). *A Comparison Between the Children of Lesbian Mothers and the Children of Heterosexual Mothers*. Unpublished doctoral dissertation, California School of Professional Psychology, Berkeley CA.

Schulenberg, J. (1985). *Gay Parenting: A complete guide for gay men and lesbians with children*. New York: Anchor Press.

Steckel, A. (1987). Psychosocial Development of Children of Lesbian Mothers. In Bozett, F. (Ed.) *Gay and Lesbian Parents*, 75-85. New York: Praeger.

Stewart, G.T., Tyler, J.P.P., Cunningham, A.L., & Barr, J.A. (1985). Transmission of Human T Cells Lymphotrophic Virus Type III by artificial insemination by donor. *Lancet* (2) 581-585.

Women and AIDS (1986), pamphlet. Women's AIDS Network (Ed.). San Francisco AIDS Foundation, San Francisco, CA.

Parenting by Gay Fathers

Jerry J. Bigner
Frederick W. Bozett

THE GAY FATHER ENIGMA

The gay father is a newly emergent figure in homosexual culture. There is little information or knowledge about these men. What is available has been based on interview and case study material using small samples rather than empirical data from samples that are more broadly representative of this population.

Gay males who are fathers have a unique and more complex social-psychological environment than other homosexual or heterosexual males. Their challenges of adjustment relate to identity concerns, acceptance of self, acceptance by family, and acceptance by other homosexuals as well as to matters more specific to parenting and custody issues. A major concern of many of these men relates to their development of a long-term, committed relationship with another man who accepts and deals with children as a central component of their relationship.

The man who is both a homosexual and a father is an enigma in our society. The term *gay father* is contradictory in nature. This is more a matter of semantics, however, as *gay* has the connotation of homosexuality while *father* implies heterosexuality. The problem lies in determining how both may be applied simultaneously to an individual who has a same-sex orientation, and who also is a parent. What complicates our understanding of this individual is that the idea of a gay father also is contradictory to the stereotypical image

Jerry J. Bigner, PhD, is Professor, Department of Human Development and Family Studies, Colorado State University, Ft. Collins, CO 80523. Frederick W. Bozett, RN, DNS, is Professor in the Graduate Program, College of Nursing, University of Oklahoma, Oklahoma City, OK 73132.

155

of a gay man. This stereotype emphasizes that gays are anti-family in their lifestyle and orientation to group living.

Pros and Cons of Gay Parenthood

PRO*

- "I have a very good relationship with my children. We may have the same kinds of problems that any single parent would have but none of them has to do with my being gay."

CON**

- "Under no circumstances should a child be allowed to be brought up in a homosexual environment. I'm not saying that the child would automatically be sexually abused by his homosexual parent but he probably would be abused by the homosexual's friends. Children who live in homosexual environments are subjected to all-night orgies and watching queens in drag. With homosexuals, one lover is not sufficient. After an hour, they want more."

PRO

- "It doesn't matter if you're gay or not. What I try and teach my children is that it's not important who you love. What is important is that you love."

CON

- "There is nothing gay about a homosexual's life. To live with a homosexual father is both unsafe and unhealthy."

* Bob, a gay father with custody of three children.
** Rev. Maurice Gordon, pastor of Lovingway United Pentecostal Church, Denver, CO.

Source: Kirchheimer, S. (1984). Gay's role as single parent. *Rocky Mountain News*, 21-S, May 10.

Researchers estimate that approximately 20 to 25 percent of self-identified gay men are fathers (Bell & Weinberg, 1978; Maddox, 1982; Miller, 1979a, b; Weinberg & Williams, 1974). This group clearly constitutes a minority within a minority in our culture. While approximately 10% of all American males are predominantly homosexual in orientation (Kinsey, Pomeroy, & Martin, 1948), the actual number of gay men who are parents cannot be accurately estimated since many are still married or are "closeted" for other reasons. (Since gays are an invisible population, most are unavailable for study. Hence, any statistics on homosexuality are, at best, only a rough estimate.)

Several researchers (Bozett, 1981a, b, 1985, 1987a; Robinson & Skeen, 1982) describe the dilemma of the man who is both gay and a father as being a victim of divided personal identity. More precisely, these individuals can be described as marginal beings who are challenged by having ties to the cultural worlds of both nongays and gays.

The process of identity development for the gay father requires a reconciliation of two polar extremes. Since each identity (heterosexual and homosexual) essentially is unacceptable by the opposite culture, the task for these men is to integrate both identities into the cognitive class called *gay father*. This process involves the man's disclosure of his gay identity to nongays and his father identity to gays, thus forming close liaisons with persons who positively sanction both identities. This process is referred to as *integrative sanctioning* (Bozett, 1981a, b, 1985, 1987a). It also involves the father's distancing himself from others who are not tolerant. At the same time, identity development is enhanced by participation in a gay lifestyle.

MOTIVATIONS FOR FATHERHOOD

There are a variety of reasons why a man who is gay may become a parent. These reasons could include the following: (1) a man might not be able to deal effectively with accepting his homosexual orientation until after several years of marriage during which children are produced; (2) a man may willfully choose to become a father even though his homosexual orientation and identity is intact; or (3) there may be a desire to become a parent because of dissatisfaction with the gay lifestyle (Bozett, 1981a, b, 1987a; Clark, 1979; Harris & Turner, 1986; Miller, 1979a, b; Voeller & Walters, 1978).

Researchers also report that while some individuals come to acknowledge their homosexual orientation after marriage, others enter into marriage fully aware of their homosexuality. Under this aegis, reasons given for marriage and involvement in a nongay lifestyle, or parenthood include: (1) a desire to conceal or even deny their homosexuality; (2) doing this as an attempt to measure the "goodness of fit" of a heterosexual lifestyle even though they know or strongly suspect that they are gay; (3) having developed a genuine affection for their female partner; (4) yielding to social pressures (from parents and other family members, especially) to adopt a conventional heterosexual lifestyle; (5) having a strong desire to escape from homophobic (fear of homosexuality) feelings through marriage; (6) escaping from a fear of loneliness by having children; or (7) simply wishing to reproduce for the same reasons held by nongay people (Bozett, 1980, 1987a; Fadiman, 1983).

The responses of a group of gay fathers have been compared with those of a group of nongay fathers on a scale that measures the values and functions of children for adults (Bigner & Jacobsen, 1989a). Gay fathers generally are similar to nongay fathers in their reasons for having children. However, some significant differences between these groups were found. Gay fathers differed from nongay fathers in two ways. Nongay fathers placed a greater emphasis on traditional values of being a parent such as continuing the family name, ensuring security in old age by having children to care for them, transmission of family traditions, and so on. In contrast, gay fathers responded differently from nongay fathers by placing greater emphasis on the function of parenthood in conveying social status and gaining acceptability as an adult member of a community.

These differences may illuminate further why some gay men become involved in heterosexual lifestyles. Many men, who later identify themselves as gay, do so only after years of trying to fit into a heterosexual lifestyle. These men marry, explore an intimate relationship with a woman, produce children, and adopt a variety of attitudes and behaviors that are representative of heterosexual orientation. Many of them report maintaining or experimenting with their homosexuality by having impersonal sexual encounters during their marriages, although these are clandestine (Bozett, 1981a, b, 1986). These men, then, may differ from other gay men in an important way. They may internalize to a greater extent the negative cultural homophobic image of homosexuals and homosexuality and actively reject a gay identification based on an inability to accept this image as part of their self-concept. This may help to explain why these men could be expected to look to heterosexual marriage and parenthood as a means of protecting themselves from disapproval and rejection by their significant others and by society in general. On the other hand, however, many gay men who have a positive, healthy gay identity may wish to become a parent for altogether different reasons such as truly enjoying children and wanting them to have a valued place in their life.

THE "LOW STATUS INTEGRATION" HYPOTHESIS

The nature of gay culture is antithetical to and conflicting with certain characteristics of the lifestyle of the homosexual man who has a history of heterosexual involvement. This man presents himself into gay culture as a father, i.e., as someone with a history of long-term emotional and financial responsibilities to others, time restrictions, different living arrangements, obligations to others who are dependent on him, and so on. Guttman (1975) has noted that men's characters often are dramatically altered by fatherhood "toward greater responsibility, selflessness, and moderation" (p. 170). More typically, gay culture is singles oriented with individuals often having few long-term commitments, few if any financial responsibilities for others, and heavy emphasis on personal freedom and autonomy. It is not uncommon for the gay father to experience discrimination and rejection from other gays who are not fathers because of these restrictions to freedom and the lack of understanding if not devaluation of the place of children in one's life. More specific research on the process and factors influencing gay mate selection should provide more accurate information on this topic.

Because gay fathers have a history of experience in a relatively long-term, committed relationship, they tend to want to replicate this same type of relationship with a man. Such liaisons present unusual strains due to feelings of jealousy toward the children often experienced by their male partner, and the knowledge that the gay father typically will maintain strong if not preferential ties and loyalties to his children.

The gay father may be viewed as being semi-integrated into two subcultures: the homosexual father versus the heterosexual parent. This person is referred to, then, as a kind of "marginal man" who does not belong fully to either social situation. He holds two social statuses that are to some degree inconsistent. Sociologists refer to this as *low status integration* (Gibbs & Martin, 1964). This means that individuals who hold partly inconsistent social statuses tend to have unique experiences as well as role conflicts. In other words, the gay father's experiences are not shared with persons who have "consistent" statuses, e.g., heterosexual fathers and gay males who are not parents. This suggests that a gay father's parental role behaviors and experiences as well as reasons to be a parent are unique. In many ways, then, low status integration may be analogous to the divorced, single-parent world, regardless of one's sexual orientation.

GAY FATHERS AND THEIR CHILDREN

There are a variety of issues that are unique to the parenting situations of gay fathers. Very little is known, however, of the quality of their parenting as compared with nongay fathers nor of the nature of their childrearing experiences in general. Likewise, little is known about the experience and perceptions of children who have a gay father.

One of the central issues relates to making one's homosexual orientation known to children. This process, in general, is termed "coming out (of the closet)," or disclosing one's homosexuality. There is much debate among gay fathers whether it is appropriate or not, when is the best time to disclose to children, and how it is best done.

Two events appear to promote disclosure to happen: (1) when parents become separated or divorced; and (2) when the father develops an intimate relationship or partnership with another man (Bozett, 1981b; Miller, 1978). When children are small, for example, the disclosure may be indirect and may occur when the father takes the children to a gay social event such as a Christmas party sponsored by a gay fathers' support group or when he openly shows affection to another man (Bozett, 1987a, b). Both direct (telling) and indirect ways of disclosure are used with older children. Based upon interview and survey studies of gay fathers (Bozett, 1980;

Harris & Turner, 1986; Turner, Scadden, & Harris, 1985; Wyers, 1987) and of interviews of the children of gay fathers (Bozett, 1988; Miller, 1979a), it appears that regardless of age of the child or means of disclosure that most children of all ages and both sexes usually respond positively.

Reasons for children's acceptance are explained in several ways: (1) gay fathers tend to teach their children to be accepting of variations in human behavior; (2) it is improbable that children of gay fathers would begin to perceive their fathers in a negative manner so abruptly after having a long history of loving experiences with them; (3) the disclosure may help to relieve family tensions in these homes since the children would be less likely after the disclosure to blame themselves for their parents' marital difficulties (Miller, 1979a).

Children's Reactions to Their Father's Homosexuality

Most children react favorably to their father's disclosure of his homosexuality. They show their acceptance both verbally and behaviorally:

- "My children wanted to see what Dad's life was like. So, we'd go out dancing in gay bars. All three of us. They would dance, and I'd dance with each of them separately. I'd dance with my son. He's very understanding. He thinks it's fine."

- "After I'd told my daughter about it (my homosexuality), she said, 'I thought you'd been fighting it all this time. I feel so relieved.' And she reached over and grabbed my hand, and she just cried with great relief. She was feeling for me. Being compassionate with me — for my feelings. I didn't have to hold anything back."

Not all children react favorably, however. These comments by adult children of gay fathers illustrate how difficult the father's sexuality may be for some children to deal with:

- "I'm embarrassed that my father is gay. A lot of times I would just like him to go away. I almost wish he would die because then

I can lie about what he was like to the future hypothetical children I'm going to have. It's not normal. Normal people don't go around doing things like that.''

- "I don't hate gays. I just hate the way they act . . . I mean my dad's fine as long as he's not acting like a fag. Sure, I'd prefer for my dad to still be in the closet. There's no conflict (that way).''

It should be noted, however, that almost all children who reject their father as being gay continue to accept him in his caregiving role as their father.

Source: Bozett, F. W. (1987). *Gay and lesbian parents*. New York: Praeger.

An over-riding fear among many children of gay fathers is what their peers will think of them if their father's gay identity becomes public knowledge. A central concern is that others would assume that they were gay as well. These children have been found to use several controlling strategies in relation to their father so they are seen by others as they want to be perceived, i.e., as not being gay (Bozett, 1987b). First, children may use *boundary control*, which has three components: (a) control of the father's behavior or asking the father to behave in ways that conceal his sexuality; (b) control of one's own behavior in relation to the father such as refusing to be seen in public with the father and his lover or gay friends; (c) controlling others in relation to the father such as not bringing friends to the father's home to keep them from coming into contact with any evidence of the father's gay lifestyle. A second strategy is *nondisclosure*. Children may be able to best control their image by simply not sharing the fact of their father's homosexuality with anyone. A third strategy is *disclosure*. While this may seem contradictory, children may tell selected others who may be potential discreditors and that by controlling who knows about the father's sexuality, then their image is protected. There are, however, factors that determine the degree and extent to which children use these controlling strategies. They are *obtrusiveness* or how discernible the child thinks the father's homosexuality is, and *mutuality* or the degree of identification the child has with the father. In addition, the child's age and if he or she lives with the father also are important factors. The less obtrusive the child believes the father's homosexuality to be and the more feelings of mutuality or connectedness the child has with the father, the less the child will use controlling strategies. Additionally, older children who live independently of their gay father employ controlling strategies less often.

PARENTING OF GAY FATHERS

There is no evidence of any kind that demonstrates that living with a homosexual parent has any significant negative effects on children. In fact, it appears that gay parents are as effective and may be even more so in some ways than nongay parents. Scallen (1981) compared gay and nongay fathers in a study using the Eversoll Father Role Questionnaire. He found that gay fathers were more endorsing of paternal nurturance, less endorsing of economic providing as a main ingredient of fathering behavior, and somewhat less traditional in their overall approach to parenting. Other research has found that: (1) most gay fathers have positive relationships with their children; (2) the father's sexual orientation is of little importance in the overall parent/child relationship; and (3) gay fathers try harder to create stable home lives and positive relationships than what would be expected among traditional heterosexual parents (Turner, Scadden, & Harris, 1985).

Several studies have examined specific parenting behaviors of gay fathers (Bigner & Jacobsen, 1989b; Harris & Turner, 1986; Miller, 1979b; Riddle, 1978; Scallen, 1981). The consensus of these studies suggests that homosexuality is not incompatible with effective parenting. No differences have been reported between heterosexual and homosexual fathers in problem-solving, providing recreation for children, encouraging their autonomy, handling problems relating to childrearing, having relatively serious problems with children, or having generally positive relationships with children. Gay fathers are reported to have greater satisfaction with their first child and fewer disagreements with partners over discipline of children.

When gay fathers are compared with nongay fathers in their responses to the Iowa Parent Behavior Scale, the gay fathers are found to be more strict and to consistently emphasize the importance of setting limits on children's behavior (Bigner & Jacobsen,

1989b). They report going to greater lengths than nongay fathers in promoting cognitive skills of children by explaining rules and regulations. As such, they may place greater emphasis on verbal communication with children. Gay fathers tend to be less traditional or more authoritative with children and to be somewhat strict in the execution of their control over children. Generally, gay fathers are found to be more sensitive and responsive to the perceived needs of children than nongay fathers. Gay fathers also appear to go to extra lengths to act as a resource for activities with children. They seem no different from nongay fathers in their expression of intimacy toward children except that they appear less willing to be demonstrative toward their partner in their children's presence than are nongay fathers (Bigner & Jacobsen, 1989b).

Several explanations can be suggested that address the differences and similarities in parenting behavior of gay and nongay fathers. First, gay fathers may feel additional pressures to be more proficient at their parenting role than nongay fathers. Factors that might motivate them to be "better" fathers could include: (1) stronger feelings of guilt about their role in fathering children, based on an increased sensitivity about their sexuality; and (2) sensitivity to the belief that they are "in the spotlight" or expected to perform better due to a fear that visitation or custody decisions could be challenged because of their sexual orientation. Second, these findings suggest that gay fathers may be less conventional and more androgynous than nongay fathers. As such, they may incorporate a greater degree and combination of expressive role functions than more traditionally sex-role oriented nongay fathers. These expressive role functions are found more conventionally in the traditional female mothering role. The cultural stereotype of the father role among traditional males is that they: (1) generally are not interested in children nor in childrearing issues; (2) view the occupational role as their primary parenting identity; (3) are less competent caregivers than women; and (4) are less nurturant than women toward children. It is possible that nongay fathers adopt this as their parenting style while gay fathers may demonstrate a blending of the qualities traditionally associated with both mother and father role images.

What is the quality of parent-child relations for those men who are gay and yet remain married and/or closeted and do not reveal their homosexuality to children? Researchers find that these relationships often are of less quality than those found among fathers who are open and honest with their children regarding their homosexuality (Bozett, 1987b; Miller, 1979a). Gay fathers who have disclosed their homosexuality to their children and to others tend to live a relatively stable lifestyle that may involve a domestic type of relationship with another man who often is a permanent partner, they tend to spend quality time with their children, and are dependable sources of caregiving (Miller, 1979a).

A principle concern of the courts, social welfare agencies, and others is that children raised by transsexual or homosexual parents will develop similar sexual identities. It should be noted that this more likely masks a deeper, more homophobic and hostile reaction about this type of alternative family rather than reflecting true concern for children. While there are no studies that investigate this issue among children of gay fathers, many respectable studies have been conducted with children of lesbian mothers (Pennington, 1987; Steckel, 1987). The consensus of these works is that homosexuality is not transmissible from parents to children by virtue of their being raised by or living in an environment with a lesbian mother. Since the issue relates to homosexuality of the parent, it is doubtful that children of gay fathers differ from children of lesbian mothers in this regard (Bozett, 1987b; Green, 1978; Miller, 1979a, b).

ISSUES OF DISCLOSURE FOR GAY FATHERS

There are many problems faced by gay fathers. One of the most pivotal is disclosure of their homosexuality to significant others ("coming out"). Nondisclosure compels the gay person to hide his true identity, and it demands relentless self-surveillance to avoid accidental slips. It exacts an extraordinary amount of psychological energy always to be on guard in both words and behavior. Continually camouflaging oneself is psychologically exhausting, and such self-denial is often exquisitely painful. The desire of most gay persons is to construct their lives socially in a form that is real, not pretend. To do this, one must disclose one's homosexuality. However, because homophobia or the irrational fear of homosexuals and homosexuality is so widespread in the United States, no gay person, regardless of the closeness of the relationship, can be assured of others' acceptance after coming out (Weinberg, 1973).

Gay men have much to lose by disclosing their homosexuality such as the personal security and intimacy provided by home and family life, economic security, and social stability. When gay men disclose to their wives, the most common outcome appears to be separation and divorce (Bozett, 1982; Hays & Samuels, 1989). It is exceedingly difficult for most women to continue to live in a spousal relationship when the man is forthright about his continued sexual engagements and relationships with other men. However, losing the legal tie to their wives is not as much a concern for gay fathers as is losing the love of their children (Bozett, 1980, 1984). This is the greatest of their fears. Although there are occasional exceptions, it appears that children rarely are rejecting of their gay fathers (Bozett, 1987), and they are much more accepting than these men anticipate. Although children can't be said to be delighted and they may not approve of homosexuality, ordinarily they neither repudiate nor disown their father. Most commonly they continue to love and relate to him as they did before. In fact, the father-child relationship has been reported to become closer based upon greater honesty and openness (Bozett, 1980, 1986, 1987b). Although disclosure of one's homosexuality usually is difficult, research bears out that in spite of increased public stigma, gay fathers achieve a sense of psychological well-being as their stigmatized careers progress (Miller, 1986).

Fundamental principles regarding the gay father's disclosure to children are presented here. These are based upon the work of Miller (1987) and Schulenburg (1985).

Guidelines for Disclosure of Homosexuality to Children

1. *Come to terms with your own gayness before disclosing to children.* This is crucial. The father who feels negative about his homosexuality or is ashamed of it is much more likely to have children who also react negatively. The father must create a setting of acceptance by first being accepting of himself.

If he tells his children when he is ready and comfortable in doing so, it is likely to be a positive experience for everyone.

2. *Children are never too young to be told.* They will absorb only as much as they are capable of understanding. Use words appropriate to the age of the child. Details may be added as they grow older.

3. *Discuss it with children before they know or suspect.* When children discover their father's sexual orientation from someone other than the father, they often are upset that their father did not trust them sufficiently to share the information with them. It is exceedingly difficult for children to initiate the subject, and they will not bring it up even though they may want to.

4. *Disclosure should be planned.* Children should not find out about their father's homosexuality by default or discover it accidentally or during an argument between their parents.

5. *Disclose in a quiet setting where interruptions are unlikely to occur.*

6. *Inform, don't confess.* The disclosure should not be heavy or maudlin but positive and sincere. Informing in a simple, natural, and matter-of-fact manner when the father is ready is more likely to foster acceptance by the child. If possible, discuss or rehearse what will be said to children with someone who has already experienced a similar disclosure.

7. *Inform the children that relationships with them will not change as a result of disclosure.* Disclosure will, however, allow the father to be more honest. Children may need reassurance that the father is the same person as he was before. Younger children may need reassurance that the father will still be their father.

8. *Be prepared for questions.* Some questions and possible answers are:

   • *Why are you telling me this?* Because my personal life is important, and I want to share it with you. I am not ashamed of being homosexual, and you shouldn't be ashamed of me either.

   • *What does being gay mean?* It means being attracted to

other men so much so that you might fall in love with a man and express your love physically and sexually.

- *What makes a person gay?* No one knows although there are a lot of theories. (This question may be a child's way of asking if he or she also will be gay.)
- *Will I be gay, too?* You won't be gay just because I'm gay. It's not contagious, and it doesn't appear to be hereditary. You will be whatever you're going to be.
- *Don't you like women?* (The child might be asking, "Don't you like Mom?" or "Do you hate Mom?" If this question is asked by a daughter it also may mean, "Don't you like me?" or "Do you hate me?") I do like women but I'm not physically (or sexually) and romantically attracted to them like I am to men.
- *What should I tell my friends about it?* A lot of people just don't understand so it might be best to keep it in the family. You can discuss it with me any time you want. If you want to tell a close friend, go ahead and try it out. But the friend might not be accepting, and he or she might tell others. You should be prepared for those possibilities. If you do tell somebody, let me know how it turns out.

While these guidelines are rather general in nature, it is suggested that factors within the family such as the health status of children and other family members are crucial in considering the timing of disclosure.

IMPLICATIONS FOR PRACTITIONERS

Implications for Educators

Much ignorance regarding homosexuality is due to the propagation of myths. It is important for educators in many disciplines and at all educational levels to dispel myths, impart facts, and promote values clarification. Myths applying to homosexuals include the notions that gay males are sexually attracted to children, that because they do not reproduce biologically they "recruit" children into homosexuality, and that they are likely to sexually molest children.

These myths have no basis in fact. Child molestation, for example, primarily is known to be perpetuated by heterosexual rather than homosexual men (Geiser, 1979). Another myth is that children of gays will also become gay. Homosexuality is not contagious nor inherited. Indeed, if heterosexual parenting is insufficient to ensure that children will also be heterosexual, then there is no reason to conclude that children of homosexuals also will be gay. However, because approximately 10 percent of the United States population is gay (Kinsey, Pomeroy, & Martin, 1948), it is likely that some children of homosexual parents also will be gay. If there is any substance to the psychoanalytically held notion that a weak or absent father contributes to the development of children's homosexuality (especially that of a son) and that warm, accessible, nurturing fathers promote the development of masculinity in sons (Lamb, 1981), then it follows that the loving attention of a gay father also should contribute to heterosexuality of their children.

Implications for Family Law Professionals

There is no evidence that being gay is a liability as far as parenting ability is concerned. In issues of child custody and visitation, judges commonly assume that gay fathers are less adequate as parents and role models than are heterosexual fathers. "Gay" seems to imply an inability to parent or of committing potential psychological harm to children. There is, however, no relationship between one's ability to parent and one's sexual orientation. The man's gay identity should be kept out of legal disputes relating to custody and visitation rights if possible as it has no bearing in this regard. When sexual orientation of a father does become an issue, it is often focused upon unduly to the exclusion of relevant concerns. Experts contend that it is not the sexual orientation of the parent that is of importance but rather other aspects of the situation such as the father's devotion to his children, his good sense of child management, his ethical standards, and the quality of home life he is able to provide for them. The courts often express concern with potential child molestation from either the father or his gay friends, that children also will become gay, that the home life is immoral, or that children may contract AIDS in this environment. This last concern about AIDS has special significance today. It is important here to stress that the transmission of AIDS is through intimate sexual contact, sharing intravenous drug equipment, or through contaminated blood products and not via the casual contact that occurs between a father and his children. All these myths need to be dispelled.

There is another concern. This is that the children of gay fathers will be embarrassed and stigmatized by their peers. If the father's homosexuality is known to the children's peers, it is likely that they will be teased since much of society is homophobic. Although society also is largely racist, minority children are not removed from their homes if they are harassed because of this. Likewise, many parents harbor religious and political views that are unpopular but no one suggests that their children live elsewhere because of exposure to these views. Despite society's bigotry, this does not justify the removal of children from the homes of parents who do not conform to majority points of view or behavior. Although living with a gay parent may create some conflict for children, this can be a strengthening experience. Moreover, the children in these homes may grow up to be more tolerant and understanding of differences between individuals than might otherwise be expected (Rivera, 1987).

Implications for Therapists

The myths about homosexuality previously mentioned need to be repudiated equally with counselors, especially those trained in the psychoanalytic tradition which considers homosexuality to be pathological.

It is extremely difficult to explain the incredibly agonizing pain that is often suffered by gay fathers and is frequently accompanied by suicidal ideation and occasionally by suicide attempts. The conflict between concern for wife, children, and home, and the desire to maintain a socially acceptable lifestyle, against the backdrop of the (almost) uncontrollable sexual drive for men and the behavior that frequently accompanies it, culminates in intense self-disgust, self-degradation, loneliness, and despair—feelings that are more than many of these men think they can bear. Therefore, it is imperative that

> they receive assistance from understanding, sympathetic, and
> . . . skilled therapists. (Bozett, 1985, p. 345)

Homophobic therapists should not accept clients whose gay identity is an issue. In addition to individual therapy, it is wise to counsel gay fathers to seek peer support from other gay fathers. In many cities in the United States, Canada, and several other foreign countries, there are local chapters of the *Gay and Lesbian Parents Coalition International*[1] which can provide assistance in this regard. Aloneness often makes gay fathers' lives very difficult. Because there is little or no recognition for paternity by gays in general, the nurturing support gained from participation in gay parent support groups may be crucial. It may be the only therapy needed or it may be a significant adjunct to psychotherapy. Moreover, therapists often need to assist gay fathers in realizing that their homosexuality is not the source of their stress but rather the source lies with society's attitudes toward homosexuality. Elevating these men's self-concepts and self-esteem also is basic to solving many of their other problems.

PSYCHOLOGICAL FATHERS: A PARENTHETICAL NOTE

In addition to what has been discussed, there are ramifications for what Giveans and Robinson (1985) refer to as "psychological fathers." These are men who assume temporary caretaking roles such as nurses, day care workers, preschool teachers, and others. There may be hesitancy on the part of some individuals or institutions to employ men in these roles, fearing that if they are gay that the children in their care may be at risk. Unfortunately, within the recent past, there have been several well publicized cases in the media of child molestation by male caretakers in day care centers. Even so, it is unlikely that most men in these positions are gay and, if they are gay, it is even more unlikely that they are attracted to young children. It has already been pointed out that it is rare for a gay man to be a pedophile. Of course, it behooves service agencies to screen applicants in order to avoid these problems and the multiple sequelae that result. However, it is equally crucial *not* to screen out men who are gay from these positions. Gay men often possess a unique nurturing sensitivity that is a highly desirable attribute for those who serve in caretaking roles and who also are models of masculinity for children.

SUGGESTIONS FOR FURTHER RESEARCH

The most urgent need is for longitudinal study of gay father families. What is it like for children to grow and develop within this family form? The advantages and disadvantages as well as the joys and sorrows that occur in association with the passage of time in these families needs to be discovered. This research should be conducted by academicians from various disciplines and should employ psychological measurements in addition to sociological and ethnographic data. Such studies also could identify differential effects of this family form on sons and daughters as well as on their psychological development beyond puberty. Appropriate comparison groups using lesbian mother families and heterosexual family units could be employed in order to ascertain similarities and differences as well as strengths and weaknesses of each. In addition, all of the research to date has been conducted with white, middle- to upper-class, highly educated urban samples. Research is needed using subjects who vary from these demographic characteristics and approximate more closely the characteristics of the general population. Furthermore, little is known about variations of the gay father family such as those that function as stepfamilies. It is important to conduct research and to publish findings so that practitioners in various disciplines can begin to understand the individual members of these families as well as the families as systematic units so they can base their practice on research rather than on hunch, bias, or stereotype. For additional suggestions for further research see Bozett (1985, 1987a, b).

CONCLUSION

Gay men marry and become fathers for a variety of reasons. Their fate has been eloquently described by Cory (1951):

The [gay] married man is a part of no world at all, precisely because he partakes of two disparate ones. Living in two societies that commingle without intermingling, he seeks to belong to both and therefore falls short of full integration in either. Wherever he turns, he is a minority—not only in the world at large but even in his small world of escape. (p. 20)

Although research is limited, it appears that gay fathers are at least equal to heterosexual fathers in the quality of their parenting. Moreover, gay fathers who have disclosed their homosexuality to their children appear to have a closer relationship with them than would normally be expected between father and child in relationships where disclosure has not occurred. It is important to understand that although the losses may be great by coming out to family and friends, the psychological health of gay fathers generally improves after doing so (Miller, 1986). The authors recommend disclosure of homosexuality to one's children if the father is comfortable with defining himself as gay and if other circumstances are favorable. Guidelines for disclosure have been provided.

Educators, social workers, lawyers and judges, and counselors in various disciplines need to be sufficiently informed about homosexuality so that myth is separated from fact. Only if this is the case will gay fathers and their families be treated objectively and fairly by representatives of our social institutions.

NOTE

1. The address of the Gay and Lesbian Parents Coalition International is P.O. Box 50360, Washington, D. C. 20004.

REFERENCES

Bell, A., & Weinberg, M. S. (1978). *Homosexualities: A study of diversity among men and women.* New York: Simon & Schuster.

Bigner, J., & Jacobsen, R. B. (1989a). The value of children for gay versus nongay fathers. *Journal of Homosexuality, 18,* 163-172.

Bigner, J., & Jacobsen, R. B. (1989b). Parenting behaviors of homosexual and heterosexual fathers. *Journal of Homosexuality, 18,* 173-186.

Bozett, F. W. (1980). Gay fathers: How and why they disclose their homosexuality to their children. *Family Relations, 29,* 173-179.

Bozett, F. W. (1981a). Gay fathers: Evolution of the gay father identity. *American Journal of Orthopsychiatry, 51,* 552-559.

Bozett, F. W. (1981b). Gay fathers: Identity conflict resolution through integrative sanctioning. *Alternative Lifestyles, 4,* 90-107.

Bozett, F. W. (1982). Heterogeneous couples in heterosexual marriages: Gay men and straight women. *Journal of Marital and Family Therapy, 8,* 81-99.

Bozett, F. W. (1984). Parenting concerns of gay fathers. *Topics in Clinical Nursing, 6,* 60-71.

Bozett, F. W. (1985). Gay men as fathers. In S. Hanson & F. W. Bozett (Eds.), *Dimensions of fatherhood* (pp. 327-335). Beverly Hills, CA: Sage.

Bozett, F. W. (1986). *Identity management: Social control of identity by children of gay fathers when they know their father is a homosexual.* Paper presented at the Seventh Biennial Eastern Nursing Research Conference, New Haven, CT.

Bozett, F. W. (1987a). Gay fathers. In F. W. Bozett (Ed.), *Gay and lesbian parents* (pp. 3-22). New York: Praeger.

Bozett, F. W. (1987b). Children of gay fathers. In F. W. Bozett (Ed.), *Gay and lesbians parents* (pp. 39-57). New York: Praeger.

Bozett, F. W. (1988). Social control of identity by children of gay fathers. *Western Journal of Nursing Research, 10,* 550-565.

Clark, D. (1979). Being a gay father. In B. Berzono & R. Leighton (Eds.), *Positively gay.* Millbrae, CA: Celestial Arts.

Cory, D. W. (1951). *The homosexual in America.* New York: Greenburg.

Fadiman, A. (1983). The double closet. *Life Magazine, 6,* 76-78; 80; 82-84; 86; 92-100.

Geiser, R. L. (1979). *Hidden victims: The sexual abuse of children.* Boston: Beacon.

Gibbs, J., & Martin, W. (1964). *Status integration and suicide: A sociological study.* Eugene, OR: University of Oregon Press.

Giveans, D. L., & Robinson, M. K. (1985). Fathers and the preschool-age child. In S. M. H. Hanson & F. W. Bozett (Eds.), *Dimensions of fatherhood* (pp. 115-140). Beverly Hills, CA: Sage.

Green, R. (1978). Sexual identity of 37 children raised by homosexual or transsexual parents. *American Journal of Psychiatry, 135,* 633-646.

Guttman, D. (1975). Parenthood: A key to the comparative study of the life cycle. In N. Datan & L. Ginsberg (Eds.), *Life-span developmental psychology: Normative life crises.* New York: Academic Press.

Hays, D., & Samuels, A. (1989). Heterosexual women's perceptions of their marriages to bisexual or homosexual men. *Journal of Homosexuality, 18,* 81-100.

Harris, M., & Turner, P. (1986). Gay and lesbian parents. *Journal of Homosexuality, 12,* 101-113.

Kinsey, A. C., Pomeroy, W. B., & Martin, C. E. (1948). *Sexual behavior in the human male.* Philadelphia: Saunders.

Maddox, B. (1982). Homosexual parents. *Psychology Today, 56*, 62-69.

Miller, B. (1978). Adult sexual resocialization: Adjustments toward a stigmatized identity. *Alternative Lifestyles, 1*, 207-234.

Miller, B. (1979a). Gay fathers and their children. *Family Coordinator, 28*, 544-552.

Miller, B. (1979b). Unpromised paternity: The lifestyles of gay fathers. In M. P. Levine (Ed.), *Gay men* (pp. 239-252). New York: Harper & Row.

Miller, B. (1986). Identity resocialization in moral careers of gay husbands and fathers. In A. Davis (Ed.), *Papers in honor of Gordon Hirabayashi* (pp. 197-216). Edmonton, Canada: University of Alberta Press.

Miller, B. (1987). Counseling gay husbands and fathers. In F. W. Bozett (Ed.), *Gay and lesbian parents* (pp. 175-187). New York: Praeger.

Pennington, S. B. (1987). Children of lesbian mothers. In F. W. Bozett (Ed.), *Gay and lesbian parents* (pp. 58-74). New York: Praeger.

Riddle, D. (1978). Relating to children: Gays as role models. *Journal of Social Issues, 34*, 38-58.

Rivera, R. R. (1987). Legal issues in gay and lesbian parenting. In F. W. Bozett (Ed.), *Gay and lesbian parenting* (pp. 199-227). New York: Praeger.

Robinson, B., & Skeen, P. (1982). Sex-role orientation of gay fathers versus gay nonfathers. *Perceptual and Motor Skills, 55*, 1055-1059.

Scallen, R. M. (1981). An investigation of paternal attitudes and behaviors in homosexual and heterosexual fathers. *Dissertation Abstracts International, 42*, 3809-B.

Schulenburg, J. (1985). *Gay parenting*. Garden City, NY: Doubleday.

Steckel, A. (1987). Psychosocial development of children of lesbian mothers. In F. W. Bozett (Ed.), *Gay and lesbian parents* (pp. 75-85). New York: Praeger.

Turner, P. H., Scadden, L., & Harris, M. B. (1985). Parenting in gay and lesbian families. Paper presented at the Future of Parenting Symposium, Chicago, Illinois.

Voeller, B., & Walters, J. (1978). Gay fathers. *Family Coordinator, 27*, 149-157.

Weinberg, G. (1973). *Society and the healthy homosexual*. Garden City, NY: Anchor Press/Doubleday.

Weinberg, M., & Williams, C. (1974). *Male homosexuals: Their problems and adaptations*. New York: Oxford University Press.

Wyers, N. L. (1987). Homosexuality in the family: Lesbian and gay spouses. *Social Work, 32(2)*, 143-148.

Children of Gay and Lesbian Parents

Julie Schwartz Gottman

SUMMARY. The purpose of this chapter is to review research literature concerning children of gay and lesbian parents. The review includes studies that compared children of lesbian mothers to children of heterosexual mothers on gender identity, gender role, sexual orientation, and varying aspects of psychological health and adjustment. Experiences and perceptions of children of gay fathers are also reviewed. The author's study found that adult-aged daughters of lesbian mothers did not significantly differ from adult daughters of heterosexual mothers on gender identity, gender role, sexual orientation, and social adjustment. Clinical and legal implications were drawn, and suggestions for future research were made.

INTRODUCTION

To many people, the terms "lesbian mother" and "gay father" are confusing and contradictory. It is commonly believed that children are only conceived by heterosexual couples. Homosexuals don't have children, since they relate sexually to members of only their own sex. Neither the premise nor conclusion is true. It is estimated that there are well over 1.5 million lesbian mothers and one million gay fathers in this country (Task Force on Sexuality, D.C. Chapter NOW, 1974; Schulenberg, 1985). At least six million children are estimated to have gay or lesbian parents (Schulenberg, 1985). Through modern methods of conception such as artificial insemination, these numbers are increasing (Pies, 1985).

This paper will explore several issues regarding children of lesbian and gay parents. Custody court disputes, research literature,

---

Julie Schwartz Gottman, PhD, currently works as a clinician and training consultant at the Seattle Professional Practice Institute, 555 116th Ave. N.E., Suite 255, Bellevue, WA 98004.

and the author's study will be reviewed. Judicial and clinical implications based on the research results will follow. Finally, suggestions will be offered for future research.

In the past, lesbian mothers and gay fathers hid their identities. If they acknowledged their sexual preference, they risked losing either their children or their lovers. During the last twenty years, however, times have changed. Increasing numbers of lesbians and gays have accepted and declared their sexuality. In addition, they have attempted to hold onto their children during court custody disputes. In turn, mental health and legal professionals have had to face social stereotypes about lesbians and gays and their abilities to parent.

Nowhere has this confrontation taken place more dramatically than in the judicial system. When parents divorce, the courts are commonly called on to settle custody disputes over the children. The best interest of the child is considered along with parental "fitness." When a parent is known to be gay or lesbian, the court frequently awards custody to either the other parent or a third party. In most of these cases the courts do not require evidence that the parent's homosexuality harms the child. It is often assumed.

Such cases are numerous. For example, in *Nadler v. Superior Court* (1967), the judge awarded custody to the father with weekly visits by the mother only in the presence of an adult third party. The judge stated, "We are dealing with a four-year-old child on the threshold of its development . . . just cannot take the chance that something untoward should happen to it." In *Townend v. Townend* (1975), custody was not awarded to a lesbian mother who lived with her lover, because the relationship was viewed by the judge to be "clearly to the neglect of supervision of the children." No explanation is given as to how the children were unsupervised. In *Koop v. Koop* (1980), child custody was awarded to the father. After the children ran away from him four times, custody was given to a half sister rather than to the mother. Again, the mother's lesbianism was assumed to be harmful. She finally won back custody five years later. Another set of children were placed in foster care, because, as the judge stated, "continuous existence of a homosexual relationship in the home where a minor is exposed to it involved the necessary likelihood of serious adjustment problems (*In re Tammy F.*, 1974).

The courts have also been concerned that children "might develop a propensity towards homosexuality themselves" (*Jacobson v. Jacobson*, 1981). They have claimed that homosexual practices are a crime, and "the devastating effect of that lifestyle upon children has been established" (*L. v. D.*, 1982). By whom it has been established was not made clear.

The most difficult cases involve mothers who engage in lesbian relationships in the home. In *In re Jane B.* (1976), a father won custody on remand after the children had lived with their mother for five years and after he discovered the mother's homosexuality. The court found that the lesbian relationship created an "improper environment for the child." The court severely restricted the mother's visitation rights. The child was prohibited from staying overnight with the mother, from being in her home when any homosexuals were present, and from being involved by the mother in any homosexual activities or publicities. No reasons relating to best interests of the child were given, and no evidence supported the conclusion that exposure to homosexuality would be detrimental to the child.

In sum, few courts have recognized the need to prove that a parent's homosexuality is harmful to their child. Custody may be challenged at any time and children taken away when parental homosexuality is discovered. Thus, most lesbian and gay parents live in constant fear of losing their children.

There is scant research on the children of gay and lesbian parents. However, what there is seems to contradict the above judicial decisions. This research along with a recent study by the author is next reviewed.

REVIEW OF THE LITERATURE

Children of Lesbian Mothers

A number of studies have examined variables in children of lesbian mothers. The variables have included gender identity, gender role, sexual orientation, self-concept, self-esteem, and social adjustment.

First, a word on gender identity and gender role. The two terms are often muddied together. Here, the terms are defined as follows:

Gender identity refers to the individual's experience of self as basically male or female. Gender role refers to behaviors and attitudes that society positively sanctions for members of one sex and negatively sanctions for members of the opposite sex (Shively & De Cecco, 1977; Spence & Helmreich, 1978). Gender identity confusion is often inferred from gender role behavior. Such inferences neglect the fact that identity and behavior are not the same, although they may be imperfectly correlated. Cognitive processes mediate and distinguish self-identity from behavior.

With these distinctions in mind, most of the studies of gender identity actually measured gender role. The measures used included toy preferences, sex-typed play activities, TV program choices, peer relationship choices, and garment preferences. These measures have limited reliability and validity. The children studied ranged from 3 to 17 years old. A control group of children of heterosexual women was usually included. One study also included a group of children of transsexual parents (Green, 1978).

These studies all reported no significant differences on gender role measures between children of lesbian mothers and control group children (Golombok, Spencer, & Rutter, 1983; Green, 1978; Hoeffer, 1981; Kirkpatrick, Smith, & Roy, 1981; Mandel & Hodvedt, 1980).

Another study compared variables in eleven children raised by lesbian couples and eleven children raised by heterosexual couples. The children were three and four years old. The measures included a Q Sort administered to parents and teachers, a projective Structured Doll Technique interview with the child, and a structured parent interview. Again, no significant differences were found in gender role (Steckel, 1985). Two other studies compared groups on the Bem Sex Role Inventory. No significant differences were found in group scores (Mandel & Hotvedt, 1980; Rees, 1979).

Two investigations of gender identity employed a projective measure, the Draw-A-Person Test. The results again indicated no significant differences between groups of children of lesbian mothers and control groups (Green, 1978; Kirkpatrick et al., 1981).

Methodological flaws limit implications of the above findings. None of the studies presented statistical analyses, nor did they control for the presence of a male role model in the home. Gender role and gender identity were often not differentiated. The desire to appear socially acceptable was also not accounted for. In addition, subject ages were limited, with the majority of subjects studied under 12 years old. Taking these flaws into account, the findings suggest that compared to children of heterosexual women, children of lesbian women exhibit socially sanctioned sex-typed behavior. Daughters tend to express feminine gender role and sons masculine gender role. Also, daughters and sons appear to respectively possess feminine and masculine unconscious gender identity.

Studies of sexual orientation in children of lesbians mothers are sparse given the sample age limits. In one study where 16 subjects had an average age of 22 years old, about 60% of the subjects reported at some time questioning their sexual identity. However, the study employed no control group, so it is not known whether or not this response typified a developmental issue common to all children. Seventy-six percent of the sample identified themselves as heterosexual but perceived sexual orientation as fluid, that is, it could shift in the future (Paul, 1985).

In sum, the effects of parental sexual orientation on children's sexual orientation remain unclear. The study reported later in this chapter attempts to shed light on this issue.

A small number of studies have also explored social adjustment in children of lesbian mothers. They are limited in their scope but provide preliminary findings.

Golombok et al. (1983) compared 37 children of lesbian mothers with 38 children of heterosexual mothers. Parents and teachers evaluated the children's emotional and social behaviors. The measures used had established reliability and validity. No significant differences between groups were found on the measures. No statistical analyses were presented, so the methodology cannot be analyzed.

Kirkpatrick et al. (1981) conducted a more controlled study. They compared 20 children of lesbian mothers to a comparison group of children of single heterosexual mothers on standard projective measures of adjustment, the WISC (Wechsler Intelligence Scales for Children), and on structured interviews. The children ranged in age from 5 to 12 years. Variables controlled included socioeconomic status of the mothers, age and birth order of the children, and length of absence from the home of the fathers or other adult males. The groups of sons and daughters did not differ significantly on any social adjustment measures. However, over half the sample in both groups demonstrated moderate or severe disturbance. Earlier in the study, both lesbian and heterosexual mothers had reported severe marital discord prior to and during their divorces. Thus, the authors reasoned that they were observing maladjustment typical in children of divorce.

Mandel and Hotvedt (1980) stated similar findings. They compared children of lesbian and heterosexual mothers on the Bene-Anthony Family Relations Test and a structured interview. The children were 3 to 11 years old. No significant differences appeared between the groups on either measure. However, the children exhibited problems often seen in children of divorce.

One other study focused on self-concept. Puryear (1983) compared 15 children of lesbian mothers and 15 children of heterosexual mothers on the Piers-Harris Children's Self-Concept scale and on kinetic family drawings. The children were 6 to 12 years old. No major differences in self-concept and family view were found between the two groups. Children in both groups were more affected by father's availability than mother's sexual orientation.

Steckel (1985) studied independence, ego functions, and object relations in 22 three- and four-year-old children of lesbian and heterosexual mothers. All the lesbian mothers of the children had female lovers living in the home, and all the heterosexual mothers had either male lovers or a husband living in the home. A structured parent interview, a Q-Sort administered to parents and teachers, and a projective Structured Doll Technique interview with children were used. No significant differences were found between the groups. However, children of heterosexual mothers as perceived by their mothers and teachers tended to be more domineering, more actively self-assertive, and more involved in power struggles. The author suggested that the differences could be related to the sex of the co-parent and not to the sexual orientation of the mother.

Rees (1979) compared 12 children of lesbian mothers to 12 children of heterosexual mothers. The children ranged in age from 10 to 20 years, yielding small numbers per age level. Kohlberg's Moral Dilemmas Test and Rotter's Locus of Control Test were administered. No significant differences were found between group scores.

Huggins (1986) measured self-esteem in 36 adolescent children, 18 with heterosexual mothers and 18 with homosexual mothers. The Coopersmith Self-Esteem Inventory was used. It has adequate reliability and validity. A number of extraneous variables were controlled. There were no significant differences found on self-esteem scores between groups. In children of lesbian mothers, those with highest self-esteem also reported positive feelings about their mothers' lesbianism. Their mothers had also had long-term lovers in the home.

Relatively small sample numbers and lack of statistical analyses limit the conclusions of the above studies. However, the findings tentatively suggest that children of lesbian mothers do not demonstrate greater social maladjustment than children of heterosexual mothers.

Children of Gay Fathers

Most notable about studies of children of gay fathers is their scarcity. Despite estimates that these children may number in the millions, only one study focuses on them while two others include them in broader investigations. This gap in the literature may reflect a two-fold prejudice against gay fathers. First, fathers are often relegated to the shadows when compared to mothers in parental importance. Second, gay men are often stereotyped as anti-family. Taken together, gay fathering is perceived as an anomaly. In reality, it is estimated that there are several million children of gay fathers in this country (Bozett, 1987).

Bozett (1980, 1987, 1988) has conducted the most thorough research on children of gay fathers. He based his results on interviews of 19 children. Theoretical constructs issued out of the data rather than prior to collecting it. The subjects were 13 females and 6 males ranging in age from 14 to 35. Two of the males identified themselves as gay, and one female reported that she was bisexual. The remainder stated that they were heterosexual.

The children first affirmed their father positively as a parent figure. Many considered him a friend, confidante, and advisor. However, heterosexual children expressed concern that they might be seen as gay if their father's homosexuality was perceived by others.

Thus, they employed social control behavior of their fathers, themselves, and others to mitigate against being seen as gay.

Children used three social control strategies. First, in "boundary control," children attempted to limit father's expression of his homosexuality. They also limited their own behavior with father and others' contact with father. This strategy helped them avoid embarrassment due to father's "differentness."

Secondly, children might disclose to a rare few people that father was gay. Sometimes children told no one, or they deceptively referred to father's lover as a housemate or uncle. This again ensured that they wouldn't be seen as gay and thus become social pariahs.

Finally, children disclosed to a larger number of people in order to "prepare" them to meet father. This might have been one way that gay children also disclosed their own identity.

The use of control strategies depended on four influential factors: mutuality, obtrusiveness, situational and maturational factors. Mutuality referred to how much the child identified with the father. Obtrusiveness referred to how overt the child perceived his father's homosexuality to be. Situational factors included varying living arrangements, and maturational factors related to the child's age.

Bozett concluded the study with hypotheses that related the child's attitudes and social control strategies to both the factors listed above and the child's perceptions of society as homophobic.

This study contributes to the literature the first view of children's methods of coping with parental homosexuality, given their need to socially survive in a homophobic culture. However, since it lacked the rudiments of a more controlled study, its findings are preliminary. Control groups, operationalized concepts and statistical analyses were not included. Thus, further research would be needed to test the author's hypotheses.

Several other studies include children of gay fathers in their samples. Miller (1979) interviewed gay fathers about their children. Among 27 daughters and 21 sons, fathers reported that one son and three daughters were gay. Bozett (1981a, b) also interviewed fathers who said that of their 25 children overall, none were gay (although not all children were old enough to have their sexual orientation assessed). To encourage traditional gender role development, fathers reported that they encouraged play with sex-typed toys (Harris & Turner, 1986).

In the above studies, investigators did not directly observe children. They also did not employ control groups, operationalize concepts, nor perform statistical analyses. Thus, their contributions must be considered preliminary and indicative of trends needing further research.

Only one study attempted a statistical approach. Paul (1986) investigated experiences and perceptions in 16 children with a gay or bisexual father, two of whom also had a lesbian mother. Again the findings were limited by a lack of a control group and small sample size.

Several findings were of interest. First, the child's initial reactions to news of father's homosexuality or bisexuality were age-dependent. Positive responses abruptly declined in number when children were informed of father's homosexuality in their teens as opposed to earlier. When informed in post-teen years, positive responses again increased. Thus, a trough-like effect emerged, signifying adolescence as the most difficult time for children to initially deal with paternal homosexuality. Children might have also undergone discomfort during adolescence despite being informed earlier. This was not surprising, given that adolescence was a time of high peer affiliation needs and individual sexual identity development. What was surprising was that children who learned of their father's homosexuality as teens were apt to report feeling closer to their gay or bisexual father. It appeared that an initial crisis could engender growth of the parent-child relationship.

Closeness to the gay or bisexual father was also positively related to self-esteem and negatively related to masculinity on the Bem Sex Role Inventory. These correlations were stronger for sons than daughters. However, quality of parent-child interactions more strongly influenced all children's reported closeness to their parent.

Most of the children sampled went through a period when they questioned their sexuality. This typifies most adolescents, however, their concerns gain in significance, since others might have expected that they would be homosexual or bisexual. Respondents reported a greater openness to alternative lifestyles, although most identified themselves as heterosexual.

A final issue for the children studied was the pull between peer relationships and family loyalties. Over half the sample at some time feared peer ostracism. They also felt pressured to exercise caution in disclosing information about their father's lifestyle. They feared not only for themselves but also for their parent, especially when a father's child custody or job security could be endangered by a poorly timed disclosure. Most respondents chose friends that fit into the family, rather than attempting to make their family fit their friends.

This study again indicated that father-child relationships did not necessarily engender pathology when father was gay or bisexual. Children appeared to experience effects of father's homosexuality when they questioned their own sexuality and strategized about peer and family relationships. It should be noted that when conflicts existed for these children, they often resulted from the child's perception of society as homophobic. The child was then compelled to protect his or her own budding identity development from homophobic stereotypes operating in the culture. The study thus affirmed that the problem wasn't with the parent, it was with the culture. Again, the study lacked a control group and employed only a small number of subjects. However, its statistical analyses and reliable measures moved the literature towards a more scientific look at the influence of paternal homosexuality on children.

SUMMARY

In general, none of the above studies on children of lesbian mothers and gay fathers reported negative effects on children relative to their parent's sexual orientation. Children did not appear deviant in gender identity, sexual orientation, or social adjustment. Issues that emerged during their upbringing related more to society's rejection of homosexuality than to poor parent-child relationships. Most social adjustment problems occurred also in control groups, the common denominator being a history of divorce in the family.

There are limits to the above findings. Control groups, valid and reliable measures, and larger sample sizes are often missing. Almost all the studies focused on younger children. Unfortunately, it is difficult to predict sexual orientation, gender identity, and social adjustment in children of homosexual parents without looking at later adult development.

The remainder of this section describes a study conducted by the author (Schwartz, 1985). It attempted to address some of the above listed weaknesses in the literature. The objective of the study was to determine if gender identity, gender role, sexual orientation, and social adjustment differed in adult-aged daughters depending on their mothers' sexual orientation.

Role modeling theory underlay most of the hypotheses studied. Past studies have suggested that children model after their parents (Bandura & Huston, 1961; Hetherington & Frankie, 1967; Kagan, 1964; Lynn, 1969; Sears, 1957). In addition, congruence between the genders of model and observer strengthens the role modeling process (Hetherington & Frankie, 1967; Maccoby & Wilson, 1957). Thus, it was expected that daughters would model after their mothers.

The research on lesbian gender identity and gender role indicates greater or comparable masculinity and comparable femininity in lesbian women compared to hetersexual women (Adelman, 1977; Bell & Weinberg, 1978; Heilbrun & Thompson, 1977; Saghir & Robins, 1973; Ward, 1974). Again, based on role modeling theory, it was hypothesized that daughters of lesbian mothers would achieve higher masculinity and/or androgyny scores than daughters of heterosexual mothers. It was not expected that femininity scores would differ significantly between the groups.

Empirical and theoretical work by Storms (1980, 1981) formed the basis for studying sexual orientation. Storms suggested that patterns of sex drive development and social bonding as opposed to role modeling shape an individual's sexual orientation. Since it was not likely that either sex drive onset or patterns of social bonding significantly differed between the groups, it was also not expected that sexual orientation would significantly differ between them.

Studies demonstrating comparable social adjustment in heterosexual and lesbian women plus role modeling theory informed the hypotheses regarding social adjustment (Freedman, 1971; Mucklow & Phelan, 1979; Siegelman, 1972; Spence & Helmreich, 1978). It was hypothesized that daughters of lesbian mothers would achieve comparable or significantly higher social adjustment scores than daughters of heterosexual mothers.

In the study, adult-aged daughters of divorced lesbian mothers were compared to adult-aged daughters of divorced heterosexual mothers. All daughters of lesbian mothers had been raised with a lesbian co-parent in the home at some time during their upbringing. To control for the presence of a male role model in the home, two control groups were used. One included daughters of heterosexual divorced mothers who had remated (lived with a man or remarried while their daughter lived at home). The other included daughters of heterosexual divorced mothers who had not remated. There were 35 subjects in each group.

A number of extraneous variables were measured and controlled for using a demographic questionnaire. They included number and ages of siblings, subject's age when father left the home and when mother began dating again, daughter's age when lovers lived in the home, duration and frequency of visits between daughter and father, the quality of those visits, and whether or not the daughter had a relationship with a male at least 10 years older than she that she considered influential on her. Seven other marital, educational, and socioeconomic variables of both mother and daughter were also measured. Statistically controlling for these variables allowed a safer assumption that significant differences between the groups of daughters were due to the sexual orientation of their mothers.

The subjects ranged in age from 18 to 44 with a mean age of 24. The average educational level was two years of college. Fathers' visits numbered between 0 and 100 per year with an average of 21 per year. Subject ages when father left the home ranged from 5 to 9. On these and the other variables, there were no significant differences between groups, with one exception. Daughters of heterosexual remated mothers had significantly more older brothers than daughters of lesbian or non-remated mothers. This difference was statistically entered into later analyses.

Four variables were measured: gender identity, gender role, sexual orientation, and social adjustment. The Personal Attributes Questionnaire was used to measure the first two variables. It has adequate reliability and validity. The Masculinity and Femininity scales measured gender identity. Taken together, they allowed for a measure of androgyny. A bipolar Masculinity-Femininity scale measured gender role. The Sexual Orientation Method was used to measure sexual orientation. It is the only measure of sexual orientation with adequate reliability and validity. Separate Homosexuality and Heterosexuality Scales permitted measurement of bisexuality. To measure social adjustment, the California Psychological Inventory was employed with 18 scales assessing different aspects of adjustment. Four were focused on in statistical analyses: The scales of Dominance, Self-Acceptance, Well-Being, and Flexibility. Subjects received questionnaires in an individual meeting with the author, then returned them by mail when completed. There was a 97% return rate.

Data were analyzed using a number of statistical techniques. First, scores on the Personal Attributes Questionnaire gender identity scales did not differ significantly between groups as was hypothesized. Scores on the gender role scale did differ between groups but only in relation to the number of older brothers in the home. There was a trend for daughters with older brothers to score higher on masculine gender role. With effects of having an older brother partialled out, no significant differences in gender role were found between groups.

The groups also did not differ significantly in sexual orientation. This had been hypothesized. Approximately 74% of all three groups scored in the heterosexual range. Of the remaining 24% who scored high on the homosexuality scale, one-third of these also scored high on the heterosexuality scale, indicating bisexuality.

On all but the Well-Being scale, subject scores did not differ significantly between groups. Scores on Dominance, Flexibility, and Self-Acceptance all fell within the standardized normal range. These scores indicated that the three groups did not differ significantly in leadership ability, self-reliance, interpersonal flexibility, and self-confidence. Scores on the Well-Being scale varied again in relation to the presence or absence of older brothers in the home. The Well-Being scale measures the individual's sense of feeling secure in the world and in relationships. Higher scorers tend to minimize worries and complaints and to feel free of doubts and disillusionment. Lower scorers express awkwardness, cautiousness and apathy. Daughters of heterosexual remated mothers scored higher when they had older brothers, while daughters of lesbian mothers scored lower. However, with or without brothers, daughters of lesbian mothers tended to score highest and daughters of heterosexual non-remated mothers scored lowest when group comparisons were made. Scores of daughters of heterosexual remated mothers resembled those of daughters of lesbian mothers. It was conjectured that intimacy modeled in the home during a daughter's upbringing benefited her sense of security and well-being, regardless of the sex of the mother's partner. Scores on the remaining 14 scales of social adjustment did not significantly vary between groups.

In sum, this study found no evidence to suggest that daughters of lesbian mothers become homosexual themselves. The majority of daughters scored in the heterosexual range. In gender identity, daughters of lesbian mothers achieved scores for femininity and masculinity that closely resembled standard population norms. Finally, daughters of lesbian mothers achieved social adjustment scores that were within normal ranges and did not significantly differ from scores of the other two groups.

These findings are preliminary given their limitations. Subjects were self-selected and most came from urban centers in California. Mothers were asked to facilitate contacts with about one-third of the group of daughters of lesbian mothers. Parallel recruitment methods were not used with daughters of heterosexual mothers. It is also doubtful that the most "closeted" daughters of lesbian mothers volunteered for this study, thus the sample may have been biased towards more healthy subjects. Although a number of extraneous variables were controlled for, many were not, including parental alcoholism, conflict in the home prior to divorce, birth order, and other factors. In addition, all of the daughters' mothers had been heterosexual during the daughters' earliest years, thus the effects of mothers' homosexual orientation were not exclusively represented. There were also limits in the measures used. The Sexual Orientation Method measures fantasy, not behavior. Thus the results were not an assured representation of sexual orientation behavior.

Since the above factors limit the findings, no generalizations should be made beyond these limits. However, the findings provide a piece of evidence to suggest that mothers' lesbianism does not harm daughters' development in sexual orientation, gender identity, gender role, or social adjustment. Since the lesbian mothers lived with partners during daughters' upbringing, the findings also suggest that a homosexual relationship in the home may not be detrimental to daughters. Further study would be needed for confirmation.

The following outlines legal and clinical implications of the above studies reviewed. Suggestions are made for future research.

LEGAL IMPLICATIONS

Child custody courts often predict that a parent's homosexuality may harm a child's development if the child is allowed to remain with the parent. None of the above studies confirm this prediction. On the contrary, children of lesbian mothers and gay fathers appear to be normal in gender identity, gender role, sexual orientation, and social adjustment. Parental homosexuality does not appear to directly or indirectly harm the child. Children may have issues to contend with concerning how society perceives them when a parent's homosexuality is revealed. However, it appears that children develop strategies to protect themselves when necessary. Judicial courts may want to consider these findings when resolving a custody dispute involving a homosexual parent.

CLINICAL IMPLICATIONS

The above findings support the conclusion that children do not demonstrate pathology related to their parents' homosexual orientation. In other words, parental homosexuality does not in itself signal pathology in the family or in the child. However, there appear to be issues that the clinician should be sensitive to in children of gay and lesbian parents.

The time and manner in which parents disclose their homosexuality to children appears to be important. Too often children discover their parent's homosexuality during divorce custody disputes. Thus, they are doubly traumatized. When parents disclose their orientation later or deny it earlier, the children may have problems trusting the parent (Pennington, 1987).

Adolescents seem the hardest hit by disclosure (Paul, 1985). Clinicians at this time might help the family weather the transition. Children would not be expected to accept the parent's sexual orientation, but they would be expected to respect it. Children might also experience resentment or guilt for love/hating the parent and would need support in resolving their feelings (Pennington, 1987).

The effects of homophobia in peers and others might be another concern for clinicians working with families. Clinicians might need to support parents in being sensitive to their children's self-protective needs. References to lovers as aunts or uncles would need to be understood. Parents might also be asked to leave lovers at home when attending special occasions with their children. It would be important that the family view the children's needs as products of a homophobic culture and not examples of the children's aversion to the parent or lover.

The children would probably do best if the parent was secure in both his or her sexual identity and parental role. The family would probably benefit as well from having a strong support system that included other lesbian and gay parented families (Pennington, 1987). Clinicians might be aware that parental aloneness could predispose the child to difficulties. In these cases, formation of support systems could be encouraged.

In sum, clinicians should not consider a child disturbed solely based on the parent's sexual orientation. However, when needed clinicians could aid the child and family to relate openly and compassionately to one another given the implications of homosexuality in a homophobic culture.

SUGGESTIONS FOR FUTURE RESEARCH

The above studies are preliminary. Refinement in subject sampling, methodology, and instrumentation could deepen an understanding of the effects of gay and lesbian parenting on children. Subject sampling methods need improvement with matching of samples and control groups on more extraneous variables. More objective studies using valid and reliable measures and statistical techniques are needed to confirm hypotheses. So few of the above studies used quantitative techniques that the field is wide open for more operationalized and quantified research.

There are also many more questions to be answered. Does homosexuality in fathers affect personality variables in children? Is social adjustment affected in the long run, and if so, does it matter whether children are male or female? How about sexual orientation in later life? Does parental homosexuality affect cognitive belief systems, social attitudes, or intrapsychological processes in children? Would peer support groups composed of children of lesbian and gay parents help children cope with feeling different, especially after initial parental disclosure? These are only a few of the questions open to investigation.

New methods of conception are also leading to a new arena of questions. Do children conceived by artificial insemination and raised from birth by homosexual parents differ from children of homosexual parents who are born into a heterosexual family? Are there differences in the issues faced by children raised by two gay men compared to those of children raised by two lesbian women? Do the characteristics of these children differ? The questions are numerous and potentially encompass the full range of child development.

To study the children resulting from artificial insemination and raised by either lesbian, gay, or heterosexual couples, a longitudinal study might be used. Social adjustment measures, parent interviews, and teacher interviews given every two years could provide important data on the comparability of development in the three groups.

To study the benefits of a support group during adolescence, children of lesbian and/or gay parents could be divided into two groups. One group could be provided with a peer support group for children of gay parents with the other group being used as a control. Social adjustment measures could be employed in both groups to explore the effects of organized peer support on social adjustment.

In sum, knowledge about children of gay and lesbian parents is in its seed state. Much could be learned with methodologically sound research that explores personality, cognitions, behaviors, and developmental issues in this increasingly present population.

REFERENCES

Adelman, M. R. (1977). A comparison of professionally employed lesbians and heterosexual women on the MMPI. *Archives of Sexual Behavior, 6* (3), 193-201.

Bandura, A., & Huston, A. C. (1961). Identification as a process of incidental learning. *Journal of Abnormal and Social Psychology, 63,* 311-318.

Bell, A. P., & Weinberg, M. S. (1978). *Homosexualities: A study of diversity among men and women.* New York: Simon and Schuster.

Bozett, F. W. (1980). How and why gay fathers disclose their homosexuality to their children. *Family Relations, 29,* 173-179.

Bozett, F. W. (1981a). Gay fathers: Evolution of the gay-father identity. *American Journal of Orthopsychiatry, 51,* 552-559.

Bozett, F. W. (1981b). Gay fathers: Identity conflict resolution through integrative sanctioning. *Alternative Lifestyles, 4,* 90-107.

Bozett, F. W. (1987). Children of gay fathers. In F. W. Bozett (Ed.), *Gay and lesbian parents.* New York: Praeger.

Freedman, M. (1971). *Homosexuality and psychological functioning.* CA: Brooks/Cole.

Golombok, S., Spencer, A., & Rutter, M. (1983). Children in lesbian and single-parent households: Psychosexual and psychiatric appraisal. *Journal of Child Psychology and Psychiatry, 24* (4), 551-572.

Green, R. (1978). Sexual identity of 37 children raised by homosexual and transsexual parents. *American Journal of Psychiatry, 135,* 692-697.

Harris, M. D., & Turner, P. H. (1986). Gay and lesbian parents. *Journal of Homosexuality, 12,* 101-113.

Hetherington, E. M., & Frankie, G. (1967). Effects of parental dominance, warmth, and conflict on imitation in children. *Journal of Personality and Social Psychology, 6,* 119-125.

Heilbrun, A. B., & Thompson, N. L. (1977). Sex-role identity and male and female homosexuality. *Sex Roles, 3,* 65-79.

Hoeffer, B. (1981). Children's acquisition of sex role behavior in lesbian mother families. *American Journal of Orthopsychiatry, 51,* 536-544.

Hotvedt, M. E., & Mandel, J. B. (1982). Children of lesbian mothers. In W. Paul, J. D. Weinrich, J. D. Gonsiorek, & M. E. Hotvedt (Eds.), *Homosexuality: Social, psychological and biological issues.* Beverly Hills, CA: Sage.

Huggins, S. L. (in press). A comparative study of self-esteem of adolescent children of divorced lesbian mothers and divorced heterosexual mothers. *Journal of Homosexuality, 17* (3/4).

In re Jane B., 85 Misc. 2d 515, 380 N.Y. Supp. 2d 848 (Sup. Ct. 1976).

In re Tammy, F., 1 Civil No. 32648 (California lst Appelate District, Division 2, Aug. 21, 1973), reported in *Custody and Homosexual Parents, 2, Women's Rights Legal Report 21,* 1974.

Jacobson v. Jacobson, FLR 8:11, 2149, North Dakota, Dec. 30,1981.

Kagan, J. (1964). Acquisition and significance of sex typing and sex-role identity.

In M. L. Hoffman & L. W. Hoffman (Eds.), *Review of child development research. Vol. 2.* New York: Russell-Sage.

Kirkpatrick, M., Smith, C., & Roy, R. (1981). Lesbian mothers and their children: A comparative survey. *American Journal of Orthopsychiatry*, 5 (13), 545-551.

Koop v. Koop, in Note, "Custody-Lesbian Mothers in the Courts." *16 Gonzaga Law Review*, 147 (1980).

Lynn, D. B. (1962). Sex role and parental identification. *Child Development*, 33, 555-564.

L. v. D., 630 S.W. 2d 240 (Mo. Ct. App. 1982).

Maccoby, E. E., & Wilson, W. C. (1957). Identification and observational learning from films. *Journal of Abnormal and Social Psychology*, 55, 76-87.

Mandel, J., Hotvedt, M., & Green, R. (1979). *The lesbian parent: Comparison of heterosexual and homosexual mothers and children.* Paper presented at meetings of the American Psychological Association, New York.

Miller, B. (1979). Gay fathers and their children. *Family Coordinator*, 28, 544-552.

Mucklow, B. M., & Phelan, G. K. (1979). Lesbian and traditional mothers' responses to child behavior and self concept. *Psychological Reports*, 44 (3), 880-882.

Nadler v. Nadler, Civ. No. 177331, Sup. Ct. Cal. (1967).

Paul, J. P. (1986). *Growing up with a gay, lesbian or bisexual parent: An exploratory study of experiences and perceptions.* Ann Arbor, UMI Dissertaion Information Service.

Pennington, S. L. (1987). Children of lesbian mothers. In F. W. Bozett (Ed.), *Gay and lesbian parents.* New York: Praeger.

Puryear, D. (1983). *A comparison between the children of lesbian mothers and the children of heterosexual mothers.* Unpublished doctoral dissertation, California School of Professional Psychology, Berkeley, CA.

Saghir, M. T., & Robins, E. (1973). *Male and female homosexuality.* Baltimore: Williams and Wilkins.

Schulenberg, J. (1985). *Gay Parenting.* New York: Anchor Press/Doubleday.

Schwartz, J. (1985). *An exploration of personality traits in daughters of lesbian mothers.* Unpublished doctoral dissertation, California School of Professional Psychology, San Diego, CA.

Sears, R. R. (1957). Identification as a form of behavior development. In P. B. Harris (Ed.), *The concept of development.* Minneapolis: University of Minnesota Press.

Shively, M., & De Cecco, J. (1977). Components of sexual identity. *Journal of Homosexuality*, 3 (1), 41-48.

Siegelman, M. (1972). Adjustment of homosexual and heterosexual women. *British Journal of Psychiatry*, 120, 477-481.

Spence, J., & Helmreich, R. (1978). *Masculinity and femininity: Its psychological dimensions, correlates and antecedents.* Austin: University of Texas Press.

Steckel, A. Psychosocial development of children of lesbian mothers. In F. W. Bozett (Ed.), *Gay and lesbian parents*. New York: Praeger.

Storms, M. D. (1980). Theories of sexual orientation. *Personality and Social Psychology*, 38 (5), 783-792.

Storms, M. D. (1981). A theory of erotic orientation development. *Psychological Review*, 88 (4), 340-353.

Task Force on Sexuality. D.C. Chapter of the National Organization for Women. (1974). *A lesbian is. . .*

Ward, S. (1974). *Range of sex-role identity and self-esteem in a homosexual sample*. Unpublished Honors Thesis, University of Texas, Austin.

Gay and Lesbian Adolescents

Ritch C. Savin-Williams

OVERVIEW

Adolescents who declare their homosexuality have recently become a highly controversial, and yet, "invisible" minority in Western societies. This cultural phenomenon has emerged because increasing numbers of youth want to explore and express sexual behaviors and identities beyond the heterosexual ones that are traditionally assumed by most parents. Adolescents with a homosexual sexual orientation and who engage in homosexual behavior have always existed; how, a gay/lesbian identity is evolving.

Distinguishing among sexual orientation, behavior, and identity is a primary goal of this paper. Another is to reduce the invisibility of lesbian and gay adolescents—to social scientists, health care providers, the lesbian and gay communities, gay/lesbian youths and their parents. Finally, a third goal is to alert parents and health care providers to some of the issues, such as irrational fears, peer ridicule, lack of support, and misunderstandings, that are directly responsible for the poor physical and psychological health of some lesbian and gay youth.

In general, the above groups have been hesitant to challenge the stigmatic, legal, and moral issues involved with gay and lesbian minors. Perhaps they fear the label of "guilty by association" as well as the unique dread of stereotypes that are usually applied to

Ritch C. Savin-Williams, PhD, is Associate Professor in the Department of Human Development and Family Studies, Cornell University. Correspondence may be sent to the author at the Department of Human Development, MVR Hall, Cornell University, Ithaca, NY 14853.

This article is based on material contained in Chapter 9 of *Invisible and Forgotten: A Study of Gay and Lesbian Youths* (Savin-Williams, in press).

those who associate with gay and lesbian youth (e.g., pedophile). Theo Sandfort noted during a recent speaking tour of the United States that these negative reactions are usually more severe here than in other, more sex-positive societies such as his Netherlands. Even those most concerned with issues of homosexuality appear to assume that this sexual orientation is a prerogative only of adulthood.

But gay and lesbian youth are also frequently invisible to themselves. This is an inherent problem for minorities in American society, especially if their minority status is based on perceived "deviancy" from societal norms. This failure to come forth compounds the difficulty of finding gay and lesbian youth as research participants, thus amplifying their invisibility. As a result, social scientists either ignore gay and lesbian youth in their research or they rely on retrospective data gathering techniques that ask gay and lesbian adults to reflect on their adolescence to recall important events, feelings, and thoughts. Yet, recall data methodologies make particular and often debatable, assumptions concerning the accuracy of adult memories of childhood sexual feelings and behaviors (Boxer & Cohler, 1988; Ross, 1980).

Until recently an unspoken assumption in traditional research on homosexuality has been that all lesbians and gays are essentially very much alike. Fortunately, however, several researchers have addressed the heterogeneity within the gay and lesbian population. For example, Alan Bell and Martin Weinberg's 1978 book, *Homosexualities*, noted that variables such as age, educational level, and religious feelings influence the attitudes, behaviors, and beliefs of gays and lesbians. Their emphasis on "within group variations" resulted in a presentation of various portraits of gay and lesbian adults. Although they exploded the myth, few social scientists, health care providers, or the mass media have listened. As a result, cognizance of the diversity within the lesbian and gay population has been pre-empted by a focus — perhaps an obsession — on characteristics thought to distinguish homosexual from heterosexual people.

One source of variation is age. Gay and lesbian youth may be quite different from adults, both gay and straight, but in many important ways similar to other adolescents. For example, it is highly likely that gay and lesbian youth, similar to other youth, internalize and incorporate to some degree into their self-image their perceptions of others, such as family members. Thus, if parents reject their son or daughter because of his or her sexual orientation, then the adolescent may too reject himself or herself and develop low self-esteem or become suicidal. If indeed it proves to be the case that sexual orientation per se produces minimal differences in developmental processes, then focusing on the frequently belaboured and believed differences that have been the primary mainstay of social scientists who seem bent, whenever possible, on emphasizing gay versus straight comparisons has been a waste of time.

Thus, far more intra-gay/lesbian population studies that explore unique and diverse patterns within a homosexual sexual orientation are needed. One promising characteristic has been suggested by several researchers (Green, 1987; Harry, 1983; Hart et al., 1978) — cross-gender personality and social role orientation. With this effort social scientists increase the likelihood of learning about normal development in all of its manifestations.

SEXUAL ORIENTATION, SEXUAL BEHAVIOR, AND SEXUAL IDENTITY

Self-Label

An initial difficulty is defining the gay or lesbian adolescent to the self and to others, especially to the family. This is not an easy task during this age period for two reasons. First, to many families gay and lesbian youth do not and cannot exist. Instead, if families discover or are told of "peculiar behaviors or inclinations" the accused adolescents are viewed as homosexually behaving youths temporarily detained from their destination as heterosexual adults. Youth themselves frequently buy into this safety net.

Second, adolescents are more likely to experience cross-orientation sexual contact than are adults, but are less likely to define themselves as homosexual individuals. Only one of 1,067 youths in a recent representative sample of adolescents (Coles & Stokes, 1985) checked the "homosexual" identity box. Yet, 5% reported that they had engaged in homosexual behavior during adolescence.

In a 1985 survey of 356, 16- to 18-year-old high school students enrolled in Cornell University's Summer College, only three labeled themselves as bisexual/homosexual; five rated themselves as "more than incidentally homosexual" and 15 as "incidentally homosexual" on the Kinsey scale (Savin-Williams, in preparation). The next year, of 176 youths surveyed during the same program only one student expressed same-sex sexual attraction; another four replied "both sexes equally." Behaviorally, 12 reported past and eight current "casual" homosexual encounters; three reported genital-genital homosexual contact in their past (Savin-Williams, unpublished data). Thus, youth are far more likely to "admit" to homosexual acts than to a homosexual identity.

It is unclear from the empirical research whether cohort or developmental effects have the greatest determination for self-label as lesbian/gay. Andrew Boxer and Bert Cohler (1989) make the strong argument that because of past research efforts, primarily cross-sectional studies of the remembered past of gay and lesbian adults, little is known concerning either developmental processes or cultural/historical effects on gay and lesbian adolescents. The argument here is for a developmental paradigm, without the intention of negating or ignoring cohort effects. Indeed, it is probably easier to come out as homosexual today as a youth than it was during previous generations who came into their adolescence before the bench-mark 1969 Stonewall encounter with the New York City police. If it were possible to control or account for historical time, I believe developmental differences in coming out would still emerge. With advancing age, especially after the increase in sexual libido and cognitive abilities during pubescence, the equation of sexual behavior and sexual identity becomes both easier and more necessary.

Definitions

An important differentiation is distinguishing among *sexual orientation*, *sexual behavior*, and *sexual identity*. A homosexual sexual orientation is thought to consist of a preponderance of sexual feelings, erotic thoughts or fantasies, and/or behaviors desired with respect to members of the same sex. It is present from an early age—perhaps at conception (see Savin-Williams, 1987a). Homosexual activity or the "homosexually stimulating experience" (Rigg, 1982) connotes sexual behavior between members of the same sex. Sexual identity, by contrast, represents a consistent, enduring self-recognition of the meanings that the sexual orientation and sexual behavior have for oneself. Although a public declaration of this status is not inherently necessary for sexual identity, there must be some level of personal recognition of this status. Affirmation, to varying degrees, may or may not follow. These definitions serve to illustrate the essential differences among sexual orientation, sexual behavior, and inner identity. Although it is likely that the three will be somewhat or highly correlated, this may be more of a future, adult than a present, adolescent reality. This issue is particularly crucial in reference to teenaged populations because it appears that many forms of sexual activity with partners varying in age, sex, and other person variables are commonplace—regardless of self-labeled or self-professed sexual orientation and identity.

The confusion is illustrated by two seemingly opposite facts: Some gay and lesbian adolescents are homosexual virgins and some heterosexual adolescents engage in extensive and prolonged homosexual behavior. Studies (Boxer, 1988; Remafedi, 1987a; Roesler & Deisher, 1972; Sanders, 1980; Savin-Williams, in press) of gay male and lesbian youths support the claim that some accept the self-label of gay/lesbian before they have had homosexual experiences. For example, in one study (Savin-Williams, in press) 5% of the males and 12% of the females were homosexual virgins. Yet, they responded on the questionnaire that their orientation was bisexual/homosexual. Among 118 youths who came to Chicago's Horizons Center, 9% of the boys and 6% of the girls had never experienced same-sex activity (Boxer, 1988). Martin Manosevitz (1970) reported that 22% of his male sample was homosexual virgins during the ages of 13-17 years and 4% during the ages 18-24 years. In Jack Hedblom's study (1973) 66% of the female sample was homosexual virgins before age 15 years and 21% at age 20 years. Barry Dank (1971) concluded: "It is theoretically possible for someone to view himself as being homosexual but not engage in homosexual relations just as it is possible for someone to view himself as heterosexual but not engage in heterosexual relations (p. 117)."

On the other hand, clearly not all adolescents who engage in homosexual behavior would identify themselves as gay or lesbian. Alfred Kinsey, Wardell Pomeroy, and Clyde Martin (1948, pp. 629 & 651) found:

> Between adolescence and 15 years of age about 1 male in 4 (27%) has some homosexual experience. The figures rise to 1 male in 3 in the later teens and appear to drop a bit in the early twenties.

Yet,

> 4 percent of the white males are *exclusively homosexual throughout their lives*, after the onset of adolescence.

Richard Pillard (1974) noted that 35% of males in his research under 19 years of age had experienced a "homosexual encounter." In the Sorensen Report (1973), 5% of the boys and 6% of the girls between the ages of 13 to 15 years responded positively to the statement, "Have you had activity with another boy [girl] or with a grown man [woman] that resulted in sexual stimulation or satisfaction for either or both of you?" (p. 432). Among 16- to 19-year olds the percentage of boys marking "yes" more than tripled to 17% while the proportion of girls remained at 6%. Marcel Saghir and Eli Robins (1973) reported 23% of their heterosexual males had homosexual contacts by age 15 years; G. V. Ramsey (1943), 31% by age 17 years; and Martin Manosevitz (1970), 23% by age 17 years.

Among females the percentages are smaller but in the same direction. In Kinsey's study (1953), by age 15 years 5% of the females had experienced homosexual contact and 2% were exclusively homosexual by sexual orientation. Ten percent of 160 women in a university dormitory had homosexual encounters (Goode & Haber, 1977). Others (Manosevitz, 1970; Ramsey, 1943; Saghir & Robins, 1973; Sorensen, 1973) reported similar statistics and conclusions.

Alan Malyon (1981) speculated that about nine in ten reports by youth of same-sex erotic interest are made by those predominantly heterosexual in orientation. However, Gary Ross-Reynolds (1982, p. 70) concluded: "The majority of adolescents who engage in homosexual behavior do not continue this practice into adulthood.

Conversely, as many as 31% of gay adults engaged in no homosexual behavior until they were out of high school." This quote illustrates the difficulty of equating homosexual behavior with either sexual orientation or identity.

On the other hand, there is ample evidence that "pre-"gay/lesbian adolescents are more likely than others to engage in homosexual behavior and to do so for a longer period of time. For example, Alan Bell, Martin Weinberg, and Sue Hammersmith (1981a & b) reported that 95% and 70% of their homosexual men and women, respectively, but only 20% and 6% of their heterosexual men and women had been sexually aroused by a member of the same sex before they reached 19 years of age. Only 2% and 0% of the latter rated their pre-adult sexual behaviors as predominantly homosexual, as opposed to 56% and 44% of the homosexual men and women who so reported. In another sample of gay men and women (Saghir & Robins, 1969; Saghir, Robins, & Walbran, 1969), 87% had homosexual contacts before the age of 19 years. In a West German sample of women, 52% had homosexual contacts by the same age (Schafer, 1977). Compared to heterosexuals, Martin Manosevitz (1970) noted:

> The homosexuals appeared to have been more active in total frequency of sexual behavior earlier, but this difference disappears by adolescence. They seemed to start earlier, and the direction of their activities was towards same-sexed partners . . . Then many shifted to male and female partners during adolescence and early adulthood. (p. 401)

During childhood (5-9 years) 41% of the homosexual males had same-sex sexual activity and this proportion steadily increased to 59% during preadolescence (10-12 years), 70% during adolescence (13-17 years), and 96% during late adolescence and youth (18-24 years). The percentages of heterosexuals engaging in homosexual behavior were considerably lower and decreased rather than increased after preadolescence: 5% (childhood), 25% (preadolescence), 15% (adolescence), and 5% (late adolescence) (Manosevitz, 1970). In a study of gay male youths between the ages of 16 and 22 years, Thomas Roesler and Robert Deisher (1972) reported that the majority described early, prepubertal homosexual activity (e.g., mutual body exploration or curiosity based sex play). Of 29 homosexual or bisexual male youths, 15 to 19 years of age, 28 had past homosexual encounters, but most of these occurred during early adolescence (Remafedi, 1987a). Paul Van Wyk and Chrisann Geist (1984) documented among Kinsey's sample that the more elevated the homosexual score the greater the likelihood of prepubertal sexual contact with boys or men for homosexual men.

Andrew Boxer (1988) noted two pathways of "initiation into sexual identity formation" among the Chicago gay male youths. The mean age of first same-sex activity for 75% of the males was 15.0 years; all began homosexual activity after the age of 11 years. The other cluster of males (25%) reported that their first same-sex activity, usually with a same-aged peer, occurred prior to age 9 years (mean = 6.5 years). Thus, research that treats all gay and lesbian youth as if they were engaged in identical developmental pathways may be obscuring important developmental processes and outcomes. This theme is pursued in much greater depth in a recent book on gay and lesbian youth (Savin-Williams, in press).

There can thus be little doubt that not only does homosexual behavior occur during adolescence, it may also be quite prevalent. Such behavior, however, may or may not be indicative of a homosexual orientation or identification. Given the complexity of whether one defines homosexuality by reference to orientation, behavior, or self-label and the fact that many teens experience a diversity of sexual behaviors and an emerging sexual identity over a period of several years, a process that may not be completed until young adulthood, it is difficult to assess the prevalence of a homosexual orientation among adolescents. Despite this handicap, it is abundantly clear that gay and lesbian youth exist during childhood and adolescence — with or without homosexual behavior and/or a homosexual identity.

Cross-Cultural Research

Although homosexuality is probably universal cross-culturally, it is clearly not documented in all cultures. This is perhaps due to the secretive nature in which it is carried out and the difficulty of satisfactorily applying a common definition to or empirically assessing the abstract construct of homosexuality as a sexual orientation. Because homosexual behavior is more clearly demarcated and observable, it is more frequently documented cross-culturally (Ford & Beach, 1951).

In various human cultures adolescent homosexual behavior may be viewed as a necessary outlet (because the sexes are separated), as preparatory for heterosexual activity (to learn about sex), as giving ritualized status such as manhood (a semen implant for masculinity to thrive), as playful acting out of the increased sexual libido derived from pubertal hormones, or (rarely) as an expression of a life-long sexual orientation. Homosexuality is seldom accepted cross-culturally after adolescence as a natural, life-long expression of sexuality (Ford & Beach, 1951). One extreme view is that of Warren Gadpaille (1980), who concluded that homosexuality as a preferred sexual expression is universally deemed deviant, although he noted that in some cultures homosexuality has been given an institutional role and its stigmatization has been moderated. Clearly, societies vary in how they react to the emergence of homosexual behavior among their adult citizens, including the degree to which they allow it to be overtly manifested and stigmatized. On the other hand, some cultures celebrate, perhaps even proscribing, homosexual behavior among their adolescents (e.g., Sambia in New Guinea [Herdt, 1981]). Two-thirds of modern tribes in South America consider adolescent homosexuality to be both normal and acceptable (noted in Tannahill, 1980). Other cultures tolerate/ignore homosexual behavior or, if brought out into public view, actively discourage it.

A classic example of the latter is the English public school system. In the late 19th century it kept boys secluded from girls in a monastic fashion through most of childhood and adolescence (Tannahill, 1980). With the Oscar Wilde "scandal" many well-bred Englishmen came to recognize that not only were Eton, Harrow, and Winchester "breeding grounds" for homosexual behavior but that some adolescent boys continued the behavior into adulthood. Lax laws against sodomy were then enforced with moral conviction.

Despite the fact that striking changes have occurred in the United

States over the past decade in terms of the visibility of lesbians and gays, it is instructive to note that many past, antihomosexual theories and treatment approaches remain as part of the belief system of a considerable number of professionals. A review by Sandra Schwanberg (1985) noted that this is most pronounced in psychiatry and less so in psychology, medicine, nursing, and the social sciences. Almost exclusively, however, conceptualizations of homosexuality have focused on adult sexual behavior, with only occasional reference to adolescents. Nonetheless, these general theories necessarily influence the education and training of health care personnel, and consequently the forms of health care and intervention strategies used in contacts with gay and non-gay adolescents.

Cultural shifts are evident, however, in the United States. For example, although the medical journal *Pediatrics* in 1969 recognized the importance of adolescent homosexuality for scientific and humanistic reasons, it was considered to be a "developmental deviance" (Solnit, 1969). Fourteen years later, in 1983, the position of the American Academy of Pediatrics, Committee on Adolescence, was quite different: Homosexuality as a sexual orientation is established before adolescence; homosexual behavior is common "en route to conventional heterosexual development" (p. 249); homosexual behavior may occur given particular environmental contexts (incarceration, single sex boarding schools, military barracks); problems with homosexuality are usually the consequence of social conditions rather than of mental illness; and the necessity for a positive attitude on the part of the pediatrician was emphasized.

Explanations for Adolescent Homosexual Behavior

Great effort, primarily anecdotal in nature, has been made to explain the relatively high frequency of homosexual experiences among teenagers. Some (Glasser, 1977; Rigg, 1982) argued that sexual experimentation involving exploration of bodies and reactions with same-sexed peers occurs because such activities are more familiar and therefore less threatening than similar heterosexual physical contact; reassurance is gained from mutual comparisons of size, shape, and sensations associated with changing bodies and sex organs (Sorensen, 1973). Others (e.g., Chng, 1980) viewed these "transient homosexual activities" as the product of typical adolescent crushes, hero-worshipping, and intimate same-sex friendships. Mervin Glasser (1977) proposed that few of the adolescents who have homoerotic impulses or behaviors ever become homosexual; normal boys only engage in homosexual behavior to release sexual drives thwarted by parents who are "protecting" their adolescent daughters.

Similarly, Lillian Robinson (1980, p. 22) viewed the psychodynamics of adolescent sexuality as frequently including "an allowable homosexuality . . . which, under favorable circumstances, is gradually replaced by heterosexual development." A "normal" homosexual stage in early adolescence was thought to be comparable to sleep disturbances or enuresis: Teenagers were expected to have these developmental problems and to outgrow them. This view allowed the possibility that homosexual experiences may even be necessary for some heterosexual youths. Typically, this so-called normal homosexual stage was presumed to last until early or middle adolescence, followed by a move to heterosexuality. Mervin Glasser (1977) believed that homosexual adolescents did not exist: "It is only after the process of adolescence . . . that the person can be considered homosexual" (p. 221). The fear was that if homosexual attachments became intense and exclusive then more overt homosexual activity was considered likely with a concomitant absence of motivation to "advance to sexual activity with the opposite sex." Thus, it was assumed that a homosexual sexual orientation was an achieved status, obtained through social conditioning or circumstances. Throughout these writings, it is emphasized that adolescents *must* "make the choice to progress" to heterosexuality.

The view of adolescent homosexual activities as a "normal phase" of adult heterosexual development that "need cause no anxiety that they are the harbingers of lifelong homosexuality" (Rigg, 1982, p. 828) may be soothing to concerned and frightened parents. But this perspective may be potentially a source of self-denial if not great anxiety to the teenager who is becoming aware of a developing homosexual identity that does not fit these expectations. For such individuals, homosexuality is not experienced as a temporary "phase" but rather as a comprehensive and persistent sexual orientation.

Thus, it is crucial that social scientists, health care providers, parents, and youth are aware of the following empirical evidence:

a. not all homosexual adolescents are sexually active;
b. many homosexual adolescents are heterosexually active;
c. many heterosexual adolescents are homosexually active;
d. the synchrony between sexual identity and sexual behavior is highly variable among adolescents; and
e. many of these issues evoke great stress and anxiety for adolescents of all sexual orientations.

Knowledge of a youth's self-identification as gay or straight may be relatively uninformative in regard to assessing the incidence or frequency of homosexual behavior. Although an adolescent who identifies as lesbian/gay is more likely than one who self-labels as heterosexual to engage in homosexual behavior, such individuals may also be homosexual virgins and some self-labeled heterosexual youths may be quite homosexually active.

Perhaps less so than at any other age, an adolescent's sexual self-label may be of limited significance to the researcher, the health care provider, or the parent. Consequently, when developing research projects or health educational programs in which homosexual behavior is a critical consideration, it becomes particularly salient to consider all adolescents—not just those currently aware of a bisexual or gay/lesbian identity. The importance of this issue in reference to AIDS prevention programs has been discussed in other publications (Mantell & Schinke, in press; Savin-Williams & Lenhart, in press).

PROBLEMS AND PROMISES
OF GAY AND LESBIAN YOUTH

Sickness and Health

Rose Robertson (1981) asserted that the stigmatization, whether self- or other-induced, of being a gay/lesbian adolescent can have a number of dire consequences. These include ostracism, violence, and expulsion by peers and families; substance abuse or suicide attempts; acting out behavior, especially in the sexual sphere such as in prostitution; and feelings of isolation, alienation, and confusion. Many of the youths in Gary Remafedi's (1987a) research reported that they were victims of physical assaults (30%), had been discriminated against in education and employment (37%), received regular verbal abuse from peers (55%), and saw disadvantages to being gay (100%). The most frequent psychosocial and medical problems were, in order, poor school performance (80% of those in school), mental health problems (72%), substance abuse (58%), running away (48%), and conflict with the law (48%) (Remafedi, 1987b).

Some gays and lesbians, though primarily only in large urban areas, find support services that help them cope with discrimination and homophobic attitudes and develop a positive, fulfilling lifestyle. A growing number of mental health professionals refuse to "treat" men and women who wish to change their sexual orientation. All too frequently, however, these services and professionals are available only to adults and not to adolescents.

Gay and lesbian adolescents are thus faced with both a hostile and an unbelieving world. They are told, "You can't be a homosexual and I won't allow it." For those who discover the truthfulness and inevitability of their homosexuality and decide to contradict their previously assumed sexual identity, there are few sources of psychological, social, or legal assistance. Greg Robinson (1984, p. 14) noted:

> Few individuals or organizations have been willing to challenge the myth that homosexuality is a phenomenon of adulthood. Whether due to inadequate professional knowledge, fear of jeopardizing professional positions, or simple lack of interest, personnel in youth-serving agencies and school districts (may of whom are gay themselves) have, for the most part, not been willing to speak out on behalf of gay youth.

Gay and lesbian organizations have also been reticent to assist the young gay or lesbian adolescent—perhaps because they fear the issue is too controversial (a disguised attempt to "recruit" young people) and complex (the social, legal, and economic status of dependent, minor youth), or because they lack the personnel, knowledge, and funds to offer support (Robinson, 1984).

Another societal disservice to its gay and lesbian youth is the state of sex education in the public schools and the community. Peter Freiberg reviewed these issues in a 1987 article in *The Advocate*, "Sex Education and the Gay Issue: What Are They Teaching About Us in the Schools?" Homosexuality and emotional relations among same-sexed individuals are almost universally ignored in sex education curriculum. Teachers fear the negative reactions of parents and the school board and the community furor inclusion of homosexuality in school classes would create. Unfortunately, AIDS education frequently carries the message, "Look how unhealthy homosexuality is." Indeed, gay and lesbian youths have received a renewed wave of violence with the AIDS crisis. Joyce Hunter at the Hetrick-Martin Institute reported that gay youths have been called an "AIDS factory" by their peers. Much of the anti-gay bashing is instigated by young men in their teens and early 20s. Because most such individuals have recently been in the public school system, an educational opportunity has generally been lost (Freiberg, 1987).

The mental health and educational deficiencies are due in part, it would appear, to the invisibility of lesbian and gay adolescents in society at large. This invisibility contributes to a sense of alienation and stress for the individual adolescent that is frequently noted by various theoretical models and, occasionally, by empirical evidence, and yet denied by those concerned with the education and health of adolescents. Lesbian and gay youth are uniquely at risk for health related problems and thus in need of intervention programs. For example, due to societal discrimination and powerful peer pressure, teenagers might deny engagement in dangerous sexual behavior that would handicap health assessment procedures. Such individuals might be more willing to discuss the particulars of sexual behaviors with *nonjudgmental* parents, health care providers, educators, and researchers.

The Promise

Social scientists, including lesbian and gay researchers, have focused almost exclusively on the "problems" at the expense of the "promises" of gay and lesbian youth. It is perhaps surprising, given the portrait so far presented, that most lesbians and gay adolescents appear to be psychologically and socially healthy individuals (Savin-Williams, in press). Andrew Boxer's (1988) youths reported relatively few negative feelings (30% of the girls and 20% of the boys) surrounding first same-sex attractions and fantasies. First same-sex *activity* elicited even lower levels of negative feelings among the girls (15%) and only slightly higher for the boys (25%). Gary Remafedi (1987a) reported that his 29 youths were self-accepting and satisfied with their lives. Given the choice, 15 said they would make no change in their sexuality.

The negative portrait is the result of two groups of researchers who have been traditionally concerned with gay and lesbian youth. First, sociologists of deviance have tended to focus on deviants and their identity problems and sub-cultural lifestyles. Although most researchers who assume a social labeling perspective encourage tolerance ("they are at least as good as anyone else"), by their comparisons with "normals" the implicit message is clear: Gays and lesbians are outside normalcy. Alexander Liazos (1980) maintained that researchers need to focus far more attention on the oppressors and persecutors of gay and lesbian youth—they are indeed the deviants.

Second are the clinicians and those in the helping professions who usually encounter lesbian and gay youths in crisis or with problems. This view was portrayed in Mike Hippler's 1986 article in *The Advocate* that vowed in its title to address both the promise and the problem of gay youth. In reality, however, the article was devoted almost entirely to the latter—primarily, it would seem, because the author's sources were clinicians, counselors, therapists, and youth workers. Although these professionals are beginning the crucial task of offering services to lesbian and gay youth in trouble with parents, the law, and themselves, they are not likely to provide a well-rounded portrait. On the other hand, to be fair, social scientists have provided few other sources from which to draw another perspective.

Perhaps the most frequently quoted and referenced writings on the *problems* of lesbian and gay adolescents have been produced by the staff at the Hetrick-Martin Institute for the Protection of Lesbian and Gay Youth in New York City (e.g., Martin, 1982). A recent summary of this problem-focused perspective is Emery Hetrick and Damien Martin's (1987) article, "Developmental Issues and Their Resolution for Gay and Lesbian Adolescents." They noted the problems of becoming socially, emotionally, and cognitively isolated:

> In these cases, clients often reported feeling separated affectionally and emotionally from all social networks, especially the family. They may feel afraid to show friendship for a friend of the same sex for fear of being misunderstood or giving away their secretly held sexual orientation; they may feel emotionally distanced and isolated from their families because they must be on guard at all times. (p. 31)

Other "presenting problems" included suicide, sexual abuse, drug use, and depression. Over time the adolescent develops coping strategies, but the ones reviewed were primarily maladaptive: learning to hide through deception and self-monitoring, denial of membership, identification with the dominant (heterosexual) group, self-fulfilling negativism, and gender deviance (e.g., cross-dressing). Outcomes frequently included "anxiety, alienation, self-hatred, and demoralization" (p. 41). Not until the last page of the article is there a reference to the fact that homosexually oriented youth may have a positive ("resilience") characteristic; homosexuality does not "invariably lead to unhappiness" (p. 40). Passing through adolescence is not presented as a positive experience for the young gay or lesbian.

This "clinicalization" of adolescence is not unique to the gay and lesbian youth population—it is a battle that is fought on all fronts in mainstream developmental psychology (Savin-Williams, 1987b). The negative, problem-centered approach to gay and lesbian youth, however, distorts our view and is, I believe, an inaccurate portrait.

Gay and lesbian youth are, with increasing frequency, coming out during their adolescence with great portent of positive outcomes. Occasionally this may take a quite visible form. For example, Sloan Chase Wiesen, editor of his prep school newspaper, the *Montclair Kimberley Academy News*, published a full-page editorial, "Mythcontheptions About Being Gay," during his senior year in high school. Topics covered included homophobia, coming out, AIDS, stereotypes, resources, and recommended readings. He closed with the following:

> There are no men, no women, no gays, no straights; there are only people who should be free to engage in the beautiful and harmless expression of romantic love to whomever they are drawn. Be yourself, whether that means being homosexual, bisexual, or heterosexual. If you are not yet sure what you are, that's fine too. Some people become aware of their sexuality as toddlers, some as pre-teens, some as teenagers, and even some as adults. So don't panic if you are still unsure, but never be afraid or ashamed to explore who you are and to be yourself. The only road to certain unhappiness is to pretend to be who you are not. Whatever your sexuality, you will find many others who are like you. Happy Valentine's Day.

Support groups for lesbian and gay youths have formed in high schools in several urban areas — for example, Chicago, Los Angeles, Minneapolis, and New York — but the rural lesbian and gay adolescent remains isolated.

Findings from my recent research (Savin-Williams, in press) present a perspective of lesbian and gay youths who have, for the most part, positive self-images and who are coping remarkably well in American society. The research does not negate the experiences of Damien Martin and other health care professionals or of the youths who come to them for assistance. But it does present another side of being young and gay/lesbian — a positive and promising period of the life course. I believe that we need to say this loudly and clearly in the pages of our professional journals and in the media, such that our youth and their parents can hear it and believe it.

REFERENCES

American Academy of Pediatrics, Committee on Adolescence. (1983). Homosexuality and adolescence. *Pediatrics, 72,* 249-250.

Bell, A.P. & Weinberg, M.S. (1978). *Homosexualities: A study of diversity among men and women.* New York: Simon and Schuster.

Bell, A.P., Weinberg, M.S., & Hammersmith, S.K. (1981a). *Sexual preference: Its development in men and women*. Bloomington, IN: Indiana University Press.

Bell, A.P., Weinberg, M.S., & Hammersmith, S.K. (1981b). *Sexual preference: Its development in men and women (Statistical Appendix)*. Bloomington, IN: Indiana University Press.

Boxer, A.M. (1988). Betwixt and between: Developmental discontinuities of gay and lesbian youth. Paper presented at the Second Biennial Meeting of the Society for Research on Adolescence, Alexandria, VA.

Boxer, A.M. & Cohler, B.J. (1989). The life course of gay and lesbian youth: An immodest proposal for the study of lives. *Journal of Homosexuality*, in press.

Chng, C.L. (1980). Adolescent homosexual behavior and the health educator. *Journal of School Health, 61*, 517-520.

Coles, R. & Stokes, G. (1985). *Sex and the American teenager*. New York: Harper & Row.

Dank, B.M. (1971). Coming out in the gay world. *Psychiatry, 34*, 180-197.

Ford, C.S. & Beach, F.A. (1951). *Patterns of sexual behavior*. New York: Harper & Row.

Freiberg, P. (1987). Sex education and the gay issue: What are they teaching about us in the schools? *The Advocate*, Issue 480, 42-49.

Gadpaille, W. (1980). Cross-species and cross-cultural contributions to understanding homosexual activity. *Archives of General Psychiatry, 37*, 349-356.

Glasser, M. (1977). Homosexuality in adolescence. *British Journal of Medical Psychology, 50*, 217-225.

Goode, E. & Haber, L. (1977). Sexual correlates of homosexual experience: An exploratory study of college woman. *The Journal of Sex Research, 13*, 12-21.

Green, R. (1987). *The "sissy boys syndrome" and the development of homosexuality*. New Haven: Yale University Press.

Harry, J. (1983). Defeminization and adult psychological well-being among male homosexuals. *Archives of Sexual Behavior, 12*, 1-19.

Hart, M., Roback, H., Tittler, B., Weitz, L., Walston, B., & McKee, E. (1978). Psychological adjustment of nonpatient homosexuals: Critical review of the research literature. *Journal of Clinical Psychiatry, 39*, 604-608.

Hedblom, J.H. (1973). Dimensions of lesbian sexual experience. *Archives of Sexual Behavior, 2*, 329-341.

Herdt, G.H. (1981). *Guardians of the flutes: Idioms of masculinity*. New York: McGraw Hill.

Hetrick, E.S. & Martin, A.D. (1987). Developmental issues and their resolution for gay and lesbian adolescents. *Journal of Homosexuality, 14*, 25-44.

Hippler, M. (1986). The problems of promise of gay youth. *The Advocate*, Issue 455, 42-47, 55-57.

Kinsey, A.C., Pomeroy, W.B., & Martin, C.E. (1948). *Sexual behavior in the human male*. Philadelphia: W.B. Saunders.

Kinsey, A.C., Pomeroy, W.B., Martin, C.E., & Gebhard, P.H. (1953). *Sexual behavior in the human female*. Philadelphia: W.B. Saunders.

Liazos, A. (1980). The poverty of the sociology of deviance: Nuts, sluts, and 'perverts.' In S.H. Traub & C.B. Little (Eds.), *Theories of deviance.* Itasca, IL: F.E. Peacock, pp. 330-352.

Malyon, A.K. (1981). The homosexual adolescent: Developmental issues and social bias. *Child Welfare, 60,* 321-330.

Manosevitz, M. (1970). Early sexual behavior in adult homosexual and heterosexual males. *Journal of Abnormal Psychology, 76,* 396-402.

Mantell, J.E. & Schinke, S.P. (in press). The crisis of AIDS for adolescents: The need for preventive risk-reduction interventions. In A.R. Roberts (Ed.), *Crisis intervention handbook.* New York: Springer-Verlag.

Martin, A.D. (1982). Learning to hide: The socialization of the gay adolescent. *Adolescent Psychiatry, 10,* 52-65.

Ramsey, G.V. (1943). The sexual development of boys. *American Journal of Psychiatry, 56,* 217-234.

Remafedi, G. (1987a). Male homosexuality: The adolescent's perspective. *Pediatrics, 79,* 326-330.

Remafedi, G. (1987b). Adolescent homosexuality: Psychosocial and medical implications. *Pediatrics, 79,* 331-337.

Rigg, C.A. (1982). Homosexuality in adolescence. *Pediatric Annals, 11,* 826-829.

Robertson, R. (1981). Young gays. In J. Hart & D. Richardson (Eds.), *The theory and practice of homosexuality.* London: Routledge & Kegan Paul, pp. 170-176.

Robinson, G. (1984). Few solutions for a young dilemma. *The Advocate,* 14-16.

Robinson, L.H. (1980). Adolescent homosexual patterns: Psychodynamics and therapy. *Adolescent Psychiatry, 8,* 422-433.

Roesler, T. & Deisher, R. (1972). Youthful male homosexuality. *Journal of the American Medical Association, 219,* 1018-1023.

Ross-Reynolds, G. (1982). Issues in counseling the "homosexual" adolescent. In J. Grimes (Ed.), *Psychological approaches to problems of children and adolescents.* Des Moines: Iowa State Department of Education.

Saghir, M.T. & Robins, E. (1969). Homosexuality I: Sexual behavior of the female homosexual. *Archives of General Psychiatry, 20,* 192-201.

Saghir, M.T. & Robins, E. (1973). *Male and female homosexuality.* Baltimore: Williams & Wilkins.

Saghir, M.T., Robins, E., & Walbran, B. (1969). Homosexuality II: Sexual behavior of the male homosexual. *Archives of General Psychiatry, 21,* 219-229.

Sanders, G. (1980). Homosexualities in the Netherlands. *Alternative Lifestyles, 3,* 278-311.

Savin-Williams, R.C. (1987a). An ethological perspective on homosexuality during adolescence. *Journal of Adolescent Research, 82,* 283-302.

Savin-Williams, R.C. (1987b). *Adolescence: An ethological perspective.* New York: Springer-Verlag.

Savin-Williams, R.C. (in press). *Invisible and forgotten: A study of gay and lesbian youths.*

Savin-Williams, R.C. (in preparation). The attitudes of 'privileged' adolescents toward homosexuality.

Savin-Williams, R.C. & Lenhart, R.E. (in press). AIDS prevention among gay and homosexually active adolescents: Psychosocial stress and health care intervention guidelines. In D.G. Ostrow (Ed.), *Behavioral aspects of AIDS and other sexually transmitted diseases*. New York: Plenum.

Schafer, S. (1977). Sociosexual behavior in male and female homosexuals: A study in sex differences. *Archives of Sexual Behavior, 6*, 355-364.

Schwanberg, S.L. (1985). Changes in labeling homosexuality in health sciences literature: A preliminary investigation. *Journal of Homosexuality, 12*, 51-73.

Solnit, A.J. (1969). Bisexuality gone away: The child is father to the man. *Pediatrics, 43*, 913-914.

Sorensen, R. (1973). *Adolescent sexuality in contemporary society*. New York: World Book.

Tannahill, R. (1980). *Sex in history*. New York: Stein & Day.

Van Wyk, P.H. & Geist, C.S. (1984). Psychosocial development of heterosexual, bisexual, and homosexual behavior. *Archives of Sexual Behavior, 13*, 505-544.

Ethnic Minority Families
and Minority Gays and Lesbians

Edward S. Morales

SUMMARY. Attitudes toward sexuality differ within the diverse ethnic and racial communities that exist in the U.S., and the cultural values and beliefs surrounding sexuality play a major role in determining how individuals behave within their sociological context. The family unit is the domain where such values and beliefs are nurtured and developed. An individual's value system is shaped and reinforced within the family context which usually reflects the broader community norms. Disclosure of a gay or lesbian sexual preference and lifestyle by a family member presents challenges to ethnic minority families who tend not to discuss sexuality issues and presume a heterosexual orientation.

For ethnic minority gays and lesbians the "coming out" process presents challenges in their identity formation processes and in their loyalties to one community over another. Ethnic gay men and lesbians need to live within three rigidly defined and strongly independent communities: the gay and lesbian community, the ethnic minority community, and the society at large. While each community provides fundamental needs, serious consequences emerge if such communities were to be visibly integrated and merged. It requires a constant effort to maintain oneself in three different worlds, each of which fails to support significant aspects of a person's life. The complications that arise may inhibit one's ability to adapt and to maximize personal potentials.

The purpose of this paper is to examine the interaction and proc-

Edward S. Morales, PhD, is Research Associate, Multicultural Inquiry and Research on AIDS (MIRA), Center for AIDS Prevention Studies (CAPS), University of California, San Francisco, CA 94143.

The author would like to acknowledge the staff of MIRA and CAPS for support, and Thomas Ficcarrotto, PhD, and Jeanne Miranda, PhD, for their assistance in preparing this manuscript.

esses between ethnic minority communities and their gay and lesbian family members. A framework for understanding the process of change, that occurs for the gay or lesbian person as they attempt to resolve conflicts of dual minority membership, is presented. Implications for the practitioner is also discussed.

Most of what we know about human sexuality today and the acquisition of sexual identity has been studied within the context of a White American mainstream population. In contrast, little has been written about sexuality and ethnic minorities, especially in relation to ethnic minority gays and lesbians. Attitudes toward sexuality differ within the diverse ethnic and racial communities that exist in the U.S., and the cultural values and beliefs surrounding sexuality play a major role in determining how individuals behave within their sociological context.

The family unit is the domain where such values and beliefs are nurtured and developed. An individual's value system is shaped and reinforced within the family context which usually reflects the broader community norms. Disclosure of a gay or lesbian sexual preference and lifestyle by a family member presents challenges to ethnic minority families who tend not to discuss sexuality issues and presume a heterosexual orientation.

A major problem in discussing ethnic minority issues concerns the diversity of cultures that are reflected among ethnic minorities which include Blacks, Latins, Asian Americans, Pacific Islanders and Native Americans. Although these groups may share the common experience of prejudice and discrimination in American society and are commonly viewed as minorities, the variety of cultures and languages restricts the global generalities one can make concerning ethnic and racial minorities as a whole. However, there may be some common experiences and processes that are applicable to two or more minority groups. Although there may be other groups that may consider themselves ethnic minorities and the nomenclature of these groups may change over time, the author will limit the term "ethnic minorities" to mean people of color, Blacks/African American, Latins/Hispanics, Asian Americans, Pacific Islanders and Native Americans.

For ethnic minority gays and lesbians the "coming out" process presents challenges in their identity formation processes and in their loyalties to one community over another. Ethnic minority gay men and lesbians are a rarely acknowledged part of either the homosexual or racial/ethnic communities in which they live and function. Ethnic gay men and lesbians need to live within three rigidly defined and strongly independent communities: the gay male and lesbian community, the ethnic minority community, and the society at large. While each community provides fundamental needs, serious consequences emerge if such communities were to be visibly integrated and merged. A common feeling engendered by this complexity in lifestyle is one of being unable to integrate the pieces of one's life. It requires a constant effort to maintain oneself in three different worlds, each of which fails to support significant aspects of a person's life. The complications that arise may inhibit one's ability to adapt and to maximize personal potentials.

Developing a lifestyle among these three communities presents the ethnic minority gay man and lesbian with the need to develop and prioritize allegiances toward these communities and to minimize the disadvantages experienced resulting from others' misconceptions about being an ethnic and sexual minority. Each of the independent communities provided states of approach and avoidance that facilitate conditions of anxiety and tension with unforeseeable resolutions due to the political, social, and familial pressures that are beyond the control of the individual. To live as a minority within a minority leads to heightened feelings of isolation, depression and anger centered around the fear of being separated from all support systems, including the family. Ethnic minority families may find a need to re-examine their value systems concerning sexual preferences if the lesbian or gay family member is to remain an active and integrated member of the family. The processes of change are unique given the complexities of multiple minority membership and different minority groups.

The purpose of this paper is to examine the interaction and processes between ethnic minority communities and their gay and lesbian family members. A framework for understanding the process of change, that occurs for the gay or lesbian person as they attempt to resolve conflicts of dual minority membership, is presented.

ETHNIC MINORITY GAYS AND LESBIANS

Research has demonstrated that approximately 10 percent of the male population is gay and that about 6 percent of the female population is lesbian (Kinsey, Pomeroy & Martin, 1948: Kinsey et al., 1953). These percentages appear to hold across various national, cultural and ethnic groups (Gebhard, 1972; Gebhard & Johnson, 1979; Shively & DeCecco, 1978). Based on the 1980 census figures, there are 240 million people in the United States of which 25 percent of them are of an ethnic minority (U.S. Census, 1981). Applying these statistics to the percentages reported above, there are approximately 19 million gay men and lesbians in the U.S. of whom 4.8 million are of an ethnic minority. These gay men and lesbians are a substantial minority within a minority.

What does it mean to be an ethnic minority gay man or lesbian? For ethnic minority gays and lesbians, life is often living in three different communities: the gay/lesbian community, the ethnic minority community and the predominantly heterosexual White mainstream society. Since these three social groups have norms, expectations, and styles, the minority lesbian or gay man must balance a set of often-conflicting challenges and pressures. The multi-minority status makes it difficult for a person to become integrated and assimilated. Within the mainstream society, ethnic minority gays and lesbians experience prejudice and discrimination for their ethnic identity, as well as for their sexual orientation. In the gay and lesbian community the social values mirrors that of the mainstream society in relation to their perception of ethnic minorities which includes negative stereotyping and prejudicial attitudes about ethnic and racial minorities. Hence, ethnic minority gays and lesbians experience discrimination for their ethnicity within the gay and lesbian community. In the ethnic minority communities the social norms and values concerning homosexuality foster homophobic attitudes and consequently gays and lesbians within minority communities face disapproval and rejection.

Another way to view the lives of ethnic minority gays and lesbians is to consider them as both a *visible* and *invisible minority*. As a visible minority they have no choice but to cope with being the object of racist practices. As an *invisible minority* they can be discrete about their sexual orientation and hope to minimize the homophobic reactions. Consequently, the potential support they can receive from the three communities is compromised by the communities' racist and homophobic attitudes. In contrast White gays and lesbians do not experience racism in the mainstream society. As an *invisible minority* they can choose to remain silent and not "come out" or remain invisible. However, the homophobic attitudes of mainstream society and ethnic minority communities limit the support for gays and lesbians. Thus, remaining invisible usually means suffering in silence.

Goffman (1963) described a process individuals experience as a function of their known identity as a minority. He used the concept of discredited for those who were of a racial or ethnic minority group and discreditable for those who required disclosure in order to be identified as a minority. For the discreditable the issue is managing the tension generated during social contacts, whereas for the discreditable the issue is managing information about the potential tensions that could be generated if their minority status was disclosed or revealed. The discredited individual must learn coping mechanisms to manage the reactions and interactions from those who discredit. The discreditable individual ". . . must face unwitting acceptance of himself by individuals who are prejudiced against persons of the kind he can be revealed to be" (p. 42, Goffman, 1963). Concealing identity allows for protection from social consequences. Applying this process to ethnic minority gays and lesbians, one can expect the development of a sophisticated decision making process that is central to well functioning coping mechanisms. Social interactions would need to be assigned to either visible or invisible minority status for an appropriate response. In situations where social interactions are viewed as a reaction of dual minority status, managing the tension generated during the social contact would seem to be the response of choice, since the visible or "discreditable" status is revealed.

Some of the social consequences faced by ethnic minority gays and lesbians have been reported and documented through surveys and testimonies to commissions. In a survey of ethnic minority gay men and lesbians in San Francisco (Morales & Eversley, 1980), respondents felt they were discriminated against by the straight community and the gay community for either being ethnic and/or gay or lesbian. Discrimination was reported to occur in a variety of settings that included: (a) the work place (80%), (b) gay friends (43%), (c) straight friends (80%), (d) public places (53%), (e) seeking housing (63%) and (f) seeking work (66%). Other forms of discrimination included situations where ethnic minority gays and lesbians have been denied admission to gay and lesbian establishments, harassed by management, or ignored upon request for service.

In a study examining the prevalence of substance abuse in the gay and lesbian community in San Francisco, Morales and Graves (1983) found that the ethnic minority subgroup sampled had the highest percent of unemployment (21%) compared to White gay men (13%), White lesbians (16%), and the White bisexual and heterosexual (14%) subgroups. Even though variables such as level of education, academic degrees, years of employment, and years of residence were the same for all groups in the study sample, ethnic minority gays and lesbians average a yearly income of $4,000 to 6,000 less than White gay men and White bisexual/heterosexual subgroups.

Two surveys of gay bars in San Francisco were performed in February 1982 and in October 1982 to determine the number of ethnic minorities employed in those businesses by the Black and White Men Together of San Francisco (1983). The report noted that in February 1982 9 percent and in October 1982 10.8 percent of the total number of employees (N = 300; N = 306, respectively) were ethnic minorities. According to the 1980 census in San Francisco 52 percent of the population were ethnic minorities. Despite the organization's attempts to publicize this employment discrimination problem in the gay community little to no action was noted in the report. On September 8, 1983 the report of the two surveys was forwarded to the Human Rights Commission of San Francisco for their response to the matter.

In response to the report from the Black and White Men Together of San Francisco and other complaints received the Human Rights

Commission of San Francisco held hearings and developed a report on those employment discrimination issues in the lesbian/gay community. Winnow (1984) documented the findings of the Commission related to the employment and hiring practices of lesbian and gay businesses. The findings of the Commission included:

1. That the institutionalized racism existing in the mainstream society also exists in the Lesbian/Gay community;
2. That Lesbian/Gay people of color are under-represented in the Lesbian/Gay business workforce;
3. That applicant pools and apprenticeship programs do not currently exist in the Lesbian/Gay business community to draw qualified applicants from the population;
4. That the hiring practices of Lesbian/Gay businesses are primarily accomplished through the system of an "old boy/girl network";
5. That voluntary affirmative action programs, by and large, are non-existent;
6. That Lesbian/Gay people of color and their allies fear reprisal in their attempts to address unfair employment practices regarding race, color, national origin, and ethnicity;
7. That business associations serving the Lesbian/Gay community have not encouraged minority participation, nor do they have the structures to deal with grievances, nor have they sought to remedy under-representation of Lesbian/Gay people of color in their member businesses;
8. That extensive education on racism and affirmative action and restructuring of business practices for Lesbian/Gay businesses needs to be undertaken; . . .
11. That Lesbian/Gay media do not currently have adequate representation of Lesbian/Gay reporters and staff of color, and issues of race and concerns of minority Lesbians and Gay men are not sufficiently addressed;
12. That Lesbian/Gay people of color feel frustrated at their invisibility and are at the edge of boycotting and taking other strong actions if the issues of racism and exclusionary hiring and employment practices are not addressed and ameliorated;
13. That the Human Rights Commission needs to actively work

with the Lesbian/Gay business community, political and community organizations and media to address, educate, and ameliorate the findings of unfair hiring and employment practices now occurring. (pp. 54-55)

In a more profoundly difficult circumstance, the history of the AIDS epidemic has also highlighted this conflict of allegiance. Over 72 percent of AIDS cases occur in gay/bisexual men and over 41 percent of the total cases are ethnic minority group members (CDC, 1988). Until September 1986 (CDC, 1986), statistics concerning the combination of ethnic minority gay and bisexual men with AIDS have been unpublished and unavailable, thus hindering efforts to understand and help ethnic minority gay and bisexual men. From the standpoint of the ethnic and racial communities, the AIDS epidemic is seen as a "White gay male disease." From the standpoint of the gay and lesbian community, efforts to involve and inform the ethnic minority communities about this epidemic have been minimal.

As the processes of identity develop among ethnic/racial minority gays or lesbians, conflicts in allegiances may occur. A common example of this conflict occurs when gay men and lesbians move into ethnic and racial minority urban neighborhoods. A displacement of ethnic and racial minorities from their homes, due to the large increases in rents in response to the increasing demand for housing, has created much tension between these communities. As community tensions build, ethnic minority gay men and lesbians may feel conflicting loyalties.

As a result of these reactions from the three different communities, ethnic minority gays can feel lost among these communities and refer to this process as "schizy" or "living three lives." Some ethnic minority gays and lesbians restrict their "coming out" because they feel they have much more to lose in terms of their careers and friendships (Morales & Eversley, 1980; Winnow, 1984). In contrast the achievement of an affirmative ethnic/racial and gay/lesbian identity can provide a profound sense of empowerment which can be further reinforced through positive role models.

ATTITUDES OF ETHNIC MINORITIES
TOWARD GAYS AND LESBIANS

Although there are many differences within ethnic minority communities there are some similarities among these groups. The nuclear and extended family plays a key role and constitutes a symbol of their ethnic roots and the focal point of their ethnic identity. The importance of a supportive family context for the survival and psychological well being of the ethnic minority individual has been well documented (McGoldrick, Pearce & Giordano, 1982; Smith, Burlew, Mosley & Whitney, 1978). Unlike Whites who mirror the mainstream society, ethnic minorities are more of a *visible minority*. As a *visible minority* they are readily identified across all segments of society and are an easy target for discrimination and racist practices. Their minority status, combined with their culture and language, strengthens their identity and pride as a community and provides a protected environment for their members.

Ethnic minorities sometimes deny that lesbians and gay men exist within their communities and claim that homosexuality is a "White people's problem." For those who choose to "come out" in the ethnic community, reactions range from moderate acceptance to tolerance of being stigmatized and treated as an outcast. Such ostracism is extremely threatening because of the close relationship and identification with their family and ethnic community. They feel deeply about their cultural roots, such that being an outcast from the ethnic community can result in chronic feelings of anger and isolation.

The attitudes of ethnic minorities toward gays and lesbians tend to be traditional and conservative. Brown and Amorso (1975) studied the attitudes of West Indian college students and compared these data with the responses of Canadians and Brazilians. Results suggested that "cultural sex-negativism" and sex-role stereotyping were important variables and were related to antihomosexual prejudice. In addition, Brazilian students scored significantly more homophobic than West Indians and Canadians respectively.

In a study by Carrier (1977) attitudes of Mexican respondents toward gays were stated to be negatively viewed, with the majority of respondents viewing homosexuality as bad, repugnant or im-

moral. In another study Carrier (1976) reported that sharply dichot-
omized gender roles in Mexico contributed to the stereotyping of
homosexual men as passive and effeminate. Among the Mexican
men who reported homosexual contacts in these studies, the expectation of males were to only play the active or inserter role, which
would enable the male not to be identified as homosexual. In general, the Mexican gay man is expected to remain in the "closet"
and never to associate with effeminate men in public. In addition,
coming out to the family was perceived to be shameful to family
members and to those who were identified as gay. The expectation
of single males in Mexican families is that they must live with the
family unless they marry or move to a distant location for career
purposes.

Hidalgo and Hidalgo (1976) studied the Puerto Rican lesbian
community and reported that 90 percent of the sample indicated that
the Puerto Rican culture makes it difficult for gays and lesbians to
"come out" without experiencing serious consequences, such as
ostracism, from their families, friends, employers, employees and
neighbors.

Warren (1980) refers to "covering" as a style of adaptation facilitated by Asian American families who emphasize educational
achievement over social interactions. Aoki (1983) reported that gay
and lesbian Asian Americans incorporate this adaptation mechanism and conceal their sexual orientation to their family. If achievement oriented activities are pursued, then the family expectations
can potentially be met, despite the absence of any indications of
heterosexual activity.

In a survey investigating barriers to treatment for gay and lesbian
substance abusers, Morales and Graves (1983) reported that 14.3
percent of the ethnic minority substance abuse counselors and administrators scored within the homophobic range on the Weinberg
Homophobic Scale (1973), as compared to 4.6 percent of the White
counselors and administrators. Whether these differences reflect
real attitudinal differences or demonstrate more frank and honest
responses to questions on the homophobic scale by ethnic minorities requires further investigation. Nevertheless, it appears that homophobia is a serious and important problem among ethnic minorities. These data suggest that ethnic gays and lesbians are targets for

expressing homophobic attitudes both from the larger mainstream society and their ethnic communities including health care providers.

IDENTITY FORMATION OF MINORITY PERSONS

Coming to grips with one's identity as an ethnic and racial minority gay man or lesbian involves a process of awareness of this multiple minority status. Different dynamics are involved in the evolution of ethnic and racial minority identity in contrast to the emergence of sexual minority status. One of the first studies to note the conflicts experienced by ethnic minority gay men and lesbians was Cory and LeRoy (1963). In their study they introduced the concept of a double stigma and viewed the lives of gay Puerto Ricans and gay Blacks as being compounded by a rock-bottom social status. Hendin (1969) in his study of 12 Black male suicides in Harlem reported four cases of gay men who resorted to suicide in reaction to the double-stigma of a racial and sexual minority. Their contact with White men as sexual partners was reported to be an unsatisfactory form of escape from feelings of personal inferiority and rejection. In a study of Black gay and bisexual men, Johnson (1982) reported that Black men who have sexual relationships with other men may identify themselves either as gay or bisexual. Those who saw themselves as gay tended to identify more with the gay community, whereas those who saw themselves as bisexual tended to identify themselves more with the Black community.

In a survey of Cuban lesbians Espin (1987) reported, that given a forced choice 11 of the 14, Cuban lesbian respondents preferred to be among White lesbians than heterosexual Cubans. Their reasons centered around three major points: (1) that sexual identity and emotional romantic fulfillment were of great importance to the respondents; (2) that one cannot hide being Cuban and there was no choice but to be Cuban; and (3) that hiding a part of one's identity by remaining in the closet was perceived to be more stressful than being openly identified. The forced choice question presented a conflict for one respondent who objected to such a forced choice. She perceived the question to be a function of racism and homophobia and that Latina lesbians are an identity within themselves and reflective of true life choices.

Several theoretical models have been proposed for conceptualizing the identity formation and development of which three will be summarized: (1) for ethnic minorities (Atkinson, Morton & Sue, 1979), (2) lesbians and gays (Vivienne Cass, 1979), and (3) ethnic minority lesbians and gays (Morales, 1983). These models have been useful in understanding the identity formation process for these groups and have been useful in both therapy and research.

Ethnic Minorities

As the awareness of multiple identities becomes clearer and more differentiated, the process of change toward a positive and integrated identity begins. Atkinson, Morton and Sue (1979) developed a model of identity development for ethnic minorities that describes a process of identity formation through developmental stages.

Stage One: *Conformity*, is characterized by a preference for the dominant cultural values over one's ethnic culture. The dominant culture is perceived as superior over one's ethnic culture and a set of negative beliefs surrounding one's own culture facilitates feelings of self-hatred and low self-esteem.

Stage Two: *Dissonance*, is characterized by conflict and confusion over values and beliefs held by the dominant society and by their ethnic society. The individual begins to challenge the dominant culture's values and beliefs in order to resolve the conflicts and confusions.

Stage Three: *Resistance and Immersion*, presents an active rejection of the values and beliefs of the dominant culture and the acceptance of the values and beliefs of their ethnic culture. Increased participation in one's ethnic communities activities and exploration of its history reinforces the sense of belonging and strengthens the identity with their ethnic roup.

Stage Four: *Introspection*, presents an intensification of the stage three process where the individual rigidly believes the values of their ethnic group to the point of experiencing conflict between loyalty to one's ethnic community and a sense of personal autonomy.

Stage Five: *Synergistic Articulation and Awareness*, is characterized by a sense of self-fulfillment and integration. The conflicts experienced in the earlier stages have been resolved and the individual develops a better sense of control and flexibility. Broader social issues and a sense of multi-culturalism develops.

This model proposes a developmental aspect to the stages suggesting that people may characterize one stage and move to the remaining stages in a progressive developmental manner. This model is useful for identifying the types of conflicts, cognitive dissonances in developing decisions, and predicting behaviors that reflect the processes of the stages progressively. For example, the anger that develops and evolves as a person moves from one stage to another changes from being internalized through self-hatred and low self-esteem to an outwardly expression of the internalized anger by rejecting the dominant culture's values and beliefs. This process of change can be mistaken for an antisocial disorder or an obsessive compulsive disorder expressed through a self righteous, ethnocentric attitude. Foreign born individuals, who are also raised in their country, may not experience conflicts in their ethnic identity as do ethnic minorities born and raised in the U.S. They may identify themselves very strongly to their culture and perceive the value systems of the U.S. as a different cultural experience.

Lesbians and Gay Men

Vivienne Cass (1979) developed a six stage model of identity development or the "coming out" process for gays and lesbians. Cass' model is based upon interpersonal congruency theory with each stage representing a particular set of conflicts with resolutions that lead to the next stage.

Stage 1—*Identity Confusion*, presents the realization that the person is engaging in homosexual behavior and that they may be homosexual; Stage 2—*Identity Comparison*, presents conflicts and feelings of alienation arising from a new identity and the need to understand the norms and values of other homosexuals; Stage 3—*Identity Tolerance*, presents an increased commitment to a homosexual lifestyle and identity and a sense of tolerance rather than acceptance of their sexual orientation; Stage 4—*Identity Acceptance*, is characterized by an increased participation in the gay and lesbian community, by the development of positive gay and lesbian friendships, and by the development of a sense of validation of their sexual identity; Stage 5 — *Identity Pride*, is characterized by the incongruencies that exist between the individual's sense of pride and acceptance as a gay or lesbian and the rejection experienced by society. Confrontational strategies are used to challenge societal rejection and is often characterized by "us versus them" dichotomy (e.g., heterosexuals versus homosexuals) and devaluation of heterosexuality; Stage 6 — *Identity Synthesis*, presents more of an integration and a greater tolerance of diversity with the personal and public sexual identities being synthesized into one image and a greater ability to receive considerable support from the environment. At this stage sexual orientation is seen as one aspect of the self and completes the identity formation process.

A unique psychological phenomenon of lesbians and gays is the "coming out" process. This model presents a developmental understanding of this process and is useful in predicting behavior. One similarity to the Atkinson, Morton and Sue (1979) model is the evolvement of a sense of righteousness in relation to their sense of affiliation to their respective minority community. The importance of historical, sociological and political influences are also similarly important factors in these models. Where they seem to differ is in the type of identification and the likelihood for the process to reoccur. For example, ethnic minorities achieving Stage Five of the Atkinson, Morton and Sue model usually means that their developmental identification processes ends and a process of integration begins. However, for lesbians and gays the coming out process is continuous and reoccurs in the various areas of their life. Coming out to family, friends, employer, and community are different and seem to involve a reoccurrence of the different stages and the conflicts they represent.

Ethnic Minority Gays and Lesbians

Morales (1983) proposed an identity formation model for ethnic minority gays and lesbians that incorporates the dual minority status of this group. This process seems to center around five different states. Each state is accompanied by decreasing anxiety and tension through the management of the tensions and differences. As cognitive and lifestyle changes emerge the multiple identities become integrated leading toward a greater sense of understanding of one's self and toward the development of a multi-cultural perspective.

State 1: *Denial of Conflicts* — During this phase the person tends to minimize the validity and reality of discrimination they experience as an ethnic person and believe they are treated the same as others. Their sexual orientation may or may not be defined, but they feel their personal lifestyle and sexual preference have limited consequences in their life. The focus of therapy centers around developing a more accurate picture of how the environmental stresses affect their functioning and how their multiple identities can be assets in their personality and lifestyle.

State 2: *Bisexual versus Gay/Lesbian* — The preference for some ethnic minority gays and lesbians is to identify themselves as bisexual rather than gay or lesbian. Upon examining their sexual lifestyles there may be no difference between those who identify themselves as gay/lesbian as compared to those identified as bisexual. The focus of therapy may be to explore the sense of hopelessness and depression resulting from the continued feelings of conflict.

State 3: *Conflicts in Allegiances* — The simultaneous awareness of being the member of an ethnic minority as well as being gay or lesbian presents anxiety around the need for these lifestyles to remain separate. Anxiety about betraying either the ethnic minority or the gay/lesbian communities, when preference is given to one over the other, becomes a major concern. The need to prioritize allegiances in order to reduce the conflict becomes the focus in therapy.

State 4: *Establishing Priorities in Allegiance* — A primary identification to the ethnic community prevails in this state and feelings of resentment concerning the lack of integration among the communities becomes a central issue. There are feelings of anger and rage stemming from their experiences of rejection by the gay community because of their ethnicity. The need to re-examine the feelings of anger and rage as they relate to their experiences becomes a central focus in therapy.

State 5: *Integrating the Various Communities* — As a gay or lesbian person of color the need to integrate their lifestyle and develop a multi-cultural perspective becomes a major concern. Adjusting to the reality of the limited options currently available for gay and lesbian people of color becomes a source of anxiety facilitating feelings of isolation and alienation. The focus of therapy centers around reassuring them that they are aware of the various dynamics they experience and can better predict outcomes and consequences.

This model proposes states rather than stages suggesting that individuals may find themselves at one or more states rather than at a particular stage. For example a person may identify with being bisexual yet live an exclusively lesbian/gay lifestyle (State 2), and have a strong identity to their ethnic minority community (State 4). The models of Atkinson, Morton and Sue, and of Cass, can be integrated and applied using these States. Hence, this multi-state individual can be in Stage 1 of Cass' model and Stage 3 of Atkinson, Morton and Sue's model. Such a person may experience much anxiety about others knowing his/her sexual preference, decide to identify as a bisexual in reaction to the lack of support they feel in the gay and lesbian community due to discrimination and prejudice, and reject the dominant society's beliefs and values because of its history of oppressing minorities.

Many ethnic minority lesbians and gays develop effective coping mechanisms and are successful in managing the conflicts they face. These well functioning individuals serve as role models for other minority gays and lesbians. The process could be enhanced by the development of formal organizations and support groups within the minority gay and lesbian community. Community organizations can serve to strengthen a positive image and provide a vehicle for minority gays and lesbians to grow as a community and maintain a support system. Some existing organizations include Gay Latinos Unidos in Los Angeles, Gay Tejanos Unidos in Texas, National Coalition of Black Lesbians and Gays, Gay Native Americans in San Francisco, and Pacific Friends in Berkeley.

ETHNIC MINORITY FAMILIES'
REACTIONS AND ROLES

A major difference between American family structures and ethnic family constellations centers around the integration of the extended family within its support system. For the ethnic person the family is the basis of their roots and the focal point of their ethnic identity. "Coming out" to the family tends to involve both the nuclear and extended family systems. Such a family collective is the major support system for the ethnic persons and is the source of great strength and pride. In other words the family is the emotional bond for the conscious self and personal psychology. For minority lesbians and gays coming out to the family not only jeopardizes the intra-family relationships, but also threatens their strong association with their ethnic community. As a result minority gays and lesbians may run the risk of feeling uprooted as an ethnic person.

Families and friends of minority lesbians and gay men can be a source of much support. Anxieties about rejection from families and friends may become exaggerated and may lack a realistic perspective. It is important for minority gays and lesbians to examine the consequences and benefits of coming out to family members on a case by case basis. A change in the quality of the relationship can be expected upon disclosure. Such change may result in a more intimate and mature relationship. With parents this may mean changing the parent-child role into an adult-adult role where a sense of mutual respect develops. In any case, comparing worse and best case scenarios may be a useful way to prepare for disclosure. Books and literature on sexual orientation written for family and friends, as well as familiarity on obtaining additional information, can be of help.

Some minority families hold traditional values that are reinforced with their religious beliefs. Within these value systems heterosexual lifestyles are considered to be the norm, and family members are expected to marry and to continue the traditional family system. Gay and lesbian lifestyles are incongruent with these value systems. Upon disclosing one's sexual identity the family may be faced with a crisis. The challenge for the family centers around its ability to be flexible and to adapt the normative expectations of its members, rather than to be rigid and to reject other lifestyle alternatives that exist within the family. Some families may decide to accept their gay or lesbian family member's lifestyle including the lover but not discuss the matter. Other families may be more active in discussing the issues in a supportive way. In any case, respect for the beliefs and values of all family members is the basis for maintaining unity in the family.

Garay (1978) proposed that Latino families respond to the coming out process in a manner corresponding to the stages of grief and mourning. The first stage, denial, is the initial reaction of avoiding or denying the emotional contents of the situation. The second stage, reproach, is characterized by anger, mutual accusations and/or some form of aggression. The third stage, compromise, is characterized by seeking a cause for homosexual behavior in which someone is at fault. The fourth stage, acceptance, is characterized by incorporating the individual and their primary partner into the family unit. This grief process may extend to the issues of AIDS which complicates the coming out process and may be an unspoken source of anxiety and stress to all family members.

Risk Factors for AIDS Among Ethnic Minority Gay and Bisexual Men

Little attention has been given to the needs and concerns of gay and bisexual minority men yet they represent 20 percent of all of the adult AIDS cases in the U.S. (CDC, 1988). Since the identification of AIDS in 1981, there has been a volume of research related to the diagnosis, treatment, and prevention of AIDS. Yet, there are only two studies currently funded on the practices and lifestyles of Black homosexual men and none on other minority men.

Gay and bisexual men constitute the largest AIDS risk group among Black, Latin and other minority groups AIDS cases (45%, 51%, and 86% respectively) and represent 20 percent of the total AIDS cases in the U.S. (CDC, 1988). Excluding the AIDS cases in the New York and Miami metropolitan areas, the majority of the minority cases with AIDS are gay and bisexual men.

Certain sexual risk behaviors of minority gay men contribute to the spread of AIDS. Bell and Weinberg (1978) reported racial difference in the preference for sexual activities in their sample of gay men. Blacks expressed a second order preference for anal intercourse as compared to Whites, whose second order preference was hand genital contact. The majority of White men preferred receiving fellatio or being active during anal intercourse, while more Blacks reported a preference for passive anal intercourse.

Denial of risk for HIV infection is the first barrier ethnic minority gays and bisexuals face. The process of identity formation as an ethnic minority gay person is a mediating factor in the realization of the risk for AIDS. For example, since the individual may not yet define himself as homosexual, he may rationalize that "only homosexuals and IV drug users are at risk and, therefore, I am not at risk." Such an individual does not perceive himself at risk for AIDS regardless of his history of homosexual activity. As certain behaviors are identified as modes of HIV transmission, the individual may realize his status of risk and, thereby, challenging his own denial. This may generate a state of anxiety and potential crisis along with questions about his HIV status and his sexual lifestyle. The discovery of his HIV status will also play an important role in the identity formation process. If he is HIV negative he may re-examine his sexual lifestyle and support system. If he is HIV positive he will need to respond to his state of health and decide how can he maintain his support system in both the gay and ethnic communities. These events may lead to changes in his identity and to some resolution of the conflicts in his allegiance to the different communities.

IMPLICATIONS FOR PSYCHOTHERAPY

The issues presented may seem an arduous challenge for minority gays and lesbians. The limited resources and support for minority lesbians and gays may facilitate feelings of despair and frustration. On the other hand, one can be more optimistic by examining the functional support networks and strategies for coping that minority gays and lesbians have used throughout their life. Within the ethnic community and within the family there are reservoirs of strength through relationships and experiences. For persons conflicted with their sexual identity the experience of being an ethnic minority can be applied toward understanding and coping with an affirmative sexual identity. This analogy is useful in developing a sense of pride and reassurance about their strength and survival instincts in confronting feelings of despair, fear and anxiety.

The role of the psychotherapist can be beneficial in developing an awareness of the processes ethnic minority gays and lesbians face and in reassuring them of their ability to cope with their stresses. It is important that the therapist be knowledgeable and trained in the areas of ethnic minorities and gay and lesbian lifestyles. Some clients find themselves frustrated in teaching therapists with limited knowledge and training the issues and processes minority gays and lesbians experience and through their frustration with this process drop out of therapy. In other cases, therapists have assumed the erroneous philosophy that the common human experience is the essence of the therapy process and cultural issues have limited relevance. Treating depression, paranoia, and troubled relationships are viewed as shared human experiences and, therefore, treated similarly for all clients. What is missed in this generic approach to therapy are the dynamics of the therapy process that include the client's perceptions of the issues and of the coping mechanisms developed within her or his cultural experiences. For instance, in the Latino culture using an assertive, confrontational response, may be perceived as a sign of disrespect and rebellion. On the other hand, incorporating "sympatia" (the importance of friendliness and empathy) may lead to the same goal without alienating family members and being disrespectful.

Many therapists wonder whether matching the client and counselor according to sexual orientation and ethnicity/race is preferred in psychotherapy. In other words, assuming that a therapist is knowledgeable, trained and experienced in ethnic minority and gay and lesbian issues, does ethnicity/race of the counselor offer an advantage or disadvantage to the client? Similarly, does the sexual orientation of the therapist offer an advantage or disadvantage? These questions have led to many heated debates. Rather than viewing the questions as "either or" it is useful to examine the advantages and disadvantages of same ethnicity/race and sexual orientation in the therapeutic dyad. When the ethnicity and sexual orientation is varied the transference and counter-transference issues can become more intensified. Careful consideration should be given to the counter-transference since this is most likely subjected to misinterpretations by the therapist. Similarly, the intensity of the transference can be misdiagnosed or misinterpreted as a personality disturbance rather than the anger and rage the client experiences as they move from one stage of identity development to another.

Another consideration centers around how the therapist is a role model for clients by being an ethnic minority and having the same sexual orientation as the client. There are advantages to the use of role models in changing behavior such as enhancing rapport, facilitating learning, encouraging an identification process, and providing a positive role model. Some disadvantages may include the development of a dependence and viewing the therapist as infallible and perfect. Also the interpretation of sexual issues in the therapy session are often different when the sexual orientation of the therapist varies. In any case, supervision and consultation is advised along with careful consideration to the effects of ethnicity/race and sexual orientation have on the therapeutic alliance.

As experts in changing behavior and in conflict resolution therapists can be useful for persons confronted with the challenges of a dual minority. Managing the social tensions as a function of a *visible* and *invisible minority* will remain as the central theme for minority gays and lesbians. Therapists can use their skills in the assessment and evaluation of the coping mechanisms being used as the individual faces the different states of identity in life. Using the resources in the community can be of great therapeutic value for ethnic minority gays and lesbians. Literature, rap groups, workshops, and conferences are increasingly available to minority gays and lesbians, and these resources are useful in developing an affirmative identity and receiving peer support.

The combined diversity of cultures and sexual lifestyles provide a rich source of information concerning the human experience. More research and theoretical models concerning minority gays and lesbians are sorely needed. Weighing the psychological processes of change, in combination with the changing societal norms and values within a multi-cultural context, is the plight of the minority lesbian and gay man. The challenge of therapists and social scientists is to observe and acknowledge this interactive process while maintaining objectivity in a multi-cultural societal context of continued change in norms and values.

REFERENCES

Aoki, B. (1983). Gay Asian Americans: Adapting within the family context. Paper presented at the 91st National Convention of the American Psychological Association, Anaheim, California, August.

Atkinson, D., Morton, G., & Sue, D. (1979). *Counseling American Minorities*. Dubuque, IA: William C. Brown.

Bell, A. & Weinberg, M. (1978). *Homosexualities: A Study of Diversity Among Men and Women*. New York: Simon and Schuster.

Brown, D. & Amoroso, M. (1975). Attitudes towards homosexuality among West Indian male and female college students. *Journal of Social Psychology*, 97(2), 163-168.

Carrier, J. (1976). Family attitudes and Mexican male homosexuality. *Urban Life*, (Oct.), 5(3), 359-375.

Carrier, J. (1977). "Sex-role preference" as an explanatory variable in homosexual behavior. *Archives of Sexual Behavior*, 6(1), 53-65.

Cass, V. (1979). Homosexual identity formation: A theoretical model. *Journal of Homosexuality*, 4(2), 219-35.

Centers for Disease Control, Center for Infectious Diseases (September, 1986). AIDS Activity-Weekly Surveillance Report-United States, Atlanta, Georgia.

Centers for Disease Control, Center for Infectious Diseases (June 20, 1988). AIDS Activity-Weekly Surveillance Report-United States, Atlanta, Georgia.

Cory, D. & LeRoy, J. (1963). *The Homosexual and His Society a View From Within*. New York: Citadel Press.

Espin, O. (1987). Issues of identity in the psychology of Latina lesbians. In Boston Lesbian Psychologies Collective (Eds.), *Lesbian Psychologies*. Urbana and Chicago, IL: University of Illinois Press.

Ford, C. & Beach, F. (1951). *Patterns of Sexual Behavior*. New York: Harper Press.

Garay, C. (1978). The Hispanic family and its homosexuals: A minority in the minority. Paper presented at the Second Biannual Convention of COSSMHO, Houston, Texas.

Gebhard, P.H. (1972). Incidence of overt homosexuality in the United States and Western Europe. In J.M. Livinghood (Ed.), NIMH Task Force on Homosexuality: Final report and background papers. DHEW Publication No. (HSM) 72-9116. Rockville, MD: National Institute of Mental Health.

Gebhard, P.H. & Johnson, A.B. (1979). *The Kinsey Data: Marginal Tabulations of the 1938-1963 Interviews Conducted by the Institute for Sex Research*. Philadelphia: W.B. Saunders.

Goffman, E. (1963). *Stigma: Notes on the management of spoiled identity*. Englewood Cliffs, NJ: Prentice-Hall, Inc.

Hendin, H. (1969). *Black Suicide*. New York: Basic Books.

Hidalgo, A. & Hidalgo, C. (1976). The Puerto Rican lesbian and the Puerto Rican community. *Journal of Homosexuality*, 2(2), 109-121.

Johnson, J. (1982). The influence of assimilation on the psychosocial adjustment of Black homosexual men. Unpublished dissertation, California School of Professional Psychology, Berkeley, California.

Kinsey, A.C., Pomeroy, W.B., & Martin, C.R. (1948). *Sexual Behavior in the Human Male*. Philadelphia: W. B. Saunders.

Kinsey, A.C., Pomeroy, W.B., & Martin, C.R. (1953). *Sexual Behavior in the Human Female*. Philadelphia: W. B. Saunders.

McGoldrick, M., Pearce, J., & Giordano, J. (1982). *Ethnicity and Family Therapy*. New York: The Guilford Press.

Morales, E. & Eversley, R. (1980). A survey of ethnic gay men and lesbians in San Francisco. Unpublished report.

Morales, E. & Graves, M. (1983). *Substance abuse patterns and barriers to treatment for gay men and lesbians in San Francisco*. Monograph, S.F. Prevention Resource Center, San Francisco, California.

Morales, E. (1983). Third world gays and lesbians: A process of multiple identities. Paper presented at the 91st National Convention of the American Psychological Association, Anaheim, California.

Shively, M. & DeCecco, J. (1978). Sexual orientation survey of students on the San Francisco State Campus. *Journal of Homosexuality*, *1*, 29-39.

Smith, W., Burlew, A., Mosley, M., & Whitney, W. (1978). *Minority Issues in Mental Health*. Menlo Park, CA: Addison-Wesley.

United States Department of Commerce-Bureau of the the Census 1980 (1981). Census of population and housing.

Weinberg, M. (1973). *Society and the Healthy Homosexual*. New York: St. Martin's Press, 1973.

Warren, C. (1980). Homosexuality and stigma. In J. Marmor (Ed.), *Homosexual Behavior: A Modern Reappraisal*. New York: Basic Books.

Winnow, J. (1984). Investigations into employment and hiring practices of lesbian/gay businesses, specifically regarding race, color, national origin and ethnicity: Findings, recommendations, and support documentation. A Report by the Human Rights Commission of San Francisco, San Francisco, California.

Older Lesbian and Gay People: Responding to Homophobia

Richard A. Friend

SUMMARY. Using a theoretical model of lesbian and gay identity formation, this paper examines the complex relationships between families and older gay and lesbian adults as a way to better understand the extensive variations individuals have in their relationships with themselves, presentation of self, relationships with others and their behaviors. Three potential styles of lesbian and gay identity formation are described in order to highlight the structures and dynamics involved in issues for gay and lesbian elders and their families. It is argued that by challenging heterosexism and by minimizing homophobia, older lesbian and gay people experience a successful aging process. While individuals who are lesbian and gay have great potential to age with a sense of power, pride and fulfillment, so do the families from which they came and those they have created.

Analyses of traditional definitions of family and family arrangements are often challenged by the inclusion of older lesbian and gay people. These older adults, like younger gay and lesbian people, are often viewed as antithetical to, and potentially dangerous for the continued existence and stability of the American family. Concerns and fears flourish that somehow lesbian and gay people threaten this vital, yet fragile institution. It is argued that at times of social stress, those stigmatized as sexually marginal are viewed as even more dangerous (Rubin, 1984). Given the current economic and sociopolitical climate, the New Right discourse of preserving the family from destruction by homosexuality reflects these fears. This climate

Richard A. Friend, PhD, is on the faculties of the Human Sexuality Education Program at the University of Pennsylvania and the College of Allied Health Sciences at Thomas Jefferson University. Correspondence may be directed to the author at The University of Pennsylvania, Graduate School of Education, 3700 Walnut Street, Philadelphia, PA 19104.

is one important reason why an analysis of the relationships between homosexuality and the family is necessary.

While homosexuality may be perceived as posing a threat to traditional families, gay and lesbian elders are also challenged to struggle with the homophobia inherent in traditional family structures. This paper analyzes a variety of ways these older lesbian and gay adults respond to this challenge.

Young gay and lesbian people who come out are often told by family members, "You may think this is what you want now, but imagine how lonely you will be when you are old." While this assertion by family may reflect a genuine concern for a loved one's future happiness, it also contains anti-gay messages as well as a negative view of aging. The lesbian or gay person may hear this as, "We love you, but not as the way you are." How families and their older gay or lesbian relatives respond to each other is a function of how each manages the issues of homophobia, heterosexism and ageism.

Using a theoretical model of lesbian and gay identity formation, this paper examines the complex relationships between families and older gay and lesbian adults as a way to better understand the extensive variations individuals have in their relationships with themselves, presentation of self, relationships with others and their behaviors. Three potential styles of lesbian and gay identity formation are described to highlight the structures and dynamics involved in issues for gay and lesbian elders and their families. It is argued that by challenging traditional heterosexist arrangements and assumptions, and by minimizing homophobia, older lesbian and gay people experience an aging process that is more successful than both heterosexuals and their gay and lesbian age peers who have not challenged these ideologies. While individuals who are lesbian and gay have great potential to age with a sense of power, pride and fulfillment, so do the families from which they came and those they have created.

REVIEW OF THE LITERATURE

Given that there are an estimated 3.5 million people over 60 years of age living in the United States who are gay or lesbian (Dawson, 1982), this group is best described as diverse (Kimmel,

1978). The most common images of older lesbian and gay people available in our culture are negative. Older lesbian women are frequently described as loners who lack feeling and attractiveness (Berger, 1982a). The view of older gay men is also bleak. They are often described as depressed, lonely, oversexed and lacking the support of family and friend structures (Kelly, 1977). By contrast, however, in reviewing the research literature, a very different view of the lives of older gay and lesbian people emerges.

According to Kelly (1977) the popular negative stereotypes described above do not apply to the lives of the older gay men he studied. On the contrary, the majority of older gay men (Berger, 1982a, 1982b; Friend, 1980; Kimmel, 1978; Francher & Henkin, 1973; Weinberg, 1970) and older lesbian women (Almvig, 1982; Dunker, 1987; Martin & Lyon, 1979; Raphael & Robinson, 1980) studied are happy, psychologically well adjusted, have high levels of self-acceptance and are adapting quite well to the aging process.

Today's older lesbian and gay adults were all born and have lived the majority of their lives through a socio-historical period of active hostility and oppression toward homosexuality (Almvig, 1982; Dawson, 1982; Dunker, 1987; Kimmel, 1977, 1978). The struggle for these women and men, therefore, has been to form a positive identity, or sense of self as a gay or lesbian person given the context which defines them in only negative and oppressive ways. For working-class and minority lesbian and gay seniors, this kind of victimization has been compounded even further by the absence of access to other cultural, economic and institutional sources of power and privilege. Unfortunately, these gay and lesbian elders are least represented in the research samples and, therefore, the least is known about the joys and pains of their lives.

Dunker (1987) describes the impact of these socio-political processes on older lesbian women.

> Defining "old" as being more than sixty-five means that all of us older lesbians were born before 1922. We've lived through some tremendous economic, scientific, social, and political changes. . . . But we are still struggling with the same old oppressions of ageism, sexism, poverty, and racism, and we're still at the bottom of the economic pile. (Dunker, 1987, p. 73)

Given this socio-historical context, a significant aspect of the lives of older lesbian and gay people involves responding to and managing heterosexism. Heterosexism is defined as the assumption that everyone is or should be heterosexual (Friend, 1986). This ideological assumption is the basis for the system of valuing and privileging heterosexuality relative to homosexuality. This results in the social construction of homosexuality as negative, dangerous and/or potentially pathological. Social historians have described this transhistorical construction of homosexuality as moving from sin to crime to sickness (Boswell, 1980; Bullough & Bullough, 1977; Foucault, 1978; Katz, 1976; Weeks, 1977).

As a socially constructed belief system, heterosexism contributes to the development of homophobia. Homophobia is defined as the irrational fear and hatred of homosexuality in one's self and others (Weinberg, 1972). Given the heterosexist social context which devalues and abhors homosexuality, Herek (1984) argues that this fear and hatred of homosexuality is often seen as appropriate and functional by individuals who experience it. Herek (1986) suggests, in fact, that to be "a man" in contemporary American society one must be homophobic.

The common stereotypic images of older gay and lesbian people emerge out of this heterosexist social context and reflect as well as reinforce fears of homosexuality. What accounts for the disparate views of the lives of older lesbian and gay people when comparing the research literature with common stereotypic images?

THE FRIEND MODEL OF LESBIAN
AND GAY IDENTITY FORMATION

Friend (in press) has developed a model of identity formation which explains some of the diverse types of lives older gay and lesbian people lead. He suggests that there is a range of potential responses to the process of developing a lesbian and gay identity within the heterosexist socio-historical context described above. According to the Friend model, those older gay and lesbian people whose identities conform to the stereotype of loneliness, depression and alienation reflect a group of people who respond to heterosexism by internalizing the beliefs and as a result experience extreme internalized homophobia. As a group, they represent one end point of the range of potential identities according to the Friend model. This group is labeled as "Stereotypic Older Lesbian and Gay People" and are the people identified by the popular images and can be used to confirm the belief that these stereotypes are accurate.

The other end point of the continuum reflects the group labeled as "Affirmative Older Lesbian and Gay People" and are those individuals most likely to be described in the research literature. These older lesbian and gay adults, who are psychologically well adjusted, vibrant and are growing older successfully, represent people who respond to heterosexism by deconstructing its negative assumptions and reconstructing an identity which values and affirms homosexuality. By developing a sense of self which includes a level of comfort and acceptance of homosexuality, this style of managing heterosexism results in the minimization of internalized homophobia.

Within the mid-range of Friend's identity continuum model are the lives of men and women who accommodate to heterosexism by conditionally accepting some aspects of homosexuality while still believing that heterosexuality is inherently better or superior to homosexuality. This group is called "Passing Older Lesbian and Gay People" by the Friend model. This group's members have not challenged the prevailing heterosexist belief system and still experience moderate levels of internalized homophobia. They will, however, either situationally or conditionally accept some aspects of homosexuality, and hence themselves. Some older people in this middle group may in certain instances label themselves as gay or lesbian but they are motivated by a strong investment in passing as heterosexual, or "at least" not appearing to be stereotypically lesbian or gay.

The Friend model is used here as a conceptual framework for understanding family issues for older gay and lesbian adults. The three groups of older lesbian and gay people described by the Friend model represent different places along a proposed identity continuum and reflect only three potential styles of identity formation. Given that this model is constructed as a linear continuum, it has some inherent limitations. For example, there are certainly other styles of identity formation along this continuum which are theoretically possible and worth delineating. This model is also limited by its own linear structure. Weinberg (1984) argues for example, that it is not clear if social identities develop in a unilinear fashion and, therefore, linear models are problematic because they ignore the fact that people are flexible, creative and individualistic in their developmental patterns.

There is tremendous individual variability between and within people who are managing and/or responding to oppression. A weakness of this model is that it does not clearly account for these unique responses. The Friend model is intended to be a conceptual aid used predominately for heuristic purposes. It is offered here to facilitate the understanding of a set of complex and dynamic family processes. As such, it is acknowledged that there are other developmental sequences that can be adapted by individuals and that result in the same or different identities than those described here.

The individual examples which reflect divergence from this model are very important for what they teach about the exceptional and resourceful ways individuals respond to their social environment. It is not the purpose of this discussion, however, to focus on these examples. With regards to these individuals, it is important to note that their courage, despair, creativity, anger and resourcefulness across the life span reflect this great variability among people. This paper focuses on the broader social structures as they impact on groups of people and hence is limited in its applicability to "all cases."

STEREOTYPIC OLDER LESBIAN AND GAY PEOPLE

As a result of internalizing the pervasive heterosexist beliefs, individuals described as "Stereotypic Older Lesbian and Gay People" conform to and reflect the negative images which are commonly used to depict all older gay and lesbian people. In describing persons he works with who are characteristic of this group, Dawson (1982) explains,

> When today's older gays were young, they faced an unrelieved hostility towards homosexuality that was far more virulent than it is today. . . . The need for secrecy caused an isolation which imperiled their most intimate relationships. And the greatest damage was done to those gay people who *believed*

what society said about them, and thus lived in corrosive shame and self-loathing. (p. 5)

While the majority of the men Kimmel (1977) studied were happy and well adjusted, those he labeled as "loners" lived lives "of relatively little sexual intimacy. Typically these men had repressed their sexuality and were often fearful that their homosexuality would be discovered" (p. 388). Likewise, Almvig (1982) and Dunker (1987) both note that although homosexuality in general, and lesbianism in particular, has gained increased social acceptance recently, many older lesbians have led very invisible lives punctuated by secrecy and personal danger.

Persons in this group are likely to believe that if members of their family of origin were to suspect or find out about their homosexuality, they would withdraw their socio-emotional support. Historically, many feared that their families might use their homosexuality as grounds for institutionalization. Given that the public conversions about homosexuality and families were most likely to describe lesbian and gay people who were cut off by their families of origin, institutionalized and subjected to other forms of victimization, many of these fears were legitimate within this historical context.

Secrecy is a major characteristic of this group of older gay and lesbian people. In hiding and keeping parts of themselves from their families and friends, distance is created in these interpersonal relationships. Described as loners, these men and women may have very little contact with their families of origin, or contact which is void of any genuine intimacy and honest sharing.

Having internalized extremely negative notions about their own homosexuality, the women and men in this group distance themselves from other lesbian and gay people as well. Given that people in the "Stereotypic" group may actively avoid openly gay and lesbian people, their opportunities to challenge the heterosexist belief systems which they have internalized is limited.

The type of low self-esteem which results from this sort of internalized homophobia may also result in men and women in this group who lead lives punctuated by very little intimacy with non-gay and non-lesbian people as well. This sort of isolation reflects the assumption that "no one would want to be close to me."

The social psychological processes of heterosexism and ageism [negative attitudes and overt discrimination based on age (Schaie & Geiwitz, 1982)] are consistent with each other. Internalizing heterosexist and homophobic identities allows people in this group to view aging as a punishment for a life poorly lived.

This set of social arrangements results in some particular individual psychological effects. As mentioned earlier, internalizing heterosexism is the foundation of internalized homophobia. The dynamics of this process leads to feelings of guilt, anxiety, self-hatred and low self-esteem. Not only does it interfere with the ability to form close relationships with others, it can lead to despair, depression and suicide.

Internalizing ageist ideology can also facilitate "gerontophobia," the fear of one's own aging and the elderly (Turner, 1985). Gerontophobia may result in greater despair (Erikson, 1963) as a life stage issue among the elderly, as well as the hatred of their age peers.

The "Stereotypic" group which is characterized by emotional distance and loneliness reflects persons whose family relationships can be described as isolated and fragmented. This differs from persons who have freely chosen to remain single (uncoupled) as a family style. Those who actively choose singlehood are likely to have socio-emotional support systems. "Stereotypic Older Lesbian and Gay People" in contrast, are unlikely to have these kinds of support systems.

PASSING OLDER LESBIAN AND GAY PEOPLE

Within the mid-range of the Friend model are the "Passing Older Lesbian and Gay People." This group believes the heterosexist ideologies with which they were raised, while also acknowledging and conditionally accepting their homosexuality. As a result, their level of internalized homophobia is slightly less than the "Stereotypic" group, yet still plays an active role in mediating the tone of their lives. Many manage the conflict of believing that heterosexuality is superior, and conditionally accepting their own homosexuality by marrying heterosexually and/or distancing themselves from anything defined as stereotypically lesbian or gay.

While some members of the "Stereotypic" group may marry heterosexually as well, their level of self-acceptance is lower due to a higher degree of internalized homophobia. For those members of this middle group who do build gay or lesbian relationships, they do so in a way which allows them to appear, or pass as heterosexual.

The families of origin of members of this group may not be aware of the older lesbian or gay person's sexual orientation since this family member is trying to "pass." Some family members may know, but are frequently invested in having this person hide, as well. The gay or lesbian person's sexual orientation may never be discussed and/or family members may help provide ways to maintain this person's "cover." These family members also accept and endorse the prevailing heterosexist ideology and therefore, have an investment in *not* being seen as a family that has an older lesbian or gay member or someone perceived to be gay or lesbian.

Historically, many lesbian and gay people have married heterosexually assuming this was their only option for some degree of happiness (Dunker, 1987; Bozett, 1984; Martin & Lyon, 1973; Miller, 1977). Many of these older persons who are married may wait for their spouse to die before coming out and managing heterosexism in a different fashion (Dunker, 1987). "Passing" for many may have meant marrying and the risk of of coming out to family members perceived as too great. According to Dunker (1987) for many older lesbians

> the risks are too great, especially the risk of exposing their deception to people who love them as they have always known them. Combined with an older person's usual resistance to change, fear of causing pain to those they love is reason enough to continue in the closet. (p. 76)

Not all non-heterosexual people who marry are necessarily trying to "pass"; many are, in fact, happily married bisexual people. Wolf (1985) reports on couples where the husband's bisexuality was known and suggests that there is mutual satisfaction with the quality of the marital relationship. Matteson (1985) states that there is an increase in marriages involving bisexual partners where the relationship is established for positive reasons rather than as an escape from homosexuality. Matteson compared acknowledged and secretive bisexual marriages. In the former type of marriage, the husband's sexual orientation is known and these men "not only accepted their homosexual experience but also affirmed and felt positive about being homosexual" (Matteson, 1985, p. 167).

It is argued here that "Passing Older Lesbian and Gay People" who are married are more likely to be in marriages which Matteson describes as "secret." The negative messages about homosexuality they have internalized would most likely prevent them from sharing about their homosexual orientation with their marital partner. Given the history of heterosexist discourse, being secretive and trying to pass is probably more representative of older gay and lesbian people who marry, than younger lesbian and gay who can more freely choose *not* to marry. In fact, Matteson (1985) reports that husbands in "secret" marriages were older then husbands in "acknowledged" marriages.

As mentioned earlier, married or unmarried, older gay and lesbian adults who try to pass as heterosexual may still have some contact with other lesbian and gay people and may even form long term primary relationships with someone of the same sex. A great deal of energy and effort, however, is spent in appearing to be heterosexual, even within these relationships. Given marginal or conditional self-acceptance, there is a perceived need to live in two mutually exclusive worlds. One is the public world of heterosexuality and the other is a more secret and private gay and lesbian world. This compartmentalization can lead to a fragmented sense of self and a lack of authenticity in interpersonal relationships. According to Minton and McDonald (1983/84), "In choosing to hide an essential part of the self, individuals are left with a gnawing feeling that they are really valued for what others expect them to be rather than for who they really are" (p. 102).

This marginalization can lead to a splitting off of sexual and emotional relationships, especially for men. Other men may be used for sex with no or little emotional attachment, where their heterosexual family or marriage is used for intimacy. Yet these latter relationships are marginalized as well, by sexual limitations and limits in interpersonal honesty.

There is a great deal of effort, both physical and psychological, which is required in "passing." This energy is reflected in the often complicated styles of living which individuals who are trying to pass create. Living arrangements may include separate bedrooms, telephones or even housing, for the purpose of concealing a same-sexed relationship. Martin and Lyon (1979) report on a lesbian couple who wrote:

> We are in our fifties, have been together for 18 years, but have never declared our love for each other in front of a third party. When we shut our doors at night we shut the world out. We have no gay friends that we know of. We are looking for companions, friendship and support, but in the lesbian organizations we've contacted we find only badge-wearing, drum-beating, foot-stomping social reformers. They consider our conservative life "oppressed," and we think of their way of life as "flagrant." There must be more like us, but how do we meet them? (pp. 140-141)

Psychologically marginal or conditional self-acceptance can compound feelings of anxiety which are not uncommon for people in this group. Hightened levels of anxiety and self-consciousness are generated by the fear of being "found out" and the energy expended in preventing this from happening. Given the perceived need to "pass," the emotional costs can be high. There may, as a result, be an absence of emotional supports in times of need or crisis. According to Martin and Lyon (1979),

> Other women who had been in lesbian relationships of long standing poured out their grief over the death of a lover. These couples had no gay friends, and the surviving partner felt bereft and alone. True, some of them had straight friends or relatives who knew, but it had never been discussed. (p. 140)

For those "Passing Older Lesbian and Gay People" who choose to marry, their family relationships may reflect other common family "issues." The older gay man in this group may indulge in secret extramarital affairs (not unlike married heterosexual men and women) although his partners may be other men. Men in this group may rationalize that they would only be "cheating" on their wives if their affair were with another woman. Older lesbian women in this group may find little sexual fulfillment in their marriages. This is not unlike many married heterosexual women who have internalized the sexist notion that female sexuality should be focused on her partner's (assumed to be male) pleasure and her own is secondary or not important at all.

AFFIRMATIVE OLDER LESBIAN AND GAY PEOPLE

"Affirmative Older Lesbian and Gay People" develop their identities by managing heterosexism in a particular way. They deconstruct heterosexist ideology by challenging its assumptions and examining critically whether being an older lesbian or gay person necessarily means living a life described by the stereotypes.

Frequently stereotypes are maintained by viewing persons who do not fit the image as "exceptions" (Babad, Birnbaum & Benne, 1983). Deconstructing heterosexism involves challenging the somewhat arbitrary nature of stereotyping, as well as its purpose as a form of social control. Those who do not conform to the stereotypes, while they may be exceptional, need not be exceptions. Once heterosexist notions are challenged and deconstructed, the individual is then able to reconstruct their identity on their own terms. For many, this means reconstructing what it means to be gay or lesbian as positive and valuable. These are the older lesbian and gay adults most likely to be described in the research literature.

Within the body of scholarly writing, the vast majority of older gay and lesbian people are described as attaining high levels of self-acceptance and psychological adjustment; even within the oppressive contexts through which many were raised (Almvig, 1982; Berger, 1982a, 1982b; Dunker, 1987; Francher & Henkin, 1973; Friend, 1980, 1987; Kelly, 1977; Kimmel, 1977, 1978; Raphael & Robinson, 1980; Weinberg, 1970). This degree of self-acceptance may also result in members of this group being more willing and accessible to participate in research projects.

Harry (1986) discusses this type of source-related sampling bias as it impacts on research on gay men. He argues that access to research samples is limited to lesbian and gay people who have some level of association with the gay and lesbian communities. Given that the oldest and the youngest age groups are least likely to be involved in these types of community resources, Harry (1986) concludes that "our studies of homosexuality are largely studies of active gays, those for whom their sexual orientation constitutes a lifestyle" (p. 22). Therefore, those who have internalized hetero-sexist discourse and have either repressed their sexuality of "hide" it to some degree are not easily available for research.

For similar reasons, members of the "Affirmative" group may be more reflective of those older lesbian and gay people who re-spond to community outreach. Senior Action in a Gay Environment (SAGE) is a New York based program providing social services for older gay and lesbian people. These inter-generational service func-tions help to enhance the quality of life for all the people who are involved in SAGE. As Executive Director, Dawson (1982) indi-cates that the largest percentage of older adults with whom he works are vibrant, active and independent.

It is more likely that members of the "Passing" group who use social service programs would shy away from groups like SAGE, opting for more "traditional" senior centers. Those in the "Stereo-typic" group would avoid contact with most types of social service programs given their long-standing pattern of isolation. At the same time, this is the population both in greatest need and most likely to be targeted by agency outreach.

For some, the process of challenging heterosexism and recon-structing a positive and affirmative lesbian or gay identity may in-volve both personal and political activism. For some this activism can express a form of resistance to the definitions of self imposed by others. Foucault (1978) argues that one function of resistance is to gain self-empowerment by reconstructing the meaning of a ho-mosexual identity—an attempt to control one's own sexuality and one's destiny. These women and men may be engaged in a purpose-ful attempt to challenge and change the oppressive hegemony of socio-sexual ideologies.

According to one older gay man for example,

> The candle of being an activist was lit and I am very greatful for it because it has helped me since then to actively fight my illness. And I hope I will be around to fight for a longer time. I will fight for any minority discrimination, whether it be Black,

Jewish, elderly or gay/lesbian. I will always fight. As long as I live, I hope I have the spirit to fight. (Pioneer Productions, 1984)

As a result of this type of activism, the affirmative identity developed reflects this process of resistance and empowerment.

For some, being engaged in purposeful social change may be an important source of reconstructing a positive gay or lesbian identity. For other members of the "Affirmative" group, however, self-acceptance and social integration may not be a conscious socio-political activity. Rather, forming an affirmative identity may simply illustrate people living lives that comfortably and individualistically reflect who they are, without a focused attempt to necessarily change dominant socio-sexual ideologies. Explaining this process, a 69-year-old lesbian says,

> For many years, homosexuals, men and women, had to live in a heterosexual world and absorb the guilt and the shame and the stereotyping that was foisted upon us. We felt sick. We felt queer. But after a while. . . . I began to dispell all that internalization and realize that I was a human being. I was a moral woman and I had raised a wonderful family. My children and my grandchildren loved me and respected me. And there must be a reason for that. Because I'm a respectable and respectful citizen, living my life the best way I could. And I developed a very strong identity of what I was—I'm a lesbian woman and I live like one. I defy anyone else to pass judgment on the way I live and my personal health. (KYW-TV, 1985)

Members of the families of origin for people in the "Affirmative" group are more likely to know about the sexual orientation of their older lesbian and gay relatives. Responses to this knowledge reflect the range from acceptance to rejection. The potential for family acceptance is greater than rejection, however. Friend (1980) reports, in fact, that the older gay men studied found that they did not lose any family supports when they came out, even though they had anticipated this loss occurring.

The older gay or lesbian person who has gone through the process of deconstructing prevailing heterosexist discourse and establishing a positive sense of self can serve as both a role model for this process and as a source of information for their families of origin. This can aid individual family members in their own process of challenging heterosexism and internalized homophobia. Knowing the value of community support, the "Affirmative" older gay or lesbian person may encourage their family members to participate in groups like Parents and Friends of Lesbians and Gays (PFLAG), for example. Here family members can get support along with other families who are confronting issues of heterosexism and homophobia.

Like the older lesbian or gay person who has engaged in establishing an affirmative identity, their family members have the potential to participate in a similar process. In this way they can develop an affirmative identity of what it means to be part of a family with someone who is an affirmative older gay or lesbian person.

For those family members who have so strongly internalized the heterosexist beliefs, engaging in a process to confront their own homophobia may not be something they choose or feel capable of doing. The costs for this stance include not being able to share in, or learn from the lives of their older lesbian and gay family members. According to one older lesbian grandmother, for example, her hopes for what she can teach her family are:

> I think the legacy I would like to leave as a Black lesbian mother is to have my children have loving relationships. To learn to respect each other. Learn to respect *women* as human beings. I feel we have a double struggle. That is to say gay men and lesbians of color, to change what society thinks we should or shouldn't be. (Pioneer Productions, 1984)

Had her family rejected her, they would have robbed themselves of the opportunity to learn a very valuable and meaningful lesson.

If part of deconstructing heterosexist notions and reconstructing homosexuality as a positive and affirmative identity involves confronting the somewhat arbitrary ways in which sexual feelings get defined as "appropriate" and "inappropriate," then this same type of analysis can apply to the ways in which traditional gender roles are socially constructed. As a result, throughout their lives, older

gay and lesbian adults who have challenged these socially constructed notions have had the potential for greater freedom to learn
and engage in skills which may be considered "non-traditional"
along gender role lines.

Greater gender role flexibility may allow older lesbian and gay to
have developed more ways of caring for themselves which feel
comfortable and appropriate. These skills may be less developed or
less comfortable for older heterosexual men and women who are
either used to having, or expecting a wife or husband to care for
them. The recently widowed heterosexual wife, for example, may
feel uncomfortable learning about the maintenance of her car if this
had always been seen as her husband's job. The widowed heterosexual husband may have to struggle with learning to cook or do
laundry if these are behaviors he always viewed as more appropriate
for his wife.

Challenging the arbitrary social construction of gender roles in
this way may be more threatening to older heterosexual people than
older gay and lesbian adults. In many ways the root of hetero*sexism*
is sexism. If a function of sexism is to insure that boys and girls
grow up to be defined as "real" men and women, this definition
includes being heterosexual. Men who are seen as "too sensitive"
and women who are thought to be "too independent" not only violate traditional gender role expectations, they are also negatively
labeled as homosexual. In this way, a homophobic label is used to
enforce a sexist sentiment. Lesbian and gay people who affirm their
identity are not going to feel as threatened if people "wonder about
them" as a result of their gender role behavior. Having addressed
these issues earlier in life, affirmative older gay and lesbian people
may feel more comfortable engaging in non-traditional gender role
behaviors than their heterosexual age-peers who find themselves
forced to because of necessity.

In western culture, what it means to be an older person is also the
result of particular socially constructed beliefs and attitudes. These
attitudes, as mentioned earlier can be defined as ageist. While the
views of aging and older people are generally negative, there is also
a double standard whereby views about older women are frequently
more negative than those about older men (Bennett & Eckman,
1973; Francher, 1962; Green, 1981; Palmore, 1971; Sontag, 1975).

Ageism and the resulting gerontophobia can also be challenged and reconstructed in positive and affirmative ways.

Access to diverse models of what it means to be an older person is essential for persons engaged in this process of confronting ageism. These models must include older people who are active, productive, sexual and self-determining individuals. A diversity of styles of adjusting to growing old provides evidence to the individual that stereotypical images are arbitrarily constructed and, therefore, have the potential for change.

Older lesbian and gay people who have had experience in reconstructing what homosexuality and gender mean are also more likely to be able to transfer this analysis to the process of deconstructing and reconstructing ageist identities for themselves as older people. Additional research is needed to more fully understand the separate relationships between this identity deconstruction/reconstruction process along these socially constructed dimensions of self (e.g., sexual orientation, gender and age). Other dimensions to explore must include race, social class, ethnicity and ability/disability status. This type of analysis is essential for more fully understanding the lives of older gay and lesbian people. As Dunker (1987) suggests,

> Old lesbians, out or closeted, have had to develop certain skills and character traits in order to survive, as do other oppressed minorities. . . . we've had to develop a degree of solid, stubborn self-confidence and courage. These qualities depend on a clear and pervasive sense of self-worth. We have *had* to be autonomous and in charge of our own lives. These skills are even more necessary for minority women . . . who have . . . . always had to support themselves, and they have had to deal with the double oppression of race and sex. (p. 76)

The survival skills Dunker refers to are part of what Kimmel (1978) calls "crisis competence." He argues that in managing the potential crisis that being lesbian or gay means in our culture, "it may provide a perspective on major life crises and a sense of crisis competence that buffers the person against later crises" (Kimmel, 1978, p. 117).

The survival skills involved in crisis competence are functional in regard to adjusting to aging. An example of this is reflected in the fact that part of the process of challenging heterosexism involves addressing the potential loss of family or origin and friends. As discussed earlier, family members may pull away or may be expected to withdraw from older gay and lesbian relatives. The older lesbian and gay person, therefore, has to respond to this by preparing some psychological response in anticipation of this potential loss. These skills function in managing other age-related crises of loss, such as forced retirement, and the loss of family members or friends due to death or moving away. These are common age-related losses which older gay and lesbian people may be more "competent" in managing given anticipatory preparation, than their heterosexual age peers.

Crisis competence may also be reflected in taking other protective stances in planning for the future. This is characteristic of "Affirmative Older Lesbian and Gay People." Given changing family patterns and greater longevity it is no longer fair to assume that children or extended family will provide for their older family members. While many adults grow old believing in and expecting this type of support, Dawson (1982) reports that gay people he works with "have been less likely to assume that their families would provide for them in old age" (p. 6) and are more likely to have carefully planned for their own future security. By considering the potential loss of family support earlier in their lives, older lesbian and gay people may be better prepared for the realities of old age.

Crisis competence, gender role flexibility and reconstructing the personal meanings of homosexuality and aging so they are positive, have the potential for powerful effects on the individual psychology of older gay and lesbian adults. Members of the "affirmative" group have adopted a set of beliefs which promote their self-worth and are likely to be proficient in skills which aid daily living and a sense of competence and empowerment. These beliefs and behaviors have a positive impact on one's feelings of self-acceptance and self-esteem.

For many "Affirmative Older Lesbian and Gay People" another potential resource is the development of an expanded definition of "family." Francher and Henkin (1973) report that older gay men who were rejected by their families replaced these supports with a strong network of friendships. Bell and Weinberg (1978) describe these friendship circles as functioning as a "surrogate family." According to Almvig (1982) "'family' for the older lesbian can be made up of a current lover, past lovers and friends, besides her own blood-line family" (p. 148).

Friend (1980) reports that the older gay men in his sample reinforced family supports with those of friends. In anticipation of losing family support, a family of friends was created. Friend (1980) concludes that this helps the adjustment process by providing a broad base of support to rely on in times of need.

Self-selected family networks suggest that "Affirmative Older Lesbian and Gay People" are saying "you can pick your family *as well as* your friends." These self-selected and self-defined families provide systems of support and care which are functional in meeting the needs of these lesbian and gay people as they grow old.

"Affirmative Older Lesbian and Gay People" are also more likely to find strength in the resources of an empowering gay and lesbian community. In many locations, opportunities for cultural, social, political and religious activities are open to older lesbian and gay people. Almost every major religious denomination, for example, has a gay and lesbian congregation and/or caucus. Some large urban areas have organizations like the New York based SAGE, as well. "Affirmative Older Lesbian and Gay People" are also more likely to choose to live in places where these resources are available.

As mentioned previously, many "Affirmative Older Lesbian and Gay People" have planned ahead for their own futures. Dunker (1987) argues that this type of planning is essential. For example, planning for health care may include establishing adequate disability and health insurance programs. Having knowledge of health care and legal systems policy, prior to a crisis is important in planning. Older lesbian and gay people who have a clear will and power of attorney, for example, are better equipped to manage hospital policies which may exclude lovers and friends from decisions regarding care and even visiting privileges (Kimmel, 1978; Martin & Lyon, 1979).

Some blood relatives may use the fact of homosexuality or an open gay or lesbian relationship as evidence of incompetence, or in contesting a will. The older lesbian or gay person who wants to ensure that funeral arrangements, personal and joint property and living will decisions are respected must plan in advance. The bereavement process following the death of a lover or friend can be helped greatly if these issues are addressed in advance. Older gay and lesbian people who have a comprehensive system of support, including family of origin, family of friends, lover and community are more likely to have the resources for managing these issues.

CONCLUSIONS

Several conclusions and recommendations emerge as a result of this discussion. First, additional research is needed to verify and refine the Friend model of identity formation as it is used here to understand the lives of older lesbian and gay people. Given that the "Stereotypic" and "Passing" groups are least represented in the literature, additional research, information and services in relation to these groups are necessary.

Also, in understanding the full range of experience among this diverse group of older people, examination of the impact of race, social class, ethnicity and ability/disability status must be addressed. Conclusions drawn on upper and middle class, well educated white, able-bodied people (mostly men) are very limited.

A cohort analysis which examines the identity management process by older versus younger lesbian and gay people is also needed. This type of research will provide valuable insight about the extent to which differences between age groups are a result of aging or are a function of living in different socio-historical periods. This will further aid in a valuable understanding not only of the lives of these women and men, by also about the transhistorical vs. context specific nature of heterosexism.

With the increasing visibility and voice of the conservative New Right, it is especially important to renegotiate the social constructions of sexuality. Given this context, whereby all of us are impacted upon by heterosexism, we can learn important lessons from understanding the various ways in which older gay and lesbian adults have managed these issues in their lives. For younger lesbian and gay people they can serve as valuable and valued role models for establishing affirmative identities and self directed futures. In addition, the older person may be provided with a sense of generativity by guiding the next generation (Erikson, 1963).

For heterosexual people, affirmative older gay and lesbian people can serve as positive role models as well. For example, heterosexual adults have the potential to enjoy closer relationships with friends and family of the same sex if they learn to renegotiate heterosexism in a way which affirms their sexuality without devaluing homosexuality. In this way they can minimize the homophobia which often interferes with intimacy in heterosexual relationships. Also, the heterosexual person who challenges heterosexism and its inherent sexism has the potential for experiencing greater comfort in their gender role expressions. As discussed earlier, this may be functional in adjusting to the aging process. As role models, therefore, older lesbian and gay adults who affirm themselves can be sources of inspiration and power for women and men of all ages and sexual orientations.

REFERENCES

Almvig, C. (1982). *The invisible minority: aging and lesbianism*. New York: Utica College of Syracuse University.

Babad, E.Y., Birnbaum, M. & Benne, K.D. (1983). *The social self*. Beverly Hills: Sage Publications.

Bell, A.P. & Weinberg, M.S. (1978). *Homosexualities*. New York: Simon and Schuster.

Bennett, R. & Eckman, J. (1973). Attitudes toward aging: a critical review of recent literature and implications for future research. In C. Eisdorf and M. Powell Lawton (Eds.), *The Psychology of Adult Development and Aging*. Washington D.C.: American Psychological Association.

Berger, R.M. (1980). Psychological adaptation of the older homosexual male. *Journal of Homosexuality*, 5, 161-175.

Berger, R.M. (1982a). The unseen minority: Older gays and lesbians. *Social Work*, 236-242.

Berger, R.M. (1982b). *Gay and gray*. Urbana: University of Illinois Press.

Boswell, J. (1980). *Christianity, social tolerance and homosexuality*. Chicago: University of Chicago Press.

Bozett, F.W. (1984). Parenting concerns of gay fathers. *Topics in Clinical Nursing*, 6 (3), 60-71.

Bullough, V. & Bullough, B. (1977). *Sin, sickness and sanity: A history of sexual attitudes*. New York: New American Library.

Dawson, K. (November 1982). Serving the older gay community. *SIECUS Report*, 5-6.

Dunker, B. (1987). In The Boston Lesbian Psychologies Collective (Ed.), *Lesbian Psychologies*. Urbana: University of Illinois Press.

Erikson, E. (1963). *Childhood and society*. New York: W.W. Norton and Co.

Foucault, M. (1978). *The history of sexuality volume 1: An introduction*. New York: Vintage Books.

Francher, S.J. (1962). American values and the disenfranchisement of the aged. *Eastern Anthropologist*, 22, 29-36.

Francher, S.J. & Henkin, J. (1973). The menopausal queen. *American Journal of Orthopsychiatry*, 43, 670-674.

Friend, R.A. (1980). GAYging: Adjustment and the older gay male. *Alternative Lifestyles*, 3, 231-248.

Friend, R.A. (1987). The individual and social psychology of aging: Clinical implications for lesbians and gay men. *Journal of Homosexuality*, 14 (1/2), 307-331.

Friend, R.A. (in press). A theory of successful aging. *Journal of Homosexuality*.

Green, S.K. (1981). Attitudes and perceptions about the elderly: Current and future perspectives. *Aging and Human Development*, 13, 95-115.

Herek, G.M. (1984). Beyond "homophobia": A social psychological perspective on attitudes towards lesbians and gay men. *Journal of Homosexuality*, 10 (1/2), 1-21.

Herek, G.M. (1986). On heterosexual masculinity. *American Behavioral Scientist*, 29 (5), 563-577.

Harry, J. (1986). Sampling gay men. *The Journal of Sex Research*, 22 (1), 21-34.

Katz, J. (1976). *Gay american history*. New York: Thomas Y. Crowell Company.

Kelly, J. (1977). The aging male homosexual: Myth and reality. *The Gerontologist*, 17, 328-332.

Kimmel, D.C. (1977). Psychotherapy and the older gay man. *Psychotherapy: Theory, Research and Practice*, 14, 386-393.

Kimmel, D.C. (1978). Adult development and aging: A gay perspective. *Journal of Social Issues*, 34, 113-130.

KYW-TV. (1985, November). *People are talking* (Television broadcast). Philadelphia.

Martin, D. & Lyon, P. (1979). The older lesbian. In B. Berzon and R. Leighton (Eds.), *Positively gay*. Millbrae, CA: Celestial Arts.

Matteson, D.R. (1985). Bisexual men in marriage: Is a positive homosexual identity and stable marriage possible? *Journal of Homosexuality*, 11 (1/2), 149-171.

Miller, B. (1979). Unpromised paternity: Life-styles of gay fathers. In M.P. Levine (Ed.), *Gay men: The sociology of male homosexuality*. New York: Harper and Row.

Minton, H.L. & McDonald, G.J. (1983/1984). Homosexual identity formation as a developmental process. *Journal of Homosexuality*, 9, 91-104.

Palmore, E. (1971). Attitudes toward aging as shown by humor. *The Gerontologist*, 11, 181-187.

Pioneer Productions (1984). *Silent pioneers* [Film]. New York: Pioneer Productions.

Raphael, S.M. & Robinson, M.K. (1980). The older lesbian. *Alternative Lifestyles*, 3, 207-229.

Rubin, G. (1984). Thinking sex: Notes for a radical theory of the politics of sexuality. In C. Vance (Ed.), *Pleasure and danger: Exploring female sexuality*. Boston: Routledge & Kegan Paul.

Schaie, K.W. & Geiwitz, J. (1982). *Adult Development and Aging*. Boston: Little, Brown and Company.

Sontag, S. (1975). The double standard of aging. In *No longer young: The older woman in America*. Proceedings of the 26th Annual Conference on Aging, The University of Michigan, Wayne State University, 31-39.

Turner, J. (1985, May). Personal Communication.

Weeks, J. (1977). *Coming out: Homosexual politics in Britain, from the nineteenth century to the present*. London: Quartet.

Weinberg, G. (1972). *Society and the healthy homosexual*. New York: St. Martin's.

Weinberg, M.S. (1970). The male homosexual: Age-related variations in social and pychological characteristics. *Social Problems*, 17, 527-537.

Weinberg, T.S. (1983). *Gay men, gay selves: The social construction of homosexual identities*. New York: Irvington.

Weinberg, T.S. (1984). Biology, ideology, and the reification of developmental stages in the study of homosexual identities. *Journal of Homosexuality*, 10, 77-85.

Wolf, T.J. (1985). Marriages of Bisexual Men. *Journal of Homosexuality*, 11 (1/2), 135-148.

Institutional Religion
and Gay/Lesbian Oppression

J. Michael Clark
Joanne Carlson Brown
Lorna M. Hochstein

SUMMARY. While gay men and lesbians have been consistently involved in the institutional forms of Judaeo-Christianity throughout history, those institutions have themselves failed to accept or support openly gay individuals or couples, either professionally, liturgically/pastorally, or doctrinally. Judaeo-Christianity has instead encouraged homophobia in society, thereby fostering antigay oppression which dehumanizes gay individuals, undermines gay couplings, and exacerbates familial tensions between gay and nongay relatives. The United Methodist Church's struggle over the ordination of gays/lesbians and Catholicism's most recent antigay promulgation provide two case studies for examining the dilemmas which institutional religion poses for gay/lesbian people.

Although gay men and lesbians have consistently been active participants in the institutional forms of Judaeo-Christianity throughout history, institutionalized religion has just as consistently failed to accept or support *openly* gay individuals or their relationships, either professionally, liturgically and pastorally, or doctrinally. Boswell (1980), for example, has described the extent to which gay men were drawn to pre-Thomist (pre-twelfth century) Roman Ca-

J. Michael Clark, MDiv, PhD, 738 Myrtle St. N.E., #10, Atlanta, GA 30308; Joanne Carlson Brown, PhD, is Professor of Church History and Ecumenics, St. Andrews College, Saskatoon, Saskatchewan S7N 0W3 Canada; Lorna M. Hochstein, PhD, is Clinical Director, Bellville Counseling Associates, 25 Huntington Ave., Boston, MA 02116.

Research was partially supported by a 1987-1988 Research Assistance Grant, American Academy of Religion, to J. M. C.

tholicism, and both Curb and Manahan (1985) and DeStefano (1986) have reported that both gay priests and lesbian nuns still constitute a disproportionately large percentage of Catholic clergy, official church doctrine notwithstanding. Apart from the clergy, gay men and lesbians have formed either officially recognized or unofficial support groups within virtually every Christian denomination and have even established their own denomination of churches (the Universal Fellowship of Metropolitan Community Churches) and a loose federation of synagogues (the World Congress of Gay and Lesbian Jewish Organizations) (cf. Saslow, 1987). This seeming plethora of gay/lesbian religious involvement notwithstanding, the vast majority of gay men and lesbians—and certainly those who are openly gay—actually find themselves outside either affirmative theological discourse or institutionalized religion; many of them are, in fact, quite hostile toward a western religious heritage whose official doctrine and tradition, both Jewish and Christian, are unabashedly homophobic and "heterosexist" (cf. Clark, 1987a, 1989). This ongoing antipathy is not without serious implications for gay men and lesbians, as well as for their nongay families of origin.

At the professional level, the ordained clergy is virtually closed to *openly* gay men and lesbians. Only the United Church of Christ, the Unitarian Universalists, and Reconstructionist Judaism, among traditional denominations, have clearly stated policies endorsing the ordination of gays/lesbians. Unfortunately, the independent, congregationally autonomous nature of these three denominations means that ordination does not guarantee gay/lesbian clergy access to actual parish ministry (cf. Comstock, 1987). In all other denominations a declaration or discovery of homosexuality can actually result in disciplinary action and even dismissal (cf. Sherwood, 1987). Similarly, at the liturgical/pastoral level, gay men and lesbians—particularly those in committed, coupled relationships—find little, if any, support. Among nongay traditional denominations, only the Unitarian-Universalists and some Episcopalian dioceses offer rituals to bless, sanctify, and support gay/lesbian couples. Fortunato (1985) fears that even these meager offerings are less an affirmation of the maturity, commitment, and value of gay/lesbian couples, than merely one subtle means on the part of these churches to discourage gay male promiscuity in the wake of AIDS.

Finally, at the doctrinal level, most denominations still fail to completely accept *any* unmarried and yet sexually active people, thereby automatically excluding gay men and lesbians. At best, a number of religious institutions will concede that "constitutional homosexuality" is not a matter of choice, while insisting nevertheless that homosexual *acts* are still sinful. This insistence upon separating sexual orientation from actual sexual fulfillment, upon "loving the sinner" but "hating the sin," belies a fundamental homophobia. This homophobia is grounded in a stubborn refusal either to thoroughly reject the rigid Mosaic condemnation of homosexuality in Leviticus or to reconsider the traditional antigay interpretation of the biblical Sodom and Gomorrah stories. Despite selective adherence to, or generally nonliteral interpretations of, the bulk of Leviticus' moral code, and despite accumulated biblical scholarship which contends that inhospitality toward strangers and *not* homosexuality was the real "sin of Sodom" (Edwards, 1984, Horner, 1978, McNeill, 1976, Nelson, 1977), institutionalized Judaeo-Christianity continues to act inhospitably, if not hostilely, toward sexually active gay men and lesbians. Gay/lesbian individuals within the majority of religious denominations consequently encounter religious as well as social obstacles to the processes of developing self-acceptance and self-esteem. At the same time, they also encounter subliminal messages which endorse secrecy, celibacy, and/or the absence of coupled sexual intimacy as the burden they must somehow bear (cf. Boyd, 1984, 1987, Morton, 1985). Their nongay families of origin are thereby actually discouraged, rather than encouraged, to accept and support their gay/lesbian adult children and/or their partners and relationships. Religious doctrine thus exacerbates the tensions and alienation already potentially present between gay people and their families.

A homophobic or heterosexist bias permeates twentieth century western culture and society so thoroughly as to make separating social attitudes from their roots in religious belief systems virtually impossible. Even Boswell (1980), who insists that the Church prior to the twelfth century refused to make specific pronouncements against homosexuals and even fostered homosexual intimacy within its own ranks as a result, does admit that, by sanctifying and codifying cultural homophobia from the twelfth century onward, the Church ultimately gave homophobia its blessing and thus insured that the subsequent symbiotic development of Church and society would exclude homosexuality from any degree of moral acceptability. Once homophobia became official Christian policy, the Church could endorse and later encourage antigay violence and pogroms. As a result, gay men and lesbians could be attacked and killed with impunity – and frequently by law – until well into the nineteenth century (Crompton, 1978). Crompton (1978) convincingly argues that the Levitical code and institutionalized Judaeo-Christianity together have informed all genocidally antigay legislation from the first century through the Nazi holocaust, during which some quarter-million gay men died (cf. Plant, 1986, Clark, 1987b). This absolute fusion of a heterosexually majoritarian culture with religiously mandated homophobia has led Morton (1985) to conclude that "compulsory heterosexuality or homophobia . . . appears to find in patriarchal religion its foremost stronghold" (p. xxx). Thus, far from providing religious support and/or spiritual nurture, even for gay/lesbian believers, institutionalized Judaeo-Christianity has actually been the arbiter of homophobic judgment, fostering rejection and alienation not only within gay/lesbian individuals and gay/lesbian relationships, but also between gays/lesbians and both their families of origin and their native cultural ethos (cf. Clark, 1987c).

Fortunato (1983) has described the resultant "gestalt of [gay] oppression" as a "constant, chronic feeling of not belonging, of being threatened and rejected," a feeling which is internalized and interwoven with the earliest processes of gay/lesbian self-discovery and self-examination (p. 86). Early in these processes, oppression includes self-denial (the denial of one's homosexuality), religious doubt (the seeming irreconcilability of gay/lesbian identity, homosexual behavior, and one's spirituality), and the consequent guilt and senses of unworthiness, loneliness, and fear of disclosure (Fortunato, 1983). Once an individual is publically identifiable as gay, oppression broadens to include a wide range of experiences, including the potential loss of a job or the denial of one's right to practice his/her profession. Job security and the hope of advancement dissolve as one is ignored, passed over, or worse, never even allowed admittance to the professional system (such as with the majority of institutionalized religious forms) (Fortunato, 1983, Goodman et al., 1983).

Unlike all other minorities, openly gay people frequently experience rejection and avoidance not only by church/synagogue and society, but by their natural familial support systems as well, which in turn encourages gay ghettoization (cf. Fortunato, 1983, Dunkel and Hatfield, 1986). Even in the relative "safety in numbers" of an urban gay ghetto, however, homophobia still includes incidents of verbal and physical abuse (antigay violence) and the virtual absence of either ecclesiastical or secular/legal protections. Gay/lesbian sex is still criminal in 26 states, making any public display of affection acceptable for heterosexuals utterly taboo for gay people; gay/lesbian aliens may be denied entry into the U.S.; gay/lesbian parents may lose not only custody of, but even visitation rights to their children; and, all gay people are subject to police harassment and, when antigay crimes are reported, often find themselves punished (blaming the victim) and their attacker(s) set free (Goodman et al., 1983, cf. Fortunato, 1983). Moreover, coupled gay and lesbian relationships enjoy *no* legal or financial benefits or social support, no tax breaks, no spousal insurance benefits, and no public ceremonies to hallow their relationships. Gay partners cannot "marry," "divorce," or bequeath with any assurances. Same sex couples may even experience difficulties in finding housing or tolerant landlords (cf. Fortunato, 1983, Goodman et al., 1983). With the few exceptions noted above, institutionalized religion has made little effort to provide the support and relief for gays/lesbians lacking in law and society. More often than not, the religious system has actually exacerbated the homophobia already extant in both spheres.

In addition to this generalized homophobia and its clear implications for gay men and lesbians, the occurrence of AIDS — primarily among gay men in the U.S. to date (cf. Lieberson, 1986) — has meant a redoubling of oppression and discrimination. Fed by fear of AIDS, both homophobia and antigay violence have steadily increased during the last decade and, once again, institutionalized Judaeo-Christianity has been slow to respond, at best, and blatantly hostile, at worst. The Religious Right, for example, has consistently used the AIDS health crisis as an opportunity to stand in judgment over both gay people and any society which even marginally permits homosexuality to exist unpunished in its midst (Clark, 1987c). With certain noteworthy exceptions (Bohne, 1986, Clark, 1986, 1987c, Fortunato, 1985, 1987, Hancock, 1985, Howell, 1985, Nelson, 1986, Shelp et al., 1986, Stiles, 1986), the religious and pastoral care systems have moved *very* slowly to respond compassionately to the AIDS crisis, thereby leaving pastoral care of persons-with-AIDS (PWAs) primarily upon the shoulders of voluntary AIDS-support services organizations (cf. Clark, 1986, 1987c).

Despite the full weight of religious pronouncements against them, as well as the absence of liturgical and pastoral support for them, gay men and lesbians continue to battle for ordination in traditional denominations, to argue against homophobic biblical interpretations, and to develop and nurture gay-supportive religious forms. Within the Judaeo-Christian tradition, for example, Boyd (1984, 1987), Clark (1986, 1987a, 1989), Fortunato (1983, 1987), Heyward (1984), and McNeill (1983, 1988) have begun to develop liberation theologies borne in and from gay/lesbian existence. Outside the Judaeo-Christian tradition, Clark (1987a) and Thompson (1987) have reported and described the rich variety of "alternative spiritualities" which gay men and lesbians are pursuing (cf. Evans, 1978, Grahn, 1984, Walker, 1980, Wright and Inesse, 1979). Moreover, Fortunato (1983) and Topper (1986) go so far as to contend that confronting and penetrating the experience(s) of oppression and consequent loss actually enable spiritual deepening for gay people. And, Fortunato (1987) and Shelp et al. (1986) have argued that the gay/lesbian community's confrontation with AIDS, with redoubled homophobia, and with premature suffering and dying in the 1980s is leading that community toward both a more profound compassion and a deeper appreciation for the genuine pluralism of all humanity. Thus, in spite of official religious rejection and even condemnation, gay men and lesbians are increasingly living out of a prophetically mature religious/spiritual dimension (cf. McNeill, 1988, Clark, 1989).

Such a panoramic review of institutionalized religion's historical and present policies toward homosexual persons and their effects upon gays/lesbians, their coupled relationships, and their relationships with nongay family members can be vividly illustrated by two cases in point. Within mainline Protestantism the United Methodist Church's failure to develop a consistent or thoroughgoing theology of human sexuality has created confusion in terms of both ordinational policy/practice for, and overall participation by, gays/lesbians (cf. Brown, 1988). Within Roman Catholicism the most recent Papal declaration regarding gay people has not only reiterated an official condemnation of homosexuality; it has banished gay/lesbian support groups from access to church property and church funds and even goes so far as to suggest that antigay violence may be understandable (cf. Hochstein, 1987). A closer examination of these two specific situations within traditional Christianity today may, therefore, provide a still clearer picture of the dilemma(s) posed by institutional religion for gay men and lesbians and for their couplings and nongay families as well.

THE UNITED METHODIST CHURCH

While the presence of lesbians and gay men in the churches is clearly not new, policy issues and statements resulting from that presence have been on Protestant denominational agendas for only a relatively short time—roughly since the late 1960s. Since that time the contemporary gay/lesbian liberation movement has encouraged gay/lesbian people in both church and society to become more vocal and more visible, which in turn has compelled the churches to respond. Unfortunately, the churches have most often responded in an inconsistent and crisis-oriented manner, attempting to affirm *all* persons as children of God who are of infinite worth and value, while simultaneously rejecting gays/lesbians for that which makes them who and what they are. As each particular challenge or person or specific issue has come to the fore, a specific response has been generated, but no overall theological view has been developed to support or provide a framework within which to work and study. All churches, and especially their gay/lesbian members, suffer because of this "knee-jerk" pattern of response. One case in point is that of the United Methodist Church (UMC). While this case study could be repeated in numerous Protestant denominations, the UMC provides one of the best examples of the dilemma facing gays/lesbians and offers one of the best frameworks within which to remedy the theological incoherence and confusion which characterize church life.

The first official statement adopted by the UMC regarding lesbians and gay men appeared in the Social Principles Statement of 1972. At the end of a basically strong affirmation of human sexuality, the phrase "though we do not condone the practice of homosexuality and consider this practice incompatible with Christian teaching" was added as an amendment from the floor of the quadrennial General Conference, a highly unusual occurrence (cf. Brown, 1988). The "incompatible with Christian teaching" amendment was an abrupt contrast to the originally proposed statement and demonstrates perfectly the incoherence of the UMC's attitudes and policies. While the Social Principles are neither church law nor rules in any binding sense, they serve as guidelines for such rules (the quadrennially issued *Book of Discipline*). This amended statement has consequently been used over time to justify ever increasing discriminatory legislation in relation to gay and lesbian people.

During the closing hours of the subsequent 1976 General Conference, when the rules had been changed to suspend debate, new legislation was added to the UMC *Book of Discipline*. In what is now designated as paragraph 906.12, the conference gave the General Council on Finance and Administration the responsibility,

> . . . for ensuring that no board, agency, committee, commission, or council shall give United Methodist funds to any "gay" caucus or group, or otherwise use such funds to promote the acceptance of homosexuality. The council shall have the right to stop such expenditures. (*Discipline*, 1976, 906.12)

The same General Conference also refused to authorize a national church study of human sexuality, barely conceding instead to provide resources for local churches to study human sexuality on a voluntary basis. This funding legislation was seen by many individuals as a weapon not only to stop education about sexuality and gay/lesbian people, but also to exclude gay/lesbian persons from various aspects of church life. The threat of paragraph 906.12 has, in fact, been invoked many times, causing articles to be rejected for publication by UMC-affiliated or -funded publications/publishers, causing people to be dismissed from church positions because their salaries came from national church funds, and causing students to be dismissed from UMC seminaries because those seminaries receive denominational monies (Brown, 1988).

The 1976 General Conference was also the first to address the issue of homosexuality and ordination. While no specific pronouncements on gay and lesbian ordination can be found in the 1976 version of the *Book of Discipline*, the issue was hotly debated in legislative sessions. The result of those debates can be found in footnotes placed in the *Discipline* in paragraph 404 on candidacy for ordained ministry. The footnote specifically refers to paragraph 404.7 and 414.7c2 on the moral and social responsibility of ministers. These paragraphs call upon ministers

> to make a complete dedication of themselves to the highest ideals of the Christian life . . . and to exercise responsible self-control by personal habits conducive to bodily health, mental and emotional maturity, social responsibility, and growth in grace and the knowledge and love of God.

Originally referring to issues such as drinking and smoking, the footnote was placed in the 1968 *Discipline* to argue against such a single issue barring a candidate from ordination. Now in the 1976 *Discipline*, with the help of a specific reference to the Social Principles (paragraph 906.12) as the guidelines for the highest ideals of the Christian life, the issue of homosexuality was obliquely addressed. A paragraph was added to the footnote exhorting annual conference boards of ministry to elevate the standards for the ministry by carrying out more careful and thorough examinations of candidates. Ironically, the word "homosexual" is never once mentioned (and indeed does not appear in the index of the 1976 *Discipline*), but everyone involved "knew" that was what the *Discipline* addressed (cf. Brown, 1988).

The ordination issue was again on the General Conference agenda in 1980. An appeal to trust regional annual conferences to act responsibly in the matter of ordaining gay/lesbian persons carried the debate and a specific (rather than oblique) prohibition was again defeated. The issue came to a head, however, when Bishop Melvin Wheatley of the Rocky Mountain Annual Conference subsequently ordained a lesbian as an elder. An appeal was made to the Judicial Council (the UMC's "supreme court") which ruled that there was nothing in the *Discipline* which specifically barred gay/lesbian ordination. In response, the 1984 General Conference first enacted a proposal calling for commitment of clergy to "fidelity in marriage and celibacy in singleness." However, after the Judicial Council ruled that the addition of those words alone did *not* establish absolute requirements nor affect the right to parish appointment of ministerial members in good standing, the conference then proceeded to expressly prohibit the candidacy, ordination, or appointment of "self-avowed, practicing homosexuals" (cf. Brown, 1988).

The first test of this new and quite specific legislation also occurred in the Rocky Mountain Annual Conference, with the continuing struggle over the parish appointment of Julian Rush. Rush, who had been serving churches as an elder, publicly declared his homosexuality ("came out") in October 1982. Bishop Wheatley's decision to continue appointing him led to the Bishop's being charged with maladministration by members of his annual conference. Wheatley's statement that homosexuality is not a sin also led a Georgia congregation to accuse him of heresy. The committee on investigation of the Western Jurisdiction ruled that there were insufficient grounds for either charge. The controversy surrounding Rush, however, did not abate. Following the 1984 General Conference action, charges were brought against Rush by a group of Rocky Mountain ministers connected with the conservative/evangelical "Good News" movement within the UMC. After a formal inquiry, Rush was found "not guilty" on the grounds that there was no proof of "practicing" (cf. Brown, 1988). While some individuals viewed this as a victory, it really was an acquiescence by a once strongly supportive, regional annual conference to a notion that it *is* valid to bar "*practicing*" gay/lesbian people from ordination and appointment to serve a church parish.

The most recent test of this specific prohibition of ordination came during the summer of 1987 when Rosemary Denman, an elder in the Maine Annual Conference, was tried for being a "self-avowed, practicing homosexual.'' Denman had discovered her lesbian identity in 1984; after the General Conference action, Denman asked for a leave of absence to enable her to sort out what she was called to do. When she requested an extension of this leave of absence, her bishop, George Bashore, along with the Board of Ministry, refused to grant it because of her lesbian lifestyle. Bashore then filed a formal complaint against her, asking that her clerical orders be rescinded. As was her right, Denman then requested an ecclesiastical trial, which was held on 24 August 1987. After nine hours, the jury of thirteen UMC ministers suspended Denman from her ministry until the next annual conference (1988). While the most lenient verdict possible, the verdict was still clearly a conviction. Ironically, Denman had actually decided, *before* Bashore initiated action against her, that she would transfer her membership and clerical orders to the Unitarian Universalist Association. Bashore could have simply allowed her to transfer to that denomination, which has no prohibition against gay/lesbian clergy, because he knew both that she was planning the transfer and that the transfer would not violate the statutes of her new denomination. He pressed charges solely because he believed that her lesbian identity and practices invalidated her "good standing" with the UMC (cf. Brown, 1988).

Because of its specific legislation, the UMC cannot accept lesbians and gay men of integrity into the ministry. It thereby violates its own Social Principles which not only call for the protection of the civil rights of gays/lesbians, but which also affirms that human sexuality is a good gift of God. These 1984 pronouncements are the consequence of an incoherent and almost non-existent theology of sexuality and are likely to be in the *Discipline* for a long time, unless a new and coherent theology can be constructed. The UMC's Wesleyan tradition of doing and testing theology by means of the "Quadrilateral" is one of the best ways of approaching this task. The "Quadrilateral" integrates scripture, tradition, reason, and experience, and thereby provides a solid framework within which to critique the currently unsatisfactory theology and to suggest a possible constructive approach. The "Quadrilateral" also supports a contextual approach to both biblical study and theology. Indeed, this is the only authentic basis for a gay/lesbian theology (or for any liberation theology).

Out of gays'/lesbians' experience of love—the love of God and the love of other persons—comes a gay/lesbian view of reality: It is only in relation that the world makes sense; but it is also experience which provides gays/lesbians with their greatest challenge. Lesbians and gay men have suffered horribly, not only at the hands of society, but more particularly at the hands of the churches. The very policies of the churches perpetuate this suffering. While these policies have forced or encouraged many gays/lesbians to leave the churches, particularly the UMC (Brown, 1988), these experiences of oppression can also be sources of gay/lesbian strength. A passionate commitment to justice and love springs from this context, the crucible in which gay/lesbian theology can be created. Moreover, there is hope in the UMC, for while the church as a whole may be slow in responding, a context where true ministry can occur has already been created in some individual UMC churches which have defiantly become reconciling congregations, churches which support and invite the full and mutual participation of lesbians and gay men (cf. Brown, 1988).

THE ROMAN CATHOLIC CHURCH

(1) "Tim" is 37, has been married eleven years, and has three daughters. He came to therapy because he was no longer able to ignore his attraction to men. Although he had been aware of his homosexual feelings prior to marriage, he believed they were morally wrong and also believed marriage and family would enable him to eliminate those feelings. "Tim" loves his wife and daughters and has tried to live a "good" life. He agonizes about hurting his wife and losing his children. He worries about offending God. And yet, "Tim" is a gay man and knows he must leave his family and accept what being gay means for his life.

(2) "John" is a 28-year-old heterosexual who came to therapy grieving over the death of his gay brother from AIDS. He was hurt and angry about his Church's harsh judgment of the brother he loved. Though he resisted the idea intellectually, he was deeply upset by the possibility that his brother was condemned by God because he was gay and, unable to depend upon a sympathetic response from friends and colleagues if they learned of his brother's

gayness and AIDS, he had told few people about the cause of his brother's death. He fears that the stigma attached to his brother's life will color his own and he is ashamed of that fear. "John" cannot turn to the Church for help; he believes that he must choose between loving his brother and remembering him as a good, grace-filled man, or continuing his affiliation with the Church.

(3) "Carla" is 33 and has been in a lover relationship with "Ann" for eight years. "Carla" and "Ann" describe their relationship as one akin to "marriage." "Carla" told her parents about her lesbian identity five years ago because she was "tired of lying and pretending and being vague," and because she hoped her disclosure would lead to a better relationship with her parents. Although her parents said they had suspected her lesbianism for some time, they responded to having their suspicions confirmed in a uniformly negative and condemning way. Her mother said "Carla" was sick, sinful, and disgusting, and that the least "Carla" could do was be celibate. Despite "Carla's" ongoing efforts to be patient with her parents, their attitude has not changed. Her mother recently said that if she has to choose to accept "Carla's" lesbianism or never see her again, she will sever her ties with "Carla," because she cannot support her daughter's "immoral" lifestyle.

"Tim," "John," "Carla," "Ann," and their parents and siblings are all Roman Catholics; yet, none of these people felt able to turn to their Church for comfort, support, or advice at an important moment in their lives. While Catholicism is not solely responsible for the homophobia affecting these individuals and their families, for their guilt or sensitivity to judgment, or for their poor self-esteem, the Church is at least partially responsible for causing and, more importantly, for perpetuating this pain. The official teaching of the Church regarding homosexuality is one of condemnation and judgment. As such, it has a far-reaching effect on lesbians, gay men, and their parents and other relatives.

The most recent document about homosexuality, published by the Vatican and approved/endorsed by Pope John Paul II, is *On the Pastoral Care of Homosexual Persons* (Ratzinger, 1986). The thesis of this pastoral letter is that homosexual behavior is not a "morally acceptable option" (sec. 3) and that even the *inclination* toward homosexual behavior (a homosexual orientation) is a "more or less strong tendency toward an intrinsic moral evil" (sec. 3). Ratzinger (1986) uses both scripture and tradition to support this belief, citing the usual passages in Leviticus (18.22, 20.13), the story of Sodom and Gomorrah, and certain Pauline and Deutero-Pauline passages (Romans 1, I Corinthians 6, I Timothy 1) to conclude that the Bible consistently judges homosexual behavior as immoral. He then adds that homosexual behavior is also wrong because homosexual unions cannot transmit life, because pro-gay views jeopardize the family, because sexuality is only good within marriage, and because homosexual behavior annuls the meaning, symbolism and goals of God's sexual design (secs. 6-7). Since all homosexual behavior is morally wrong, the Church requires lesbians and gay men to live a life free from all sexual expression (sec. 12). The remainder of the document encourages Catholic bishops to withdraw all support from organizations which do not actively promote this teaching and to support legislation which defends/promotes traditional family life (sec. 17). Because the majority of American Catholics are still taught to accept the pronouncements of the Church and to respect and obey the Pope on theological matters, such a document clearly has both an influential and a negative effect on lesbians, gay men, and their partners and relatives (Henley and Pincus, 1978).

Like most nongay people, most lesbians and gay men long for a loving, long term relationship to sustain and support them throughout their lives. They also long for acceptance by and connection to their families of origin. Many factors contribute to the difficulty of sustaining such familial and love relationships over time. But, for Roman Catholic lesbians and gay men, the teaching and attitude of the Church are an additional inhibiting factor. Many people continue to believe that gay people are deviant, sick, or abnormal. Debilitating though these labels may be alone, however, they are often less damaging to a gay person's sense of self than the labels "bad" or "immoral." The label "bad" strikes at the core of an individual's senses of self-worth and personal value, and also engenders a deep sense of shame which is difficult to reverse. The individual unwittingly becomes the label (McNeill, 1976, p. 166). Rather than accept a gay/lesbian identity and the Church's negative, labelling judgment, some lesbians and gay men marry and make a valiant effort to live according to the goals of God's "sexual design" (sec.

7). Many of these marriages end in divorce, however, and thus add further guilt and regret to the gay/lesbian person's burden (cf. Ross, 1983).

In their study, *American Couples*, Blumstein and Schwartz (1983) concluded that social sanction is the single most important factor which holds heterosexual marriages together. Lesbian and gay male couples have neither social nor religious sanction. The partners bring to their relationship the knowledge that their religious tradition believes any sexual relationship with a member of the same sex is sinful and offensive to God. Not only is their love, their relationship, and their sexuality not supported by the hierarchical Church or the local Church community, the Church actively devalues such relationships and encourages their dissolution. It may then point to the instability of gay/lesbian relationships as a sign of their inherent "badness." For those who truly believe the Church's teaching, the beloved partner becomes an occasion of sin and temptation, a path away from God. One partner may project his/her internalized homophobia on the other partner and thereby devalue the very person he/she loves and the relationship he/she claims to value.

The Church's teaching on homosexuality thus poses a conflict of loyalty for lesbians and gay men (McNaught, 1979). The Church appears to force a choice between loyalty to the Church or loyalty to the gay/lesbian person's own sense of self. The result is that many gay men and even more lesbians have physically left the Church (many lesbians also object to the pervasive sexism of the Church; homophobia in addition to sexism frequently proves intolerable). Thus one member of a couple may be a devout Catholic and the other a bitter, angry, and hurting ex-Catholic. The non-practicing partner may be angry with the other's continued involvement in this religious institution and view that involvement as complicity with the oppressor (McNaught, 1979). God and the Church become sources of further friction within the relationship.

The teaching of the Church also affects the parents and extended families of lesbians and gay men. These relatives have been socialized by society and Church to view lesbians and gay men as immoral and deviant. Most people simply assume that all of their family members are heterosexual; parents do not expect or even consider the possibility that their child might grow up to be gay or lesbian. It is usually a shock, therefore, to discover an adult child's gayness, and parents are often embarrassed and ashamed. They wonder what they did wrong and they seek to hide this information from friends, neighbors, and other relatives. Tragically, the Church offers no supportive guidance or education to these nongay family members: There are no formal guidelines for maintaining or (re)building a relationship with a gay/lesbian child and his/her partner, no help in moving on after the self-revelation is shared, no clear reassurances that a gay/lesbian child is still loved by God. The Church's negative assessment of the gay/lesbian adult child fosters isolation, lowered self-esteem, and an unwarranted sense of parental failure. The Church offers no safe, non-judgmental place for parents and relatives to turn with their own grief, disappointment, shame, and confusion about their adult child's life. Parents often choose, therefore, to lie about their son or daughter and to create heterosexual social lives for them, along with elaborate reasons for their continued unmarried life and same-sex "roommate." These lies, of course, result in further alienation of family members from one another, from neighbors and friends, and from God and Church. For relatives of gay men dying with AIDS, these lies may involve falsifying the real nature of the illness and thus preclude the special support and care needed by the family in order to come to terms with the death of a family member from a frightening and socially unacceptable disease (cf. Clark, 1987c).

Parents may also believe that they must choose between their daughter or son and the Church. An adult child's self-revelation may set off a religious and spiritual crisis in the family as the parents struggle to reconcile the Church's judgment with their own knowledge of their child's goodness. Sometimes parents, too, leave the Church in anger and pain. More often, relatives of gays/lesbians may use the Church's teaching as a moral club with which to berate their gay/lesbian relation in the hopes of effecting change. Some families similarly use the Church's teaching as a reason to sever all ties with the gay relative, or as a reason to remain ignorant about the gay relative's life. The Church's teaching, therefore, easily becomes one more source of conflict and tension between gay men, lesbians, and their families.

This Church teaching is not just one opinion among many. It is a serious teaching, and its rejection by any of the faithful should be the exception rather than the rule. Nevertheless, it is important to note that this official position is not an unchangeable, infallible teaching. It is simply the current doctrinal position of Roman Catholicism. Because it is not infallible, it contains the theoretical possibility of error and is ideally open to change and correction (Curran, 1987). Although the Church certainly does not encourage or support dissent or dialogue about doctrinal matters among its faithful, such dissent and dialogue continue (Gramick and Furey, 1988). Although the official Church widely disseminates and quotes this document, the Church is not monolithic. Less vocal, less public theologians view a homosexual orientation and sexual behavior as valid Christian possibilities and perceive gay men and lesbians as good, healthy people who are open to the grace of God (Baum, 1974, Fehren, 1972, McKenzie, 1982, McNaught, 1979, McNeill, 1976, Nugent, 1983, Woods, 1977). Groups such as Dignity, the Conference of Catholic Lesbians, and New Ways Ministry affirm and support gays/lesbians and their families from within the larger parameters of the Church. These groups are operated by Catholics for Catholics, and make a serious attempt to provide emotional and spiritual help to gay/lesbian Catholics and their families. Similarly, respectable scriptural scholars and Church historians propose a more sophisticated, less simplistic interpretation of scripture and tradition and thereby raise serious questions about the uniformity and consistency of Church opinion and teaching on this matter (Bailey, 1975, Boswell, 1980).

Fortunately, there is also an increasingly tolerant, liberal, and "unorthodox" opinion expressed by some of those ministering within the Church. Many priests, as well as male and female religious (some lesbian or gay themselves), are knowledgeable about and sensitive to the pastoral needs of gay/lesbian people (cf. DeStefano, 1986). Many of these religious do not accept or support the official teaching of the Church, although they must disagree quietly and privately or risk censure. They can and do, however, offer models of acceptance not often seen in official Vatican representatives. While these alternative voices are frequently muffled by the powerful voice of the Vatican, they exist nevertheless and can be used to rebuild self-esteem, to encourage autonomous thinking, to provide affirmation of intrinsic value, and thus to aid lesbians, gay men, and their families to recover from the intrapsychic and interpersonal damage perpetuated by the official Church.

CONCLUSION

Overall, gay men and lesbians, as well as their coupled relationships and their nongay family members, are together cast into a paradoxical situation. While religious institutions, with the few noted exceptions, continue to reject homosexuality and/or gay sexual fulfillment, gay men and lesbians themselves continue to insist upon their innate created goodness, upon the value of their relationships, and upon their right to spiritual nurture. While many gays/lesbians are finding or creating that spirituality outside institutional forms, others are joining individual, sympathetic congregations and/or clergy to worship together. The paradox of official rejection and occasional "unofficial" acceptance, however, only perpetuates existing tensions among gays/lesbians, their committed partners, and their nongay family members. Too often the official positions and pronouncements of various churches and synagogues still alienate gay men and lesbians from these institutions and separate gay and nongay family members from one another. Clearly, a great deal of work remains to be done within institutionalized religion before any genuine and thoroughgoing reconciliation will be possible.

REFERENCES

Bailey, D. (1975). *Homosexuality and the western Christian tradition*. Hamden, CT: Shoe String.

Baum, G. (1974, 15 February). Catholic homosexuals. *Commonweal*, 479-482.

Blumstein, P. & Schwartz, P. (1983). *American couples*. New York: Morrow.

Bohne, J. (1986). AIDS: Ministry issues for chaplains. *Pastoral Psychology*, *34*(3),173-192.

Boswell, J. (1980). *Christianity, social tolerance, and homosexuality*. Chicago: Univ. Chicago.

Boyd, M. (1984). *Take off the masks*. Philadelphia: New Society.

Boyd, M. (1987). Telling a lie for Christ? In M. Thompson (Ed.), *Gay spirit, myth and meaning* (pp. 78-87). New York: St. Martin's.

Brown, J. C. (1988). Persons of sacred worth, but: The failure of mainline Protestantism to create a viable theology of sexuality. *Quarterly Review*. In press.

Clark, J. M. (1986). AIDS, death, and God: Gay liberational theology and the problem of suffering. *Journal of Pastoral Counseling, 21*(1),40-54.

Clark, J. M. (1987a). *Gay being, divine presence*. Garland, TX: Tanglewüld.

Clark, J. M. (1987b). *Pink triangles and gay images*. Arlington, TX: Liberal Arts.

Clark, J. M. (1987c). Special considerations in pastoral care of gay persons-with-AIDS. *Journal of Pastoral Counseling, 22*(1),32-45.

Clark, J. M. (1989). *Someplace to start: Toward an unapologetic gay liberation theology*. San Francisco: Harper & Rowe. Under review.

Comstock, G. D. (1987). Aliens in the promised land? *Union Seminary Quarterly Review, 41*(3-4),93-104.

Crompton, L. (1978). Gay genocide from Leviticus to Hitler. In L. Crew (Ed.), *The gay academic* (pp. 67-91). Palm Springs: Etc.

Curb, R. & Manahan, N. (Eds.). (1985). *Lesbian nuns*. Tallahassee: Naiad.

Curran, C. (1987). Academic freedom and Catholic institutions of higher education. *Journal of the American Academy of Religion, 55*(1),107-121.

DeStefano, G. (1986). Gay under the collar: The hypocrisy of the Catholic church. *The Advocate*, no. 439, 43-48.

Dunkel, J. & Hatfield, S. (1986). Countertransference issues in working with persons with AIDS. *Social Work, 31*(2),114-117.

Edwards, G. R. (1984). *Gay/lesbian liberation, a biblical perspective*. New York: Pilgrim.

Evans, A. (1978). *Witchcraft and the gay counterculture*. Boston: Fag Rag.

Fehren, H. (1972, September). A Christian response to homosexuals. *U.S. Catholic*, 6-11.

Fortunato, J. E. (1983). *Embracing the exile*. New York: Seabury.

Fortunato, J. E. (1985). AIDS: The plague that lays waste at noon. *The Witness, 68*(9),6-9.

Fortunato, J. E. (1987). *AIDS, the spiritual dilemma*. San Francisco: Harper & Row.

Goodman, G. et al. (1983). *No turning back*. Philadelphia: New Society.

Grahn, J. (1984). *Another mother tongue*. Boston: Beacon.

Gramick, J. & Furey, P. (Eds.). (1988). *The Vatican and homosexuality*. New York: Crossroad.

Hancock, L. (1985). Fear and healing in the AIDS crisis. *Christianity and Crisis, 45*(11),255-258.

Henley, N. & Pincus, F. (1978). Interrelationships of sexist, racist, and anti-homosexual attitudes. *Psychological Reports, 42*(1),83-90.

Heyward, I. C. (1984). *Our passion for justice*. New York: Pilgrim.

Hochstein, L. M. (1987). Roman Catholic statements on lesbians and gay men: A clinician's perspective. Unpublished paper, presented American Academy of Religion annual meeting (6 December), Boston.

Horner, T. (1978). *Jonathan loved David*. Philadelphia: Westminster.

Howell, L. (1985). Churches and AIDS: Responsibilities in mission. *Christianity and Crisis*, *45*(20),483-484.

Lieberson, J. (1986). The reality of AIDS. *The New York Review*, *32*(22),43-48.

McKenzie, T. (1982, August). Why gay Catholics won't be locked out of the church. *U.S. Catholic*, 6-12.

McNaught, B. (1979). Gay and Catholic. In B. Berzon & R. Leighton (Eds.), *Positively gay*. Millbrae, CA: Celestial Arts.

McNeill, J. J. (1976). *The church and the homosexual*. Kansas City: Sheed, Andrews, & McMeel.

McNeill, J. J. (1983). Homosexuality, lesbianism, and the future: The creative role of the gay community in building a more humane society. In R. Nugent (Ed.), *A challenge to love* (pp. 52-64). New York: Crossroad.

McNeill, J. J. (1988). *Taking a chance on God: Liberating theology for gays, lesbians, their lovers, families, and friends*. Boston: Beacon.

Morton, N. (1985). *The journey is home*. Boston: Beacon.

Nelson, J. B. (1977). Homosexuality and the church. *Christianity and Crisis*, *37*(5),63-69.

Nelson, J. B. (1986). Responding to, learning from AIDS. *Christianity and Crisis*, *46*(8),176-181.

Nugent, R. (Ed.). (1983). *A challenge to love*. New York: Crossroad.

Plant, R. (1986). *The pink triangle*. New York: Henry Holt.

Ratzinger, J. (1986). *On the pastoral care of homosexual persons*. Boston: Daughters of St. Paul.

Ross, M. W. (1983). *The married homosexual man: A psychological study*. Boston: Routledge & Kegan Paul.

Saslow, J. M. (1987). Hear, O Israel: We are Jews, we are gay. *The Advocate*, no. 465, 38-41,44-49,108-111.

Shelp, E. E., Sunderland, R. H., & Mansell, P. W. A. (1986). *AIDS, personal stories in pastoral perspective*. New York: Pilgrim.

Sherwood, Z. (1987). *Kairos, confessions of a gay priest*. Boston: Alyson.

Stiles, B. J. (1986). AIDS and the churches. *Christianity and Crisis*, *45*(22), 534-536.

Thompson, M. (Ed.). (1987). *Gay spirit, myth and meaning*. New York: St. Martin's.

Topper, C. J. (1986). Spirituality as a component in counseling lesbian-gays. *Journal of Pastoral Counseling*, *21*(1),55-59.

Walker, M. (1980). *Visionary love*. San Francisco: Treeroots.

Woods, R. (1977). *Another kind of love*. Chicago: Thomas More Assn.

Wright, E. & Inesse, D. (1979). *God is gay*. San Francisco: Tayu.

AIDS:
Impact on the Gay Man's Homosexual and Heterosexual Families

INTRODUCTION

AIDS, the end-result of human infection by a small, 10 nm diameter the Human Immunodeficiency Virus (HIV), is actually an amalgamation of diseases associated with severe immune deficiency (Ho, Pomerantz, & Kaplan, 1987). Diseases which are presumptively diagnostic of AIDS include *pneumocystis carinii* pneumonia and primary lymphoma of the brain (CDC, 1987). Since 1982, more than 69,000 cases of AIDS have been reported to the Centers for Disease Control (CDC) and estimates are that 40 times more people are infected with HIV (San Francisco Health Department, 1988; Institute of Medicine, 1986).

In contrast to the early days of the epidemic (1982-1984), onset of AIDS is preceded by well-defined prodromal syndromes. The first syndrome is an acute flu-like illness lasting 3 to 14 days after infection (Biggar, 1987; Farthing, Brown, Staughton, & Cream, 1986). A latent phase, known as asymptomatic, seropositivity, follows. Eventually, patients develop AIDS-Related Complex (ARC), a variable illness characterized by a series of vague constitutional symptoms, such as lymphadenopathy, fatigue, fever, weight loss, and night sweats (Pinching, 1986). Because the HIV entered the homosexual/bisexual community early in the epidemic, these men are at high risk for becoming infected and developing AIDS.

Nancy C. Lovejoy, RN, DSN, is Assistant Professor, School of Nursing, University of California, San Francisco, San Francisco, CA 94143.

The current tendency to diagnose patients in the prodromal phases of HIV infection has increased survival times. In fact, data from the three-year San Francisco General Hospital Cohort Study suggest that only 22% of homosexual men ($N = 111$), who seroconvert, will develop AIDS within one year of diagnoses (Moss et al., 1988); and projections are that only 50% will develop AIDS within six years of diagnoses. Factors associated with increased risk of progression among homosexual men include: multiple sexual partners, a history of sex with someone with AIDS (Polk et al., 1987), and use of certain sexual behaviors (receptive fellatio, anal intercourse, douching prior to intercourse) (Goedert et al., 1987; Winkelstein et al., 1987).

FAMILY RESPONSES TO AIDS

Health care providers, who render AIDS care, report that disclosure of a diagnosis of HIV infection is devastating to the patient and his family members, invariably, raising the specter of death and disfigurement (Miller, 1988; Ross & Rosser, 1988). For the patient's homosexual family, that is, gay friends, lovers, or partners, who are voluntarily bonded together for mutual social and economic development, disclosure is followed by concern about personal vulnerability to AIDS: "What is going to happen to my health?" For the patient's heterosexual family, i.e., persons who are bonded together by blood, marriage or adoption, disclosure may unexpectedly reveal the patient's homosexuality or involvement in a homosexual family. These unexpected revelations may result in bitter accusations: "My son would never have gotten AIDS if it hadn't been for you!"

Clinicians suggest that, after disclosure of the patient's diagnosis, affective responses and reactionary concerns of family members follow predictable patterns known as the AIDS adjustment process. The adjustment process occurs in phases: crisis, transition, acceptance, and preparation for death and bereavement (Nichols, 1985). Under optimal conditions, the adjustment process results in acceptance and preparation for an altered future (Forstein, 1984; Holland & Tross, 1985; Miller, 1987; Nichols, 1985). The purpose of this review is to detail current knowledge of the impact of an

AIDS-related diagnosis on the patient's homosexual and heterosexual family members. Unresolved family issues/concerns requiring research will also be addressed.

PHASE ONE: CRISIS

The crisis phase, which immediately follows news of the diagnosis, is characterized by shock and denial, alternating with anxiety.

Shock

Manifestations

Affectively, shock is characterized by lack of emotion, apathy, despair, withdrawal, and severe physical symptoms (heart palpitations, parasthesias, syncopy, and diaphoresis) that may require medical attention. When in shock, family members may experience a "period of emotional ventilation, including crying and hysterical speech" (Miller, 1987, p. 1672), leaving them temporarily unable to make complex decisions.

Shock at the diagnosis may abruptly alter family structure and functions. Homosexual family members, who are bereft of emotional resources or prone to AIDS hysteria (i.e., unnatural fear of AIDS) may abandon patients. Heterosexual family members, who are intolerant of the homosexual lifestyle or AIDS may withdraw support while others may rush to offer assistance (Holland & Tross, 1985). Robinson, Skeen, and Walters (1988), who surveyed the attitudes and reactions of parents with adult gay children in the United States to AIDS ($N = 702$), suggest that older parents are less likely to reject patients rather than younger parents, possibly because they have significantly more positive attitudes towards AIDS than their younger counterparts. Similarly, parents with liberal leanings have more positive outlooks towards AIDS than conservative parents and are, therefore, more likely to support patients following diagnoses than parents with conservative leanings.

Although family members recover from shock following news of the patient's diagnosis, they report being shocked by a myriad of other factors over the course of the AIDS trajectory (Baumgartner, 1985; Cecchi, 1986; Geis, Fuller, & Rush, 1986; Peabody, 1986).

Family members, who have not dealt with the health care system since, "My son was born" or "I needed shots for school," find medical terminology, cost of care, and the complex health care system shocking. "We need help with the details of how the health bureaucracy works," report shocked family members.

Early in the epidemic, homosexual family members interviewed by Geis et al. ($N = 9$) reported being shocked at inconsistencies in infection control measures: "One day they tell you it's regulation to wear gloves and gown, then the next day they say it doesn't matter . . ." (Geis et al., p. 49). Family members also reported finding homophobic attitudes and AIDS hysteria (Cecchi, 1986; Lovejoy, in preparation). In fact, survey data (Douglas, Kalman, & Kalman, 1985) showed that many health care professionals were referring to AIDS as the "WOG" (wrath of God) and that 9% of nurses and interns ($N = 128$) surveyed believed that homosexuals deserved getting AIDS. However, research suggests that, in high incidence areas, many of these sources of shock have been removed. For example, recent research suggests that homophobic attitudes and AIDS hysteria among health professionals decrease as knowledge of AIDS and numbers of contacts with AIDS cases increases. Klimes, Catalan, Bond, and Day (1988), surveying 400 psychiatric health workers from acute and community settings in Oxford, England found that the better informed professionals were about HIV, the more positive their overall attitude towards caring for HIV positive patients ($p < .001$) and AIDS sufferers ($p < .01$). Surveying 2,351 hospital workers, Henry, Campbell, and Willenbring (1988) found that positive behaviors and attitudes toward AIDS patients correlated with lower homophobia scores, confidence in AIDS-related medical information, and greater number of contacts with AIDS patients ($p < .0001$). Unfortunately, homosexual families in high incidence areas find ambiguity or uncertainty about AIDS information among health professionals, shocking. Wrote one respondent in a recent survey: "Tell them to learn about as much about AIDS as we do because we're well-informed" (Lovejoy & Moran, 1988).

Over the course of the AIDS trajectory, homosexual families may also experience shock at the perceived or real "injustices of the social system," such as, inequities inherent in retirement benefits.

On learning that the company his partner worked for eight years would not award retirement account monies to him, one shocked homosexual partner, exclaimed, "Why don't they just give him the money from his retirement account; he'll never live long enough to see it now!" Other sources of shock are evictions, firings, rejections, and dismissals following disclosure of the AIDS diagnosis (Fettner & Check, 1985). When the patient's illness progresses, family members are shocked by the physical and mental changes seen in patients. "My son John, a physician, was the sweetest, gentlest man before his illness. But before he died, he would lose his temper over nothing at all," reported one shocked and saddened mother. Said Peabody (1986) of her son's experience with AIDS, "I never could get used to his thinness . . ." Regardless of the amount of grief work the family has done, learning that the patient's condition is irreversible is another serious shock. Collective shock at the relentless toll AIDS has taken on their families, many homosexual men are demanding that more be done to stop AIDS: "We need to seek more support from the current administration for AIDS research."

Interventions

When in shock, family members need a quiet, supportive environment and time to accept an altered reality (Miller, 1987). All family members are helped by being able to talk with health professionals, who are experienced with AIDS, listen, and act as "positive role models." From clinical experience, Miller (1987) also reports that it is crucial for health professionals to provide families with a lifeline (telephone numbers of the clinic, community agencies concerned with HIV, etc.) during the first few days following disclosure of the patient's diagnosis. Partners also need immediate counseling about safe sex, infection control, and health boosting behaviors (Miller, 1988). In addition, close family members need to be observed for signs of symptoms, suicidal activity, high levels of anxiety, depression, obsessional disturbances, and symptoms requiring medical interventions. Families, who are sufficiently shocked, will need written information regarding follow-up ap-

pointments and dissuaded from making complex decisions until re-
covered (Schoen, 1986).

Denial

Manifestations

On hearing the news of the diagnosis, family members may temporarily deny this unwelcome information. Signs of denial include
anger, depression, use of impersonal words when describing the
patient's illness, and/or avoidance of the health care system (Kiening, 1978a). The family member's denial is usually selective. In
other words, family members may acknowledge that the patient is
ill but deny aspects of the illness, such as, its terminal prognosis.
This type of denial helps family members cope with day-to-day
routines of living (Lazarus & Folkman, 1984).

Interventions

In the early phases of the AIDS trajectory, health professionals
can support the family's use of denial unless it compromises their
health or the health of others (Abrams, Dilley, Maxey, & Volberding, 1986). Therapeutic interventions include selectively challenging denial when it precludes: (a) partner's acceptance of the need to
use safe sex or undergo antibody testing or (b) family member's
performance of needed infection control measures (Miller, 1987).
Family members whose beliefs or behaviors are so challenged will
need to be assessed carefully for signs of depression—a normal
response to removal of denial as mental defense against anxiety.

Anxiety

Manifestations

AIDS anxiety pervades the lives of families of homosexual
men even before disclosure of the diagnosis. In cities where visible
numbers of men are sick and dying from AIDS, AIDS anxiety can
cause homosexual family members to become preoccupied with
AIDS-like symptoms or obsessional worrying about AIDS to the

point of occupational dysfunction (Morin, Charles, & Malyon, 1984). Fletcher et al. (1988), who measured anxiety of homosexual men presenting for anonymous AIDS testing ($N = 38$) with the Spielberger Anxiety Scale (Spielberger, 1979), found that men who tested seropositive were more anxious prior to learning test results than men who did not test HIV seropositive. Robinson, Skeen, and Walters (1988), surveying parents with adult gay children ($N = 702$), found that about half were concerned about their children's AIDS risk and a significant number worried about the health conditions of their children's sexual partners.

Research and clinical observations indicate that anxiety levels rise following news of the diagnosis. In fact, Miller reports that following disclosure of HIV antibody assays, "partners (and family members) often have higher and more chronic levels of psychological morbidity arising from knowledge of the patient's HIV infection than . . . patients themselves" (p. 1673). Fletcher et al.'s (1988) prospective study showed that anxiety escalated among patients, who tested seropositive ($N = 38$). Family anxiety also does not seem to abate over the AIDS trajectory. Comparing patient and homosexual family members ratings on the Spielberger Anxiety Scale (Spielberger, 1979), Church, Kocsis, and Green (1988) found that family members in all phases of the AIDS trajectory were more anxious than patients ($N = 40$). Anxiety was promoted by questions about what is going to happen, the impact of the patient's illness on their lives, contagion; ignorance of treatments, drugs, and drug protocols; and uncertainty about the future, particularly if infected themselves (Lovejoy, Moran, & Paul, 1988; Lovejoy, & Moran, 1988).

Related research shows that family members of patients, who are seriously ill, may attempt to quell their anxiety through relentless information-seeking (described below), the use of exercise, meditation or other non-somatic anxiety-reducing measures (Lovejoy et al., 1988). If anxiety is somaticized, family members may develop hypertension, migraine headaches, and recurrent herpes infections (Lovejoy, 1986). If AIDS anxiety is not reduced, Harowski (1988) suggests that pre-existing psychiatric illnesses may be exacerbated.

Interventions

Because family members are likely to be anxious throughout the AIDS trajectory, family health assessments involve observation for overt and covert signs of anxiety: rapid speech; insomnia; poor hygiene; withdrawal; signs of sympathetic stimulation (i.e., hyperventilation, tension, hyperviligence); and disorientation to time, place, or person. Sources of anxiety, such as continued use of high risk sexual behaviors (anonymous sexual partners, unprotected anal sex), also need to be examined. Clinicians generally concur that anxious family members respond favorably to clear, rational discussions of known routes of infection, safe sex, available treatment options and services, and the practical consequences of disclosure: ineligibility for life insurance, dental and medical treatment, and some types of employment as well as loss of employment (Miller, 1987; Ross & Rosser, 1988). Family members also benefit from learning to manage and monitor patients' symptoms and to separate AIDS myths from misconceptions (Miller, 1987; Ross & Rosser, 1988). When family members repeatedly seek consultations with physicians, exhibit dependence in all relationships, or feel socially isolated, referrals to behavioral psychologists or psychiatrists may be warranted (Miller, 1987).

PHASE TWO: TRANSITION

Emotions and mental mechanisms of the crisis phase gradually give way to alternating waves of anger, depression, guilt, and fear. Causal factors of the diagnosis are actively sought. Other family member concerns expressed during this phase of adjustment are homophobia, social support, sexuality, and sickness roles.

Fear/AIDS Hysteria

Manifestations

Family members find AIDS frightening because it is incurable, and "You don't know what will happen next!" Due to early sensationalized media reports (Salisbury, 1986), family members are also fearful of contagion. AIDS hysteria, or the rampant fear of contagion, may also be fueled by unconscious forces, such as, fear of latent homosexual impulses. Other fears held by family members include fear of scorn, quarantine, disclosure, and mandatory testing. These fears may discourage participation in research. Family members are also frightened by losing their loved one (Helquist, 1984). Fear of separation may cause family members to either withhold affection from patients or maintain vigils, i.e., maintain watchful surveillance over patients, particularly during hospitalizations.

Interventions

According to Schietinger (1986), one of the most powerful ways of cutting through fear is to invite a person, who has successfully coped with AIDS, to meet with family members and describe his experiences (Helquist, 1984). Family members can also be helped by expressing their fears and identifying issues prompting this response. Anecdotal reports also suggest that group support sessions assist family members to clarify sources of fear and facilitate decision-making (Salisbury, 1986; Schoen, 1986).

Anger

Manifestations

Anger, i.e., intense displeasure, is an integral part of homosexual family life (Feinbaum, 1986; Kiening, 1978b). Joseph et al. (1984) state that part of the anger stems from fear that hard-earned gains in civil liberties and social acceptance may be lost due to the epidemic. Other sources of anger for homosexual men include perceived lack of public support for AIDS issues: "We need to get rid of Reagan. . . . We need to get more money into education and medications. . . . I think we should quarantine Africa!"

Families are also angered by actual or potential loss of control, independence, and rejection (Helquist, 1984). Lovers may be angry with patients for endangering their health (Ross & Rosser, 1988). In addition, interviews ($N = 9$) showed that lovers are angered by the lack of standardized medical treatment protocols, insensitive health care personnel, misdiagnoses, and research protocols that "treat patients like guinea pigs" (Geis et al., 1986). Clinical observations also indicate that partners are angered by inadequacies in the health care system: non-existent benefits, excessive or lost paperwork, the Medicare spend-down policies that leave patients without medical insurance when they need it most, and other barriers to health care services (Bernstein, 1986; Cecchi, 1986; Peabody, 1986).

The heterosexual family, who may not have known about the patient's homosexuality, may experience anger at the loss of "expected grandchildren," their son's violation of Judeo/Christian traditions, or their son's lover: "Sex between men is unnatural." Interestingly, Robinson et al., determining the attitudes and reactions of parents with adult gay children ($N = 702$) to the AIDS epidemic, found that a sizeable number of them secretly wished that AIDS were more prevalent among heterosexuals so their children would not be the target of so much negativism.

Both sets of families become angry during the pre-bereavement and mourning process (Caplan, 1974). This anger is exacerbated when hetero- and homosexual families have not developed mutually supportive roles during the patient's illness. In these instances, there may be bitter arguments over funeral arrangements, financial settlements, and disposal of possessions (Geis et al., 1986). In all instances, the family's anger may be displaced onto caregivers and others through verbal outbursts, passive-aggressive behavior, sarcasm, fault-finding, withdrawal, and stubborn silence (Dilley, Ochitill, Perl, & Volberding, 1985; Feinbaum, 1986).

Interventions

Family members, who are angry, can be helped to manage their anger through acts of empathy and sensitivity, including sensitive explanations of medical procedures, protocol eligibility requirements, and health care regulations. Direct confrontations regarding sources of anger are generally counterproductive (Kiening, 1978b). If anger persists in a family group despite therapeutic interventions, health professionals need to discern whether attitudes of health personnel are at issue.

Depression

AIDS-related depression may be due to organic or non-organic causes. Non-organic causes of depression include anger turned inward, and unconscious conflicts about how the disease is acquired or its meanings (Kubler-Ross, 1969; Morin, Charles, & Malyon, 1984; Volberding, 1985). Among homosexual family members who are HIV seropositive, depression may be due to HIV infection of the brain (Navia, Jordan, & Price [1986]). Depression may also be provoked by psychosocial factors, such as, loss of social support, financial security, and inability to respond to all the demands of the illness. Data from a three-year prospective of a group of 227 HIV seropositive men showed that depression was significantly associated with subsequent symptom development (Joseph, Kessler, Ostrow, Phair, & Chmiel, 1988). Donlou, Wolcott, Gottlieb, and Landsverk (1985) found that following diagnosis, ratings on the Profile of Mood States (POMS) Questionnaire (McNair, Lorn, & Droppleman, 1971) by outpatients with systemic symptoms of AIDS or ARC of six-months duration ($n = 21$) were more depressed than pre-bone marrow recipients ($n = 5$), chronic renal failure patients ($n = 22$), and healthy college men ($n = 320$). However, these studies do not indicate whether HIV seropositive patients were in coupled relationships nor do they distinguish psychosocial from organic depression.

Interventions

Non-organic depression may be counteracted by providing family members and patients with information and choices (Schoen, 1986). Assisting family members to express feelings associated with depressed states and providing sympathetic interpretations of illness events is also useful. Depressed family members also respond well to having positive role models (Lovejoy et al., 1988). If depression is chronic, antidepressants may be indicated (Ross & Rosser, 1988).

Guilt

Manifestations

AIDS-associated guilt stems from violation of the prevailing code of ethics or sense of propriety. This response was fostered by early media reports depicting AIDS as the result of a "me" generation of behavior and "divine retribution" for sexual promiscuity (Harowski, 1988). Clinical observations suggest that guilt experienced by homosexual couples may also be fostered by past promiscuity, infidelity, and internalized homophobia (Schoen, 1986). If not relieved, the guilt-ridden partner may be driven from the relationship. On the other hand, parents may ponder what they did to cause their son to assume such a high risk lifestyle: "Where did we go wrong?" Family members also experience several types of guilt during the bereavement process (described below), including parental-role guilt, death-causation guilt, moral guilt, survival guilt, and grief guilt (Miles, 1985).

Interventions

Health professionals may help relieve guilt by helping family members express their concerns and challenge misconceptions promoting guilt (Schoen, 1986). For example, partners can be informed that the incubation period for AIDS is so variable that they may be unjustly accusing themselves of transmitting the virus to the patient. Parents, who are struggling with guilt over their son's homosexuality, may be assured that human sexuality encompasses a range of expressions and that male homosexuality is considered to be normal by the American Psychiatric Association, should the patient express no desire to change this orientation (American Psychiatric Association, 1985; Quadland & Shattls, 1987).

Social Support

Manifestations

Social support helps family members adjust, i.e., form new, stable identities; examine sources of pain and pleasure; reassess the value of courage, commitment, affection and concern for others;

and learn to appreciate quality rather than quantity of life (Nichols, 1985, p. 766). Anecdotal reports suggest that the quality of support available to families affected by AIDS is marred by AIDS hysteria, stigmatization and rejection. Recent interviews suggest that social support experienced by homosexual men may also be adversely influenced by the AIDS deaths of so many friends: "There are big holes in my life . . . my friends are no longer available." Concerned homosexual family members are also beginning to suggest that society needs to legitimize relationships between homosexual couples in order to increase the probability that these relationships will survive illness and the dying process. As one patient simply stated: "Health care professionals can help gay people by 'societal OKs' for developing long term relationships" (Lovejoy et al., in preparation).

Research suggests that homosexual men ($N = 60$) generally find their social support more distressing than heterosexuals ($N = 50$), making them at higher risk for stress-mediated immunosuppression (Mann, Kocsis, & Green, 1988). In fact, Wolcott, Namir, Fawzy, Gottlieb, and Mitsuyasu (1986), found that satisfaction with social support among newly diagnosed patients with AIDS (3 months post diagnosis) ($N = 50$) was inversely related to numbers of illness concerns, negative attitudes toward homosexuality, greater emotional distress, and poor health status. Satisfaction with social support was directly related to participation in a coupled relationship, underscoring the importance of working with partners to save coupled relationships. Donlou et al. (1985) found that scores on the Resource and Social Supports Questionnaire ranged widely (13 to 60) among 21 male homosexual/bisexual outpatients diagnosed with AIDS or ARC for six months or longer. Homosexual, rather than heterosexual family members, were seen as being important sources of support by the sample. In contrast, Hewitt (1988), conducting a clinical and epidemiological analysis of AIDS patients treated in Buffalo during 1981-1986, found that a significant number of patients chose to return to their heterosexual families, unexpectedly straining the resources of local and state governments. Factors prompting homecoming decisions were: poor overall health and loss of independence in self-care, loss of health insurance through former employment, desire to die at home, and an impulsive decision to be with the family after the initial shock of the diagnosis. In some instances, homosexual partners accompany patients. As one partner confided, "Tom wanted to come back to San Francisco to be near his folks. That's all right with me . . . he needs to be with them . . . but I am not sure how it will work out."

The literature does not describe the quality of social support experienced by patients prior to homecoming or factors influencing the quality of support between heterosexual and homosexual families during the course of the AIDS trajectory. Also, little is known about the social support systems of heterosexual family members, although anecdotal reports suggest that heterosexual families, whose sons live out of town, may simply choose not to tell their social networks about the diagnosis. "They may suspect, but they don't know," reported one mother at a recent AIDS conference.

Interventions

Homosexual family members, particularly caregivers, need to be supported throughout the transition phase through intensive counseling and, in later phases, by supportive activities provided by local and national organizations, such as, the National Association of People with AIDS (NAPWA) within the gay community (Miller, 1987; NAPWA, 1988a). Self-help or support groups also seem to offer support to family members, who are ego-syntonic (Kelly & Sykes, 1988; Ross & Rosser, 1988). Heterosexual and homosexual family members, who accompany patients to unfamiliar cities or hospital settings, may also benefit by referrals to "Helping Hands" programs which offer social support to out-of-town guests.

Information-Seeking

Manifestations

Information-seeking is a predictable response to novel situations judged to be threatening (Lazarus & Folkman, 1984; Lenz, 1984). Information-seeking serves several purposes: identifying available choices, making informed decisions, and maximizing effective problem-solving. Due to the fact that some health care experts made statements about the syndrome without sufficient scientific data to support their reports early in the epidemic (1984) (Salisbury, 1986), some homosexual men are reluctant to seek information about AIDS from health care professionals, preferring instead to procure information from gay organizations and self-help groups (Harowski, 1986; NAPWA, 1988a).

Anecdotal reports suggest that homosexual and heterosexual family members want to know: "What causes AIDS?" . . . "Can it be treated?" . . . "What community resources are available to me?" . . . "How can I cope?" (Helquist, 1984). Families also want to know about finances, AIDS organizations, how the virus is transmitted, accessibility of drugs and therapies, and how to obtain legal assistance to obtain a will or to protect the patient's rights (Salisbury, 1986; NAPWA, 1988b). Early in the epidemic (1985), Moran, Lovejoy, Viele, Dodd, and Abrams (1988) found that 54.1% of homosexual men attending outpatient clinics wanted more information about safe sex. By 1987, Lovejoy and others (Lovejoy & Moran, 1988; Lovejoy et al., 1988) found that the majority (about 80%) of HIV positive men attending outpatient HIV clinics ($N = 30$; $N = 178$) wanted more information about "ways to build your health and immune system," indicating that the informational needs of families may be changing over the course of the epidemic. About half of the men also wanted to know how to manage the side effects of treatments, counseling and financial services, stress reduction methods, and ways to fight off depression.

Interventions

Clinicians suggest that both heterosexual and homosexual families need to have misinformation corrected and to receive accurate information about treatment options, prognosis, financial obligations, and available social services (Helquist, 1984). They also need to be provided with information about the five stages of dying as outlined by Kubler-Ross (1986) (i.e., denial and isolation, anger, bargaining, depression, and acceptance) in a timely and appropriate fashion. Furthermore, family inquiries need to be answered very simply; and anxieties that prompt questions, explored (Nichols, 1985). Because information-seeking is influenced by the credibility of the source of information (Harowski, 1986), Williams (1986) recommends that AIDS information be made available by persons or media judged to be acceptable to homosexual and heterosexual family members. Bor and Miller (1988) report that staff can avoid being overwhelmed by the informational needs of family members by asking a series of questions that focus concerns, i.e., the specific nature of problems being faced, the worst aspect of these problems, strategies that might be used for coping with the problems, and the impact of these concerns on the family, sexual partner, friends and others.

Sexuality

Manifestations

Prior to the AIDS epidemic, sexual promiscuity and instant sex were valued aspects of the homosexual lifestyle (Reece, 1988). "Back then, I was very, very good," typifies the wistful musings of patients with AIDS. With the discovery that the epidemic was venereally-propelled, both HIV infected and noninfected gay men began adopting safer sexual behaviors, i.e., reducing the numbers of partners, forming coupled relationships, using condoms and spermicides, and avoiding douching prior to anal intercourse (Moran et al., 1987; Lovejoy et al., 1988).

There are few studies of the sexual dilemmas faced by homosexual family members who are undergoing the transition phase of adjustment. However, Church, Kocsis, and Green (1988), interviewing homosexual partners of AIDS patients ($N = 40$), found that sexual relationships were significantly altered by the patient's diagnosis. Geis et al. (1986) found that partners of patients with AIDS ($N = 9$) curtailed performance of intimate sexual activities and increased use of masturbation and fantasy. Partners also worried about, "who would find them sexually attractive," after discovering that they were lovers of patients with AIDS. Patients worry about HIV-related impotence. "Mark would love it if I could have an erection, but I can't," reported one frustrated patient (Lovejoy, Paul, & Moran, 1988).

Related studies suggest that partners may be beset with questions about the relative safety of certain sexual behaviors: "What is the risk of oral sex and 'pre-cum'?'' . . . "Are there measures that can be taken after sex to prevent infections?'' . . . "If you clean well, is external rimming safe? . . . What if you first rubbed nonoxynol-9 lubricant around the rectum?'' . . . "What [sex] is really safe and possibly safe? . . . How safe is possibly safe?'' (Lovejoy et al., 1988; Lovejoy, in preparation; Moran et al., 1988). Homosexual men want research conducted on "the safety of oral sex . . . ,'' "the actual risk of various oral sexual acts just short of ejaculation,'' and "more definite answers about passage of virus, i.e., saliva, 'precum,' sucking without ejaculation'' (Lovejoy et al., 1988).

Related research also suggests that homosexual men are more likely to perform unsafe sex under certain conditions. By self-report, homosexual men are likely to practice unsafe sex when: under the influence of marijuana or alcohol, in the "heat of the moment,'' challenged to prove themselves, in long-term monogamous relationships, depressed, or condoms are not available (Lovejoy et al., 1988; Lovejoy & Moran, 1988). Data from a three-year prospective study ($N = 466$) conducted by Stall, McKusick, Wiley, Coates, and Ostrow (1986) suggest that men who drink during sexual activity, are about twice as likely as men who do not drink, to practice unsafe sex. Risk of unsafe sex is also greater if there is illegal drug use (e.g., marijuana). Early data from the Multicenter AIDS Cohort Study (MACS) ($N = 987$) also suggest that use of unsafe sexual behaviors is positively related to lack of knowledge about safe sexual behavior, low perceived risk of AIDS, and belief that medicine will soon find a cure for AIDS (Ostrow et al., 1986). In contrast, Prieur (1988), conducting in-depth interviews with 63 gay men attending gay bars in Oslo, found that AIDS knowledge did not distinguish between these groups of men who did and did not practice safe sex. Instead, data from this study suggest that men, who practice unsafe sexual behaviors without knowledge of partner's HIV status, are less socially open homosexuals, are not members of any gay organizations, are not involved in long-term coupled relationships or well-defined social networks, suggesting that any improvement of a gay man's social situation will probably have AIDS prevention as a side-effect.

Interventions

Because difficulties in the sexual relationship may result in breakdown of the partnership, leaving patients more vulnerable to the adverse effects of AIDS, Miller (1987) advocates taking a brief history of the partner's sexual history, social support network, and usual mechanisms for coping with stress in order to identify appropriate interventions (Ross & Rosser, 1988). These interventions may include counseling regarding future sexual options, vectors of HIV transmission, HIV antibody testing, and information regarding the effects of AIDS on sexual functioning. Partners need to know that patients may become impotent either because of HIV infiltration of the autonomic nervous system or psychogenic causes: fear of infecting others, lowered positive self-image, or depression with its attendant problems in affection, closeness, and intimacy. Partners will also need to be forewarned that patients may revert back to use of high risk behaviors (either because they feel their life may end anyway or because of a revenge motive) (Ross & Rosser, 1988). Therefore, partners need to be encouraged to rely on safe sex practices until patients adjust to their diagnoses.

Partners can be assured that sexual dysfunction related to anxiety may be amenable to restructuring strategies, such as, hypnosis and imagery (Harowski, 1988). Relief from unwanted or unsafe sexual behaviors may be gained by:

- ego-dystonic individuals from one-to-one discussions about sexual assertiveness, sexual limit-setting, making sexual requests of partners, trust, affection, and sexuality (Morin et al., 1984)
- by ego-syntonic individuals by therapy groups which focus on open discussion of driving forces toward sexual promiscuity and developing self-limiting contracts (Quadland, Shattls, Jacobs, & D'Eramo [1986])
- safe sex educational programs which include presentations of safer sex activity in an affirmative, erotically appealing manner and use of explicit, erotically appealing videos and slides (D'Eramo, Quadland, Shattls, Schuman, & Jacobs [1988])

Patients indicate that they would be helped if health care professionals would: "Just ask questions about our sexual needs . . . and feel good talking about any problems." . . . "Deal directly with sexual questions." . . . "Be direct with asking questions about sexual habits and informing patients about safe sex habits." . . . "Take our sexual problems seriously." . . . "Not be afraid to use street language in your answers." Inflated promises of successful therapies should be avoided (Ostrow et al., 1986).

Altered Roles

Manifestations

During the transition phase of adjustment, family members adjust their roles to accommodate the demands of the illness situation, shifting priorities and responsibilities. Although initial meetings between heterosexual and homosexual families are tense, mothers are often reassured by the love between partner and son, but fathers are less comforted (Helquist, 1984). If unable to accept each other, homosexual and heterosexual families may find themselves in love triangles — bitter struggles over who will assume responsibility for the patient's medical management (i.e., who and when to call for medical assistance), financial management (e.g., medical bills, insurance, bank accounts, charge accounts, outstanding loans, inheritance, etc.), emotional support and physical care (Nichols, 1985). Incidence of these triangles seem to be related to patients' inability to express "first loyalties" to one or the other set of families.

Related research shows that family members commonly adopt the "perpetrator" role (Lovejoy, 1987). In this role, the family member seeks to perpetrate normalcy. Occasionally, a family member may adopt the actress or actor role, pretending that the patient will get well or that a vaccine will be developed in time to save the patient's life. This pretense is difficult to maintain and inhibits the patient from discussing death-related concerns. As the burden of care increases, the extended caregiving role is adopted. Family members learn how to move adult patients in and out of bed, change sheets and clean bedridden patients, who are experiencing multisystem failures. The family learns new ways of communicating and caring as the patient's depression, rage, loss of mental acuity, or organic euphoria impair routine ways of relating.

Occasionally, family members become totally absorbed in the patient's illness. This immersion seems to be a gradual process that begins with a heightened love, growing sensitivity to patient needs, intense identification with the patient, and self-neglect. As the patient's situation deteriorates, those who are immersed report experiencing a sense of stagnation. These caregivers are in danger of developing patient burnout, and, unless rescued from this state, may lose their will to live (Lovejoy, 1986).

Interventions

Much of the acrimony experienced by families meeting for the first time can be avoided if patients and their homosexual families are counseled in advance about role alternatives and patients are encouraged to identify first loyalties. Patients, who want partners to act in their behalf, need to be advised to legalize these wishes with a durable power of attorney document and will. During the role transition process, families can be assisted in setting realistic expectations of themselves and patients, identifying effective coping mechanisms, and coached to relate with patients in new ways when AIDS dementia strikes: "Don't argue with them," "Don't make complex demands," and "Keep patients oriented with signs and labels on household items." Families also need to be referred to respite services at appropriate intervals.

PHASE THREE: ACCEPTANCE

During the acceptance phase of adjustment, patients and family members live within the limitations set by the illness and anticipate an altered future. Patients may make arrangements for dependents, who will survive them. Family members may initiate programs in self-care in order to better care for the patient. Although, the period is marked by hope, medical crises may cause family members to re-experience emotions and concerns expressed during previous phases of adjustment.

Hope

Hope, according to theorists, is a complex of feelings and thoughts associated with the fundamental belief that there are solutions to significant human needs and problems (Lange, 1978; Stotland, 1969). The hopeful person is characterized by vibrancy, energy and drive, a sense of well-being, optimism, interdependence, and selective denial that is aware of the precariousness of the situation (Stotland, 1969). Many family members maintain hope through renewed spiritual involvement. Homosexual family members also seem to restore meaning to their lives by becoming involved in altruistic activities or engaging in meditation and metaphysics.

If families are bereft of hope, they experience despair, apathy, the desire for revenge, or suicide. Although there are no studies of the suicide rates among family members affected by AIDS, related research shows that suicide rates among patients with AIDS is not escalating. Reviewing data from 1982 to 1986, Engleman et al. (1988) found that the rate of suicides per 100,000 in San Francisco, a major AIDS epicenter, has not changed significantly since the beginning of the epidemic (range 40.5% to 43.6%). Large well-designed studies, however, have shown that gay men tend to attempt suicide two to seven times more often than heterosexuals, particularly when there are histories of alcohol abuse, drug abuse, and interrupted social ties (Saunders & Valente, 1987).

Interventions

Hope may best be restored by providing members with sufficient information to resolve problems and set realistic, concrete goals—one to five years into the future. Prior to setting goals, it is constructive to review the family member's past successes.

Self Care

Manifestations

During the acceptance phase of adjustment, family members become increasingly concerned about improving their own health. This concern may be prompted by the need to increase their ability to care for the patient or themselves after the patient's death. Although reportedly over one billion dollars were spent in 1987 on AIDS self care by patients, little is known about the money spent by affected family members, who may or may not be seropositive (Boris, 1988). Research suggests that seronegative men in and out of committed relationships ($N = 284$) are adopting a variety of self care behaviors (see Table 1) (Lovejoy & Moran, 1988; Lovejoy et al., 1988; Moran et al., 1988) and that these behaviors may offer subjective health improvements. As one young man reported of his AIDS routine: "I still swim, as I have regularly done over the last six years . . . I am convinced that swimming, a good diet, and no drugs has maintained my health even though I am HIV positive and

Table 1

AIDS Self Care Behaviors

Category	Exemplars
Nutrition	Take lechtin, amino acids
Improved hygiene	Stop putting unclean hands to face
Symptom surveillance	Keep a close watch on my body; have regular check-ups
Stress reduction	Use visualization, meditation, or yoga; take hot baths
Cognitive strategies	Seek information; live day-to-day; use more open communication; value relationships
Alternative therapies	Use acupuncture or other nonconventional healing strategies
Physical fitness	Exercise regularly; jog
Social support	Belong to men's groups
Safe sex	Avoid going to bathhouses; reduce sexual contacts

have a T4 cell count of 88'' (Lovejoy et al., 1988, p. 158). Studies of the effects of self care on objective measures of health have not been reported.

Interventions

Health professionals have a responsibility to convey essential information about self care to family members following diagnosis. The emphasis should be on promoting health and competence in preventing disease transmission: disinfecting household objects contaminated with blood or other high titer body fluids, wearing gloves if hands are cut when handling body fluids, trying not to share drinking cups that have not been washed prior to use, and recognizing symptoms requiring immediate follow-up care (Helquist, 1984). Family members report that it is helpful to observe experts performing requisite tasks so that they can attend to needed motions and attitudes (Lovejoy, 1986).

PHASE FOUR:
ANTICIPATORY MOURNING AND BEREAVEMENT

Families prepare for the patient's death through anticipatory mourning. Usually, this episode begins when the patient begins to withdraw his emotional investment in others; but, in the case of AIDS, the process may begin in the transition phase of adjustment when family members renegotiate roles in anticipation of the patient's probable need for custodial care (Carlson, 1978). During anticipatory mourning, family members help the patient complete his unfinished business, provide assurance that the patient's wishes will be respected, and give the patient permission to let go of life. Anticipatory mourning involves crying, trembling, moaning, restlessness, sighing, and retreat from others. When mourning, family members may become so anxious that it is difficult for others to be around them. Whether anticipatory mourning unequivocally facilitates the process of bereavement has yet to be established.

Bereavement

Manifestations

Bereavement begins after the patient's death and may not be completed for months or years afterward (Carlson, 1978). Carlson (1978) suggests that the process is initiated by an obsessional review of events leading up to the patient's anticipated death. The review may be conducted alone or with others. The purpose of the review is to allow "the person to be able to integrate the loss both emotionally and cognitively" (Carlson, 1978, p. 95). During the review, persons are normally very emotional, profoundly sad, depressed, guilt-ridden, and isolating. Suicide may be contemplated and enacted.

Following the death of the patient, the post-bereavement process is prolonged by secondary losses resulting from the patient's death, such as, loss of sexual gratification, social support, financial security, or loss of dignity when funeral directors refuse to accept the patient's body (Carlson, 1978; Cecchi, 1986). In the case of AIDS, secondary losses of the heterosexual family include loss of a son "they thought they knew." For homosexual family members, secondary losses involve threatened loss of health.

Research suggests that bereavement is more intense for survivors below age 45 than for those who are older (Ball, 1977; Parkes, 1964). Parents with short preparation for death express more guilt feelings than parents with longer preparation time, and mothers express more guilt than fathers (Demi, 1978). Research also suggests that bereavement is so common in homosexual communities that it is known as the second AIDS epidemic (Martin & Dean, 1988). In fact, of the 199 homosexual men in New York City, who reported having lost at least one close homosexual family member from 1981 through 1985, 67% had been bereaved once, 18% had been bereaved twice, and 15% had been bereaved three times or more. AIDS bereavement was associated with psychological symptoms, such as demoralization, traumatic stress response, sleep disturbance, recreational drug use, and sedative use. The bereaved in this sample reported heavy use of psychological consultations, with consultations increasing 4-fold among those bereaved once and 5 times among those bereaved 3 times or more (Martin & Dean, 1988). There was no sign of adaptation among those suffering from multiple deaths.

Interviews of homosexual and heterosexual family members (N = 11), who maintained hospital vigils during the dying interval, also suggest that they received suboptimal care during the terminal phase of the patient's illness. For example, one study showed that, although family members wanted to be present at the patient's death, few (3/11) were. Family members (6/11) also reported that no support was available to them immediately after the patient's death, although they wanted staff to help them adjust (Rubin & Wu, 1988).

Intervention

Although limited in scope, research strongly suggests that families need more support from health professionals during the mourning and bereavement interval. They need to be assured that the patient is comfortable and to be given accurate information about the patient's condition (Rubin & Wu, 1988). Following the patient's death, survivors, who do not use religious bereavement mechanisms, are vulnerable to pathologic grief responses (Gelcer, 1983). For these families, preventative care may involve formal bereavement programs which help survivors complete the bereavement process and develop new roles (Constantino, 1981; Janson, 1986). In one exemplary program, trained personnel visit family members at the funeral and two weeks, 1 month, 3 months, 6 months, 9 months, 12 months, and 13 months after the death of a loved one (Janson, 1986). Contact is also made on dates having significance for the family: birthdays, special holidays, and the first anniversary of the death. Bereavement visits serve to assist survivors understand and interpret normal grief behaviors, develop effective coping skills and functional ways of dealing with the loss of a loved one, encourage the renewal of old relationships, develop new support systems in the community, and minimize any unnecessary stress during the first year of bereavement. Whether formal bereavement services can reduce the bereavement crisis in homosexual community needs to be determined in future research.

DISCUSSION

The relative paucity of knowledge regarding family responses during the AIDS adjustment process and factors which influence optimal outcome is alarming in view of the important role the family plays in the quality of life experienced by patients with AIDS. The number of atheoretical, descriptive studies offers the concerned health professional little more than suggested, guidelines for practice. Although a few experimental studies address substantive issues, such as, how to alter health endangering behaviors, little is known about the interpersonal relationships of heterosexual and homosexual family members affected by AIDS or interventions which help both sets of families adapt to the demands of the illness. Family studies that would provide useful information include:

1. Factors contributing to pathologic triangulation between homosexual and heterosexual family members.
2. Role transitions, role negotiations, and interventions which promote the development of complementary role structure and function between the patient's homosexual and heterosexual families.
3. The effects of self care behaviors on objective and subjective measures of family member health over the AIDS trajectory.
4. Information-seeking behaviors of homosexual and heterosexual family members, determinants of the informational search, the quality of the informational network, and the effects of specific information programs on the homosexual and heterosexual family member's ability to cope.
5. Determinants of immersion and interventions which ameliorate its detrimental effects.
6. The effects of structured bereavement programs on homosexual family members experiencing AIDS bereavement.
7. The quality of social support/life experienced by homosexual and heterosexual families during and after homecoming.
8. Causes and consequences of AIDS-related celibacy/impotence in homosexual families.

In order to generate a scientific basis for clinical practice, future studies need to test hypotheses derived from well-established explanatory or predictive theories. Theories which may stimulate the generation of useful knowledge include: family structure and function theories (Minuchin, 1974), role transition theories (Golan, 1981; McCubbin & Patterson, 1982), coping theories (Lazarus & Folkman, 1984), and Seligman's (1975) theory of learned helplessness. In addition, multi-centered prospective studies are needed to determine if family responses are affected by geographical location or incidence of AIDS cases. There is also a great need for qualitative studies to extract the intricate dynamics and deep feelings of family members in the context of being involved with a significant person who has AIDS. Quantitative, survey, questionnaire, or pen/pencil approaches, while helpful in establishing correlational relationships, do not provide the depth of understanding necessary for the development of appropriate interventions.

REFERENCES

Abrams, D., Dilley, J. W., Maxey, L. M., & Volberding, P. A. (1986). Routine care and psychosocial support of the patient with the Acquired Immunodeficiency Syndrome. *Medical Clinics of America*, 70(3), 707-720.

American Psychiatric Association. (1985). *Diagnostic and Statistical Manual of Mental Disorders*. University of Cambridge: Press Syndicate.

Ball, J. F. (1977). Widows' grief: The impact of age and mode of death. *Omega*, 7, 307-333.

Baumgartner, G. H. (1985). *AIDS: Psychosocial Factors in the Acquired Immune Deficiency Syndrome*. Springfield: Charles C Thomas.

Bernstein, P. H. (1986). Aids for AIDS. *Caring*, 5(6), 47-51.

Biggar, R. J. (1987). Epidemiology of human retroviruses and related clinical conditions. In S. Broder (Ed.), *AIDS modern concepts and therapeutic challenges* (pp. 91-121). New York: Marcel Dekker, Inc.

Bor, R. & Miller, R. (1988). The essentials of AIDS counselling for the clinician (Abstract No. 9524). *Fourth International Conference on AIDS*, Stockholm, Sweden.

Boris, V. (1988). Exploitation of AIDS patients trading with false hopes, panaceas and pseudo-therapies (Abstract No. 8071). *Fourth International Conference on AIDS*, Stockholm, Sweden.

Caplan, G. (1974). Foreword. In I. Glick, R. Weiss, & C. Parkes (Eds.), *The first year of bereavement* (pp. vii-xi). New York: Wiley.

Carlson, C. E. (1978). Grief. In C. E. Carlson, B. Blackwell (Eds.), *Behavioral concepts and nursing intervention* (pp. 87-112). Philadelphia: J. B. Lippincott Company.

Cecchi, R. (1986). Living with AIDS: When the system fails. *American Journal of Nursing, 86*, 45, 47.

CDC. (1987). Revision of the CDC case definition for Acquired Immunodeficiency Syndrome. *Morbidity & Mortality Weekly Report, 36*(15), 3S-15S.

Church, J. A., Kocsis, A. E., & Green, J. (1988). Effects on lovers of caring for HIV infected individuals related to perceptions of cognitive, behavioral, and personality changes in the sufferer (Abstract No. 8592). *Fourth International Conference on AIDS*, Stockholm, Sweden.

Constantino, R. E. (1981). Bereavement crisis intervention for widows in grief and mourning. *Nursing Research, 30*(6), 351-353.

Curran, J. W., Jaffe, H. W., Hardy, A. M., Morgan, W. M., Selik, R. M., & Dondero, T. J. (1988). Epidemiology of HIV infection and AIDS in the United States. *Science, 239*, 610-619.

D'Eramo, J. E., Quadland, M. C., Shattls, W., Schuman, R., & Jacobs, R. (1988). The "800 Men" project: A systematic evaluation of AIDS prevention programs demonstrating the efficacy of erotic, sexually explicit safer sex education on gay and bisexual men at risk for AIDS (Abstract No. 8086). *Fourth International Conference on AIDS*, Stockholm, Sweden.

Demi, A. S. (1978). Adjustment to widowhood after a sudden death; Suicide and non-suicide survivors compared. In M. V. Batey (Ed.), *Communicating Nursing Research: Vol. 11* (pp. 91-99). Boulder, CO: Western Interstate Commission for Higher Education.

Dilley, J. W., Ochitill, H. N., Perl, M., & Volberding, P. A. (1985). Findings in psychiatric consultations with patients with Acquired Immune Deficiency Syndrome. *American Journal of Psychiatry, 142*(1), 82-85.

Donlou, J. N., Wolcott, D. L., Gottlieb, M. S., & Landsverk, J. (1985). Psychosocial aspects of AIDS and AIDS-Related Complex: A pilot study. *Journal of Psychosocial Oncology, 3*(2), 39-55.

Engleman, J., Hessol, N. A., Lifson, A. R., Lemp, G., Mata, A., Rutherford, G. W., Goldblum, P., Bott, C., & Stephens, B. (1988). Suicide patterns and AIDS in San Francisco (Abstract No. 8597). *Fourth International Conference on AIDS*, Stockholm, Sweden.

Farthing, C. F., Brown, S. E., Staughton, R. C. D., Cream, J. J., & Muhlemann, M. (1986). *A colour atlas of AIDS*. London: Wolfe Medical Publications.

Feinbaum, S. (1986). Pinning down the psychosocial dimensions of AIDS. *Nursing and Health Care, 7*(5), 255-257.

Fettner, A. G. & Check, W. A. (1985). *The truth about AIDS: Evolution of an epidemic*. New York: Holt, Rinehart & Winston.

Fletcher, M. A., O'Hearn, P., Ingram, F., Ironson, G., Laperriere, A., Linas, N. G., & Schneidermen, N. (1988). Anticipation and reaction to anti-HIV test results: Effect on immune function in an AIDS risk group (Abstract 9515). *Fourth International Conference on AIDS*, Stockholm, Sweden.

Forstein, M. (1984). AIDS anxiety in the "worried well." In S. Nichols, & D. Ostrow (Eds.), *Psychiatric implications of acquired immune deficiency syndrome* (pp. 50-60). American Psychiatric Press: Monongraph Series.

Friedland, G. H. & Klien, R. S. (1987). Transmission of the Human Immunodeficiency Virus. *New England Journal of Medicine, 317*(18), 1123-1135.

Geis, S. B. & Fuller, R. L. (1986). Lovers of AIDS victims: Psychosocial stresses and counselling needs. *Death Studies, 10*, 43-53.

Gelcer, E. (1983). Mourning is a family affair. *Family Process, 22*, 501-516.

Goedert, J., Biggar, R. J., Lemlbye, M., Mann, D. L., Vilson, S., Gail, M. H., Grossman, R. J., DiGioia, R. A., Sanchez, W., Weiss, S. H., & Blattner, W. A. (1987). Effect of T4 count and cofactors on the incidence of AIDS in homosexual men infected with human immunodeficiency virus. *Journal of the American Medical Association, 257*(3), 331-334.

Golan, N. (1981). *Passing through transitions.* New York: The Free Press.

Harowski, K. J. (1988). The worried well: Maximizing coping in the face of AIDS. *Journal of Homosexuality, 14*(2), 299-306.

Henry, K., Campbell, S., & Willenbring, K. (1988). AIDS-related knowledge attitudes and behaviors among employers at a U.S. Hospital (Abstract 9110). *Fourth International Conference on AIDS,* Stockholm, Sweden.

Helquist, M. (1984). *The family's guide to AIDS: Responding with your heart.* San Francisco AIDS Foundation, San Francisco Department of Public Health and the California Department of Health Services.

Hewitt, R. G. (1988). Homecoming cases of AIDS: The impact of AIDS patients who come home on a low incidence region for the syndrome (Abstract No. 9575). *Fourth International Conference on AIDS,* Stockholm, Sweden.

Ho, D. D., Pomerantz, R. J., & Kaplan, J. C. (1987). Pathogenesis of infection with Human Immunodeficiency Virus. *New England Journal of Medicine, 317*(5), 278-286.

Holland, J. C. & Tross, S. (1985). The psychosocial and neuropsychiatric sequelae of the Acquired Immunodeficiency Syndrome and related disorders. *Annals of Internal Medicine, 103*, 760-764.

Institute of Medicine. (1986). *Confronting AIDS: Directions for public health, health care, and research.* Washington, D.C.: National Academy Press.

Janson, M. A. H. (1986). A comprehensive bereavement program. *Quarterly Review, 12*(4), 130-135.

Joseph, J. G., Emmons, C. A., Kessler, R. C., Wortman, C. B., O'Brien, K., Hocker, W. T., & Schaefer, C. (1984). Coping with the threat of AIDS: An approach to psychosocial assessment. *American Psychologist, 39*, 1297-1302.

Joseph, J. G., Kessler, R. C., Ostrow, D. G., Phair, J., & Chmiel, J. (1988). Psychosocial predictors of symptom development in HIV infected gay men (Abstract No. 8587). *Fourth International Conference on AIDS,* Stockholm, Sweden.

Kelly, J. J. & Sykes, P. (1988). Helping the helpers: A support group for caretakers of persons with AIDS (Abstract No. 8081). *Fourth International Conference on AIDS,* Stockholm, Sweden.

Kiening, Sr., M. M. (1978a). Denial of illness. In C. E. Carlson & B. Blackwell (Eds.), *Behavioral Concepts: Nursing Intervention* (pp. 211-225). New York: J. B. Lippincott Company.

Kiening, Sr., M. M. (1978b). Hostility. In C. E. Carlson & B. Blackwell (Eds.), *Behavioral Concepts: Nursing Intervention* (pp. 128-140). New York: J. B. Lippincott Company.

Klimes, I., Catalan, J., Bond, A., & Day, A. (1988). Knowledge and attitudes of health care staff to HIV infection (Abstract No. 9108). *Fourth International Conference on AIDS*, Stockholm, Sweden.

Kubler-Ross, E. (1969). *On death and dying.* New York: Macmillan.

Lange, S. P. (1978). Hope. In C. E. Carlson & B. Blackwell (Eds.), *Behavioral Concepts: Nursing Intervention* (pp. 171-190). New York: J. B. Lippincott Company.

Lang, W., Anderson, R. E., Perkins, H., Grant, R. M., Lyman, D., Winkelstein, W., Royce, R., & Levy, J. A. (1987). Clinical immunologic and serologic findings in men at risk for Acquired Immunodeficiency Syndrome. *Journal of the American Medical Association, 257*(3), 326-330.

Lazarus, R. S. & Folkman, S. (1984). *Stress, Appraisal, and Coping.* New York: Springer Publishing Co.

Lenz, E. R. (1984). Information-seeking: A component of client decisions and health behavior. *Advances in Nursing Science, 6*(3), 59-72.

Lovejoy, N. (1986). Family responses to cancer hospitalization. *Oncology Nursing Forum, 13,* 33-38.

Lovejoy, N. (1987). Roles played by hospital visitors. *Heart and Lung, 16*(7), 573-575.

Lovejoy, N., Moran, T., & Paul, S. (1988). Self-care behaviors and information needs of seropositive homosexual/bisexual men. *Journal of Acquired Immune Deficiency Syndrome, 1*(3), 155-161.

Lovejoy, N. & Moran, T. A. (in press). The health promoting beliefs, behaviors, and informational needs of homosexual/bisexual men with AIDS or ARC. *International Journal of Nursing Studies.*

Lovejoy, N. & Moran, T. (in preparation). Self-care behaviors and informational needs of seronegative homosexual/bisexual men with AIDS or ARC.

Lovejoy, N., Paul, S., & Moran, T. (in preparation). Characteristics of celibate and noncelibate men diagnosed with AIDS or ARC.

Mann, J., Kocsis, A. E., & Green, J. (1988). Role of life-events and social support in HIV infection (Abstract No. 8078). *Fourth International Conference on AIDS*, Stockholm, Sweden.

Martin, J. P. (1986). Challenges in caring for the person with AIDS at home. *Caring, 5*(6), 13-20.

Martin, J. L. & Dean, L. (1988). The secondary epidemic of AIDS-related bereavement (Abstract No. 8069). *Fourth International Conference on AIDS,* Stockholm, Sweden.

McCubbin, H. I. & Patterson, J. M. (1982). *Family stress, coping, and social support.* Springfield, IL: Charles C Thomas.

Miles, M. S. (1985). Emotional symptoms and physical health in bereaved parents. *Nursing Research, 34*(2), 76-81.

Miller, D. (1987). Counseling. *British Medical Journal, 294*(6588), 1671-1674.

Minuchin, S. (1974). *Families and family therapy*. Cambridge: Harvard University Press.

Morin, S., Charles, K., & Malyon, A. (1984). The psychological impact of AIDS on gay men. *American Psychologist, 39*, 1288-1293.

Moran, T. A., Lovejoy, N., Viele, C. S., Dodd, M. J., & Abrams, D. I. (1988). Informational needs of homosexual men diagnosed with AIDS or AIDS-related complex. *Oncology Nursing Forum, 15*(3), 311-314.

Moss, A. R., Bacchetti, P., Osmond, D., Krampf, W., Chaisson, R. E., Stites, R., Wilber, J., Allain, J. P., & Carlson, J. (1988). Seropositivity for HIV and the development of AIDS or AIDS related condition: Three year follow-up of the San Francisco General Hospital cohort. *British Medical Journal, 296*(6624), 745-750.

Navia, B. A., Jordan, B. D., & Price, R. W. (1986). The AIDS dementia complex: I. Clinical features. *Annals of Neurology, 19*(6), 517-524.

NAPWA. (1988a). People with AIDS: Partners in the provision of services (Abstract no. 9528). *Fourth International Conference on AIDS*, Stockholm, Sweden.

Ostrow, D. G., Joseph, J., Monjan, A., Kessler, R., Emmons, C., Phair, J., Fox, R., Kingsby, L., Dudley, J., Chmiel, J. S., & Van Raden, M. (1986). Neuropsychiatric aspects of AIDS. *Psychopharmacology Bulletin, 22*(3), 678-683.

Parkes, C. M. (1964). Effect of bereavement on physical and mental health—A study of the medical records of widows. *British Medical Journal, 11*(1), 274-279.

Peabody, B. (1986). Living with AIDS: A mother's perspective. *American Journal of Nursing, 86*, 45-46.

Pinching, A. (1986). Immunology. In P. Jones (Ed)., *Proceedings of the AIDS Conference 1986* (pp. 71-80). Ponteland, Newcastle upon Tyne: Intercept.

Polk, B. F., Fox, R., Brookmeyer, K., Kanchanarakasa, S., Kaslow, R., Visscher, B., Rinaldo, C., & Phair, J. (1987). Predictors of the Acquired Immunodeficiency Syndrome developing in a cohort of seropositive homosexual men. *New England Journal of Medicine, 316*(2), 61-66.

Price, P. M. & Scimeca, A. M. (1984). The epidemic of the 80's: AIDS. *Cancer Nursing, 6*, 283-290.

Prieur, A. (1988). A psycho-social description of some gay men with a high risk behavior (Abstract no. 4083). *Fourth International Conference on AIDS*, Stockholm, Sweden.

Quadland, M. C. & Shattls, W. D. (1987). AIDS, sexuality, and sexual control. *Journal of Homosexuality, 14*(1/2), 277-298.

Quadland, M. C., Shattls, W. D., Jacobs, R., & D'Eramo, J. (1986). "800 Men": A safer sex education program. Unpublished report in progress. New York: Gay Men's Health Crisis, Inc.

Reece, R. (1988). Special issues in the etiologies and treatments of sexual problems among gay men. *Journal of Homosexuality, 14*, 43-57.

Robinson, B. E., Skeen, P., & Walters, L. (1988). Psychosocial impact of the

AIDS threat on parents of gay children in the United States (Abstract No. 8586). *Fourth International Conference on AIDS*, Stockholm, Sweden.

Ross, M. W. & Rosser, B. S. (1988). Psychological issues in AIDS-related syndromes. *Patient Education and Counseling, 11,* 17-28.

Royse, D. & Binge, B. (1987). Homophobia and attitudes toward AIDS patients among medical, nursing, and paramedical students. *Psychological Reports, 61,* 867-870.

Rubin, H. & Wuz, A. W. (1988). Family expectations in AIDS terminal care (Abstract No. 9541). *Fourth International Conference on AIDS*, Stockholm, Sweden.

Salisbury, D. M. (1986). AIDS: Psychosocial implications. *Journal of Psychosocial Nursing, 24*(12), 13-15.

San Francisco Public Health. (July, 1988). Reported AIDS cases.

Saunders, J. M. & Valente, S. M. (1987). Suicide risk among gay men and lesbians: A review. *Death Studies, 11,* 1-23.

Schietinger, H. (1986). A home care plan for AIDS. *American Journal of Nursing, 86,* 1021-1028.

Schoen, K. (1986). Psychosocial aspects of hospice care for AIDS patients. *American Journal of Hospice Care, 3*(2), 32-34.

Seligman, M. E. P. (1975). *Helplessness*. San Francisco: Freeman.

Spielberger, C. D. (1979). *Understanding stress and anxiety*. New York: Harper & Row.

Stall, R., McKusick, L., Wiley, J., Coates, T., & Ostrow, D. G. (1986). Alcohol and drug use during sexual activity and compliance with safe sex guidelines for AIDS: The AIDS Behavioral Research Project. *Health Education Quarterly, 13*(4), 359-371.

Vachon, M. L. S., Rogers J., Lyall, W. A., Lances, W. J., Sheldon, A. R., & Freeman, S. J. J. (1982). Predictors and correlated of adaptation to conjugal bereavement. *American Journal of Psychiatry, 139,* 998-1002.

Volberding, P. A. (1985). The clinical spectrum of the Acquired Immunodeficiency syndrome: Implications for comprehensive patient care. *Annals of Internal Medicine, 103,* 729-733.

Williams, L. S. (1986). AIDS risk reduction: A community health education intervention for minority high risk group members. *Health Education Quarterly, 13*(4), 407-421.

Winkelstein, L., Lyman, D. M., Padian, N., Conant, M., Samuel, M., Wiley, J. A., Anderson, R. E., Lang, W., Riggs, J., & Levy, J. A. (1987). Sexual practices and risk of infections by the human immunodeficiency virus. The San Francisco Men's Health Study. *Journal of the American Medical Association, 257*(3), 321-325.

Wolcott, D. L., Namir, S., Faway, F. I., Gottlieb, M. S., & Mitsuyasu, R. T. (1986). Illness concerns, attitudes towards homosexuality, and social support in gay men with AIDS. *General Hospital Psychiatry, 8,* 395-403.

The Shaman:
The Gay and Lesbian Ancestor
of Humankind

Kris Jeter

Once upon a time there was a beautiful princess named Caenis who was the daughter of King Elatus of Lapith Thessaly. Caenis enjoyed her singlehood, and some say her love of women, and refused to marry. One day, as she walked along the seashore, Poseidon raped her. Poseidon then decided to rectify his assault by granting Caenis a wish. Caenis chose to be transformed into a man invulnerable to death by sword so that she would never again be subjected to the disrespect and indignity of rape. Poseidon granted her wish. Caenis was now named Caeneus and became a chief of the Lapiths of Thessaly. One night during a wedding ceremony, inebriated Centaurs attacked the Lapiths, determined to abduct and rape the women. Caeneus killed six Centaurs, including their leader. The remaining Centaurs fought him and found that their weapons would not kill Caeneus, and so pummelled Caeneus with rock boulders and fir trees. Some storytellers say that Caeneus was pounded into Ge – Ghia, Mother Earth – and was metamorphosed once again into her female form, Caenis. Others, including Ovid, say that the seer Mopsus saw the spirit of Caeneus transmute into a flamingo with shiny wings and fly into the sky. Whether in the earth or heavens, Caenis/Caeneus, empathetic of the ways of both men and women, is known as a wise one, a shaman.

Kris Jeter, PhD, is Associate Director of Mentor and Learner Relationships for the Jean Houston Human Capacities Training Program and Director of Programs and Communications for The Possible Society. Address correspondence to 800 Paper Mill Rd., Newark, DE 19711.

317

THESIS

The Greek myth of Caenis/Caeneus, tells of a shaman, a lover of women who lived as a woman as well as a man, who could journey in the underworld and fly in the heavens and uphold the dignity of humankind. The thesis of this article is that individuals who have been able to live in the worlds of both the female and male sexes, by such actions as cross dressing; assuming varied gender roles; surgically reversing sexual organs; and/or realizing an ambisexual, gay, or lesbian life style have often been acknowledged historically by hunting and agricultural cultures as spirit guides transcending the bounds of everyday consciousness.

In hunting cultures, some individuals have felt called to become shamans. A number of these shamans have crossed gender lines. They have been known to possess the knowledge of the great bear, totem animal, fire, X-ray art, and spear. In agricultural cultures, ambisexual deities have been worshiped and held as role models. Shamans from the farming lands have been known to make permanent sex changes. Persons within the time-honored roles of shaman, often willing to actively empathize with both genders, have been able to heal individuals, families, and societies through actions as attorney, counselor, healer, magician, mortician, naturalist, philosopher, poet, priest, prophet, smith, spiritual guide, and weathermaker.

In this analytic essay, I shall relate the evolution of human society to the development of the position of the shaman. The historical stages are:

1. The pre-gender, pre-kinship society
2. The gender, kinship hunting society
3. The matrifocal agricultural society and
4. The patrifocal agricultural society with remembrances of ambisexual deities.

I shall briefly discuss general characteristics of the shaman and differentiate the shaman of the hunters and the shaman of the farmers. My purpose in writing this analytic essay is to illuminate the shaman as one position of status held since the beginning of humankind by individuals who temporarily or permanently inhabit the realms of both the female and male sexes. The shaman's compassion with both sexes and harmony with all life was the basis of a wisdom which was sought after by tribal members to provide insight to personal, family, and community situations.

In this time of the AIDS epidemic, the identification of a positive ancestor of gays and lesbians is most important (Roberts). AIDS, a disease originally named GRID or Gay-Related Immune Deficiency, as of 31 March 1989, has killed 52,435 individuals, primarily gay men, Hatians, and recreational drug users in the United States alone (Centers for Disease Control). With each diagnosis, gay men have faced economic hardship, fears of contagious infection, heartache, hostility, isolation, rejection, remorse, shame, and social stigma. The knowledge that one ancestor, the shaman, was a healer across the cultures and throughout the ages of the world, provides hope in a time of helplessness and hopelessness. From this suffering of the heart, mind, and soul may emerge a mythic structure reminisent of the shaman which centers on healing, not only the ills of the specific individual, but also the ills of our modern culture. AIDS may be the harbinger of a new humanity in which the immune systems of all individuals, nature, and societies are nourished, cared for, and protected. A necessary transformation from "me as self" to "we as unity" occurs. The whole system changes (Sussman and Jeter). The powers of the Shaman are being remembered and reclaimed.

THE SHAMANS OF THE HUNTERS

Salvatore Cucchiari has hypothesized that the earliest stage of human society was the ambisexual, pre-gender, pre-kinship society. This society had two non-exclusive functional roles: the Child Tenders and the Foragers. The Child Tenders worked close to the base camp, nurturing children, building a haven. The Foragers worked outside of the base camp obtaining and trading supplies. Fire was taken from nature where lightning had struck or spontaneous combustion had occurred. At the base camp, fire was tended and nurtured. Although the Child Tender role and the Forager role required different physical skills and travel abilities, the roles were not considered unalterable, dualistic, nor were they authoritatively assigned. Rather, the two roles were shared. The proportion of humans to assets was constantly reevaluated.

As trade expanded from exchange of things to exchange of people, Cucchiari has contended, a gender, kinship society developed. The Proto-Woman was assigned the role of Child Tender and the Proto-Man was assigned the role of Forager. The Proto-Woman was portrayed in art with large hips and breasts, often with a child being suckled on the left breast next to the heart beat. Meanwhile, the Proto-Man was represented as a variety of animals, totems of the hunter. Norms of behavior developed establishing rules of incest and taboos, demanding female dependency, sexual ownership, and exclusive heterosexuality so that offspring could be identified.

Edward Carpenter has suggested that those women who did not want to tend children and those men who did not want to forage developed new occupations. Being dissimilar and distinct, they felt impelled to contemplate nature with the talents of both the Proto-Woman and Proto-Man and to visualize, conceive, and invent new arts and sciences. These inventions were considered magical and divine and this Proto-Human became known as the shaman.

During Upper Paleolithic times, 33,000 B.C.E.-17,000 B.C.E., hunters and gatherers decorated caves in France and Spain. The cave art is X-ray drawings of pregnant female animals and animals pierced with spears. Both art themes address the food supply of the community: the fertile animal and the successful hunt.

André Leroi-Gourhan's research on these caves can be utilized to date the time when the pre-gender, pre-kinship culture became a gender, kinship culture. Leroi-Gourhan has distinguished three spacial areas of the caves and has assigned meanings to the cave art. The portal was painted with images of those animals that threatened the human the most: the bear, lion, and rhinoceros, all symbols of masculinity. The outer areas contained pictures of the ibex and stag, also symbols of masculinity. The inner sanctum has portraits of huge herbivores, the bison, horse, mammoth, and oxen, symbols of the female.

The caves, a number of which extend one mile beneath the earth's surface, represented the womb and were the site for spiritual initiation and rebirth. Because the cave layers and caves of the Mousterian era hold an equal number of male and female symbols, that era is thought to be pre-gender, pre-kinship. The cave layers and caves of the following eras are progressively represented by more male symbols and fewer female figures and symbols, thus marking the beginning and endurance of the gender, kinship era.

The great bear resided in Asia, Europe, and North Africa. The bear walks as a human. When skinned, the bear is remarkably identical to the human being. Myths tell that the bear taught the human how to survive. The bear, like the shaman, is a loner during most of the year. In the summer, the bears gather at the streams to feast on fish, such as the salmon that swim upstream to mate. These loners during the annual feast cooperate and share the bounty. In winter, the bears enter hibernation, allowing the life force to sleep, dream, and rejuvenate.

Cross-cultural myths have told of a male bear who marries a female human and permits himself to be slaughtered by his brother-in-law if people will forever conduct bear ceremonies. The cross-cultural rituals of bear ceremonies contain recurring characteristics. The hunters make offerings, invoke blessings, and prophetize boons before their pursuit for game. Either before or after the hunt, they participate in rituals of atonement, at oneness with the bear. The dead bear is received by the community with respect and treated as a prized visitor. The flesh — and the potency — of the bear are eaten in communion. The skeleton of the bear is either preserved in a cave or buried underground so that the bear can be born again as quarry for the hunter (Edsman).

The shaman may be considered the brother-in-law, the rememberer of the bear ceremonies. In Australia, where there are no bears and in later day Americas, similar ceremonies honor indigenous animals, totem animals.

Joseph Campbell and Andreas Lommel have traced the early transformation of geography and humankind as affected by the ice ages. During the last of the four glacial ages, 70,000 B.C.E.-40,000 B.C.E., as the ice glaciers melted and the European barren tundra lands became thick woodlands, the large animal herds traveled from the south to the northeast. The animals were pursued by the Paleolithic hunters, across Northern Asia, down the Pacific islands to Australia, across Northern America, and down the Americas to the Cape. The hunter's motto was not "To be, or not to be," but rather, "To eat, or to be eaten" (Campbell, page 51).

During this era, two technological advances occurred of great importance: the generation of fire and production of flint and obsidion spears. The shaman's role was especially transformed with these advances.

Around 48,000 B.C.E., humans learned to generate and ignite fire by creating friction between sticks. No longer were they only dependent upon fire provided by nature and nurtured by gifted ones, perhaps women, perhaps shamans. Fire was used to clear jungles and woods, cook food, detain wild animals, provide heat, expel game out of the woodlands, and reinforce spear points. Fire was a metaphor for life. Myths and rituals have told of a family's extinguishing of its hearth fire when a family member died.

The sacred perpetual fire was differentiated from the profane new fire. The perpetual fire held the memory of the origins of life from heaven and the history of conscious tending. The profanity of new fire has been described in mythology and practice. Prometheus stole fire from the deities. The name of Prometheus was probably derived from the Sanscrit word, *math*, which means "to steal, rob, take away" and the Sanscrit word, *manth* , which means "to stir, churn; to produce fire by rapidly whirling a dry stick in another dry stick." Moreover, Prometheus stole from humans the need for sacred perpetual fire. New fire became associated by some cultures with heterosexuality; it was begat by female and male rubbing sticks (Edsman). Shamans, especially shaman women, became the keepers of the sacred hearth, rememberers of the perpetual fire.

The hunters used the tools they had slowly developed since the beginning of time: water-worn pebble tools and choppers; bifacial hand axes; and the refined flake-tools. Then, about 38,000 B.C.E., first in the Near East and then in Asia and Europe, flint and obsidian pieces with comparable sides were pounded and formed for particular functions. The flint and obsidian pieces were attached to tree branches to become spears. No longer did humans have to be physically next to an animal to make a kill. Rather, the human could stand at a distance, throw the spear, and kill the animal. Art and myths depict the Great Hunt of animals by the atlatl or spearthrower. The Shaman possessed the knowledge of the animals, the force of wind and propellation, and the generation of fire to construct spears.

It is hypothesized that during this era, the last of the four glacial ages, as human beings, *homo sapiens* mediated death through ritual. At Shanidar, 250 miles north of Baghadad in the Zagros Mountains, there is a cave with a 175 foot wide entrance with a depth of 132 feet. A dig of 45 feet in depth, has uncovered 100,000 years of history. At the level of 60,000 B.C.E., an infant, two women, and a man were buried with floral arrangements composed of eight different types of blossoms still used today in Iran as healing herbs. At the level of 40,000 B.C.E., the body of a forty-year-old man born with a disabled shoulder, whose right arm had been surgically amputated beneath the elbow, has been found. The Paleolithic humans appear to have been concerned with life and death (Solecki).

Researchers at other digs have identified bodies placed in fetal position on a pallet of uterus-shaped conch shells in domed-chambers resembling the vagina and uterus. The body was decorated with red ochre and appeared as the newborn, shrouded in blood. Oswald Spengler specified the "Recognition of Death" (*Blick auf den Tod*) as the point of origin of consciousness of a culture. "There is no such thing as death; there is but a passing on." Since the beginning of time, the woman had welcomed and greeted the human being at birth. With the "Recognition of Death," the shaman, often the male psychopomp, assumed the role of welcoming and greeting the human being to death, to "passing on."

Between 40,000 B.C.E. and 30,000 B.C.E., the oceans swelled and flooded over the landbridges, cutting off travel from Asia to Australia and the Americas. When the earth became cold again between 30,000 B.C.E. and 20,000 B.C.E., the landbridges reemerged, and the pre-gender, pre-kin Mousteroid tradition, which marked the culmination of the Neanderthal human, was passed northward over the continents with the migrating humans. The Mousteroid tradition was based on the Neanderthal worship of the Master Bear and it readily adapted itself to each environment to which it spread.

Again, the oceans gorged and flooded over the landbridges. They reemerged between 11,000 B.C.E. and 8,000 B.C.E. The Aurignacoid tradition which also originated in the caves of France and

Spain during the first epoch of the upper paleolithic culture spread over the arctic region from Europe to Asia and down the Pacific and America landbridges. The Aurignacoid artistic tradition also spread, portraying in X-ray style, the muscles and skeleton of animals, and the foliage and roots of plants (Lommel).

With both migrations across continents, shamans were required by the hunters to remember the old traditional wisdom and to mediate between the hunter with the animal. The shaman, as X-ray artist, knew the skeletal essence of life (Kuhn). The shaman culture of the hunter has five distinct characteristics.

1. All shamans except those from Australia have worshipped the bear. Emil Bachler found caves in the German and Swiss Alps which contain pre- and early-Mousterian tools and the remains of the cave bear, lion, and panther placed about the cave carefully in a deliberate fashion. He discovered stone cabinets containing cave bear skulls and wall shelves housing cave bear skulls and lengthy bones and hypothesized the existence of a Bone-offering Cult, a Bear Cult in which the cave bear was the Animal Master. To expand Oswald Spengler's and Joseph Campbell's theory, it appears that the point of origin of the consciousness of the Mousterian culture occurred when the "Recognition of Death" of not only humans but animals, such as the bear, occurred.

2. Shamans have recognized an animal as the totem ancestor, the trustee, the attendant, the alter-ego, of an individual, family, or tribe. Usually among hunting societies, the animal that is the primary source of food is the major totem. Generation after generation of a family has participated in the ritual of holy communion with the totem deity, injesting its strengths and virtue with each bite of food.

3. The shaman, especially the female shaman, has been the keeper of the sacred perpetual fire. Fire is life. It is used to warm the inner and outer body (Edsman).

4. Animals and plants have been represented in art as if an X-ray. The internal organs and skeleton are drawn. Lifelines from the mouth to the lung or stomach are pictured. The heart is emphasized. Vertebrae, such as ribs, are outlined.

5. Art and myths have depicted the Great Hunt of animals by the atlatl or spear-thrower. The spear is a weapon with a long shaft and sharp blade which is thrown or thrust through the hunted being.

THE AMBISEXUAL DEITIES AND THE SHAMAN
OF THE FARMER

Agriculture, the deliberate seeding, nurturing, and harvesting of plants for food began relatively recently in our human evolution. In the Mesopotamian highlands, farming communities developed around 7,500 B.C.E. as evidenced by digs in Catal Huyuk, Turkey; Jericho, Jordon; Jarmo, Iran; and Tepe Sarab, Iran. The art of agriculture later progressed in the valleys of the Nile River and the Tigris-Eurphrates River.

The advent of agriculture has been associated with the cultivation, enrichment, and refinement of the arts, the intellect, and society. Etymologically, the word, culture, is derived from the Latin word, *cultura*, which means to till, to cultivate the soil (Neilson).

Agricultural societies evolved from gender and kin groups to stratified communities of persons with specializations. Anthropomorphic female deities were worshiped with the offering of gift-sacrifices. Human skulls were preserved. Sanctuaries were adorned with ornate paintings and sculptures, often of birds of prey, bulls, and leopards.

Marija Gimbutas in *Goddesses and Gods of Old Europe* and Riane Eisler in *The Chalice and The Blade* synthesized research in archeology, art, economics, history, literature, politics, and sociology into a theory about the existence of Old Europe. From 7,000 to 3,500 B.C.E., humans lived in large circular-shaped villages. Life was revered and peace was valued. The female, recognized to be the bearer of life, was worshiped as deity in temples, whose two-storied architecture mirrored the advancement of that civilization. Community life was egalitarian and matrilineal. Grains and vegetables were cultivated and animals were domesticated. Seas were navigated and ceramics, marble, sea shells, and volcanic glass were traded. By 5,000 B.C.E., this culture of the chalice as the vessel of life had spread from the Aegean to the Adriatic coast, the Danube basin, to Bohemia, Germany, Holland, Moravia, and Poland. This was a period of mutual group life where women and men shared equally in the ways of the culture.

Then copper was mined and used in Bulgaria, Romania, and Yugoslavia. The horse was domesticated, wheeled vehicles were constructed, and trade multiplied. The Krugan people from lands north of the Black Sea, who had forged the blade — the tool of conquest — out of copper with other minerals, swept down into Old Europe in three waves, 4,000 B.C.E., 3,500 B.C.E., and 3,000 B.C.E. Villages were small settlements of houses built partially underground. On the hilltops, chieftains lived in fortresses. The blade, the cutting edge of weapons, was revered in war.

The male, as conqueror, was worshiped as deity. For the first time, story lines contained scenes of rape, division, and destruction of female deities. Community life was patriarchal and patrilocal. Fewer and fewer figurines, multi-colored ceramics, or temples were created. Cultural evolution was abruptly detoured. Now, Old Europe, long sustained by acts of cooperation and partnership, was dominated by Krugans. By 3,000 B.C.E., the culture of the blade, the weapon of death, had spread across Europe, overtaking the culture of the chalice. The cult of individualism was in power; force was an instrument to obtain individual ends. Groups were forged with steel and existed because of the power and domination of the male leader. The group of the former period which had had a life of its own and emphasized equities relationships and shared decision-making became an archaic form.

Although the male deities gained status, the memory of the powers of the female deities were never completely erased. Plants, especially cereals, became mainstay of the human diet. The breast of the female gave milk; the efforts of the female gave the staff of life. Ritual lovers were proffered to female deities to ensure fertility.

Whereas hunters emphasized the differences between females and males, planters identified the creator as ambisexual and accorded highest respect to ambisexual shamans. The worship of the ambisexual creator and rituals of castration and transvestism spread from the Near East to Southeast Asia and Middle America.

Hermann Baumann has named thirty-seven particular regions where mythologies on the worship of ambisexual deities and powers have spread from the Mesopotamian highlands west to the lands around the Mediterranean sea, Europe, and Africa and east to Indonesia, South Asia, the Far East, Australia, Oceania, North America, and South America. He has also specifyed forty-seven tribes in Eurasia, Africa, Madagascar, Burma, India, Indonesia, the Near East, Northeast Asia, the South Seas, and America who had ritualized the permanent sex change of castration and the non-permanent sex change of transvestism.

A. L. Kroeber has proposed that the majority of native North Americans tribes have had positions for individuals who have chosen to cross sexual roles. The Spaniard explorers called these individuals *mujer-hado* or man-witch-woman (Hay). The French explorers named these individuals *berdache*, a word derived from the Italian *berdasia*, derived from the Arabic *bardaj*, derived from the Persian word *barah*; all of these terms mean "kept boy" or "male prostitute" (Angelino and Shedd). It is assumed that native Americans, noting the European settlers' prejudice, felt pressure to hide or discourage the individuals who crossed sexual roles, at least from Europeans (Luri).

Native American mythology is rich with references to crossing gender. In a Kamia creation myth, Warharmi, a female transvestite, and Madkwahomai, her two male twins created without fertilization, contain the seeds required for agriculture (Katz, 1976). In a Navaho creation myth, homosexuals distributed all of the riches to the world (Niethammer). Many Navaho myths portray cattle, humans, and sheep as shamans (Reichard). A Sinkaietk myth tells of the male Coyote who dressed as a woman to leave the home of the Cougar (Cline et al.). A Tlingit myth speaks of the eighth child of a human woman and the sun who is "half-man, half-woman" (de Laguna).

Sue-Ellen Jacobs has reviewed anthropological literature and designated 87 native North American tribes who embrace individuals who cross gender roles and are accorded the status of healer, oracle, ritual leader, and shaman. In twenty of these tribes, women assume masculine ways.

The foremost Shamans were the transformed female or male, the ambisexual human, mirroring the image of the ambisexual deity. Accompanying these rituals were archaic megalithic temple complexes.

Marie Delcourt has studied the ambisexual in the ancient literature and recent folk practices of Mediterranean peoples. Myths associate transvestism with heroic acts. There are myths of men who cross dress, such as Achilles, Dionysos, Hymenaeus, and Leucippos; and myths of women who cross dress such as Leucippe and Procris. The consistent connection between cross dressing and sexual intercourse indicates that transvestism was simply not a rite of passage, but rather a ritual of power. The power of fertility was celebrated in festivities which involved transvestism for Artemis, Aproditos, and Dionysos. Rituals in which men dressed as women included those for Dionysos, Heracles of Cos, and Hercules Victor of Rome. A ritual in which women dressed as men was in honor of Artemis of Lacedemonia. Both sexes cross-dressed for rituals to Aphroditos of Cyprios and Hybristika of Argos. Throughout time, transvestism has been used to camouflage the new-born infant, the newly wed, and the pregnant woman from evil spirits.

THE SHAMAN

The word, shaman, is derived from the Tunguz word, *saman*. The shaman is the master of ecstasy. At will, the shaman's soul can take flight to heaven, traverse the earth, and plummet into the underworld. Shamans use trance work within the context of the tradition of the land. This involves knowledge of breath control, genealogy, the language of animals and humans, mythology, plant hallucinogens, spirits, and techniques.

The shaman either inherits the profession or experiences a vocational calling. The call often occurs to those who are recluse, generally adolescents, although, perhaps adults. They will experience the "shaman's sickness," labeled by psychiatrists as hysteria, mental unbalance, and physical torment. They hear voices, see visions, and feel the need to be a shaman or else, by refusal, court death.

The initiate will experience bodily dismemberment and the falling away of flesh from the skeleton. The novice perceives that the spirits are genuinely annihilating the ego, severing or stewing it, and then reconstructing the leftovers into a new shaman, competent of sensing the secret interiors of humans. The shaman dies and is born anew. Only then can the shaman form a tender, private, enduring intimacy with the soul's beloved. In hunting societies, the beloved is an animal and the shaman can become that animal. In planting societies, the beloved is a human of the opposite sex. The soul's beloved is constantly acknowledged and praised.

A significant number of shamans are gay or lesbian. The majority cross dress to allow increased movement, assume powers of the opposite sex, and perform rituals (Light).

The shaman often wears a mask of her or his ancestors, so that the ancestor's powers are always available. A drum and drum stick or a rattle are used to evoke and retain spirits for rituals. The pectoral, a circular piece of polished copper, is used to view the future. Feathers are held and worn so that flight can be taken and time and space traversed.

The shaman mediates between men and women, animals and humans, plants and humans, and heaven and earth. The shaman balances life forces, promoting equilibrium between humans and nature. Individuals, families, and communities are counseled by the shaman to consciously harmonize emotional, intellectual, physical, and spiritual temperaments with the ways of the universe.

CONCLUSION

Once upon a time, a boy named Tiresias was born to Chariclo, a nymph and friend of the goddess Athenia, and Udaeus, a Theban nobleman. One day, while hiking on Mount Cithaeron or Mount Cyllene, Tiresias saw two serpents engaged in sexual lovemaking. Tiresias struck, almost to the point of death, the female with his staff. Instantly, Tiresias was transformed into a woman. Seven years later, Tiresias happened to once again see serpents, perhaps the same serpents as before, engaged in sexual lovemaking. Tiresias struck and killed the male with her staff and was instantly transformed once again into a man.

One day, Hera and Zeus were engaged in an argument about who gains the greatest ecstasy from sexual lovemaking, men or women. Hera held that men experienced the greatest enjoyment, and Zeus said that women did. Tiresias was called upon to settle the argument because he had experienced life as both a man and a woman. Tiresias proclaimed that a woman had nine times more pleasure than a man in sexual lovemaking. The enraged Hera instantly blinded Tiresias. To compensate for his wife's action, Zeus cleansed Tiresias' ears so that he would comprehend the language of the birds. Zeus also gave Tiresias the boon of unerring prophecy. As the years ensued, some say for seven generations, Tiresias advised Creon, Dionysus, Laodamas, Oedipus, Odysseus, and Pentheus and others of their future.

Some storytellers say that after a long life, Tiresias, while traveling with his daughter Manto, was captured and transported to Delphi to be offered to Apollo as the booty of war. Other storytellers say that Tiresias accompanied Manto when she moved to Colophon, Asia Minor. Here Tiresias died and seers gathered to officiate the ritual for his death.

The Greek myth of Tiresias tells of a shaman, a human who lived as a woman as well as a man, who could communicate with the winged birds and forsee the future. The thesis of this article is that individuals who have been able to live in the worlds of both the female and male sexes, by such actions as cross dressing; assuming varied gender roles; surgically reversing sexual organs; and/or realizing an ambisexual, gay, or lesbian lifestyle have often been acknowledged historically by hunting and agricultural cultures as spirit guides transcending the bounds of everyday consciousness.

Shamans, as ambisexuals, androgynes, celibates, hemaphrodites, gay males, lesbians, transvestites, and other intersexes, have consciously contemplated the life force and their expression of this vitality. Ecstasy, enthusiasm, and passion are fueled by their knowledge and experience of the feminine and masculine, animal and plant, celestial and underground worlds. Individuality and uniqueness rather than egocentrism and egotism are expressed. Brooding and contemplation balance action and motion. Shamans utilize skill, strength, and stamina rather than aggression, assault, and assertion.

For 70,000 years, the shaman, willing to actively empathize with both genders, has been able to heal individuals, families, and societies through her or his actions as an attorney, counselor, healer, magician, mortician, naturalist, philosopher, poet, priest, prophet, smith, spiritual guide, and weather-maker. Shamans with their "ability to abide in the sphere of ambiguity uniquely empowers them to restore order" from chaos (Orion, 1988). It is the healing and ordering power of this position to which we return, in attention and in memory, to remember the sources of healing and power — to summon the shaman — in ourselves.

REFERENCES

Angelino, H. and C. L. Shedd. A Note on Berdache. *American Anthropologist.* Vol. 57, 121-125, 1955.

Bachler, E. *Das apline Palaolithikm der Schweitz im Wildkirschli, Drachenloch und Wildenmannlisloch.* Schwizerische Gesellschaft fur Urgeschichte, Monographien zur Ur- und Fruhgeschichte der Schweiz. Volume 2. Basel, Switzerland: Birkhauser, 1940. 260.

Baumann, H. *Das Doppelte Geschlecht: Ethnologische Studien zur Bisexualitat in Ritus und Mythos.* Berlin, West Germany: Dietrich Reimer, 1955.

Beane, W. C. and W. G. Doty, (Ed). *Myths, Rites, Symbols: A Mircea Eliade Reader.* Vol. 2. New York: Harper Colophon Books, 1976.

Boswell, J. *Christianity, Social Tolerance, and Homosexuality: Gay People in Western Europe from the Beginning of the Christian Era to the Fourteenth Century.* Chicago, IL: The University of Chicago Press, 1980.

Briggs, K. M. *The Fairies in Tradition and Literature.* London, England: Routledge and Kegan Paul, 1967.

Brodzky, A. T., R. Danesewich, and N. Johnson, (Eds). *Stones, Bones and Skin: Ritual and Shamanic Art.* Toronto, Ontario, Canada: The Society for Art Publications, 1977.

Campbell, J. *The Way of the Animal Powers: Historical Atlas of World Mythology.* Vol. 1. London, England: Times Books Limited, 1984.

Carpenter, E. *Intermediate Types Among Primitive Folk.* London, England: George Allen and Company, 1914.

Cavin, S. *Lesbian Origins.* San Francisco, CA: Ism Press, Inc.,1985.

Centers for Disease Control. *Statistical Analysis for the Centers for Disease Control.* Atlanta, GA: Centers for Disease Control, 30 April 1989.

Cline, W., R. S. Commons, M. Mandelbaum, R. H. Post, and L. V. W. Walters. *The Sinkaietk or Southern Okanagon of Washington.* Edited by Leslie Spier. General Series in Anthropology. Vol. 6. Menasha, WA: George Banta Publishing Company, 1938.

Cornford, F. M. *Principium Sapientiae: The Origins of Greek Philosophical Thought.* Cambridge, MA: The Syndics of the University Press, 88-106, 1952.

Cucchiari, S. The Gender Revolution and the Transition from Bisexual Horde to Patrilocal Band: The Origins of Gender Hierarchy. *Sexual Meanings: The Cultural Construction of Gender and Sexuality.* Edited by S. B. Ortner and H. Whitehead. Cambridge, England: Cambridge University Press, 1981.

Damon, G., J. Watson, and R. Jordan. *The Lesbian in Literature: A Bibliography.* Second Edition. Reno, NV: The Ladder, 1975.

de Laguna, F. Tlingit Ideas about the Indian. *Southwestern Journal of Anthropology*. Vol. 10, 172-179, 1951.

Delcourt, M. *Hermaphrodite: Myths and Rites of the Bisexual Figure in Classical Antiquity*. Translated from the French by Jennifer Nicholson. London, England: Studio Books, 1961.

Dodds, E. R. The Greek Shamans and the Origin of Puritanism. *The Greeks and the Irrational*. Berkeley and Los Angeles, CA: 135-178, 1951.

Dover, K. J. *Greek Homosexuality*. Cambridge, MA: Harvard University Press, 1978.

Eaton, E. (Mahad'yumi). *The Shaman and the Medicine Wheel*. Wheaton, IL: The Theosophical Publishing House, 1982.

Edsman, C. M. Bears. Translated from Swedish by Verne Moberg. *The Encyclopedia of Religion*. Edited by Mircea Eliade. Vol. 2. New York: Macmillan Publishing Company, 1987.

Edsman, C. M. Fire. Translated from Swedish by David Mel Paul and Margareta Paul. *The Encyclopedia of Religion*. Edited by Mircea Eliade. Vol. 5. New York: Macmillan Publishing Company, 1987.

Eisler, R. *The Chalice and the Blade: Our History, Our Future*. San Francisco, CA: Harper and Row, 1987.

Eliade, M. *Myths, Dreams, and Mysteries: The Encounter between Contemporary Faiths and Archaic Realities*. Translated from French by Philip Mairet. New York: Harper Colophon Books, 1975.

Evans, A. *Witchcraft and the Gay Counterculture*. Boston, MA: Fag Rag Books, 1978.

Foster, J. H. *Sex Variant Women in Literature*. Tallahassee, FL: Naiad Press, 1985.

Gimbatas, M. *Goddesses and Gods of Old Europe*. Berkeley, CA: University of California Press, 1982.

Goldberg, B. Z. *The Sacred Fire*. Secaucus, NJ: Citadel, 1958.

Grahn, J. *Another Mother Tongue: Gay Words, Gay Worlds*. Boston, MA: Beacon Press, 1984.

Grahn, J. *The Highest Apple: Sappho and The Lesbian Poetic Tradition*. San Francisco, CA: Spinsters, Ink, 1985.

Greenberg, D. F. *The Construction of Homosexuality*. Chicago, IL: The University of Chicago Press, 1988.

Grottanelli, C. Agriculture. *The Encyclopedia of Religion*. Edited by Mircea Eliade. Vol. 1. New York: Macmillan Publishing Company, 1987.

Hay, H. Review of the Hammond Report (1887). *Homophile Studies*. Vol. 6, 1-212, 1963.

Hicks, D. *A Maternal Religion: The Role of Women in Tetum Myth and Ritual*. Special Report Number 22. De Kalb, IL: Northern Illinois University Center for Southeast Asian Studies, 1984.

Jacobs, S. E. Berdache: A Brief Review of the Literature. *Colorado Anthropologist*. Vol. 1, 25-40, 1986.

Jeter, K. *Austrailian Dream Time: A Multi-Media Illustrated Lecture*. Newark, DE: Beacon Research, 1988.

Jeter, K. A Historical, Interdisciplinary Analysis of the Animal and Human Social Ecosystem. *Pets and the Family*. New York: The Haworth Press, 1985.

Katz, J. N. *Gay American History: Lesbians and Gay Men in the U.S.A.* New York: Crowell, 1976.

Katz, J. N. *Gay/Lesbian Almanac: A New Documentary*. New York: Harper and Row, 1983.

Kroeber, A. L. *Handbook of the Indians of California*. Berkeley, CA: California Book Company, Ltd., 1953.

Kroeber, A. L. *Handbook of the Indians of California*. Bureau of American Ethnology. Bulletin 78. Washington, DC: U.S. Government Printing Office, 1925.

Kuda, M. J. (Ed). *Women Loving Women: A Select and Annotated Bibliography of Women Loving Women in Literature*. Chicago, IL: Womanpress, 1975.

Kuhn, H. *Auf den Spuren des Eiszeitmenschen*. Abridged Edition. Wiesbaden, West Germany: F. A. Brockhaus, 94-95, 1953.

Lefkowitz, M. R. *Women in Greek Myth*. London, England: Gerald Duckworth and Company, Ltd., 1986.

Leroi-Gourhan, A. *The Art of Prehistoric Man in Europe*. London, England: Thames and Hudson, 1968.

Leroi-Gourhan, A. *Les Religions de la Préhistoire*. Paris, France: Press Universitaires de France, 31-36, 1964.

Leroi-Gourhan, A. The Evolution of Paleolithic Art. *Scientific American*. Vol. 218, 59-66, 1968.

Lewis, I. M. The Shaman's Career. *Religion in Context: Cults and Charisma*. Cambridge, England: Cambridge University Press, 1986.

Light, D. A. P. Personal Correspondance. 12 September 1988.

Lommel, A. *Die Unumbal: Ein Stamm in Nordwest-Australien*. Hamburg, West Germany: Museum fur Volkerkunde, 1962.

Murray, M. *The God of the Witches*. London, England: Oxford University, 1952.

Murray, M. *The Witch-Cult in Western Europe: A Study in Anthropology*. London, England: Oxford University Press, 1921.

Niethammer, C. *Daughters of the Earth: The Lives and Legends of American Indian Women*. London, England and New York: Collier, 1977.

Norton, R. *The Homosexual Literary Tradition: An Interpretation*. Brooklyn, NY: The Revisionist Press, 1974.

Nowack, M. and S. Durrant. *The Tale of the Nisan Shamaness: A Manchu Folk Epic*. Seattle, WA: University of Washington Press, 1977.

Orion, L. Old World Shamanism of the Siberians and Eskimos and the New World Shamanism of the Huichol Indians. Unpublished Paper, State University of New York at Stony Brook, May, 1982.

Orion, L. Personal Correspondence. 14 September 1988.

Raymond, J. G. *A Passion for Friends: Toward a Philosophy of Female Affection*. Boston, MA: Beacon Press, 1986.

Reichard, G. A. *Navaho Religion: A Study of Symbolism*. New York: Bollingen Foundation, 1950.

Reichard, G. A. *Social Life of the Navajo Indian with some Attention to Minor Ceremonies*. Columbia University Contributions to Anthropology. Vol. 7. New York: Columbia University Press, 1928.

Roberts, M. Personal Communication. 2 January 1989.

Roscoe, W. *Living the Spirit: A Gay American Indian Anthology*. New York: St. Martin's Press, 1988.

Russell, J. B. *Witchcraft in the Middle Ages*. Ithaca, NY: Cornell University Press, 1972.

Rutherford, W. *Shamanism: The Foundations of Magic*. Wellingborough, Northamptonshire, England: The Aquarian Press, 1986.

Saslow, J. M. *Ganymede in the Renaissance: Homosexuality in Art and Society*. New Haven, CT: Yale University Press, 1986.

Sergent, B. *Homosexuality in Greek Myth*. Translated from French by Arthur Goldhammer with a Preface by Georges Dumézil. Boston, MA: Beacon Press, 1986.

Sobol, D. *The Amazons in Greek Society*. London, England: Barnes, 1972.

Solecki, R. S. Shanidar IV, a Neanderthal Flower Burial in Northern Iraq. *Science*. Vol. 190, 880-881, November 28, 1975.

Spengler, O. *Der Untergang des Abendlandes (The Decline of the West)*. Two volumes. Munich, West Germany: C. H. Beck'sche, Volume 1, page 216, 1923.

Sussman, M. B. and K. Jeter. Marriage and Parenting in the United States. Paper presented at the XXIVth International CFR Seminar on Marriage, Parenthood, and Social Policy, Singapore, 3 May 1989.

Torrey, E. F. *Witchdoctors and Psychiatrists: The Common Roots of Psychotherapy and its Future*. New York: Harper and Row, 1986.

Villoldo, A. and S. Krippner. *Healing States: A Journey into the World of Spiritual Healing and Shamanism*. New York: Simon and Schuster, 1987.

Weed, S. Personal Correspondence. 1 October 1988.

Whitehead, Harriet. The Bow and the Burden Strap: A New Look at Institutionalized Homosexuality in Native North America. *Sexual Meanings: The Cultural Construction of Gender and Sexuality*. Edited by S. B. Ortner and H. Whitehead. Cambridge, England: Cambridge University Press, 1981.

Williams, W. L. *The Spirit and the Flesh: Sexual Diversity in American Indian Culture*. Boston, MA: Beacon Press, 1986.

Williamson, H. R. *The Arrow and the Sword*. London, England: Faber and Faber, 1947.

Zolla, E. The Bisexual Shaman. *The Androgyne: Reconciliation of Male and Female*. New York: Crossroad, 1981.

Homosexuality and Family Relations: Glossary of Terms

Activism: A deliberate set of actions directed to effect change, usually in response to oppression.

Affirmative: Feeling positive about one's self; valuing one's self.

African American: Persons who are of African descent, Negro race, usually born and reared in the United States, and live in the U.S. Other terms used to denote this group include Black, Afro-American, and Black American.

Ageism: Negative attitudes and overt discrimination based on age.

AIDS: One or more of the diseases identified by the Centers for Disease Control (1987) as being presumptively indicative of infection with the HIV (Human Immunodeficiency Viral) virus.

AIDS bereavement: Unresolved mourning following the deaths of multiple friends/lovers due to AIDS.

AIDS hysteria: Rampant, unfounded fear of HIV transmission or infection.

AIDS myths: Fabrications related to contagion or progression of HIV infections.

AIDS related complex (ARC): Pre-AIDS signs and symptoms that include fever greater than 100, weight loss of 10% or greater or more than 15 pounds, and lymphadenopathy involving two or more extra linguinal sites.

AIDS trajectory: Clinical course associated with HIV infection.

Asian American: Persons who are of Asian descent, Mongoloid race, usually born and reared in the United States, and live in the U.S.

Bisexual: Persons who are sexually attracted to both women and men.

Black: Persons who are of African descent, Negro race, usually born and reared in the United States, and live in the U.S. Other terms used to denote this group include African American, Afro American, and Black American.

Coming out: A developmental process by which an individual develops a gay identity and acknowledges that identity to the self and discloses it (comes out) to others.

Constitutional homosexuality: A homosexual orientation which, predetermined by whatever complex of factors, is *not* viewed as a matter of choice; the opposite of constitutional heterosexuality.

Crisis competence: The ability to manage and/or respond to crises.

Deconstruction: To analyze, challenge, and understand the components of a concept or identity's socially constructed meaning.

Deutero-Pauline: Writings in the New Testament that scholars believe were produced within the circle of the followers of St. Paul, but were not written by St. Paul himself (Pauline).

Discourse: Language and beliefs that reflect a particular ideology.

Ego-syntonic: A well-integrated sense of self.

Ethnic minority: Denotes persons who are Black/African American/ Afro American, Asian American, Pacific Islander, Hispanic/ Latin, Native American.

Ethnic minority gays and lesbians: Persons who are Black/African American/Afro American, Asian American, Pacific Islander, Hispanic/Latin, Native American who are affectionally and physically attracted to persons of the same sex.

Gay: Persons (usually men) who are affectionally and sexually attracted to other men.

Gay ghetto; Gay ghettoization: Urban neighborhoods with a particularly heavy concentration of gay male and/or lesbian residents, often including gay/lesbian businesses and organizations; the tendency of many gays/lesbians to seek out and migrate to such areas to reinforce gay/lesbian identity and self-acceptance.

Gender roles: Behaviors, attitudes, or feelings that are defined as "appropriate" or "inappropriate" for one or the other sex, or both.

Gender role flexibility: The ability to comfortably express and engage in a range of attitudes and behaviors independent of whether they are defined as "appropriate" or "inappropriate" for one's sex.

Gerontophobia: Fear of aging and older people.

Heterosexual: Persons whose sexual and affectional feelings and behaviors are predominately for members of the opposite sex.

Heterosexual families: Persons who are related by marriage, parentage, or adoption.

Heterosexism; heterosexist: The assumption that everyone is, or should be, heterosexual; a valuation which assumes that heterosexuality is better than homosexuality.

Hispanic: Persons who are Latino or Latina, and whose family origins are from the Caribbean, Mexico, Central America, or South America, and whose culture includes the Spanish Language.

HIV-related impotence: Loss of ability to achieve an erection due to HIV infection of autonomic nerves.

HIV positive (or seropositive): Blood tests for presence of the HIV antibody are positive.

Homecoming: Migration of HIV seropositive homosexual men from gay communities to other communities inhabited by heterosexual family members.

Homophobia; homophobic: An irrational fear of homosexuality in one's self and others.

Homosexual: Persons whose affectional and sexual feelings and behaviors are predominately or exclusively with members of their own sex. The term is considered offensive by many gays and lesbians since it is perceived as referring solely to sexuality without acknowledging the emotional and spiritual aspects of the gay and lesbian experience.

Identity: Sense of self; self-concept.

Identity foreclosure: A term used to describe the interruption of psychosexual or psychosocial development, or as an arrestment at a certain psychosexual or psychosocial developmental stage.

Identity formation: Individual identity development that occurs over a lifetime whereby one's own set of unique personality characteristics distinguish the self from others.

Ideology: A systematic body of beliefs or concepts, including theories, assertions, and assumptions.

Individuation: The development of one's own identity separate from the identities of others.

Internalized homophobia: The taking in or internalization of society's negative attitudes and assumptions about homosexuality by gays or lesbians.

Immersion: A process that leads to complete identification with the patient, self-negation, and possibly loss of the will to live.

Immunosuppression: Loss of a functional immune response.

Infallible: Incapable of error in the area of faith and morals; in the Roman Catholic Church a doctrinal teaching must be specifically deemed "infallible *ex cathedra*" by the Pope; otherwise it is considered fallible.

Invisible minority: Persons who are not considered part of the mainstream culture, whose minority identity is not externally discernable, and whose identity becomes known about only if it is disclosed.

Kinsey-type ratings: A scale (originally developed by Alfred Kinsey) used to rate one's own or other's sexual orientation on a 7 point continuum from 0-6; 0 describes exclusive heterosexuality and 6 exclusive homosexuality.

Latin: Persons who are Hispanic, and whose family origins are from the Caribbean, Mexico, Central America, or South America, and whose culture includes the Spanish Language.

Lesbian: A woman who is affectionally and sexually attracted to other women.

Mainstream society: Refers to the majority culture, values, and lifestyle of a country.

Native American: Persons who are American Indian, born, reared, and live in the United States, and whose family origins are native to the Americas, particularly the continental U.S.

Nonoxynol-9: A spermicide effective against the HIV found in some brands of condoms.

Oppression: The result of a system where one's access to power is limited or controlled.

Oral sex: Oral-genital contact.

Pacific Islander: Persons whose origins are in the islands of the Pacific Ocean.

Passing: Hiding or covering up a part of one's self. Often refers to hiding one's homosexuality by "passing" as heterosexual.

Patriarchal religion: Belief systems founded by male leaders (patriarchs) who worship a male god, and uphold strict gender role and sexual behavior separations that clearly favor conforming hetero-sexual men; e.g., both Judaism and Christianity as traditionally conceived.

Power: The ability to control and influence others.

Pre-cum: Pre-ejaculatory fluid.

Reconstruction: To rebuild and put together a concept or identity so that it differs from its usual socially constructed meaning.

Restructuring strategies: Cognitive activities designed to provide a sense of control, confidence, or positive attitude toward a situation.

Rimming: Oral-anal contact.

Sexism: Attitudes, behaviors, and beliefs that value one sex over the other.

Sexual orientation: An individual's feelings of affectional and sex-ual attraction for persons of the same, opposite, or both sexes.

Social construction: Meanings for concepts and identities provided by the ideological systems developed for their explanation.

Stereotype: Shared set of beliefs that describe attributes, personali-ties, or characteristics of people because of who they are as-sumed to be or based on the group(s) to which they belong.

Stereotypic: Conforming to a shared set of beliefs or stereotypes.

Sympatia: A Spanish term that refers to empathy, and having a high value for social and personal relationships.

T4 cell count: Immune cells that orchestrate cellular immunity. Normal T4 cell counts are greater than 400 cells per mm3.

Visible minority: Persons who are members of a culture that is not considered to be part of the mainstream, and whose identity is easily identifiable by means of race, ethnicity, and/or cultural/ linguistic characteristics.

White: Persons who are Caucasian, European descent, and who identify with the values and beliefs of other similar persons, and who represent the mainstream members of society.